**This item was purchased
through a
Title VI-a International Grant**

Reducing Poverty in Asia

Reducing Poverty in Asia

Emerging Issues in Growth, Targeting, and Measurement

Edited by

Christopher M. Edmonds

Research Economist, Asian Development Bank, Manila, Philippines

A JOINT PUBLICATION OF THE
ASIAN DEVELOPMENT BANK AND EDWARD ELGAR PUBLISHING

Edward Elgar
Cheltenham, UK • Northampton, MA, USA

Published by
Edward Elgar Publishing Limited
Glensanda House
Montpellier Parade
Cheltenham
Glos GL50 1UA
UK

Edward Elgar Publishing, Inc.
136 West Street
Suite 202
Northampton
Massachusetts 01060
USA

A catalogue record for this book
is available from the British Library

Library of Congress Cataloguing in Publication Data

Asia and Pacific Forum on Poverty (2001: Manila, Philippines)
    Reducing poverty in Asia: emerging issues in growth, targeting, and measurement/edited by Christopher M. Edmonds.
        p. cm.
    Revised papers presented at the First Asia and Pacific Forum on Poverty held at the Headquarters of the Asian Development Bank in Manila in February 2001.
    1. Poverty—Asia—Congresses. 2. Poverty—Pacific Area—Congresses.
3. Technological innovations—Economic aspects—Asia—Congresses.
4. Technological innovations—Economics aspects—Pacific Area—Congresses.
5. Asia—Economic conditions—since 1945—Congresses. 6. Pacific
Area—Economic conditions—20th century—Congresses. I. Edmonds, Christopher M., 1963–   . II. Asian Development Bank. III. Title.
HC415.P6R434   2001
339.4'6'095—dc21   2003044800

ISBN 1 84376 264 1

Printed and bound in Great Britain by MPG Books Ltd, Bodmin, Cornwall

Contents

List of Figures   vii
List of Tables   ix
List of Contributors   xiii
Foreword by Tadao Chino, President, ADB   xv
Acknowledgements   xvii
List of Abbreviations   xviii

Introduction   xxi
Christopher M. Edmonds

PART I – THE MACROECONOMY, GLOBALIZATION, AND
       PRO-POOR GROWTH

1.   Marginalization in a Globalizing World: Some Plausible   3
     Scenarios and Suggestions for Measurement
     Kaushik Basu

2.   Balanced Development: An Approach to Development Policy   20
     and Priorities
     Graham Pyatt

3.   Poverty Analysis and Measurement within a General   45
     Equilibrium Framework
     Erik Thorbecke

4.   Macroeconomic Policies and Poverty Reduction: Stylized   79
     Facts and an Overview of Research
     *Ratna Sahay, Paul Cashin, Paolo Mauro, and Catherine
     Pattillo*

PART II – TARGETING URBAN OR INDUSTRIAL SECTORS

5.   New Technologies, Competitiveness, and Poverty Reduction   109
     Sanjaya Lall

6.   Use of Information Technology for Poverty Reduction: A Case 124
     Study of Efforts in the Indian State of Andhra Pradesh
     Randeep Sudan

7.   Small and Medium Enterprise Development in Equitable Growth   143
      and Poverty Alleviation
      Dipak Mazumdar

PART III – NEW DEVELOPMENTS AND ISSUES IN POVERTY
         MEASUREMENT

8.   Poverty Lines: Eight Countries' Experiences and the Issue of   173
      Specificity and Consistency
      Abuzar Asra and Vivian Santos-Francisco

9.   Poverty Comparison in the Philippines: Is What We Know   197
      About the Poor Robust?
      Arsenio M. Balisacan

10.   Assessing the Poverty Impact of Policy- and Sector-Based Lending   220
      John Weiss

PART IV – COUNTRY STUDIES

11.   Pathways of Poverty Reduction: Rural Development and   235
      Transmission Mechanisms in the Philippines
      Arsenio M. Balisacan

12.   Structural Adjustment, Macroeconomic Policies, and Poverty   261
      Trends in Pakistan
      Abdul Razzaq Kemal

13.   The Poverty Situation and Policy in Sri Lanka   298
      Saman Kelegama

14.   Pacific Islands: Is Poverty an Issue?   319
      Christopher Lightfoot and Anthony Joseph Ryan

15.   Opening Doors to More Inclusive Societies: The Case of the   328
      Pacific Island Countries
      Vijay Naidu

Index   343

List of Figures

2.1	A Schematic Representation of the General Basis of Well-Being	23
2.2	The Equilibrium of a Household that is Both a Consumer and a Producer	32
2.3	The Marginal Efficiency of Investment Schedule	39
3.1	Flow Diagram of SAM Transactions	50
3.2	Simplified Interrelationship among Principal SAM Accounts	53
3.3a	Effect of a 30 Percent Reduction in World Export Price of Export Agriculture Crop on Income Distribution: Rural Households	68
3.3b	Effect of a 30 Percent Reduction: Small Landowner Households	68
3.3c	Effect of a 30 Percent Reduction: Large Landowner Households	69
3.3d	Effect of a 30 Reduction: Urban Low Income Households	69
3.3e	Effect of a 30 Percent Reduction: Urban High Income Households	70
3.3f	Effect of a 30 Percent Reduction: Capitalist Households	70
3.4a	Nonparametric Income Distribution for Indonesian Household Groups, 1996 vs. 1999: Agricultural Workers	74
3.4b	Nonparametric Income Distribution: Farmers with Land	74
3.4c	Nonparametric Income Distribution: Rural Low Education	75
3.4d	Nonparametric Income Distribution: Rural High Education	75
3.4e	Nonparametric Income Distribution: Rural Non-Lbf	76
3.4f	Nonparametric Income Distribution: Urban Low Education	76
3.4g	Nonparametric Income Distribution: Urban Non-Lbf	77
3.4h	Nonparametric Income Distribution: Urban High Education	77
4.1a	Human Development Index (HDI), Human Poverty Index (HPI) and Poverty Line: 1998	92
4.1b	Human Development Index (HDI), Human Poverty Index (HPI) and Poverty Line: 1998	93
4.2	Human Development Index (HDI) and Gini Coefficient	94
4.3	Histogram of Human Development Index (HDI): 1975 and 1998	98
5.1	Rates of World Export Growth by Technological Categories, 1985–1998	112
5.2	Growth Rates of Manufactured Exports by Industrial and Developing Countries, 1985–1998	113

5.3   Regional Shares of Developing Country Manufactured   114
       Exports, 1998
5.4   Values of Manufactured Exports by Leading Developing   116
       Countries, 1985 and 1998
5.5   High-Technology Products in Manufactured Exports, 1998   117
5.6   Foreign Direct Investment as a Percentage of Gross   119
       Domestic Investment, 1997
5.7   Tertiary Enrollments in Technical Subjects as a Percentage 121
       of Population, 1995
5.8   R&D by Productive Enterprises as a Percentage of Gross   121
       Domestic Product, 1995
9.1   Mean Expenditure and Poverty Line   203
11.1   Rural Growth and Rural Welfare   237
11.2   Poverty Reduction, 1988–1997: Incidence   253

List of Tables

1.1	Per Capita Income and Quintile Income, 1997	14
2.1	The Multiple Levels of Aggregation at which Causation can be Identified	25
2.2	Examples of Investment, Maintenance and Depletion for Each of the Main Types of Assets	36
3.1	A Basic Social Accounting Matrix	49
3.2	Simplified Schematic Social Accounting Matrix	52
3.3	Social Accounting Matrix for Archetype African Developing Country	64
3.4	Income and Demographic Characteristics	66
4.1	Human Development Index (HDI), 1998	95
4.2	HDI Transition Matrix	99
4.3	Macroeconomic Performance (1975–1998)	101
5.1	Rates of Growth of High-Technology and Other Manufacturing, 1985–1997	111
7.1	Percentage Distribution of Employment by Size-Groups in Manufacturing, Selected Asian Countries	149
7.2	Relative Productivity (Value Added per Worker) by Enterprise Size-Groups in Manufacturing, Selected Asian Countries	150
7.3	Classification of Republic of Korea Workers in Small-Scale Enterprises, 1971	152
7.4	Republic of Korea: Distribution of Employment in Manufacturing by Size-Groups and Relative Labor Productivity	162
7.5	Taipei,China: Distribution of Employment in Manufacturing by Size-Groups and Relative Labor Productivity	162
8.A1	Ratio of Urban to Rural Poverty Lines, Bangladesh	192
8.A2	Provincial Rankings Based on Headcount Index, Indonesia, 1993	193
8.A3	Provincial Rankings Based on Headcount Index, Indonesia, 1996–1998	194
8.A4	Regional Rankings Based on Headcount Index, Philippines, 1994	194
9.1	National Poverty Estimates, 1994 and 1997	204
9.2	Sources of the Difference in Estimates of Poverty Change	205
9.3	Mean Expenditure and Income, by Decile, and Gini Index	206
9.4	Regional Profile, 1997	208
9.5	Provinces with Highest and Lowest Poverty Incidence	209
9.A1	Estimates of Food Thresholds and Poverty Lines: Absolute Cost-of-Basic-Needs Approach	214
9.A2	Regional Cost-of-Living Indexes	217

10.1	Poverty Reduction Impact Matrix	226
10.2	Modified Poverty Reduction Impact Matrix: Removal of Fertilizer Subsidy	229
10.3	Modified Poverty Reduction Impact Matrix: Financial Sector Reform	230
11.1	Agriculture in the National Economy	238
11.2	Agricultural Growth in Asian Developing Countries	239
11.3	Average Growth Rates of Agriculture by Subsector	240
11.4	Rural Poverty Estimates—Official Methodology	241
11.5	Rural Poverty Estimates, 1961–1997	242
11.6	Standard of Living and Human Development in the Philippines, Indonesia, and Thailand	245
11.7	Indicators of Human Development in the Philippines, Indonesia, and Thailand	245
11.8	Effective Rates of Protection by Major Sector	252
11.9	Determinants of Poverty Reduction	255
12.1	Incidence of Poverty	266
12.2	Poverty Measures for Pakistan	266
12.3	Trends in the Incidence of Poverty	266
12.4	Poverty Trends in the 1990s by Rural and Urban Areas	267
12.5	World Bank: Poverty Indicator, 1984–1985 to 1996–1997	267
12.6	Poverty Indicators under Basic-Needs Approach	268
12.7	Poor/Nonpoor Transition Matrix, 1986–1987 to 1987–1988	269
12.8	Household Income Distribution in Pakistan	271
12.9	Household Income Distribution by Rural-Urban Areas	272
12.10	Trends in the Prevalence of Malnutrition	275
12.11	Budgetary Deficit in Pakistan	277
12.12	Tax Structure of Pakistan	279
12.13	Incidence of Both Direct and Indirect Taxes	280
12.14	Percentage Increase in Tax Burden by Income Groups	281
12.15	Social Indicators of Pakistan	281
12.16	Subsidies in Pakistan	282
12.17	Zakat Receipts	283
12.18	Growth in Monetary Assets	284
12.19	Growth of GDP	285
12.20	Distribution of Unemployment Rates	286
12.21	Percentage Distribution of Workers by Establishment	287
12.22	Logistic Regressions Effects of Predictors on Being Poor	288
12.23	Determinants of Poverty—Single Variable Case	290
12.24	Data on the Variables Used in Regressions	291
12.25	Multivariate Regression of Poverty	293
13.1	Social Indicators: Sri Lanka and Selected Asian Countries	299
13.2	Consumption Poverty in Sri Lanka by Sector, 1985–1986, 1990–1991, and 1995–1996	300
13.3	GDP Growth and Poverty Incidence by Region	302
13.4	Income and Human Poverty by Province	304

13.5	Income Shares Spending Units	304
13.6	Gini Coefficient	304
13.7	Welfare and Social Infrastructure Expenditure	306
13.8	Social Development Expenditure in Five-Year Periods as a Percentage of GDP	310
15.1	Human Poverty Index for Pacific Island Countries	332
15.2	Employment Status of Pacific Island Women	337

List of Contributors

Abuzar Asra is the Senior Statistician in the Division of Development Indicators and Policy Research of the Asian Development Bank, Manila, Philippines.

Arsenio M. Balisacan is a Professor in the School of Economics of the University of the Philippines, Quezon City, and Undersecretary of the Department of Agriculture of the Philippines.

Kaushik Basu is a Professor of Economics at Cornell University, Ithaca, New York.

Paul Cashin is an Economist in the Research Department of the International Monetary Fund, Washington, D.C.

Christopher M. Edmonds is an Economist in the Development Indicators and Policy Research Division, Economics and Research Department, of the Asian Development Bank, Manila, Philippines.

Saman Kelegama is Executive Director of the Institute of Policy Studies, Colombo, Sri Lanka.

Abdul Razzaq Kemal is the Director of the Pakistan Institute of Development Economics, Islamabad, Pakistan.

Sanjaya Lall is a Professor of Development Economics at Oxford University, England.

Christopher Lightfoot is a Lecturer in Economics at Melbourne University, Australia, and a consultant on economic policy and planning with extensive experience in the Pacific Islands.

Paolo Mauro is an Economist in the Research Department of the International Monetary Fund, Washington, D.C.

Dipak Mazumdar is a Professor at the Centre for International Studies, University of Toronto, Canada.

Vijay Naidu is a Professor at the University of the South Pacific School of Social and Economic Development, Suva, Fiji Islands.

Catherine Pattillo is an Economist in the Research Department of the International Monetary Fund, Washington, D.C.

Graham Pyatt is a Professor at the Institute of Social Studies, The Hague, Netherlands.

Anthony Joseph Ryan is a New Zealand-based Economist and free-lance consultant on rural development with extensive experience in the Pacific Islands.

Ratna Sahay is Advisor to the First Deputy Managing Director of the International Monetary Fund, Washington, D.C.

Vivian Santos-Francisco is a former statistics analyst at the Development Indicators and Policy Research Division, Economics and Research Department, of the Asian Development Bank, Manila, Philippines.

Randeep Sudan is Special Secretary to the Chief Minister of the Government of Andhra Pradesh, Hyderabad, India.

Erik Thorbecke is H. E. Babcock Professor of Economics and Food Economics and Director of the Program on Comparative Economic Development at Cornell University, Ithaca, New York.

John Weiss is a Professor of Development Economics in the Development and Project Planning Centre, University of Bradford, England.

Foreword

The Asian Development Bank (ADB) has worked with governments, nongovernmental organizations, and the private sector for more than three and a half decades to foster economic and social development of countries in the Asia and Pacific region. Poverty reduction has always been a goal in these efforts, but with the adoption of ADB's Poverty Reduction Strategy (PRS) in 1999, poverty reduction became the explicit, overarching objective that guides its lending, policy dialogue, and technical assistance activities in its developing member countries (DMCs). Under the Strategy, ADB is committed to host once every three years an international forum involving government representatives, civil society, nongovernmental organizations, and the development community to consider recent research on understanding the causes of and remedies for poverty in the Asia and Pacific region, and to review efforts to reduce poverty by ADB and its borrowing members. The papers included in this volume were presented at the first such forum, which was held at ADB headquarters in February 2001.

Developing Asia is home to nearly two thirds of the world's poor. The region's economic progress over the past half century has enabled many countries to grow rapidly and improve the quality of life of their impoverished citizens in a sustainable manner. High growth has reduced poverty in some DMCs, but not throughout the region. The proportion of the region's population living in absolute poverty has been halved over the last three decades, but still about one in three Asians lives on an income of less than a US$1 per day.

The region has also witnessed progress in addressing the broader social dimensions of poverty. For example, adult literacy rose from 40 percent to 70 percent between 1970 and 2000. Over the same time period, average life expectancy increased from 55 to 68 years. However, as with poverty reduction, success in social development has varied across DMCs.

The Bank's Poverty Reduction Strategy has three strategic pillars. The first pillar recognizes that pro-poor sustainable economic growth is the basis of all efforts to reduce poverty. The second pillar mandates social development as a second goal in ADB operations. The third pillar acknowledges that poverty reduction also depends on good governance and that ADB efforts should foster good governance in its DMCs. All three pillars are essential to reducing poverty in the region.

Despite a broad understanding of how the three pillars relate to one another, there is much ground for research to help clarify links between them, identify synergies among them, and determine the most effective sequencing of poverty reduction initiatives in the context of each DMC. Much of the debate at the first poverty forum, and a number of the papers in this volume, consider these issues.

This volume contains some of the papers presented at the first poverty forum, highlighting contributions from economists and other social scientists studying poverty in the economies of Asia and the Pacific. The works consider the economics of poverty and contribute to the empirical understanding of poverty in the region. Some papers develop methodologies that can be applied to improve our understanding of the characteristics and causes of poverty.

ADB is confident this collection of papers will contribute to the literature and spur debate on poverty and poverty reduction efforts in Asia and the Pacific. ADB's sponsorship of this volume underlines its recognition of the need for research to improve our understanding of poverty and of ways to reduce poverty. By supporting events such as the 2001 poverty forum, the publication of this volume, and similar efforts to foster dialogue, ADB hopes to foster rigorous scholarly work on poverty reduction in the region ADB serves.

Tadao Chino

Tadao Chino
President, ADB

Acknowledgements

Thanks are due to many individuals without whose hard work this book would not have been written. This publication emerges from the First Asia and Pacific Forum on Poverty (the Forum), a meeting of more than 300 poverty experts and stakeholder and government representatives that convened at the headquarters of the Asian Development Bank (ADB) in Manila in February 2001. Earlier versions of the chapters included in this volume were prepared for and presented at the Forum.

An initial thank you is extended to the authors who prepared the excellent chapters and patiently responded to the various rounds of editing carried out to finalize the volume. Clearly, without their strong contributions, it would not have been possible to prepare this book. Next, I must express my gratitude to the individuals that assisted in reviewing and preparing the volume. Three editors worked on the volume and did an excellent job in reviewing the chapters: Sara Collins Medina, Joyce Gorsuch, and Reggie Capuno. The preparation of the volume benefited immensely from the technical assistance of Rafaelita Jamon and Rodrigo Lachica. Rhommell Rico's desktop-publishing work for the volume was vital to its preparation. Karmina Ong provided expert administrative and secretarial support for the Forum.

Numerous people assisted in the numerous tasks involved in organizing a large forum involving so many individuals and organizations. Brahm Prakash headed the ADB Division charged with leading the efforts to organize the Forum, and he contributed much to the Forum. Arvind Panagariya provided excellent advice and helpful encouragement in the preparation of the volume in his capacity as Chief Economist of ADB. J.P. Verbiest was equally supportive and helpful in seeing the work completed in his capacity of Officer-in-Charge of the Economics and Research Department. Staff from the Poverty Reduction Unit of ADB's Strategy and Policy Department were key partners in organizing the Forum, so thanks are due to Karti Sandilya, Carolyn Heider, Isabel Ortiz, and Steven Pollard. Finally, the assistance of Edward Elgar Publishing, particularly Dymphna Evans and Caroline Cornish, in finalizing and publishing the book is duly acknowledged.

List of Abbreviations

ADB	Asian Development Bank
APSWAN	Andhra Pradesh State-Wide Area Network (India)
APVAN	Added Network Services (Andhra Pradesh, India)
BCA	Bachelor of computer applications (university degree)
BPS	Badan Pusat Statistik (National Bureau of Statistics, Indonesia)
BSNL	Bharat Sanchar Nigam Ltd. (telecommunications firm Andhra Pradesh, India)
CAR	Cordillera Autonomous Region (Philippines)
CARD	Computer-Aided Administration of Registration Department (Andhra Pradesh, India)
CARP	Comprehensive Agrarian Reform Program (Philippines)
CBN	Cost of basic needs (method of computing poverty lines)
CBSL	Central Bank of Sri Lanka
CGE	Computable general equilibrium (model of WHAT)
CPI	Consumer price index
DCI	Direct calorie intake (method of computing poverty lines)
DFID	Department for International Development (United Kingdom)
EO240	Executive Order No. 240 (Philippines)
ERP	Effective rate of protection
FAO	Food and Agriculture Organization of the United Nations
FAST	Fully Automated System for Transport (Andhra Pradesh, India)
FBS	Federal Bureau of Statistics (Pakistan)
FDI	Foreign direct investment
FEI	Food-energy intake (method of computing poverty lines)
FGT	Foster-Greer-Thorbecke (inequality coefficient)
FIES	Family Income and Expenditures Survey
GDP	Gross domestic product
GIS	Geographical information system
GNP	Gross national product
GSDP	Gross state domestic product
GVA	Gross value added
HDI	Human Development Index
HDR	Human Development Report of UNDP
HEIS	Household Expenditure and Income Survey
HIPC	Heavily indebted poor countries
HITEC	Hyderabad Information Technology and Engineering Consultancy (city in Andhra Pradesh, India)
HIV/AIDS	Human immunodeficiency virus/acquired immunodeficiency syndrome
HPI	Human poverty index
ICT	Information and communications technology
IFPRI	International Food Policy Research Institute
IIIT	Indian Institute of Information Technology, Andhra Pradesh, India

ILO	International Labour Organisation
IMF	International Monetary Fund
IRDP	Integrated Rural Development Program
JFM	Joint forest management (committee), Andhra Pradesh, India
LAC	Latin American and the Caribbean
Lao PDR	Lao People's Democratic Republic
LDC	Less developed countries
LES	Linear Expenditure System
LFS	Labor force survey
LSE	Large-scale enterprise
LSMS	Living Standard Measurement Study (of the World Bank)
MCA	Master of computer applications (university degree)
MENA	Middle East and North Africa
MIRAB	[Naidu]
MSIT	Master of Science in Information Technology (university degree)
NAFTA	North American Free Trade Agreement
NASSCOM	National Association of Software and Service Companies (India)
NFA	National Food Authority (Philippines)
NGO	Nongovernment organization
NIE	Newly industrialized economy
NLSS	Nepal Living Standards Survey
NNP	Net national product
NSCB	National Statistical Coordination Board (Philippines)
NSO	National Statistics Office (Philippines)
NWFP	North-West Frontier Province (Pakistan)
OECD	Organization for Economic Cooperation and Development
PACS	Primary Agricultural Credit Society (Andhra Pradesh, India)
PD27	Presidential Decree No. 27 (Philippines)
PHDR	Pacific Human Development Report (of the UNDP)
PIC	Pacific island country
PIDE	Pakistan Institute of Development Economics
PNG	Papua New Guinea
PRC	People's Republic of China
QUANGOS	Quasi-nongovernmental institutions
R&D	Research and development
RGDP	Regional [per capita] gross domestic product
RHS	Rural Household Survey
RQI	Rank-weighted quintile income
SAM	Social accounting matrix
SAP	Structural Adjustment Program
SITC	Standard industrial trade classification
SKIMS	Secretariat Knowledge and Information Management System (Andhra Pradesh, India)
SMART	Simple, moral, accountable, responsive, transparent (government, Andhra Pradesh, India)
SME	Small and medium enterprise
SSA	Sub-Saharan Africa

SSE	Small-scale enterprise
SUSENAS	National Socio-Economic Household Survey (Indonesia)
TEPI	Trade, Export Promotion and Industry Program (Pakistan)
TNC	Transnational corporation
TWINS	Twin Cities Integrated Network Services (Andhra Pradesh, India)
UNDP	United Nations Development Programme
UNICEF	United Nations Childrens' Fund
VAT	Value added tax
WTO	World Trade Organization
WUA	Water users' association

Introduction

Christopher M. Edmonds

Four broad themes are addressed in this volume. The first is broad macroeconomic questions relating to poverty reduction efforts in Asia. The chapters by Kaushik Basu and Graham Pyatt consider how the poor are conceptualized in current development approaches. Both authors propose reorientation in current practice to better prioritize poverty reduction efforts. Professor Basu argues that the definition of the poor should be changed from one based on absolute income-metric poverty to one based on relative poverty. Citing moral and practical considerations, he advocates that policies be focused to assist individuals whose incomes place them in the lowest quintile of the income distribution, rather than those with per capita incomes below defined poverty lines. Following the observation that globalization holds potential benefits for the entire population, he argues that policymaker concern should focus on groups that tend to be marginalized from globalization and facilitate their participation in the growth process.

Professor Pyatt favors refocusing existing approaches in policy modeling to show greater sensitivity to the varied effects of policies at different scales. He finds flaws in existing policy models, which the chapter explains tend to be based on a single scale. The chapter outlines alternative analytical approaches that permit the consideration of development policies and their effects at multiple scales (e.g., micro-, meso-, and macroeconomic levels). The chapters by Basu and Pyatt are both provocative, in that they challenge existing approaches to development policy and policy modeling, and advocate reorientations in the way the poor are identified and policies are understood.

The chapter by Erik Thorbecke continues the discussion of development policy at the macroeconomic level, showing how existing social accounting matrix (SAM) and computable general equilibrium (CGE) models can be extended to consider the effects of policy changes and economic shocks on income distribution and poverty. By adding distribution analysis to existing methods for assessing policy effects in a general economic equilibrium context, Professor Thorbecke's proposed models provide useful tools for examining the direct and indirect poverty impacts of proposed policy changes. The chapter presents a number of examples of such modeling efforts and highlights the insights gained from them.

The chapter by Ratna Sahay, Paul Cashin, Paolo Mauro, and Catherine Pattillo reviews recent research on the links between macroeconomic policies and poverty reduction and presents some new empirical results. Macroeconomic policies the chapter considers include inflation controls, trade liberalization, and external debt. The association between these macroeconomic measures and the Human Development Index (HDI) across 100 countries during the period 1975–1998 is estimated and discussed. The analysis supports the conclusion that sound macroeconomic policies in developing countries foster more rapid improvements in the HDI scores. Results also indicate that policies aimed at improving basic education and health are effective measures for fostering equitable growth.

The second theme and group of chapters are focused on the importance for reducing poverty in Asia of antipoverty interventions targeted to particular urban or industrial sectors. An area of much recent discussion concerns the role of technological innovation—in particular the implications and applications of information and communications technology (ICT)—in development and poverty reduction in the Asian region. Part II contains two chapters that consider issues in this area from markedly different perspectives. The chapter by Sanjaya Lall considers the role of technological innovation in accounting for growth in export-oriented ICT and manufacturing industries in Asia. He argues that the competitiveness of manufacturing industries in Asia's successful economies facilitated high growth and expanded job opportunities in industries that employ skilled labor. In turn, Professor Lall argues, these achievements brought about major achievements in poverty reduction. The chapter also discusses the implications of the technological underpinnings of competitiveness and growth for the current development strategies of leading East Asian countries.

The chapter by Randeep Sudan examines the role of ICT and the development of the ICT sector for poverty reduction in South Asia; in particular, it focuses on the role ICT applications have played in poverty reduction initiatives in the state of Andhra Pradesh, India. Sudan considers a number of case studies of ICT application in the state's poverty reduction efforts (e.g., information dissemination to remote areas, as a tool in anti-corruption efforts) and the effect of ICT industry expansion in the state on the poor. The author concludes that ICT development offers many valuable opportunities for application in poverty reduction efforts.

Dipak Mazumdar's chapter focuses the development of small and medium enterprises (SMEs) as a route to pro-poor growth. The chapter presents estimates that show SME development has a larger impact in reducing poverty than growth of larger enterprises. Professor Mazumdar discusses the implications this finding holds for development and poverty reduction strategies in Asia.

The third theme and set of chapters are related to the measurement and characterization of poverty in Asian and Pacific countries. The chapter by Abuzar Asra and Vivian Santos-Francisco considers the trade-off between defining a national poverty line or lines that most accurately measure poverty across the distinct situations found in a country (specificity), and defining poverty lines that provide a basis for comparing poverty incidence across geographic areas and time (comparability). The chapter reviews how the poverty lines of eight Asian countries were derived and are computed, and evaluates them with respect to the importance given to concerns about specificity and comparability of the poverty definition.

The chapter by Arsenio M. Balisacan examines common approaches to measuring poverty applied internationally, reconstructs a poverty profile for the Philippines using different approaches, and considers the results in an effort to understand how recent experience vis-à-vis growth and poverty reduction is reflected in profiles. The chapter argues that present practices used in poverty measurement in the Philippines fall short in terms of informing policy choices. Professor Balisacan constructs a new profile, applying an alternative approach to poverty measurement that seeks to address shortcomings identified in the techniques applied in official poverty measures to monitor policy performance in reducing poverty. The chapter also shows that our understanding of the poor based on poverty figures derived from survey data is quite sensitive to the measures employed to obtain the information.

The chapter by John Weiss discusses poverty measurement in the analysis of the effects of policy changes, and considers possible implications for poverty reduction of shifting development lending away from project activities and toward policy- or sector-based lending. Highlighting the lack of well-established tools for ex ante assessment of the impact of policy- and sector-based loans on poverty outcomes, the chapter notes that methodologies for evaluating the effects of projects on growth and poverty reduction are far more developed and better understood. Professor Weiss reviews the "poverty impact matrix" approach to assessing policy loan effects, but argues that experience from the past two decades militates against mechanistic application of such tools; instead, he suggests case-by-case assessment grounded in a thorough understanding of the local policy environment. By addressing the question of poverty monitoring in the context of policy reform efforts intended to spur growth and reduce poverty, this chapter returns to many of the themes addressed in the first section of the book.

The final theme and set of chapters in the volume concern country studies on poverty and poverty trends in selected Asian and Pacific countries. These provide detailed discussions of the situations of the poor and how these have evolved over time in the selected countries. These chapters also provide a useful context in which to consider the more theoretical or methodological issues that are the focus of the earlier chapters. The chapter by Arsenio M. Balisacan in this part of the book looks at the poverty situation in rural Philippines, examines the effectiveness of poverty interventions targeted on agricultural sector development, and considers more generally the role of agricultural development in poverty reduction in the country. The chapter traces the failure of rural development and the country's poor performance in rural poverty reduction to policy biases against agriculture in general and against small farms in particular.

The chapter by Abdul Razzaq Kemal reviews poverty trends in Pakistan, evaluating the factors that appear to explain why poverty increased during the 1990s. His analysis shows that macroeconomic policies carried out as part of structural adjustment packages have adversely affected output and employment, and have resulted in the country having a more regressive tax system. This has had the effect of increasing the tax burden borne by the poor at the same time as it has reduced the poor's income-earning opportunities. These changes, according to Kemal, account for much of the observed increase in the incidence and severity of poverty in the country.

The chapter by Saman Kelegama reviews the current poverty situation in Sri Lanka and shows that poverty declined little during the 1990s. The chapter identifies shortcomings in the existing poverty-reduction strategy and programs. The author identifies a number of impediments, including both structural and political factors and inadequate market liberalization, which have caused the general failure of poverty reduction efforts in Sri Lanka. *Depoliticizing* the implementation of existing poverty programs and undertaking structural economic/market reform, Kelegama argues, will facilitate greater effectiveness of existing poverty programs.

Two chapters discuss poverty in Pacific island countries. The chapter by Christopher Lightfoot and Anthony Joseph Ryan poses the question: Is poverty an issue in the Pacific? The authors answer that poverty clearly exists and is a problem in the Pacific islands, but that the cultural pride commonly expressed by Pacific islanders impedes public acceptance of this reality. Poverty in this region does not take the form of nutritional or material deprivation; instead, it results largely from greater vulnerability in the face of limited opportunities to earn cash income and income insecurity caused by frequent environmental and economic shocks. The chapter traces poverty in the Pacific islands to shortages of financial, technical, and social services; the nature and quality of governance processes; and outcomes of discrimination based on gender, ethnicity, or social status, rather than to actual material deprivation or lack of productive resources.

The chapter by Vijay Naidu argues that both relative and absolute poverty, as well as economic inequality, are becoming more pronounced in the Pacific islands. Examining the nature and extent of poverty in the region, the author recommends the opening up of country economies and polities to facilitate the development of more inclusive societies as a priority in reducing poverty. Improving the provision of basic resources to vulnerable groups and creating opportunities for productive and sustainable livelihoods are the other priority areas identified in the chapter for poverty reduction efforts in the Pacific islands.

To conclude, the materials collected in this volume highlight the contributions of sound economic research to improving the understanding of poverty in the world's most populated region, which an estimated two-thirds of the world's poor call home. Since the Asian Development Bank adopted the Poverty Reduction Strategy in 1999, with its goal of making the reduction of poverty the overarching goal of its operations, great progress has been achieved. An important part of this work has involved the development of new tools and methodologies for assessing the poverty reduction effect for ADB-financed antipoverty interventions. In this area, as well as in efforts to build capacity in developing member countries to address poverty, ADB's collaboration with leading international and regional economists has been of the greatest importance. It is hoped that this book will be a means for sharing some of the insights gained and advances achieved from these efforts with researchers and stakeholders in Asia and the Pacific.

PART I

The Macroeconomy, Globalization, and
Pro-Poor Growth

1. Marginalization in a Globalizing World: Some Plausible Scenarios and Suggestions for Measurement

Kaushik Basu

1. Introduction

One curious feature about the debate on globalization is that those who favor it see no negative fallout and those who oppose it see no silver lining. This polarization results from the reluctance of either side to concede to the other any argument that could be used to oppose its agenda. But while this strategy of not giving way on any front may be desirable for college debating competitions, it does not augur well for scientific inquiry.

Take, for instance, the side of the globalizers, those who believe that on balance globalization is a desirable process. By refusing to look at the negative fallout, these advocates of globalization do a great disservice to economic policy, since they dampen the effort to counter the negative effects. This chapter is rooted in the belief that globalization creates enormous opportunities through greater trade and the flow of capital to where it is most productive, and that its benefits typically outweigh the costs. But, though positive, it is not without negative effects. Globalization does have a tendency to marginalize some people and regions. Such claims are often made by the opponents of globalization, but are usually left at the level of mere assertion. This chapter gives some concrete examples of how globalization has a concurrent tendency to marginalize people. Once this process is properly understood, we can devise policy measures to counter the process and spread the benefits of globalization.

After discussing the fallout of globalization, this chapter will discuss how we should measure a nation's economic well-being, drawing on earlier work (Basu, 2001), which is particularly sensitive to poverty and marginalization.

2. Globalization and Marginalization

There is a large activist literature arguing that the current process of globalization will marginalize and even hurt certain sections of the population, especially those who are already on the fringes. Since some of the writers who say this are habitually pessimistic about all changes, we must ask if there is good reason to believe them. The answer in this case is yes. There are two broad routes through which globalization tends to generate forces of marginalization.

First, consider poor fishermen who use simple boats, like the catamaran in Kerala, to catch fish in the seas close to the coast. Suppose that globalization occurs and this brings in larger fishing companies, domestic or multinational does not matter, into the business. These companies, using sophisticated ships, go deeper into the sea and make larger catches. This is likely to increase the national income of this country but may well leave the coastal fishermen poorer, because their catch becomes smaller as a lot of the fish are now netted on the high seas.[1] This is a case of impoverishment through the "resource route."

There are other more indirect ways in which the resource route can leave people worse off. An increase in national income and the use of advanced technology can cause a worsening of environmental conditions. Poor farmers and fishermen, who get no direct benefit from this country's globalization and technological modernization and suffer no loss of income may, nevertheless, see their overall standard of living deteriorate. After all, the environment is now worse and, unlike the direct beneficiaries of modernization and open trade, they do not have higher incomes as a result.

Even if there is no impoverishment of resources and no environmental deterioration, there may be a more complex "market route" through which some sections of the population lose out. Consider a fisherman who owns a pond, catches x kilograms (kg) of fish each year, keeps some of it for his own consumption, and sells the rest in order to buy other necessities of life.

Suppose that he decides that he does not want to be richer and so becomes complacent that, even if the rest of the world modernizes and globalizes, he has nothing to worry about, because he will continue to do what he has always done. Now suppose technological advancement takes place in producing or catching fish or, for that matter, in the production of any other good that is a substitute for pond fish. Let us assume that environmental conditions remain unchanged. Since this man continues to catch x kg of fish each year, at first sight it seems that his welfare will remain unchanged. But as world production of fish or fish substitutes increases, the price of fish will decline. When our fisherman tries to sell a part of his catch and buy other goods, he will find that he cannot buy as many of the latter as before. His real income will have decreased.[2] This decrease is an

---

1.   Stiglitz (1998b) makes a more general point when he argues that while free trade can be a powerful instrument of progress, it can fail to create growth if the developing country does not fulfill certain institutional priors, such as having a structure that promotes domestic competition.

2.   In case there is technological advance occurring in several sectors, what this argument needs is that technological advance in the production of fish and fish substitutes be

important result that arises from the forces of globalization and techno-logical progress to marginalize large groups of people in certain traditional sectors. This may be called impoverishment through the "market route."

Of course, in principle, it is possible to compensate the losers, since the total output rises, but that seldom happens. A closely related problem occurs by virtue of the price changes that are inevitable with globalization and the opening up of an economy. A farmer who is used to facing a steady price for the good he produces (because of government protection) may suddenly have to cope with fluctuations in the global price of that good. This may prompt major changes in cropping patterns and, inevitably, adjustment costs.

Another market-route problem occurs when footloose global companies become major players in world production. By threatening to take their busi-ness to another nation, they can strike harder bargains with workers in a par-ticular country than they would have when firms did not cross international boundaries so easily. This is closely related to the issue of international labor standards, which is discussed elsewhere (Basu, 1999).

If we are to push for development while minimizing these marginalizing tendencies of globalization and technological advance, we need to measure development in ways that severely deduct points for any increase in marginalization. In the sections that follow, we discuss such a method of mea-suring development.

3. Measuring Development

The development debate appears to be, at last, coasting toward a consensus: developing nations must not focus their energies on the growth rate of their gross domestic product (GDP), net national product (NNP), gross national product (GNP), and the like, but instead try to achieve "human development" or "comprehensive development." A remarkable feature of these new goals is that everyone seems to support them, though few know what the terms mean. This is in some sense understandable. First, the terms "human" and "compre-hensive" are so enticing that no one can proclaim to be against these without sounding absurd and boorish. And since the aim of these new objectives is to go beyond narrow economic objectives to larger social and political goals, some vagueness in the target is inevitable. Attempts to give these goals sharper focus, as in the United Nations Development Programme's (UNDP) construc-

---

greater than in the production of other goods. This causes very little loss of generality: if the technological advance in the other goods sector is greater than in the fish industry, then those who produce goods that are the substitutes for the products of these other sectors but use traditional technology will now become impoverished.

tion of the human development index, have inevitably led to the criticism of arbitrariness. But even on this point one may argue that it is better to be somewhat arbitrary but have your broad objective right than to have a sharply defined but morally indefensible objective.

One aim of this chapter is to join this debate somewhat idiosyncratically. After a discussion of the concept of development as it has evolved over time (Section 4), it goes on to propose and evaluate particular goals that countries should adopt. Section 5 suggests some perspectives on measuring and evaluating the progress of nations, without claiming that these measures should be the sum total of what nations strive to achieve. Instead, the measures that are suggested should be part of the larger goal of human development.

4. The Idea of Development

By leafing through *Forbes* magazine and recent *World Development Reports* it is easy to compile the following facts. The total 1998 income of Hollywood's 50 richest individuals exceeds the total income of Burundi's entire population of seven million. If Bill Gates decided to convert into cash the *increase* in value of his total assets over the past year and consume it, he would be able to consume more than the total annual consumption of the 60 million people of Ethiopia.

These numbers reflect both the phenomenal scope for wealth and economic well-being that the modern world makes possible, and also how easy it is for this enormous potential to bypass large masses of humanity. This de facto exclusion indicates a massive failure, not in scientific achievement (technically all can be provided for), but in social and political institutions. In this unbelievably rich world, large numbers of children work 12 to 14 hours a day, even so just barely enabling their families to survive; in many countries more than 100 babies out of every 1000 live births die in the first year of life; and in many nations more than half the population has no access to electricity or safe drinking water.

Have we had the right goals? Have we striven too hard for narrow aggregate economic targets, without paying adequate attention to basic human well-being and equality?

For long stretches of history, a nation's achievement was measured by its territorial control. So progress was equated with sending out armies and armadas. Though trade could always create value simply by altering the ownership of goods and services, a large part of the global game was viewed as zero sum. As a consequence, development, which connotes advance and progress, was not an important part of the human agenda. The aim of a state or a kingdom was peace and general prosperity; expansion meant encroachment into what belonged to others.

One can see this kind of reasoning in one of the earliest books on economics, *The Arthashastra* by Kautilya, which was written around 300 BC. Despite its attempt to be a comprehensive treatise on statecraft and the economic management of a nation,[3] its obsession is with order and static efficiency: the king should have a well-defined set of laws and punish anybody who disrupts the functioning of society.

There are long tracts on the management of state finances, on how profligacy must be avoided, on fiscal discipline, and on effective tax collection. The concern for budgetary discipline is so great that, in times of financial shortage, the *Arthashastra* (Kautilya, 1999: 272) permits the king to exploit the gullibility of the masses and raise funds by "building overnight, as if it happened by a miracle, a temple or a sanctuary and promote the holding of fairs and festivals in honor of the miraculous deity" and (Kautilya, 1999: 273) "using secret agents to frighten people into making offerings to drive away an evil spirit." Despite such attention to detail and its range of concerns, which trespass the boundaries of economics, politics, and sociology (not to mention morality), what is surprising about this classic work, viewed from the edge of the 20th century, is how little it dwells on *progress* or growth of aggregate material well-being. This was generally true of early views of the good life.

With the growth in trade and breakthroughs in science and technology (of which in theory there need be no end), this view has changed. Our goals have moved away from purely tangible wealth (land and gold) and static well-being. One can have a large income, despite having very little control over land or anything tangible. By sending one's capital to distant lands, one can partake in the success of faraway places without the aid of soldiers and guns. The discovery of a new technology in one laboratory in one city can spread to faraway lands. In principle, this prosperity can be there for all and greater income over time can accrue to all. Yet that has not happened. For every People's Republic of China, whose per capita income grew at the astonishing rate of 6.7 percent per year for 30 years starting from 1965, there is a Sierra Leone, whose per capita income fell during the same period at the rate of 1.4 percent per year. For every Chile, whose per capita income grew at the more sober rate of 1.6 percent over the same 30 years, there is a Ghana, whose per capita income declined at the rate of 0.9 percent. Negative average growth over the past 30 years was also observed in Bolivia, El Salvador, Madagascar, Senegal, and several other nations (World Bank, 1998). These anomalies raise a host of new questions concerning development and distribution. What policies should Third World nations follow? What policies should global organizations such as the World Bank or the World Trade Organization follow or advocate?

With the rise in popularity of measuring and keeping tabs on national incomes, which is clearly a phenomenon of the past century, progress and

---

3.   Arthashastra literally means "doctrine of wealth."

development have also come to be measured in terms of the GNP or per capita income of a nation. This intellectual tradition, with its limited objective, helped nations focus their energies narrowly and must have played a role in the rapid growth of national incomes. But it also brought dissension and disappointment in its wake. To maximize income growth, environmental considerations were left to languish on the sidelines; often the standard of living was allowed to slide; large inequalities between classes, regions, and genders were ignored; and poverty was tolerated more than it should have been. Fortunately, that attitude has been changing.

A large number of economists have argued the need for moving beyond this narrow goal.[4] This argument is precisely the line along which Stiglitz (1998a: 31), for instance, has contested the so-called "Washington consensus." "The Washington consensus advocated use of a small set of instruments... to achieve a relatively narrow goal (economic growth). The post-Washington consensus recognizes both that a broader set of instruments [is] necessary and [that] our goals are also much broader." And Stiglitz goes on to emphasize rightly the need to focus attention on better income distribution, environment, health care, and education.

In a series of influential publications, Sen (1983, 1985, and 1999) has contributed to the broadening of the goals of development. He has argued the need to move away from the commodity fetishism of earlier approaches and toward the evaluation of development and progress in terms of functioning and capability. A function is what a person manages to do or be. A good can enable something to function but is distinct from the functioning. A bicycle is a good, whereas being able to transport oneself rapidly to work is a function. And several persons, each owning a bicycle, may be able to achieve very different kinds of functioning, depending on their other attributes: how well fed they are, their morbidity statistics, and so on. As Sen has pointed out, this approach has its roots in an intellectual heritage that goes back to Adam Smith and Karl Marx (Basu and Lopez-Calva, 2001) and was lost in the increasing fervor of evaluating the progress of nations in terms of incomes, which we have seen in the 20th century.

This broader approach to the concept of well-being and progress has generated two kinds of literature. The first formalizes this still nebulous idea (Atkinson, 1995; Herrero, 1996; Romer, 1999; and Suzumura, 1999). The second tries to put it into operation (Dasgupta and Weale, 1992; Brandolini and D'Alessio, 1998; and the *Human Developments Reports* [UNDP, 1990 et seq.]). This chapter is concerned with the more practical and policy-oriented issues of development goals; the modifications suggested take off from that concern, and the next section begins with a statement of the method used by UNDP.

---

4.   For a lucid and comprehensive account of the changing objectives of development over the last 50 years, see Thorbecke (1999).

5. Quintile Income, Quintile Growth

The UNDP, beginning with the *Human Development Report 1990*, has argued strongly for an indicator of a nation's progress, which is a weighted average of (i) the nation's literacy and educational achievement, (ii) the citizen's life expectancy, and (iii) the nation's per capita income.

More recently, the World Bank has argued for broadening development goals beyond traditional macroeconomic goals such as national income growth, fiscal health, and balance of payments stability, and to include "societal development": basic human rights, access to a just legal system, literacy, and good health (Stiglitz, 1998a; Wolfensohn, 1999). Streeten (1994) has sought to bring order to these objectives by classifying them into two categories: resource development and humanitarian progress, and giving six reasons why we should be interested in human development: (i) it is desirable as an end in itself; (ii) it can promote higher productivity and so enhance human command over goods and services; (iii) it reduces the birth rate, which is a generally desirable effect; (iv) it is good for the environment; (v) it can contribute to a healthy civil society and democracy; and (vi) it can promote political stability.

Most of these objectives are, however, related to the objectives of equality and poverty reduction, of people being included in the development process rather than being excluded or abandoned. Thus, Streeten points out how the poor are not just victims of environmental degradation but often its cause; and how human development promotes a healthy civil society by improving the lot of the poorest people and making them feel included.

This sense of inclusion suggests a natural correction for the way we evaluate different economies. Essentially this says that, in evaluating an economy's state or progress, we must focus primarily on how the poorest people are faring. A first attempt to do this is to look at economic conditions of the poorest 20 percent of the population. In other words, instead of bothering about the per capita income of the nation, we should be concerned about the per capita income of the bottom quintile of the population. Likewise, instead of equating a country's progress with the growth rate of per capita incomes in general, we should look at the growth rate of the per capita income of the poorest 20 percent of the population.

In recommending the use of these measures and therefore commending them as goals of development, this chapter is not taking issue with the advocacy of noneconomic goals, which has gathered strength in recent years with the publication of UNDP's annual *Human Development Reports* and the World Bank's new interest in "comprehensive development." This suggestion is not meant to be a denial of the larger aims of trying to achieve political stability, environmental health, and a higher general quality of human life. To understand this recommendation, it is necessary to keep two factors in mind. First, *to the extent that we do look at income and income growth*, we should instead look at per capita income of the poorest 20 percent (henceforth, "quintile income") and the per capita income growth rate of the poorest 20 percent (henceforth, "quintile growth rate") of the population. Secondly, these quintile objectives are likely to correlate better with other noneconomic indicators, such as environmental conditions and social stability,[5] for the reasons that Streeten has suggested (Aturupane, Glewwe, and Isenman, 1994).[6]

Thus, even when we decide to play the dismal scientist and focus on income, a focus on *quintile* income will automatically capture the social indicators emphasized in broader notions of human development.

Before proceeding further it is useful to write down some definitions formally. Let us define an *income profile* of a country with n persons as a vector, $x = (x_1, x_2, ... x_n)$, of nonnegative numbers, such that x_i denotes the income of person i. Without loss of generality, it will be assumed that, if x is an income profile, then $x_1 = x_2 = ... = x_n$. This simply entails renaming the citizens so that the poorest person is named person 1, the second poorest person is named person 2, and so on, with ties being broken arbitrarily. Since populations can vary, we will for explicitness use $n(x)$ to denote the number of elements in x. Now, let $t(x)$ be the largest integer r such that $r/n(x) = 1/5$.

Given a country with an income profile x, the *quintile income* of the country is denoted by $q(x)$, which is defined as follows:

$$q(x) = [x_1 + ... + x_{t(x)}] / t(x). \tag{1.1}$$

Suppose a country's income profile changes from x_t in period t, to x_{t+1} in period $t + 1$. Then the *quintile growth rate*, call it g, of this country between years t and $t + 1$ is defined as

$$g = 100[q(x_{t+1}) - q(x_t)] / q(x_t). \tag{1.2}$$

This criterion for assessing the *economic* performance of an economy stems from a combination of normative and pragmatic considerations. Suppose one looks at the gross inequalities of income that prevail in the world, as suggested by the few striking examples cited at the start of Section 2. Although the question may not arise in discussions among professional economists, the layperson often asks whether there is a case for limiting the incomes of the richest people. The answer

---

5. One cannot deny, though, that for certain kinds of social problems, such as crime, the crucial variable may be the gap between the per capita incomes of the richest and the poorest people in a society.

6. A similar exercise that broadened the idea of human well-being to more explicitly take account of political and civil liberties was undertaken by Dasgupta and Weale (1992).

to such a question should depend most crucially on what such a policy would do to the poorest people. It is indeed a shame that Bill Gates earns so much more than the average person in Burundi and, for that matter, the average person in the United States. But if it were the case that trying to curb Bill Gates' income would cause the poor people to be worse off, then there would be no case for such a curb. Not only in distributional questions such as this but in deciding on any economic policy, it seems morally appealing to check on what the policy change will do to the poorest people.[7] This is the normative consideration.

One may legitimately ask if it is reasonable to hold up the progress of a society's better-off population segment if the bottom quintile contains a disproportionate number of dysfunctional individuals. There are several possible responses to this question. First, thanks to a variety of market failures, a society's bottom quintile is likely to contain not just dysfunctional individuals but also many talented people, whose talents are not realized and nurtured because of limited access to education and credit. Second, even for the dysfunctional people, there is a moral case for transferring direct support to them by taxing the rich. Of course, if the tax becomes too large and therefore inefficient, the entire society in question will fail to thrive in the long run; by the criterion of the long-run interest of the bottom quintile itself, such a policy will turn out to be undesirable. What is attractive about this criterion is that it sets limits on how much a government should try to redistribute wealth and income to the poor through a self-referential calculation, which looks at the long-run interest of the poor. While Rawls (1971) in his abstract models could focus attention on *the* worst-off person, in reality we seldom know who the worst-off is. Indeed, thanks to earnings from the informal sector, income data for the poorest persons is very difficult to collect. However, most nations do provide information on the income or expenditure share that goes to the poorest 20 percent of the population. And so the suggestion that we concentrate on the poorest 20 percent is the pragmatic part of the recommendation.

Designing policy by focusing attention on the poorest 20 percent also has the advantage that one cannot totally ignore the effect on people outside this group. This is because if others fare too badly, they will become part of the poorest 20 percent and so will automatically come into focus. For this same reason, raising the quintile growth rate can never mean ignoring the overall growth rate of the country. For certain periods of time, a positive quintile growth rate can occur together with a negative per capita income growth rate. But if that happens for too long, there will be perfect

---

7. Answering an interviewer's question about what a "successful" economy is, Sen (*Chicago Tribune*, 28 March 1999) pointed out: "This concerns how the worst-off members of society share in that society. Neglect of people at the bottom of the ladder would indicate a failed economy."

equality of income in the country and at that point the per capita growth rate will coincide with the quintile growth rate. For this reason, the criterion being suggested here is distinct from that of mere poverty reduction. The objective of reducing poverty satisfies the property of satiation, that is, it is a self-liquidating objective: once poverty is removed there is nothing more to strive for. On the other hand, the aim of improving the lot of the poorest 20 percent can never be satisfied. It is a moving target.

The relation between this criterion and reducing inequality is more complicated. If a society is locked in a zero-sum game, then improving the condition of the bottom quintile of society is also to reduce inequality (for reasonable definitions of inequality), since in a zero-sum society one has to take from Peter to give to Paul. On the other hand, as already discussed, allowing some people to become richer may be essential to enable the bottom quintile of society to do better. In such situations, my criterion will tend to exacerbate inequality. One may of course bring in a special inequality consciousness by requiring that inequality reduction should be a lexicographically secondary objective: that is, if two policies leave quintile income the same but one of them lowers inequality, then we should choose the latter. In general, the principle worth upholding is that equality is a desirable objective as long as it does not occur at the expense of the poorest people. If some aggregate welfare has to be sacrificed for greater equality, that is worthwhile, but if poverty has to be increased in order to have greater equality, then the greater equality is not worth it.

Measuring welfare in terms of the welfare of the bottom quintile of society also has the advantage of satisfying the criteria of anonymity and the weak Pareto principle. In other words, if two societies were such that one could be made to look just like the other through a permutation of individuals, then under my criterion the two societies would be judged as equally good; and if everybody's income rose, then these societies would be considered better according to this criterion of evaluation.

There are, however, some desirable axioms that the quintile measure does not satisfy. One such axiom, the "weak transfer axiom," says that when a fixed sum of money is transferred from a rich person to a poorer person who is in the bottom quintile of society, such that the income ranking of people remains unchanged, the new income profile should be considered socially superior to the old one. When money is transferred from a person above the bottom quintile to someone in the bottom quintile, the quintile income will rise. However, when the transfer takes place between a person already in the bottom quintile to someone poorer, the quintile income remains unchanged. Hence, quintile income as a measure of welfare violates the weak transfer axiom.

Using an index that I shall call the rank-weighted quintile income may rectify this weakness. This is essentially an ordinal index that penalizes a country if, within the poorest 20 percent, income is distributed in favor of the relatively rich. Let x be an income profile. Then the rank-weighted quintile income (RQI) is denoted by $q^{\hat{}}(x)$ and defined as follows:

$$q^{\hat{}}(x) = \sum_{i=1}^{t(x)} [t(x) + 1 - i]_{x_i} / \sum_{i=1}^{t(x)} [t(x) + 1 - i] \qquad (1.3)$$

$q^{\hat{}}(x)$ is the weighted average of the incomes of the poorest 20 percent, with the weight for the poorest ith person's income being given by $t(x) + 1 - i$. Hence, the poorest person gets the highest weight, $t(x)$, and the richest person in the bottom 20-percent group gets the lowest weight of one.

By rearranging terms, the above equation can be rewritten as follows:

$$q^{\hat{}}(x) = 2q(x) - \frac{2\Sigma \, ix_i}{t(x) \, [1 + t(x)]} \qquad (1.4)$$

One can proceed in this vein and create variants that are more complex. These more nuanced measures may be pursued in the future for more sophisticated measurement of welfare based on the general idea that the welfare of a society ought to be equated with the welfare of the poorest people. But to spend more time on these measures here will distract us from our present objective. From here onward, the focus will return to quintile income and quintile growth.

Some changes in welfare criteria may be important notionally, but may make very little difference when put into practice. This possibility prompts the following question: if international organizations that display comparative income and growth information, such as in the World Bank's *World Development Reports*, instead gave data on quintile income and quintile growth, would this make important changes in rankings? If not, then the whole exercise would be academic and of little consequence from the practitioner's point of view. However, it is easy to see that the changes in rankings could be quite sharp. Table 1.1 shows the relative performance of a group of nations using the criteria of income and quintile income.

Table 1.1 takes a selection of 40 countries, which includes the world's 10 richest nations and the 10 poorest. There was one handicap in doing the calculation: for most nations, data on the share of income going to the bottom 20 percent is not available on an annual basis. Therefore, the latest available data on income shares were used. The figure in parentheses in the second column gives the year from which the share data is obtained. Subject to this caveat, it is interesting to see how large a difference the shift from per capita income to quintile income makes. Switzerland, the richest nation in terms of per capita income, drops below Norway and Denmark in terms of quintile income. The

United States, the fourth richest country, drops below the other nine richest nations. Among poor nations, Sierra Leone's per capita income of US$160 is low enough, but its quintile income is a shocking US$9. The South Asian countries are very poor, but they do relatively better viewed through the lens of quintile income.

Table 1.1. Per Capita Income and Quintile Income, 1997

I. Economy	Percentage Share of Income of Poorest 20% (various years as indicated)		GNP Per Capita in US Dollars (1997)	Per Capita Income of Poorest 20% or Quintile Income (1997)
Austria	10.4	(1987)	27,920	14,518
Bangladesh	9.4	(1992)	360	169
Belgium	9.5	(1992)	26,730	12,697
Brazil	2.5	(1995)	4,790	599
Burkina Faso	5.5	(1994)	250	69
Chile	3.5	(1994)	4,820	844
Denmark	9.6	(1992)	34,890	16,747
Egypt, Arab Rep.	8.7	(1991)	1,200	522
Ethiopia	7.1	(1995)	110	39
France	7.2	(1989)	26,300	9,468
Germany	9.0	(1989)	28,280	12,726
Guinea-Bissau	2.1	(1991)	230	24
Hungary	9.7	(1993)	4,510	2,187
India	9.2	(1994)	370	170
Indonesia	8.0	(1996)	1,110	444
Israel	6.9	(1992)	16,180	5,582
Madagascar	5.1	(1993)	250	64
Malaysia	4.6	(1989)	4,530	1,042
Mali	4.6	(1994)	260	60
Mexico	3.6	(1995)	3,700	666
Nepal	7.6	(1995–1996)	220	84
Netherlands	8.0	(1991)	25,830	10,332
Niger	2.6	(1995)	200	26
Norway	10.0	(1991)	36,100	18,050
Pakistan	9.4	(1996)	500	235
People's Republic of China	5.5	(1995)	860	237
Poland	9.3	(1992)	3,590	1,669
Romania	8.9	(1994)	1,410	627
Russian Fed.	4.2	(1996)	2,680	563
Rwanda	9.7	(1983–1985)	210	102
Sierra Leone	1.1	(1989)	160	9
South Africa	2.9	(1993–1994)	3,210	465
Sweden	9.6	(1992)	26,210	12,581
Switzerland	7.4	(1982)	43,060	15,932
Tanzania	6.8	(1993)	210	71
Thailand	5.6	(1992)	2,740	767
Ukraine	4.3	(1995)	1,040	224
United States	4.8	(1994)	29,080	6,979
Venezuela	4.3	(1995)	3,480	748
Viet Nam	7.8	(1993)	310	121

Source: World Bank (1998).

It is one thing to present data and information on the bottom quintile of societies (as this section urges), and another actually to design policy and set development goals based on these criteria. When we move on to designing policy, two issues arise. First, there is the tradeoff between economic well-being and other indicators of welfare; second, there are potential conflicts between global goals and national goals. Let me first take up the matter of the tradeoff between different goals; since there is relatively little to say on this, we can concentrate on the latter. The issue of potential conflict between global and national goals takes us into new analytical territory concerning strategic issues in policymaking and conditional morality.

Given the recent effort to make economists, international bureaucrats, and policymakers aware that "there are things in life that matter, apart from income and wealth," it is easy to believe that the focus on income was always the principal focus of nations. But, as was mentioned in the previous section, that is not so. Classical writers talked about the significance of a good quality of life in general, and this typically goes beyond material plenitude. In a letter written to Lord Carlisle on 8 November 1779, Adam Smith wrote about how Ireland could make greater progress: "It wants order, police and a regular administration of justice both to protect and to restrain the inferior ranks of people, articles more essential to the progress of industry than both coal and wood put together..." (Mossner and Ross, 1987). In discussing the alienation of labor, Marx (1844) stressed how a life in which only one's material wants are met is animalistic; freedom to choose is an essential constituent of good human life. As mentioned earlier, these traditions, via modern formalizations, have influenced the construction of the human development index.

Before proceeding further, one question worth asking is this: Even though the need to broaden our goals of development, as suggested in the *Human Development Reports*, has great normative appeal, is there a case for constructing a single index out of a composite of varied indices? While it is true that such an index can have—indeed has had—the desirable effect of mobilizing popular opinion, its conceptual underpinnings are questionable. Ray (1998) has rightly questioned the weaknesses of aggregating diverse indicators of the quality of life. There is another problem with the use of such aggregate measures, which has not always been noted. Let us suppose that we take all variables that are worthwhile and construct a strictly concave welfare function in which these variables enter as arguments. For simplicity, we often use a linear aggregator, such as the human development index, but clearly, since we have too much of one variable, we would expect the weight on that to decrease. Hence, the strict concavity is natural. What I want to argue is that if we use such an aggregate notion of welfare and do cost-benefit analysis to determine which projects are desirable, we are likely to run into important flaws in our decision making.

Note that in standard treatments of cost-benefit analysis or project evaluation, it is considered unimportant what the project is actually about. Whether it be a school or a dam, the same method of analysis is supposed to apply. This reasoning would be fine if all projects were fully specified and alternative courses of action were open to a nation. In reality, projects do not come in that form. Separate projects come up one at a time and each is typically evaluated separately. And therein lies the problem of evaluating all projects against one aggregate measure of welfare.

To see this, suppose that welfare depends on only two variables, income and literacy, and the welfare function is strictly convex. Hence, indifference curves (more precisely, superior sets) in the income-literacy space are strictly concave. Suppose there are two projects: a school and a dam. The former generates two units of literacy and causes a drop of one unit of income, whereas the latter causes a rise of two units of income and a drop of one unit of literacy. It is entirely possible that if each project were evaluated individually (as it usually is), then *by the yardstick of this all-embracing welfare function*, each would be rejected, though the combination of the two projects would be clearly desirable.

What this example suggests is that projects will either have to be bunched together and evaluated together or different projects must be evaluated against different yardsticks. Since it is virtually impossible to consider all projects at once, we are forced to rely on the latter course. In other words, we must evaluate a school in terms of what it does for schooling and literacy. If it contributes a lot to literacy without "too much" damage to other things, it must be considered desirable. Likewise, a dam may have to be evaluated in terms of what it does for income. This is not a well-defined rule for project analysis (the worth of a project depends on what other projects are *likely* to come up in the future, for which there may be no hard information), but this is close to what policy planners, through their intuition, tend to do. In this case the policy planners may be right.

To reject the use of an aggregated index is, however, no reason to reject the importance of the components of such an index. One way of capturing this is to look at a *vector* of a nation's achievements, leaving the exact tradeoffs one considers reasonable to be determined at the time of specific decisions, and perhaps varied depending on context. What this section has argued is that an important component of this vector should be quintile income. This is data that international organizations, such as the UNDP and the World Bank, should make widely available.

In addition, one can take the spirit of this proposal further and focus on the performance of the bottom 20 percent of various dimensions of well-being, such as life expectancy and health indicators. Concerning literacy, one has to be more innovative, because whenever a country has a literacy rate below 80 percent, the least literate quintile will be completely illiterate and so there will be little to distinguish between most developing nations on this score. A recent paper argues that there are two kinds of illiterate persons: an "isolated illiterate," an illiterate who lives in a household consisting entirely of illiterates; and a "proximate illiterate," an illiterate who lives in a household that has at least one literate person (Basu and Foster, 1998). The paper argues that access to a literate person, as a proximate illiterate would have, can relieve the darkness of illiteracy nonnegligibly.[8] Thus a nation in which the literacy rate is 50 percent by virtue of half the members of each household being literate is much better off than another nation in which 50 percent of the people are literate and 50 percent are isolated illiterate. An implication of this reasoning is that if we were to start bottom up, as the quintile approach would require us to do, in devising literacy programs, we would first start with the isolated illiterates.

One reason why individual nations do not give adequate attention to quintile incomes, environment, education, and minimal labor standards is that in the rough and tumble of international competition, they find little room for such soft targets. Just as, according to one theory, firms that do not maximize profit risk getting wiped out by the process of evolution, nations fear that to keep afloat in the global economy, they must achieve higher growth. Thus part of the challenge is not to persuade national leaders that quintile income matters, that the environment matters, etc.—few national leaders disagree with these priorities *in principle*—but to create global institutions that make it possible for countries to pursue these goals. This challenge requires us to understand why, even when each country wants to pursue a certain goal, in the strategic environment of the global economy it may fail to do so. That circumstance is the subject matter of the section that follows.

6. A Remark on Policy

Globalization, I argued at the start, creates opportunities for all. By allowing businesses to take advantage of gains from trade and by channeling capital to where it is most productive, globalization creates wealth in ways that were inconceivable even a few decades ago. However, this creation of wealth implies that globalization gives rise to a *potential* Pareto improvement. A potential Pareto improvement is compatible with some groups' becoming marginalized and even worse off in absolute terms. But if we measure progress in terms of the quintile measures described above, then a potential Pareto

---

8.   An empirical study by Basu, Narayan, and Ravallion (1999), based on individual income and literacy data from Bangladesh, confirms the enormous externalities of having a literate person at home. Illiterate persons who have literate family members at home seem to earn systematically more than isolated illiterate persons. Gibson (1999) finds confirmation of the same theory in his study of nutrition in Papua New Guinea.

improvement will not be cause for celebration unless it translates into progress for the poorest people.

Take the case of India since 1992. In terms of overall growth, India has made rapid progress, with its real national income growing at an average rate of over 6.5 percent per year. However, the focus on this average hides the information that India's regional distribution of income has been steadily deteriorating through the 1990s (Rao, Shand, and Kalirajan, 1999). If international organizations, such as the Asian Development Bank, shifted their focus to quintile income rather than income in general, nations would be forced to pursue policies that were equity-conscious if they wanted to move up the global charts. India would then have an additional incentive to pursue policies that coupled fast growth with better distribution.

At one level, measurement is a technical, value-free activity, with no direct relation to policy. Yet when some method of measurement becomes widely accepted and global policymakers begin to watch the charts that indicate that measure, this innocuous, statistical exercise comes to wield enormous influence on the design and implementation of policy.

References

Atkinson, Anthony. 1995. Capabilities, Exclusion and the Supply of Goods. In *Choice, Welfare and Development*, edited by Kaushik Basu, Prasanta Pattanaik, and Kotaro Suzumura. Oxford: Oxford University Press.

Aturupane, Harsha, Paul Glewwe, and Paul Isenman. 1994. Poverty, Human Development and Growth: An Emerging Consensus? *American Economic Review* 84 (May): 244–249.

Basu, Kaushik. 1999. Child Labor: Cause, Consequence and Cure, with Remarks on International Labor Standards. *Journal of Economic Literature* 37: 1083–1119.

———. 2001. On the Goals of Development. In *Frontiers of Development Economics*, edited by Joseph Stiglitz and Gerald Meier. New York and Oxford: Oxford University Press.

———, and James Foster. 1998. On Measuring Literacy. *Economic Journal* 108: 1733–1749.

———, and Luis-Felipe Lopez-Calva. 2001. Functionings and Capabilities. Forthcoming in *Handbook of Social Choice and Welfare*, edited by Kenneth Arrow, Amartya Sen, and Kotaro Suzumura. Amsterdam: North-Holland Publishers.

———, Ambar Narayan, and Martin Ravallion. 1999. Is Knowledge Shared within Households? The World Bank. Mimeo.

Brandolini, Andrea and G. D'Alessio. 1998. Measuring Well-Being in the Functioning Space. Banca d'Italia. Mimeo.

Dasgupta, Partha, and Martin Weale. 1992. On Measuring the Quality of Life. *World Development* 20: 119–31.

Gibson, J. 2001. Literacy and Intrahousehold Externalities. *World Development* 29 (1): 155–66.

Herrero, Carmen. 1996. Capabilities and Utilities. *Economic Design* 2: 69–88.

Kautilya. 1992. *The Arthashastra*. Edited by L. N. Rangarajan. New Delhi: Penguin.

Marx, Karl, 1844. *The Economic and Philosophic Manuscripts*. English translation. London: Lawrence and Wishart.

Mossner, Ernest, and Ian Ross, eds. 1987. *The Correspondence of Adam Smith*. Indianapolis: Liberty Fund.

Rao, Govinda, R. T. Shand, and K. P. Kalirajan. 1999. Convergence of Incomes across Indian States: A Divergent View. *Economic and Political Weekly*, 34: 769–78.

Rawls, John. 1971. *A Theory of Justice*. Oxford: Oxford University Press.

Ray, Debraj. 1998. *Development Economics*. Princeton: Princeton University Press.

Romer, John. 1999. What we owe our Children, They their Children, and ... University of California at Davis. Mimeo.

Sen, Amartya. 1983. Development: Which Way Now? *Economic Journal* 93: 745–62.

———. 1985. *Commodities and Capabilities*. Amsterdam: North-Holland Publishers.

_____. 1999. *Development as Freedom*. New York: Alfred Knopf.

Stiglitz, Joseph. 1989. *The Economic Role of the State*. Oxford: Blackwell Publishers.

_____. 1998a. More Instruments and Broader Goals: Moving Towards the Post Washington Consensus. WIDER Annual Lecture, The World Bank. Mimeo.

———. 1998b. Towards a New Paradigm for Development: Strategies, Policies and Processes. Prebisch Lecture at the United Nations Commission On Trade and Development. The World Bank. Mimeo.

Streeten, Paul. 1994. Human Development: Means and Ends. *American Economic Review* 84.

Suzumura, Kotaro. 1999. Consequences, Opportunities and Procedures. *Social Choice and Welfare* 16: 17–40.

Thorbecke, Erik, 1999. The Evolution of the Development Doctrine and the Role of Foreign Aid, 1950–2000. Cornell University.

UNDP (United Nations Development Programme). 1990 et seq. *Human Development Report*. Oxford: Oxford University Press.

Wolfensohn, James. 1999. A Proposal for a Comprehensive Development Framework. Washington: World Bank. Mimeo.

World Bank. 1998. *World Development Indicators 1998*. Washington: World Bank.

2. Balanced Development: An Approach to Development Policy and Priorities

Graham Pyatt

1. Introduction[1]

Given the World Bank's recognition of poverty as its "overarching" concern, the development community is now that much closer to consensus on the proposition that economic growth is not the objective of development policy nor even the most useful measure of its success: development is both different in kind from economic growth and broader in scope. Some would go much further. The capabilities approach that has been conceptualized by Amartya Sen (1970) and articulated for a wider audience by the United Nations Development Programme (UNDP) in its annual series of *Human Development Reports* (HDRs) rejects the role of prices as an index of marginal utility or as the definitive measure of scarcity. Ultimately it leads, as in the HDR for the year 2000, to the setting of targets for human development via some (unspecified) political process as an alternative to allowing markets to orchestrate the allocation of resources. Others, who also recognize that economic growth is not the ultimate objective, nonetheless maintain that, in the long run, the pursuit of economic growth offers the best prospects for raising living standards and is, therefore, not only a necessary concern of domestic policy but could be sufficient if only the political processes within a country were guided by the enlightened self-interest of its people.

Between these very different points of view lies the middle ground, much of it occupied by variants of the proposition that the *quality* of growth also matters. However, some of these variants are more explicit than others in characterizing what is meant by the "quality" of a growth process. Those variants, which typically emphasize the economic aspects of development, suggest that quality growth and "broad-based" growth are more or less synonymous. However, from an ex ante point of view there is clearly an important difference between labor-intensive growth and the central thesis of Chenery et al. (1974), which emphasizes the accumulation of assets by those who are relatively poor. And, while both of these could result ex post in growth being "broad-based," it does not then follow that growth will necessarily be "pro-poor," i.e., that the

---

1. This chapter draws on earlier work on the subject matter, and can be seen in relation to it as a report on work in progress. See Pyatt (1992, 1995, and 1996).

growth process will entail the progressive reduction of income inequalities or, *a fortiori*, that the long-run growth of average income within the poorest group in society will have been maximized, as prescribed by Rawls (1971).

The approach to development policy that is outlined here supports the notion that the quality of growth matters. However, to give content to this sentiment and, not least, to design suitable policies, we need a more specific approach to the issues, backed up by a model or conceptual framework that describes the way in which we think living standards are determined. Accordingly, an important theme in this chapter will be to outline two useful contributions toward a better model of crucial mechanisms and to develop some of their implications.

The substantive argument that begins in Section 2 of the chapter recognizes that the determinants of living standards are to be found not only at the macro (economy-wide) and at the micro (individual/household) levels of society, but also at the international level and, again, at the meso (structural) level. A first step, therefore, is to appreciate the interdependence of policies at each of these levels and the evident need for coordination.

Following this, in Section 3 three different approaches to policy formulation are discussed that offer alternative ways of translating a desire to raise living standards and a concern for the poor into operational policies that modify or supplement the role of the market in the interest of development. One of these is to set targets, as suggested above, and another, which is essentially competitive, is to make extensive use of cost-benefit analysis, if only as a conceptual framework, to guide the allocation of resources in cases of market failure and, more generally, in the public interest. A third, complementary approach emphasizes the value of empirical studies of what has and what has not worked in different countries, so that some of the lessons of history might be put to good use.

With these general considerations by way of background, Sections 4 and 5 of the chapter outline two modifications of the conventional neoclassical approach to the analysis of growth and development, which I think are improvements, i.e., they would result in more realistic models and hence are likely to lead to better (more realistic) policies. The first concerns the way in which we model the household and this is discussed in Section 4b. The second, which is introduced in Section 5b, describes production processes in the formal sector and the nature of technology. Neither is new: the former dates back to the work of Chayanov et al. (1966) and Becker (1964, 1965) and builds on the subsequent literature that views the household as being simultaneously a consumer and producer. It has various implications, not least of which is to emphasize the importance of the labor market. Similarly, the putty-clay vintage model of production processes, as pioneered by Johanson (1959) and Salter (1960) and developed subsequently by various authors, emphasizes the complementarity of labor and capital in the short term and the fact that the long term can be no different from the short term unless there is investment in the interim. Taken in conjunction, these innovations relative to standard thinking give theoretical content to what we already know empirically, namely that employment and investment should be at the center of development policy concerns.

Finally, in Section 6 the role of government is discussed. For the most part, this discussion proceeds on conventional lines that emphasize the importance of both monetary and fiscal policy. However, an implication of the alternative model of the household proposed in Section 4 is that the costs of maintaining human capital should be deducted from the standard measures of the gross domestic product to obtain a more appropriate quantification of value added. And, by implication, basic needs should be exempt from value-added tax (VAT). A further implication is that conventional institutional arrangements that support separate recurrent and development budgets make less sense when the provision of health and education services are recognized as investments in human capital. Since these budgetary arrangements can lead to major distortions in the use of public funds, it is suggested that they be reviewed.

2. Determinants of Living Standards and Levels of Aggregation

A first step in trying to give content to the notion of quality growth is to identify the basic determinants of living standards. Figure 2.1, an attempt to do so, suggests that well-being is founded on rights, which include property rights and entitlements, and therefore on a somewhat broader concept than the real asset base—land, housing, tools, etc.—on which economists have tended to focus in the past. This asset base is a stock and the main role of the economic system is to use this stock to generate a flow of goods and services via production activities, which are defined in the figure to include reproduction, i.e., the raising of the next generation. How well this process works must depend on the context within which production and reproduction take place, i.e., on the efficiency of markets, on the institutional framework (not least the family), and on the quality of governance, etc. At the next level up in Figure 2.1 we arrive at individual capabilities and opportunities, which have been endorsed as the essential objectives of development by the UNDP, through its annual series of HDRs (UNDP, 1990 et seq.).

There has been some discussion of the extent to which the capabilities approach ultimately leads to policy priorities that are different from those of the World Bank, as set out in the *World Development Report 1990* (World Bank, 1990). Here, two general observations may be helpful. First, it is clear that Sen's notion of capabilities is broader than the conventional consumption opportunity set, since it includes opportunities and entitlements that cannot be deliv-

**Figure 2.1. A Schematic Representation of the General Basis
of Well-Being**

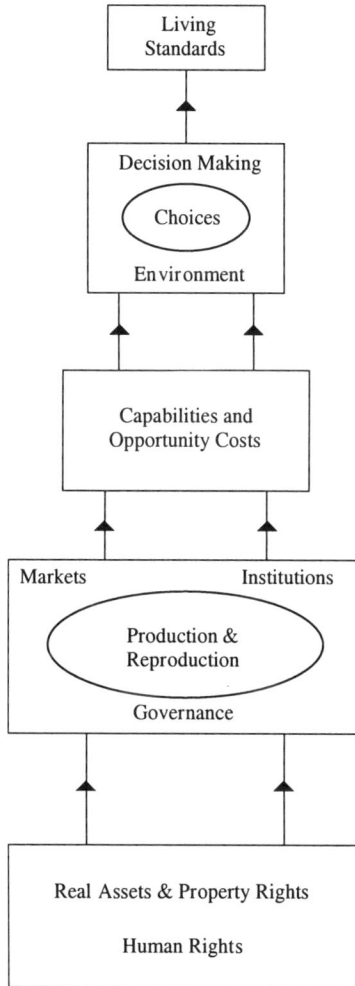

```
                    ┌─────────────────┐
                    │     Living      │
                    │    Standards    │
                    └─────────────────┘
                             ▲
                             │
                    ┌─────────────────┐
                    │ Decision Making │
                    │   ( Choices )   │
                    │  Environment    │
                    └─────────────────┘
                       ▲         ▲
                       │         │
                 ┌───────────────────┐
                 │  Capabilities and │
                 │  Opportunity Costs│
                 └───────────────────┘
                     ▲         ▲
                     │         │
           ┌─────────────────────────┐
           │ Markets      Institutions│
           │   ( Production &        │
           │     Reproduction )      │
           │     Governance          │
           └─────────────────────────┘
                  ▲         ▲
                  │         │
        ┌───────────────────────────┐
        │ Real Assets & Property     │
        │          Rights            │
        │                            │
        │      Human Rights          │
        └───────────────────────────┘
```

ered by markets and derive instead from family ties and community. It then follows that the expansion of the consumption opportunity set is a part of what Sen means by development, but not the whole story. In this sense, economic growth is characteristic of development but not synonymous with it.

A second and different point is that the way in which economic growth is conventionally measured is exceptionable. This is in part a reflection of current conventions as to what to include and what to leave out when measuring individual incomes or, at the national level, the gross domestic product. Giving more attention to nonmarket activities and basing comparisons between individuals and countries on purchasing power parities goes some way toward meeting these concerns. However, it is unlikely that such developments would be seen by the authors of the HDRs as being sufficient to meet their objections, which relate not only to what is included and what is left out, but also to the aggregation of individual capabilities using market prices as weights. To date, no alternative system of weighting has been proposed. Yet, without some system of weighting or valuation, there is no way of aggregating the various ingredients of well-being into a single aggregate measure.

Accordingly, the alternative to an explicit system of values is to analyze options in terms of vectors of capabilities and to accept the implication that policy options can, at best, be weakly ordered. Faced with this prospect, most economists would prefer to accept the opportunity cost of scarce resources as being a useful value system and hence a way of arriving at aggregates, such as total consumption; and to accept that, while total consumption so determined is a useful index of well-being, it is far from being the only measure that is interesting. Sen must be correct in suggesting that life expectation might be a useful alternative measure and that such alternatives are not perfectly correlated. It therefore makes a difference which one is chosen.

One considerable advantage that follows from a willingness to entertain a single, metric measure of living standards, based on consumption, say, is that it simplifies the quest for causes of well-being or the lack thereof, which is poverty. However, this does not mean that causes are easy to identify. On the contrary, this is a difficult area, the more so because the causes of poverty have to be understood relative to a level of aggregation if the fallacy of composition is to be avoided.

To clarify these concerns, Table 2.1 recognizes four levels of aggregation, each of which is relevant to poverty analysis and all of which can usefully be disaggregated to recognize more detail. For example, the micro level can be disaggregated further to recognize individuals as distinct from households, and this distinction is important if analysis is to address the inequality that obtains within households, often along gender lines. An example of the fallacy of composition at this level would be to suggest that because those women who have relatively more children may be better off (because their land entitlement under traditional systems may be greater and/or because their older children can help with productive and reproductive responsibilities), then all women might be better off if they had more children. Similarly, while it is true that those who are better educated tend to have higher living standards, it does not follow that increasing human capital will cause an economy to develop: it may instead lead to the pervasive unemployment of educated youth, depending on the balance between education, on the one hand, and the creation of job opportunities on the other.

Table 2.1. The Multiple Levels of Aggregation at which Causation can be Identified

Level of Aggregation	Sub-strata/Policy areas
International	Trade Policy
	International Debt
Macro	Monetary Policy
	Fiscal Policy
	Governance, including
	the Respective Roles
	of Government, NGOs,
	and Private Enterprise
Meso	Socioeconomic Groups
	Communities
	Production Sectors
	Product and Factor Markets
Micro	Households
	Individuals

Note: NGO = nongovernment organization.

At the next level up from the micro, i.e., at the meso level of analysis, we find all the structural features of an economy: the communities in which people live, the production sectors into which all economic activity is divided, and the markets through which goods and services change hands.

The distinction between the micro and meso levels of analysis is important, because it reflects the distinction between prices and quantities. At the micro level, commodity prices and wage rates are typically exogenous, so it may be reasonable to claim that low wages and high prices are causes of poverty at this level. However, at the meso level and above, wages and prices are endogenous: they depend on the interplay of demand and supply. Thus, from a meso perspective, the level of wages is determined by whatever it is that determines demand and supply in the labor market. It would then be a major fallacy of composition to suggest that if all wage rates were higher, there would be less poverty. On the contrary, it is likely that higher wage rates would cause unemployment and therefore increase poverty. Similarly, at the micro level, smallholders who achieve high yields tend to be better off. But if all smallholders were to achieve higher yields, then they would all be better off only if the price elasticity of demand for their produce was greater than one. This condition will often be satisfied, but it is not out of the question for higher output to lower prices by glutting the market.

At the sector and local level, many of the mechanisms that operate at the meso level are a translation of policies and attitudes that are set at the macro level. These include political attitudes about the role of the private sector (businesses and nongovernment organizations [NGOs]), law and order, and good governance, all of which affect poverty via, for example, their influence on investment, and therefore on growth. More importantly, they can also affect poverty and well-being directly, through human rights, for example. Otherwise, it is at the macroeconomic level that monetary and fiscal policies are determined. These are the foundations upon which the system of economic incentives is built. The best efforts of private entrepreneurs and the self-employed in the informal sector can all be frustrated by bad macroeconomic policies, which prejudice their chances of thriving. In sub-Saharan Africa, in particular, bad economic policies through the 1970s and 1980s remain a major cause of poverty today, and many countries in that region have yet to regain the level of income per head that they previously enjoyed.

The importance of macroeconomic policies notwithstanding, some blame for contemporary poverty should be apportioned at a level of aggregation above that of the nation state, viz., the international economy. In that arena, the countries of sub-Saharan Africa are small players and can hardly be responsible for the changes in the international environment which took place circa 1980–1982. At most they could be blamed for not having foreseen these changes and making appropriate contingent plans, or for reacting too slowly. But this is a blame that must evidently be shared in some measure with their advisors. Whatever the verdict of history might be on this matter, it will remain the case that the present overhang of international debts and the need to service them will remain as major problems for years to come: they may not be the only cause of poverty today, but they undoubtedly constrain the ability of governments to alleviate poverty, both now and for the foreseeable future. Sound macroeconomic policies have that much less to offer in mobilizing resources for a poverty alleviation strategy if such a strategy is crowded out by obligations to service debt.

What, then, are the causes of poverty and where are they found? The answer must be that they are found at every level from the individual to the global. It then follows that the design of strategy needs to address each and every level in turn. But the ordering is potentially crucial because, for any given level, what happens at a higher level of aggregation is (more or less) exogenous and, therefore, must be taken as given. It follows that the quest for appropriate policies must begin at the highest level and work down. Solutions to the problem of poverty must therefore start at the global level with trade issues, debt, and the international migration of labor and capital, and work down to a consideration of the lower levels only when the potential for policy interventions into the higher strata is exhausted. As we follow such a procedure, working down through the levels of aggregation, we will eventually be left with those individuals who, for one reason or another, have not been able to catch the drift of the mainstream of development as it emerges by some combination of chance and the policies that have been selected at levels beyond their influence. These are the individuals who, through no fault of their own, have been marginalized by the tide of affairs. These are the poor who are potentially destitute and therefore in greatest need of help.

3. Alternative Approaches to Development Policy

The notion of balanced development that is invoked in this chapter refers, in the first instance, to the need for balance in the allocation of resources within and between the economic and social sectors. It therefore suggests an emphasis that is hardly new: the same concern can be found in the 1961 *Report on the World Social Situation* published by the United Nations, the full title of which is "Report on the World Social Situation: with special reference to the problem of balanced social and economic development" (United Nations, 1961). More recently, this same theme has been resurrected by UNDP within the context of its annual series of HDRs. There is a surprising degree of continuity between these two sources, despite the gap of 20 years.

The starting point for the unknown authors of the UN study was to emphasize the various ways in which economic and social development are interlinked. They begin with the proposition that the "importance of economic development as a means to social ends" is well known and can be taken as being more or less self-evident. The complementary argument, that social development is important for economic growth, is then developed in stages, the first of which is to note how social factors can impede such growth in various ways. The potential obstacles are elaborated under three headings: (i) population growth; (ii) institutional factors, such as a caste system; and (iii) individual factors, which are defined to include motivations and attitudes, not least in relation to savings and entrepreneurship. Set against these potential obstacles are the many positive ways in which social development expenditures can support economic growth, the primary example being investment in human capital. Health care and education are singled out for special mention in this connection and it is suggested that there is no adequate way of distinguishing the economic benefits of such expenditures from their social implications. The report indicates that it would be (extremely) difficult to define the size of the eventual economic returns from a sewage disposal scheme or the building of a hospital and that "[the] possible contribution of [a] school to material production is beyond measurement at the present time but not beyond conception" (United Nations, 1961).

Today, some 30 years on, it may be realistic to express somewhat greater optimism over the prospects of measuring the economic benefits of a school. Indeed, it is precisely that possibility that will be invoked here to suggest that across a wide range of policy concerns, a calculus of economic costs and benefits can be conceptualized and, indeed, implemented as a way of ensuring that a sensible balance is struck between the use of resources to promote economic growth and the broader agenda that is addressed by social policy.

In adopting this position it is interesting to note that the authors of the 1961 UN report were evidently worried about something other than the technical difficulties of cost-benefit analysis. Specifically, they were concerned that precise knowledge of the interactions and interdependencies between economic and social variables "will not *fully* indicate what the pattern of development ought to be, because questions of value also come in—the value to be placed upon, say, education for its own sake" (United Nations, 1961, emphasis added). Faced with this undeniably reasonable proposition, we cannot avoid the question of what to do about it. There seem to be several possibilities. One would be to proceed, difficulties notwithstanding, to conceptualize the computation of economic costs and benefits. Back in 1961, this might not have appeared an attractive option, since the necessary theoretical developments were only just beginning to emerge. Today, however, it is much more realistic. An alternative approach, which is hinted at in the UN study, is to set targets:

> The concept of balanced development clearly means, for most people who use the term, an appropriate relation between economic and social factors—giving to each field or sector of development the attention it deserves in the total complex. It thus implies in the first instance a value or goal, something to be sought (even if only dimly perceived)... (United Nations, 1961).

This contrast between cost-benefit analysis and the setting of targets re-emerged in the early country studies undertaken by UNDP under the auspices of its HDR activities. Griffin and McKinley (1994) set out some elements of the debate to which these studies gave rise, with the case for using cost-benefit analysis as a foundation for balanced development promoted in the country study for Pakistan. To judge from the latest HDR, it seems that, within UNDP, this debate has now been resolved in favor of the alternative approach, which depends on setting targets for social objectives.

As an alternative to both of the above approaches, the 1961 UN study considers a third possibility, which is to explore the actual experience of countries by looking for patterns in cross-section data in an attempt to identify what actually seems to work and what does not. We can refer to this third possibility as the empirical approach.

In opting for the empirical approach, the 1961 UN report provides an illuminating analysis of the relationship between gross domestic product and social indicators such as infant mortality, life expectancy, school enrollment, calorie intake, etc. With due respect for the limitations of these data, various outliers are identified. For example, exceptionally good school enrollment ratios, relative to the gross domestic product, are noted for Ireland; Japan; Sri Lanka; Taipei,China; and Thailand, with a correspondingly poor performance recorded for Cuba and Venezuela. Similar results for infant mortality show Greece, Japan, and Taipei,China as doing well, while Chile joins Cuba and Venezuela as poor performers.

These analyses were undertaken in the 1961 UN study on the basis that the standard of living of a population—or better, the "level of living"—must be regarded as a set of components (health, nutrition, education, housing, employment conditions, etc.) that cannot be reduced to a single index. Insofar as the level of living is measurable, it must be expressed, not as a single quantity, but as a pattern of nonconvertible quantities. The fact that the level of living is not to be defined as per capita national income does not deny, however, the underlying importance of growth of national income for the improvement of welfare:

> It follows from the above that it is impossible to say on any systematic grounds what a country's level in health, education, or other social component should be, given its level of economic development; or, again, what percentage of its national income it should expend in these fields. If an economically under-developed country is only one-third literate and has only one-third of its children in school, there is no standard which will demonstrate that, say, one-half of the people should be literate and one-half of the children in school. Obviously, everyone should be literate and all children should be in school (United Nations, 1961).

No doubt we can all agree to that. But the issue that concerns policy today is not to determine where we eventually want to be, but how to proceed from wherever we are. It is in recognition of this practical need to proceed on an incremental basis that the UN study makes its strongest plea for comparative studies of experience in different countries:

> If countries have a long historical experience in development and a familiarity with the interactions of economic and social factors, plus an educated population aware of its needs and articulate about its values, and a leadership skilled in the analysis of alternative proposals, then the process of legislative debate and political decision may well be adequate to deal with questions of balanced development. But many less developed countries have no such historical experience to guide them. [They lack most or all of the above]. In these circumstances Governments have been interested in finding guidance in the experience of other countries (United Nations, 1961).

Given that we now have some 50 years of development experience that is reasonably well-documented, the necessary raw material for serious historical studies is increasingly available. Their unique contribution would be to set present development problems in their proper historical context and hence displace the rhetoric that can otherwise inhibit our understanding of the issues.

4. Human Capital and Living Standards

a. The money metric

In 1980, and with some reluctance, the World Bank launched the Living Standard Measurement Study (LSMS; Chander, Grootaert, and Pyatt, 1980), which has subsequently provided a major stimulus for making data available on various aspects of household living standards. In particular, it has provided data on the distribution of the money metric, which is typically measured by consumption or income per head at the household level.

Ten years later, following "the lost decade" of the 1980s, the World Bank reaffirmed its erstwhile concern with poverty and initiated a program of poverty assessments in borrowing countries. Relatively soon, these became dependent on the availability of data of the type promoted by the LSMS and a style of analysis was established that I have characterized elsewhere as the statistical approach.

This approach has three elements: first, the assumption that the living standard of each individual or household can be estimated from survey data; second, the inference that frequency distribution of the metric can be estimated; and hence, third, the conclusion that overall inequality and poverty can be measured. Insofar as all this is possible, the statistical approach can support analyses of the extent to which growth necessarily entails greater inequality and/or a reduction in poverty, via the calibration of Kuznets curves (using time-series data), the estimation of poverty elasticities, etc. Unfortunately, none of the analyses of this genre that have been reported to date are particularly persuasive and, even if they were, they are inherently incapable of taking us appreciably closer to the identification of suitable policies: they suggest that growth is important, but have little to say about the content of growth, mainly because they make little or no reference to economic structure. Similarly, at the micro level, the fact that the money metric may be correlated with individual characteristics, such as education, may imply very little that is policy relevant. In particular, it does not imply that increasing the resources devoted to education will necessarily raise living standards now or in the future, since to assume that it did would be to risk a fallacy of composition, as discussed above in Section 3.

A further source of difficulty is that poverty is defined differently in each Poverty Assessment, with the poverty line being defined independently for each country but in such a way that the incidence of poverty usually lies within a range of 30 to 50 percent. This has the dubious advantage of making poverty invariably a substantive issue to be discussed as part of the policy dialogue for each country, i.e., every country has some. The main disadvantage is that the nature of poverty and the identity of the poor vary, depending on where the line is drawn. The cross-fertilization of ideas between countries has accordingly been discouraged. For this and other reasons, a review that was undertaken in 1995–1996 of all Poverty Assessments that had been conducted in countries within sub-Saharan Africa concluded that they had generated little more than facts (correlations), as distinct from a corpus of knowledge or understanding (Hamner, Pyatt, and White, 1996). The limitations are quite basic. For example, the Poverty Assessments are typically unable to establish whether the incidence of poverty is greater or less in rural areas and whether the wage for unskilled labor has gone up or down relative to the cost of wage goods. Indeed, the Poverty Assessments for sub-Saharan Africa have little or nothing to say about employment. It is therefore not surprising that the policy recommendations promoted rarely modify or venture beyond the two-pronged approach of their antecedent, *World Development Report 1990* (World Bank, 1990), which emphasizes the importance of growth and human capital formation, with the added rider that safety nets may be needed, since the structural adjustments that are typically required to establish the preconditions for growth will inevitably result in some casualties.

b. The household as consumer and producer

The failure of the Poverty Assessments can be attributed in part to their reliance on the money metric approach. Accordingly, a better model is needed, preferably one that recognizes that individuals and households are located at the intersection of the cash and noncash economies. The main limitation of the metric approach is to assume away much of the complexity that this implies.

Figure 2.2 illustrates the interdependence of the consumption and production decisions of a household. The curve AA' represents the production opportunity set, which is defined for negative as well as positive levels of net output for each of the two commodities represented on the diagram on the understanding that a negative net-out means that the household buys in that particular commodity.

The slope of the line BB' is determined by the relative prices of the two goods, so that total revenue is maximized if the household produces the combination of goods represented by point D. From the point of view of consumption, the line BB' is the budget constraint and utility is maximized if the household consumes the combination of goods represented by point E. Hence the difference between points D and E implies that, in this illustration, the

Figure 2.2. The Equilibrium of a Household that is Both a Consumer and a Producer

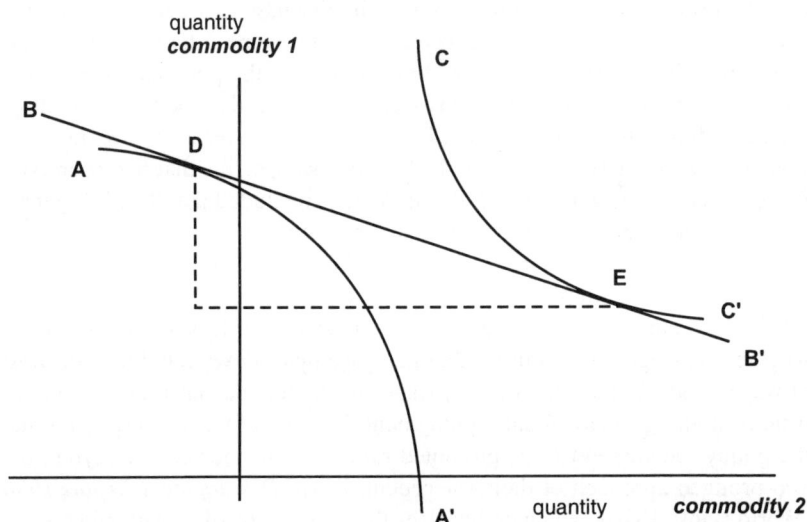

household buys *commodity 2* for both intermediate and final consumption; and it produces *commodity 1* at a level in excess of its final consumption requirements, selling the surplus in order to pay for all its requirements of producing *commodity 1*.

The salient element of this formulation is that the production opportunity set defined by the curve AA′ defines the capabilities of the household in commodity space: as capabilities expand, so will the production opportunity set. More specifically, the location of the frontier AA′ will depend, in the first instance, on the way in which a household allocates its time. On a per capita basis each household has the same time endowment, but otherwise, the circumstances of each household will differ according to the skills of its members, their complementary assets (tools, housing, land), and their access to facilities (transport, schools, health centers, etc.). The line AA′ is therefore determined by a household's *assets, access,* and *abilities*, and the dependency ratio.

Given these, the line BB′ depends on the relative prices of the goods and services that the household buys and sells, i.e., on the terms of trade that are relevant to its particular circumstances. Hence the consumption point E and, therefore, the household's living standard (to the extent that this is determined by what it consumes) will depend on access, assets, and abilities via the location of AA′ and also on the terms of trade it has to contend with for those goods that it has to buy and sell.

This characterization of the household can be modified and enriched in various ways without changing the basic implications, which are that, with a given dependency ratio, the living standard of a household can be raised by:

- encouraging the accumulation of assets (tools, housing, land, etc.);
- providing better access to basic services (markets, clinics, potable water);
- enhancing abilities via education, training, learning-by-doing, and better health care; and
- improving the household's terms of trade with the cash economy.

In particular, the model can be generalized to allow for nontraded goods, such as leisure and the caring of one member of the household for another. In this sense, the formulation can recognize the nonmarket contributions of women to the household and the demands on their time that result. These demands have an opportunity cost that is, of course, captured by the shadow price of the services provided. An additional, technical point is that the formulation suggests a direct link with the concept of human capital insofar as the location of AA' otherwise depends on the household's nonhuman capital and supporting infrastructure. An alternative interpretation, therefore, is that the location of the line AA' depends on the real assets owned by the household, supporting infrastructure, and human capital endowment.

In much the same spirit as above, the location of the line BB' can be seen as depending on a notional measure of the household's income and on prices in a way that is analogous to that which supports the money metric approach. However, the money metric approach assumes that all households face the same prices, with the relevant set of prices being the prices of final consumption goods and services. Figure 2.2 is essentially different, insofar as the only prices that matter are those of the goods and services that are actually traded: goods and services that are purchased for intermediate use such as seed and fertilizer. They also include the prices of labor services that a household might sell in the cash economy or buy in according to its needs, e.g., for plowing. The proposition that all households face the same prices (and that the opportunity costs of nontraded goods are also similar) may therefore be approximated within relatively homogeneous socioeconomic groups, but may otherwise be unsustainable. A metric might therefore be useful in analyzing inequality and poverty within such groups, but its distribution across an entire population is likely to conceal more than it reveals. Hence the statistical approach to the distribution of living standards should not be relied on. A more constructive way forward could start with the disaggregation of the population into socioeconomic categories and then proceed to explore the determinants of living standards within each group in the context of a structural (meso-level) model and accounting framework.

One particular implication of such an approach is that the results of household surveys, especially those relating to sources of cash income and expenditures, would need to be fully reconciled with, and integrated into, the national accounts in order that a consistent and coherent story might emerge about the various ways (direct and indirect) that the distribution of income and the structure of production are inextricably interwoven. One of the original ambitions of the LSMS was to promote such a synthesis, so that the design of policies at the meso level might be fully integrated into the total policy package. It is a matter for regret that this has not yet happened; meanwhile, evidence is accumulating of serious inconsistencies between what the household surveys and the national accounts have to say about trends in per capita consumption.

A further implication of the proposed approach is that the initial impact of adjustment policies at the household level will be transmitted via the household's terms of trade and job opportunities, these being the most important elements of the interface of many households with the cash economy. If agricultural price supports are withdrawn, then this will have an obvious and immediate impact on the farmers affected via their terms of trade. Similarly, the model emphasizes the sense in which the improvement of employment prospects must be a critical element in any policy package that seeks to achieve a broad-based improvement in living standards. Conversely, if the labor market collapses, then households are going to have to sell off some of their assets (if they have any) or rely on transfers (safety nets).

5. Production Technology

a. Production as a stock-flow relationship

Contemporary models of economic and social development such as in Thomas et al. (2000) typically assume that production is a stock-flow relationship, with output generated by combining the services that can be provided by different types of capital in the context of a system of incentives. The starting point for modeling production processes is therefore what is often referred to as an "AK model," within which physical capital, human capital, and environmental capital (natural resources) are normally recognized and separately distinguished (Table 2.2). Some authors add working capital and social capital to this list, but to do so raises complications. Working capital is essentially a financial asset and therefore different in kind from other forms; and both Arrow (1999) and Solow (1999) have queried the sense in which social capital is comparable to physical capital. More generally, there is a long-standing debate as to whether the stock of wealth that is accounted for by any of the different forms of capital can be usefully factored into a meaningful measure of quantity and a unit value or price. This is important, insofar as the standard AK model assumes that this issue can be resolved in favor of meaningful quantum measurement, and that quantities of different types of capital can be substituted one for another. In particular, it is typically assumed that physical capital and labor (human capital) can be substituted for each other.

An alternative formulation that does not rely on the measurement of capital is sufficient for present purposes and arguably more realistic. It assumes that stocks of physical capital, human capital, and natural resources are enumerable but not measurable, i.e., that the elements of these stocks can be listed, but there is no aggregate quantum measure for each. It then follows that, for each type of capital, new investment, maintenance, and depletion have to be interpreted directly. And the meaning of balanced development can now be extended to imply that, in principle, decisions as to what to invest in, how much to spend on the maintenance of particular assets, and how fast to deplete natural resources can all be evaluated in comparable terms using cost-benefit analysis. A balanced approach now requires that only the most attractive projects should be pursued and that, in this general sense, "crowding-out" should be avoided. It also means that, in the first instance, the balanced development of the social sectors will be achieved if, for example, rates of investment in human capital and the level of maintenance of the stock are determined on their merits relative to alternative ways of spending public revenues. In other words, we can promote a supply-side argument in support of social sector activities via their impact on human capital.

b. The putty-clay vintage model

A second sense in which the proposed treatment of different types of capital would allow an injection of greater realism into the analysis of development concerns is its potential consistency with the fact that, in the real world, the services provided by different types of capital have to be used in more or less fixed proportions that are determined via the choice of technique that is made (with or without the guidance available through cost-benefit analysis) when a new investment is undertaken. This leads to what is generally known as "the putty-clay vintage model" of production processes, the salient characteristic of which is that value added per worker is highest in the most recently installed plants, so that profit per worker decreases with the age of the technology. At any one point in time, technologies from a range of vintages will remain in operation, while the oldest plants, for which the value added per worker is less than the wage, will be obsolescent; typically, they will be scrapped.

Table 2.2. Examples of Investment, Maintenance and Depletion for Each of the Main Types of Assets

Types of Capital	Alternative Activities		
	Investment	Maintenance	Depletion
Physical Capital	Building a Road, Factory, etc. Installing New Machinery	Keeping Assets in Running Order	Scrapping (Obsolete) Assets
Human Capital	Raising Levels of Literacy	Providing Health Care	Retirement from the Workforce
Natural Resources	Exploration Activites	Protection of Fisheries	Extraction of Minerals

This formulation introduces an important asymmetry into the relationship between employment and wages. If the net output price of some activity falls, perhaps because a protective tariff is reduced, then either the wage must fall proportionately or some plants will cease to be profitable and employment will fall. However, if the net output price rises relative to the wage, there will be no increase in employment *unless and until* new investment creates new jobs. So, given a relatively sticky money wage, a fall in demand will impact directly on employment, while an increase in demand will tend to raise profits with no extra jobs being created unless and until investment in new capacity is introduced. Alternatively, given the net output price, while a rise in wages will result in a loss of jobs and output, a fall in wages will not, of itself, create new employment opportunities or an increase in output (except to the extent that any excess capacity might now come into operation.)

It follows from this description that the implications of a change in real wages in a putty-clay model are different from those implicit in the standard neoclassical model, because the latter has substitution possibilities: when real wages fall in a Solow-Swan model,[2] the capital/labor ratio falls, implying that, with a given (fixed) stock of capital, employment increases. Experience of structural adjustment programs in many countries suggests that the putty-clay formulation is more realistic. It implies that, if we want to maintain employment through a period of adjustment, the speed of current account liberalization must be closely geared to the rate at which new jobs are being created via new investment.

This empirical support for the vintage model is reinforced by theoretical considerations that are discussed in Pyatt (1964), where it is shown that the vintage model implies a relationship over time of the form

$$g = \alpha I + \rho i$$

where g is the rate of growth of output, I is the rate of growth of employment and i is investment, expressed as a reaction of the gross domestic product. Moreover, the theory also suggests that the parameter α should approximate the share of wages in value added and that ρ should be a rate of profit on new investment. Other authors have found empirical support for such a relationship, among them Scott (1982).

Similarly, several authors have explored the long-run, steady-state properties of the vintage model, including Solow et al. (1996), who find that the behavior of vintage models is very similar to that of the standard Solow-Swan neoclassical formulation. The latter can therefore be seen as a surrogate for the

---

2.   This is a model that seeks to explain growth, in particular, the role of capital and new technology.

former in the steady state, according to Solow (1970). By implication, in the real world (which is never in a steady state) the vintage model is arguably to be preferred as a point of departure for the analysis of adjustment processes and convergence, because it offers a better characterization of the likely implications of specific policies that might otherwise prove to be more severe than their proponents intended.

We have seen in the previous section that employment is an important determinant of the welfare of individuals and households. To this we can now add that, given the putty-clay model of production processes, investment in new technologies, which creates new opportunities for learning-by-doing and a demand for new skills, is an essential mechanism for raising living standards. Equally, a program of rapid liberalization is likely to result in a rapid loss of jobs. New jobs depend on new investment, which in turn may not be forthcoming without reforms, the immediate effect of which may be a loss of jobs. Clearly, policy should seek to balance this loss of old jobs against the creation of new ones.

Accordingly, the determinants of the rate of investment are important, not least the dependence of investment on incentive reforms. To bias investment in the direction of labor-intensive techniques is probably an inappropriate policy response. A more appropriate approach may be to encourage the use of modern technology in producing those goods and services, the production of which is inherently labor intensive. In other words, a quality growth strategy may well require a conscious effort to proceed, as the way opens, to raise productivity and not to attempt to catch up too quickly.

c. The marginal effect of investment

Within the formal sector of an economy, the maintenance of the stock of real assets is generally taken care of by businesses in the normal course of their operations. But decisions to build a new plant, to branch out into a new line of business, or to invest in a new type of machine are less commonplace and therefore more likely to be the subject of careful deliberation. They give rise to what Keynes referred to as the marginal efficiency of investment schedule, which requires the ranking of projects according to their internal rate of return and hence the identification of a monotonic decreasing relationship between the rate of return on the marginal project and the volume of investment. Figure 2.3 illustrates the construction and also shows, on the same graph, the volume of financing available to fund investment projects in the formal private sector as a function of the rate of interest: as the rate of return on finance increases, so is the amount of financing on offer assumed to increase.

If the rate of return on each potential investment were known with certainty, and if the market for finance were perfect (only the most rewarding projects were able to attract finance), then the market could be expected to converge on point C. In practice this is unlikely for many reasons, the most important of which are that (i) participants in this market have incomplete information and (ii) entrepreneurs who accept the consequent risks require an incentive to do so in the form of a risk premium, i.e., an expected rate of return that is in excess of the rate of interest. This risk premium will lower the rate of investment from I to I', say, while the fact that the market is less than perfect in identifying the best projects will have the effect of further lowering the rate of investment below I'. It therefore follows that both risk and market imperfections will lower the rate of investment and therefore be prejudicial to growth. Policies that reduce risk are clearly desirable, therefore, as is the development of a well-informed and efficient financial system that can mobilize the sav-

Figure 2.3. The Marginal Efficiency of Investment Schedule

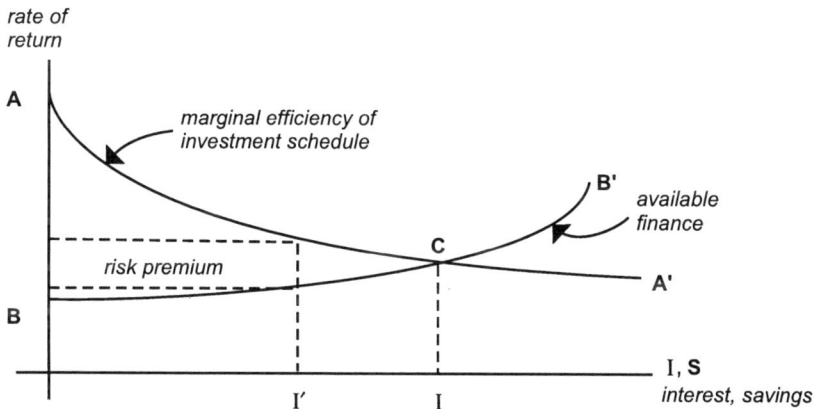

ings that are required in order to finance private investment and to discourage any tendencies towards credit rationing and "crowding-out" that might otherwise emerge. Balanced development requires that this market should work well as an important element of an overall concern to make the best use of available resources.

6. Politics and the Role of Government

a. A role for politics

The discussion in Section 4 of the household as consumer and producer can be extended without too much difficulty into a model of the informal sector, while the treatment in Section 5 of production activity in the formal sector introduces the main features of financial and nonfinancial corporate activity. It now remains to say something about the role of government and all those other nongovernment institutions, subsets of which are referred to as "not-for-profit institutions servicing households" by national income accounts, and as "quasi-nongovernmental institutions" (QUANGOs) in other contexts, etc.

Following the widespread perception in the 1980s that the governments of many developing countries were taking on too much and interfering excessively with market forces, a general consensus in the development community has favored encouragement of NGOs and the cutting back of government in size and scope so as to be more in keeping with its capacities.

While this trend is to be welcomed in general terms, two qualifications seem to be important. First, while the general perception is that NGOs are benign, reality can be less reassuring, and the regulation of both domestic and institutional NGOs is quite rightly a major concern for governments. This is an area that requires much more research and careful advice from multilateral agencies in their efforts to encourage the retrenchment of the public sector.

Second, it should be recognized that whatever the international community might think, the role of government versus that of alternative institutions is preferably a matter for resolution via domestic political processes rather than the conditionality attached to international loans. This is recognized insofar as "local ownership" of structural adjustment programs is thought to be critical to their success. But such ownership can only be achieved if the public is informed and, preferably, consulted at the formulation stage. To the extent that this is happening in some countries, there is an increasing awareness among women that the men who have previously dominated politics at all levels have not always understood the issues as well as they might.

One consequence of opening up debate on institutional forms is that greater diversity may be called for. The first example is large countries where local government is unreliable; new institutions may be needed to tap local knowledge and disburse international funds at a micro level. The second example is new thinking about land reform and the development of smallholder agriculture via QUANGOs, which may well be appropriate in particular instances. There is a wealth of successful experience in various countries upon which to draw.

Third, in reflecting on the role of government in relation to other institutional forms, it should not be forgotten that the need for change was prompted by the fact that, as of the early 1980s, the "rules of the game" changed for developing countries with an end to the net inflow of official development assistance at low or even negative real interest rates. The previous institutional arrangements were designed to encourage and distribute the proceeds of such a flow and, therefore, to serve the convenience of both bilateral and multilateral donors as well as that of the government. An issue that arises in today's new environment is whether the basic distinction of many governments between their development and recurrent budgets has now served its purpose.

b. The role of government

Once the role of government is settled relative to other institutions, there are likely to remain three areas in which government must be active:

- setting basic parameters that have a pervasive effect on economic activity at the international and macroeconomic levels;
- regulating markets and the nontransactional relationships that arise between institutions at the meso level; and
- trying to ensure that assets of all types are nurtured on a sustainable basis.

The first two of these three roles cover familiar ground and can be dealt with briefly here. Monetary policy is included under the first heading, as a part of government's responsibility for international relations and the flow of funds. Otherwise, some of the most important macroparameters are those affecting risk, notably the responsibility for a just and reliable legal system and freedom of information in the public domain.

Responsibilities under the second heading are similarly well established in the literature on fiscal policy and public finances. They include the control of monopoly, the supply of public goods, and the elimination of discrimination, all of which can be seen as elements of an incentive system that is designed to encourage the efficient use of all available resources. There is nothing in the remodeling of the household sector proposed in Section 4 that would change the standard arguments in relation to these elements of fiscal responsibility. However, in relation to general taxation, there is an important implication. If it is now recognized that the household is both a consumer and a producer, then those things that the household requires in order to produce, i.e., the basic needs of the household and regrettable necessities, such as traveling to work, should be treated as intermediate consumption, not final. They should therefore be excluded from the definition of value added (i.e., gross domestic product) and, accordingly, should be exempt from any VAT.

To some extent, the practice of excluding some basic needs from VAT is followed in all countries that have such a tax; the reformulation of the economics of the household, which is outlined in Section 4, gives a rationale for this practice.

The corollary of defining the gross domestic product so as to exclude the cost of basic needs has no similar analogue in national practices but, it can be noted, this adjustment can be seen as a shift toward the Marxian concept of surplus. Moreover, since income in excess of basic needs will be close to zero in the subsistence sector, the adjustment suggested would establish a natural origin for the scale on which the (revised) gross domestic product per capita is measured.

The importance of the third area of government responsibility emerges from the interpretation of production as a stock-flow relationship, and the emphasis here on cost-benefit analysis.

Both (poor) households and (rich) companies exploit the environment at (almost) every opportunity, creating external costs for others and benefits for themselves. An important role for government is to discourage such abuses where possible. While the National Conservation Strategies launched in Rio de Janeiro have generally failed, some governments have had success in trying to regulate abuse by creating local communities of interest or by insisting that "the polluter pays" in cases where the polluter can afford it.

The depletion of natural resources is typically easier for a government to control, since it is usually subject to the licensing of concessions. However, it is probably only in a minority of cases that the issues raised are addressed in the interest of sustaining living standards in the long run. A key issue is whether the revenues generated by depletion today can be used in ways that confer greater benefits than those that might accrue in future if extraction were deferred. From this cost-benefit point of view, there seems to be a prima facia case that most governments overestimate their absorptive capacities and discount the future too heavily.

Next, with regard to infrastructure, there is an important balance to be struck between the need to "crowd in" the private investment initiatives of households and companies, by building rural roads and an international airport, for example, and to avoid "crowding out" these same private initiatives by preempting an undue share of the financing available through credit controls, etc., as an alternative to credit rationing via interest rates.

This balance is much easier to achieve if domestic savings are buoyant, since neither of the alternatives—foreign borrowing and lower rates of investment—provide as attractive an alternative. For the corporate sector, a high savings rate implies that a large share of profits is retained within each business to finance future investment. In the household sector, the implications are similar, with the added edge that, for the poorest, the accumulation of productive assets and human capital in the sense discussed previously is the *sine qua non* of breaking away from subsistence on a sustainable basis. Private savings are therefore important.

Finally, the husbandry of human capital requires *inter alia* the allocation of funds to the social sectors—health care, education, potable water supplies, family planning, etc.—and their efficient use. This allocation sets an agenda that cost-benefit analysis can do much to rationalize, since it is evident that in many countries the allocation of resources is far from optimal. Urban bias in the provision of education and health benefits is, to some extent, inevitable, but the degree of bias is all too often excessive. It is exacerbated by a complementary bias that operates against the basic levels of service provision, such as primary education, and manifests itself in schools with no teachers, chalk, or books, and basic health care centers that lack Band Aids and aspirin. This same bias typically operates in favor of the tertiary levels—subsidized universities and sophisticated curative treatments in the hospital. Running through all this is a gender bias that diminishes the chances that girls will attend school or that the special health needs of women will be met. A root-and-branch cost-benefit analysis of all these problems would most likely result in a major reallocation of resources in favor of the poor. It would also point to the woefully inadequate levels of provision that many governments are able to sustain.

However, at the end of the day, perhaps the most serious misallocation of resources is that between capital projects and the financing of recurrent expenditures. It suggests that aid providers are prepared to finance so-called development projects (via tied aid) on a scale that is not locally sustainable. The case for doing so is obviously weak. Indeed, if the provision of basic health and education services is seen as maintenance and investment in the stock of human capital, then the justification for present practices is far from apparent. They have evident advantages. But the two-tier system they create within government results in major inefficiencies, if the main objective is the cost-effective delivery of services to those who need them the most.

References

Arrow, K. J. 1999. Observations on Social Capital. In *Introduction to Social Capital: a multifaceted perspective*, edited by P. Dasgupta and I. Serageldin. Oxford: Oxford University Press.

Becker, G. S. 1964. *Human Capital*. New York: Columbia University Press.

———. 1965. A Theory of the Allocation of Time. *The Economic Journal* (Sept.).

Chander, R., C. Grootaert, and G. Pyatt. 1980. Living Standards Measurement Study, Working Paper No. 1. *Living Standards in Developing Countries*. Washington, DC: World Bank.

Chayanov, A.V., D. Thorner, B. Kerblayb, and R. E. F. Smith, eds. 1966. *The Theory of the Peasant Economy*. Irvin, IL: Homewood.

Chenery, H., M. Ahluwalia, C. Bell, J. Duloy, and R. Jolly. 1974. *Redistribution with Growth*. Oxford: Oxford University Press.

Griffin, K., and T. McKinley. 1994. *Implementing a Human Development Strategy*. London: Macmillan.

Hamner, L., G. Pyatt, and H. White. 1996. Poverty in Sub-Saharan Africa: what can we learn from the World Bank's Poverty Assessments. The Hague: Institute of Social Studies Advisory Services. Mimeo.

Johanson, L. 1959. Substitution and Fixed Production Coefficients in the Theory of Economic Growth: a Synthesis. *Econometrica* 27: 157–176.

Pyatt, G. 1964. A Measure of Capital. *Review of Economic Studies* 30: 3.

_____ 1992. Towards Balanced Development in Pakistan. *The Pakistan Development Review* 31(4): 407–29.

_____ 1995. Balanced Development. Inaugural Address delivered at the Institute of Social Studies, The Hague. March 1955.

_____ 1996. Poverty *versus* the Poor. Dies Natalis address. The Institute of Social Studies, The Hague. Reproduced as Chapter 5 of *Identifying the Poor*, edited by G. Pyatt and M. Ward. Amsterdam: IOS Press.

Rawls, J. 1971. *A Theory of Justice.* Cambridge, Mass.: Harvard University Press.

Salter, W. E. G. 1960. *Productivity and Technical Change.* Cambridge: Cambridge University Press.

Scott, M. F. G. 1982. *A New View of Economic Growth.* Oxford: Clarendon Press.

Sen, Amartya. 1970. *Collective Choice and Social Welfare.* San Francisco: Holden-Day.

Solow, R.M. 1970. *Growth Theory: an Exposition.* Oxford: Oxford University Press.

———. 1999. Notes on Social Capital and Economic Performance. In *Introduction to Social Capital: a Multifaceted Perspective*, edited by P. Dasgupta and I. Serageldin. Oxford: Oxford University Press.

———, J. Tobin, C. C. von Weizsacker, and M. Yari. 1996. Neoclassical Growth with Fixed Factor Proportions. *Review of Economic Studies* 33(94): 79–116.

Thomas, V., et al. 2000. *The Quality of Growth.* New York: Oxford University Press.

United Nations. 1961. *Report on the World Social Situation: with Special Reference to the Problem of Balanced Social and Economic Development.* New York: United Nations.

UNDP (United Nations Development Programme). 1990 et seq. *The Human Development Report.* New York: Oxford University Press.

World Bank. 1978. *The World Development Report.* Oxford University Press.

3. Poverty Analysis and Measurement within a General Equilibrium Framework

Erik Thorbecke

1. Introduction

The fundamental reason for analyzing and measuring poverty within a general equilibrium framework rather than a partial equilibrium framework is that interaction and interdependence within a socioeconomic system matter, as does the prevailing structure of the economy. Policy measures and shocks have direct effects on sectors of production, institutions (such as different socioeconomic groups and firms), and factors of production. However, indirect effects of policies and shocks are often as important, or more so, than the direct effects.

For example, socioeconomic interaction affects poverty alleviation in a differential way through the sectoral pattern of growth. The impact of a sector's output growth on poverty alleviation can be direct, through the increase in incomes accruing to poor households that contributed through their labor or land to that sector's output growth. But another part of poverty alleviation results from the indirect effects operating through the interdependence of economic activities, i.e., the closed loop effects familiar in the social accounting matrix (SAM) literature. Assume that we are interested in the main paths through which a new textile factory in a rural site affects, directly and indirectly, the incomes of small farmers. The increase in textile output will require unskilled labor that is to be provided typically by two household groups, small farmers and landless agricultural workers. Because those two groups are likely to be relatively poor, a significant part of the incremental incomes accruing to them from earnings from work in the factory will be spent on food. The subsequent increase in food crop production, in turn, requires unskilled family labor from small farm households, thus further raising their incomes and lowering the incidence of poverty in that group.

Another example of the importance of interaction can be seen when a government subsidizes specific socioeconomic groups (e.g., the urban poor) as part of its poverty alleviation strategy. The initial effects will be to reduce poverty among this group, but because of the indirect effects of this group's spending (presumably largely on foodstuffs), the incomes of other groups (such as small farmers producing domestic food crops) may well increase. In this case, interaction in the economy would lead to an indirect reduction in poverty through the spending and respending effects of the initial beneficiaries of the subsidies. A large part of the increase in income received by the initial beneficiary group would spill over into an increased demand for goods and services that, in turn, have to be produced with different factors of production, such as unskilled labor, skilled labor, and capital. The household groups that are endowed with the factors required to satisfy this additional demand for food and consumer goods would be compensated through additional wages and other factor incomes, lowering thereby the incidence of poverty among the poor in those socioeconomic groups.

Still another example of a policy measure likely to have significant direct and indirect effects on poverty is a devaluation and trade liberalization program within a structural adjustment framework. The immediate impact of a devaluation is to increase the relative prices of tradables vs. nontradables, thereby benefiting tradable production activities. In at least some poor developing countries, farmers and agricultural workers producing agricultural export crops would benefit, assuming adequate supply response and a favorable environment. Since a part of the higher incomes is likely to be spent on consumer goods and informal services, indirect spillover effects could benefit rural nonagricultural households and urban households involved in the production of those consumer goods and services. Poverty might accordingly be reduced among those groups through those indirect effects.

There are essentially two analytical methods to estimate and simulate the effects of exogenous shocks (including policies) on poverty. The first approach relies on a SAM framework that is assumed to reflect closely the underlying socioeconomic structure and interdependence of the country or region under consideration. SAM multipliers are derived from the base-year SAM in such a way as to focus specifically on the extent to which different exogenous shocks affect household groups' incomes. Ultimately, SAM multipliers also focus on poverty alleviation and the structural mechanisms and linkages through which the initial shock contributes, directly and indirectly, to poverty alleviation. This approach is based on some limiting assumptions, such as the existence of excess capacity, unused resources, and constant prices.

The second approach relies on building a computable general equilibrium (CGE) model calibrated on an underlying SAM and reflecting not only the initial structure of the socioeconomic system, but also the behavior of the various agents and institutions. In contrast with the first method, which describes a Keynesian world, the CGE approach attempts to capture a more likely world (and set of conditions) in that, at least, some sectors in the economy operate at full capacity and some factors of production (skilled labor) are fully employed. Under those circumstances, prices can no longer be assumed to remain constant. In such a model, prices are endogenously determined so as to generate the set of prices that is consistent with "equilibrium" in an economy. When an economy is affected by an exogenous shock or a policy change, a new set of prices obtains, which, in turn, determines production, consumption, employment, and income.

Both approaches, i.e., SAM multiplier modeling and CGE models, are based on two fundamental pillars: that interaction and interdependence within a socioeconomic system matter, as does the prevailing structure. What CGEs add to the simple SAM framework is that they capture the behavior of the main actors in response to price changes.

In what follows, these two approaches are described, with relevant examples of their applicability to estimate and simulate the impact of the shocks on poverty.

2. The Social Accounting Matrix Multiplier Approach to Estimate Poverty Impact of Shocks

a. The social accounting matrix as accounting system and conceptual framework

As a data framework, the SAM is a comprehensive and disaggregated snapshot of the socioeconomic system during a given year. It provides a classification and organizational scheme for the data that is useful to analysts and policymakers alike. It incorporates explicitly various crucial relationships among variables, such as the mapping of the factorial income distribution from the structure of production and the mapping of the household income distribution from the factorial income distribution. Table 3.1 presents a basic SAM. It can readily be seen that it incorporates all the above flows—all major transactions—within a socioeconomic system.

A SAM is a square matrix in which each transactor or account has its own row and column. The payments (expenditures) are listed in columns and the receipts are recorded in rows. As the sum of all expenditures by a given account (or subaccount) must equal the total sum of receipts or income for the corresponding account, row sums must equal the column sums of the corresponding account. For example, the total income of a given institution (say a specific socioeconomic household group) must equal exactly the total expenditure of that same institution. This is the economic analog of the physicists' law of conservation of energy. Hence, analysts interested in understanding how the structure of production influences the income distribution can obtain useful insights by studying the SAM.

In the basic SAM of Table 3.1, six accounts are distinguished. Production activities produce different sectoral goods and services (e.g., textile products) by the purchase of raw materials and intermediate goods and services. In addition, these accounts pay indirect taxes to the government. The remainder is, by definition, value-added payments that are distributed to the factors of production (column 5). Production activities receipts (row 5) derive from sales to households, exports, and the government. In the present formulation of the SAM, no distinction is made between production activities and commodities. For the sake of simplicity, it is assumed that a production activity is equivalent to a corresponding commodity. In some instances, the SAM format distinguishes between production activities and commodity accounts. This would be the case when a given production activity produced different commodities, for example, so that these two sets of accounts would require different sectoral breakdowns. For this reason, many SAMs include both production activities and commodities accounts. When commodity accounts appear in a SAM, they can best be seen as representing a region's or nation's product markets.

Factors of production accounts typically include labor and capital subaccounts. They receive income (recorded in row 1) from the sale of their services to production activities in the form of wages, rent, and net factor income received from abroad or from other regions (corresponding to the value added generated by the production activities). In turn, these revenues are distributed (column 1) to households as labor incomes and to companies as distributed profits.

Institutions include households (typically broken down by socioeconomic group), companies (firms), and the government. From row 2a, it can be seen that households receive factor income (wages and other labor income, rent, interest, and profits) as well as transfers from government and from the rest of the nation and the world (e.g., remittances). Households' expenditures (column 2a) consist of consumption of goods from the region, from other regions, and from abroad, and income taxes with residual savings transferred to the capital account. Companies (row 2b) receive profits and transfers and spend on taxes and transfers, with their residual savings channeled into their capital account.

The government account (row and column 3) is distinct from administrative public activities included in the production activities account. These public services (such as education) buy intermediate goods, pay wages, and deliver public and administrative services. The government account per se allocates its current expenditures to buying the services provided by the production activities account. Other government expenditures (column 3) are transfers and subsidies to households and companies, and the remaining savings are transferred to the capital account. On the income side, the government receives tax revenues from a variety of sources and current transfers from abroad (row 3).

Table 3.1. A Basic Social Accounting Matrix

Expenditures

		1	2a	2b	3	4	5	6	Totals
		Factors of production	Households	Companies	Government	Combined capital account	Production activities	Rest of the world combined account	
			Institutions						
			Current accounts						
Receipts	**1** Factors of production						Value added payments to factors	Net factor income received from abroad	Incomes of the domestic factors of production
Institutions / Current accounts	**2a** Households	Allocation of labor income to household	Current transfers between households	Profits distributed to domestic households	Current transfers to domestic households			Net nonfactor incomes received plus indirect taxes on exports	Incomes of the domestic institutions after transfers
	2b Companies	Allocation of operating surplus to companies			Current transfers to domestic companies				
	3 Government		Direct taxes on income and indirect taxes on current expenditures	Direct taxes on companies plus operating surplus of state enterprises		Indirect taxes on capital goods	Indirect taxes on inputs	Net nonfactor incomes received plus indirect taxes on exports	
	4 Combined capital account		Household savings	Undistributed profits after tax	Gov't current account surplus			Net capital rec'd from abroad	Aggregate savings
	5 Production activities		Household expenditure on domestic goods		Gov't current expenditure	Investment expenditures on domestic goods	Raw material purchases of domestic goods	Exports	Aggregate demand— gross outputs
	6 Rest of the world combined account		Household expenditure on imported goods			Imports of capital goods	Imports of raw materials		Imports
	Totals	Incomes of the domestic factors of production	Total outlay of households	Total outlay of companies	Total outlay of government	Aggregate Investment	Total costs	Total foreign exchange receipts	

Source: Thorbecke (1991).

49

Figure 3.1. Flow Diagram of SAM Transactions

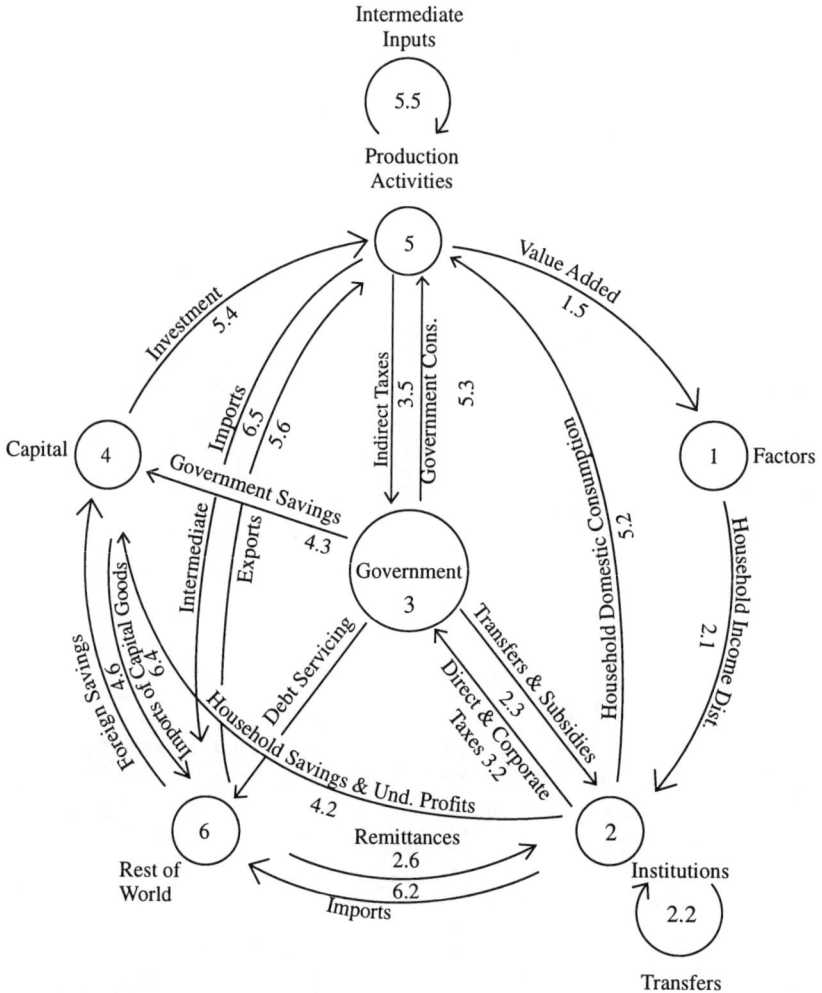

Notes: The flow diagram reflects exactly the transactions and transformations appearing in the SAM on Table 3.1. Note that transactions are numbered in a way consistent with the numbering of the accounts in Table 3.1. For example, the allocation of value added is a receipt for the Factor Account (#1) and a payment by the Production Activities Account (#5); hence, the corresponding transformation (matrix) is denoted by 1.5.

Source: Thorbecke (1991).

The fifth account is the combined capital account. On the income side (row 4) it collects savings from households, companies, government, and foreign savings. In turn, it channels these aggregate savings into investment (column 4).

Finally, transactions between domestic residents and foreign residents, respectively, are recorded in the rest of the world accounts (row and column 6). These transactions include, on the receipt side, households' consumption expenditures on imported final goods, as well as imports of capital goods and raw materials (row 6). The economy receives income from the rest of the nation and world (column 6) in the form of exports, as well as factor and nonfactor income earned. By definition, the difference between total foreign exchange receipts and imports is net capital received from abroad, or from the rest of the nation, and extraregional and foreign savings.

The SAM framework can also be used as a conceptual framework and as a basis for modeling. In this case the generating mechanisms that influence the flows in Figure 3.1 have to be spelled out explicitly and quantitatively. Whereas the SAM in Table 3.1 is a snapshot of the economy, Figure 3.1, which reproduces all of the transformations that appear in Table 3.1, can be interpreted more broadly as representing flows (over a period of one year) which, in turn, have to be explained by structural or behavioral relationships.

b. The social accounting matrix and multiplier analysis

We assume that there exists excess capacity that would allow prices to remain constant and that expenditure propensities of endogenous accounts remain constant.[1] We also assume that production technology and resource endowments are given for a particular time period.[2] Under these assumptions, the SAM framework can be used to estimate the effects of exogenous changes and injections, such as increases or decreases in the demand for specific products (sectoral outputs), on the whole socioeconomic system. To derive and illustrate the underlying logic of this methodology, the SAM accounts need to be partitioned into endogenous and exogenous accounts. It has been customary to consider government, the rest of the world, and capital as exogenous and the factors, institutions (household groups and companies), and sectoral production activities as endogenous.[3] The resulting simplified SAM appears in Table 3.2, and the corresponding endogenous flows appear in Figure 3.2. Note that the exogenous accounts have been combined in Table 3.2 and the sum of

---

1.   Subsections 2b to 2d follow closely the methodology developed in Thorbecke and Jung (1996) and Pyatt and Round (1979).
2.   The SAM is basically a snapshot of transactions occurring at one point in time (a given year). Dynamic changes in technology or resource endowment would be reflected by a new SAM with different coefficients.
3.   The standard justification for taking the government account as exogenous is that policy measures are, at least in a limited way, under the control of the government—

the exogenous injections is also consolidated into one vector (hence x_i, $i = 1$, 2, 3 represents the sum of injections from abroad, investment, and government expenditures affecting i). Likewise l_i''s represent the corresponding leakages.

Thus the simplified and truncated SAM shown in Table 3.2 consolidates all exogenous transactions and corresponding leakages and focuses exclusively on the endogenous transactions and transformations. Five endogenous transformations appear. The matrix T_{13} allocates the value added that is generated by the various production activities into income that accrues to the various factors of production; matrix T_{33} shows the intermediate input requirements (input/output transactions); and T_{32} reflects the expenditure pattern of various institutions, including household groups, on the commodities (equivalent to production activities) that they consume. Matrix T_{21} reflects the mapping of factorial income distribution into household income distribution (by household group). It tells us the sources of income of the different categories

Table 3.2. Simplified Schematic Social Accounting Matrix

		Expenditures				
		Endogenous accounts			**Exogenous**	**Totals**
		Factors	**Institutions (Households and companies)**	**Production Activities**	**Sums of other accounts**	
		1	**2**	**3**	**4**	**5**
Receipts		*Endogenous accounts*				
Factors	1	0	0	T_{13}	x_1	y_1
Institutions, (households and companies)	2	T_{21}	T_{22}	0	x_2	y_2
Production activities	3	0	T_{32}	T_{33}	x_3	y_3
		Exogenous accounts				
Sum of other accounts	4	l_1'	l_2'	l_3'	t	y_x
Totals	5	y_1'	y_2'	y_3'	y_x'	

of households, which, in turn, reflect the resource endowment possessed by various types of households. Finally, T_{22} gives the interinstitutional transfers, such as transfers among different types of households or between companies and households.

---

an assumption that would, incidentally, be debated by public choice advocates. In the absence of a sound and robust theoretical explanation of private investment behavior, it is also conventional to assume private investment and its pattern to be given exogenously. Finally, with regard to the rest of the world account, it is assumed that exports (but not imports) and some other transactions depend on overseas variables and can hence be taken as exogenous.

**Figure 3.2. Simplified Interrelationship among Principal SAM Accounts
(production activities, factors, and institutions)**

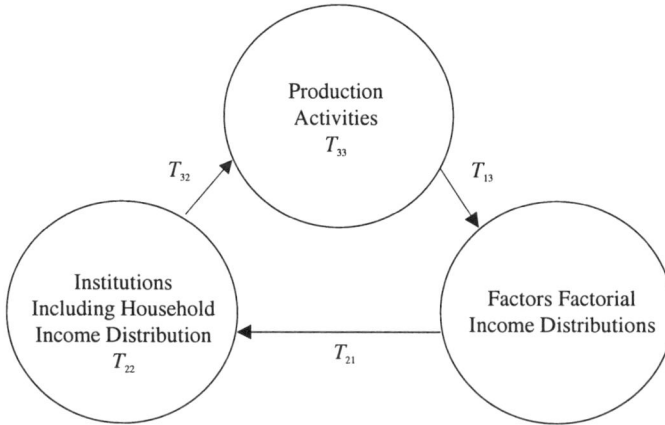

Source: Thorbecke and Jung (1996).

The logic underlying the scheme in Table 3.2 and Figure 3.2, as will be seen shortly, is that exogenous changes (the x's) in Table 3.2 determine, through their interaction within the SAM matrix, the incomes of the endogenous accounts: (i) factor incomes [vector y_1], (ii) household and companies incomes [y_2], and (iii) incomes of the production activities [y_3].

For analytical purposes, the endogenous part of the transaction matrix is converted into the corresponding matrix of average expenditure propensities. These can be obtained simply by dividing a particular element in any endogenous account by the total income for the column account in which the element occurs.[4] From Table 3.2 it can be seen that A_n is partitioned as follows:

$$A_n = \begin{bmatrix} 0 & 0 & A_{13} \\ A_{21} & A_{22} & 0 \\ 0 & A_{32} & A_{33} \end{bmatrix} \tag{3.1}$$

4. To be exact, the matrix of average expenditure propensities consists of two parts: A_n, which is the square matrix of average expenditure propensities for the endogenous accounts, and A_l, which consists of the so-called leakages, or the proportions of each endogenous variable that leak out as expenditure into any one of the three accounts. While the transaction matrix is expressed in money flows, the A_n and A_l matrices are expressed as ratios, with each column adding up to exactly unity.

From the definition of A_n, it follows that in the transaction matrix, each endogenous total income (y_n) is given as

$$y_n = A_n y_n + x \tag{3.2}$$

which states that row sums of the endogenous accounts can be obtained by multiplying the average expenditure propensities for each row by the corresponding column sum and adding exogenous income x.

Equation (3.2) can be rewritten as

$$y_n = (I - A_n)^{-1} x = M_a x \tag{3.3}$$

Thus, from (3.3), endogenous incomes y_n (factor incomes, y_1; institution incomes, y_2; and production activity incomes, y_3, as shown in Table 3.2) can be derived by premultiplying injection x by a multiplier matrix M_a. This matrix has been referred to as the accounting multiplier matrix because it explains the results obtained in a SAM and not the process by which they are generated. The latter would require the specification of a dynamic model including the different SAM accounts and variables.

One limitation of the accounting multiplier matrix M_a, as derived in equation (3.3), is that it implies unitary expenditure elasticities (the prevailing average expenditure propensities in A_n are assumed to apply to any incremental injection). While this assumption may be defensible for all other elements of A_n, it is certainly unrealistic for the expenditure pattern of household groups (A_{32}). A more realistic alternative is to specify a matrix of marginal expenditure propensities (C_n below) corresponding to the observed income and expenditure elasticities of the different agents, under the assumption that prices remain fixed.[5] In this case, C_n formally differs from in the following way:

$$C_{13} = A_{13}, C_{33} = A_{33}, C_{21} = A_{21}, C_{22} = A_{22}, \text{ but } C_{32} \neq A_{32}.$$

Expressing the changes in incomes (dy_n) resulting from changes in injections (dx), one obtains

---

5.   Since the expenditure (income) elasticity for household group h and commodity (product) i: εy_{hi} is equal to the ratio of the marginal expenditure propensity (MEP_{hi}) to the average expenditure propensity (AEP_{hi}), it follows that the matrix of marginal expenditure propensities, C_{32}, can be readily obtained once the expenditure elasticities and average expenditure propensities (A_{32}) are known, for example:

$$\varepsilon y_{hi} = \frac{MEP_{hi}}{AEP_{hi}}; MEP_{hi} = \varepsilon y_{hi} AEP_{hi}$$

$$dy_n = C_n dy_n + dx \ (4) = \left(I - C_n\right)^{-1} dx = M_c dx \qquad (3.4)$$

This has been termed a fixed price multiplier matrix (Pyatt and Round, 1979) and its advantage is that it allows any nonnegative income and expenditure elasticities to be reflected in M_c.[6]

c. Multiplier decomposition to estimate impact of a change in demand for and output of different production activities on mean incomes

In the present context, it is desired to estimate the impact that different production activities have on poverty alleviation, which requires identification of the effect of each production activity on each household group's income, the incidence of poverty in each group, and the extent to which the poor in each group share in their group's income growth.[7] Depending on the technology used, the factor endowment of the socioeconomic groups, and the extent of interlinkages on the demand and supply sides (the degree of integration of the economy), certain production activities contribute more to the growth of household groups' incomes than others. As is shown subsequently, income growth in turn contributes to poverty alleviation, depending on the sensitivity of the adopted poverty measure to income.

Equation (3.5) shows how the matrix of marginal expenditure propensities (C_n) is partitioned:

$$C_n = \begin{bmatrix} 0 & 0 & C_{13} \\ C_{21} & C_{22} & 0 \\ 0 & C_{32} & C_{33} \end{bmatrix} \qquad (3.5)$$

Hence equation (3.4) can be written in explicit form as

$$dy_1 = C_{13} dy_3 + dx_1 \qquad (3.4a)$$

---

6. Note that the consumption function implicit in the above formulation has total household income as its argument. Thus, the expenditure elasticities have to be estimated as a function of total income, rather than as a function of disposable income or total consumption. Furthermore, price effects are ignored by definition. Notwithstanding the clear superiority of fixed fixed-price multipliers compared to accounting multipliers in reflecting actual consumption behavior, the latter continue to be used in much applied work, because they can easily be derived from limited data.

7. It should be noted that the methodology developed here is applicable to any exogenous shock, such as government subsidies to specific socioeconomic groups and/or an increase or decrease in specific export activities. In the present illustration, we assume that an exogenous shock, such as public investment or a change in export demand originating abroad, generates an increase in sectoral output.

$$dy_2 = C_{21}dy_1 + C_{22}dy_2 + dx_2$$
$$dy_3 = C_{32}dy_2 + C_{33}dy_3 + dx_3$$

that yields

$$dy_1 = C_{13}dy_3 + dx_1$$
$$dy_2 = (I - C_{22})^{-1} C_{21}dy_1 + (I - C_{22})^{-1} dx_2 \qquad (3.4b)$$
$$dy_3 = (I - C_{33})^{-1} C_{32}dy_2 + (I - C_{33})^{-1} dx_3$$

We are focusing on the contribution that different production activities make to income growth. Starting with an exogenous change in demand for a given production activity (dx_3), we want to know the impact on incomes of the different household groups (dy_2) and, more specifically, on the additional incomes accruing to the household groups. Thus, we concentrate on that part of the fixed price multiplier matrix that links production activities to household groups (M_{c23}).[8] Let m_{ij} be an element of this matrix; it shows the total direct and indirect effects of an increase of one unit in the demand for (and the output of) production activity j on the incremental incomes received by socioeconomic (household) group i.

Thorbecke and Jung (1996) have shown that M_{c23} can be decomposed multiplicatively into two different matrices, which represent what they coin distributional (D) and interdependency (R) effects, respectively:

$$M_{c23} = R \cdot D \qquad (3.6)$$

where dimensions of matrices M_{c23} x R, and D, are household groups multiplied by production activities, household groups multiplied by household groups, and household groups multiplied by production activities, respectively. Fixed price multipliers and distributional effects corresponding to each pair of production activity and household group can be obtained directly from matrices M_{c23} and D, respectively.

The distributional effects represent the initial effects of a change in output of the respective production activities on the incomes of the various socioeconomic groups. The strength of the distributional effects depends mainly, as is shown next, on the technology in use (e.g., how labor-intensive it is and how much it relies on the factors of production possessed by household groups), and the factor endowment of the households (e.g., how much unskilled labor and land they possess). In turn, the interdependency effects capture the direct and indirect effects of spending and respending by the particular household group under consideration, and other groups that benefited, income-wise, from the exogenous output injection. Interdependency effects reflect the ex-

---

8. M_{c23} is the matrix constituted by comprising the columns of production activities and rows of socioeconomic household groups of the fixed price multiplier matrix, M_c.

tent of integration within the economy on both the demand and supply sides. The more consumers spend on domestic goods and services, and the more diversified their consumption pattern, the larger these effects. Likewise, the greater the intersectoral linkages on the production side and the transfer linkages among household groups, the higher the interdependency effects. In the following subsections, distributional and interdependency effects will be defined and discussed in more detail.

i. Distributional effects

Distributional effects originate with an exogenous change in output of a given production activity (dx_3). Say that textile output is increased by one unit. In order to produce this additional unit, intermediate inputs such as cloth, other fibers, and fuel may be required, which in turn need other intermediate inputs to be produced. The first, second, and higher order effects are captured by the matrix $(I - C_{33})^{-1}$. Likewise any increase in sectoral output requires primary inputs such as unskilled labor, capital, and land. The demand for these factors of production is given by matrix C_{13}. In turn, additional income will flow to the household groups, depending on their factor endowment. This transformation is represented by C_{21}. If the prevailing textile technology requires much unskilled labor, then socioeconomic groups that are well endowed with this factor, such as the rural landless and the urban uneducated, will benefit. When factors owned mostly by a household group composed mostly of poor are used intensively by a specific production activity, the distributional effects will be large and vice versa. Finally, income transfers occur between and among different socioeconomic groups and are captured by $(I - C_{22})^{-1}$

Thus, from the above discussion, the total distributional effects are defined as

$$D = (I - C_{22})^{-1} C_{21} C_{13} (I - C_{33})^{-1} \tag{3.7}$$

D can be broken down multiplicatively into its three components:[9]

$$D_3 = (I - C_{22})^{-1}; D_2 = C_{21} C_{13}, \text{ and } D_1 = (I - C_{33})^{-1}, \text{ i.e.,}$$

$$D = D_3 D_2 D_1 \tag{3.7a}$$

where D_3 stands for the transfer effects, D_2 for the direct distributional effects, and D_1 for the intersectoral production effects.

To recapitulate, D_3 represents the interhousehold transfers, D_2 represents the income flows accruing to household groups from the factors used in the

---

9.   An additive decomposition is impossible in this case, since the dimensions of the matrices differ.

production process and owned by those groups, and D_1 represents input-output interlinkages on the production side.

ii. Interdependency effects

While the distributional effects capture the initial impact of a change in sectoral output on incomes, the interdependency effects capture the spending and respending effects. The initial incremental incomes received by the households are, in turn, spent on food, clothing, and other commodities. To satisfy this additional demand, a corresponding output has to be produced requiring intermediate and primary inputs that ultimately generate an additional indirect flow of incomes for the poor. Thus, interdependency effects aggregate the impact of the initial first round of spending and subsequent rounds of respending by the household groups. As mentioned previously, interdependency effects reflect the degree of integration in the socioeconomic system on the production and expenditure sides. What we call interdependency effects (R), in the present context, are equivalent to the closed loop effects identified by Pyatt and Round (1979) in their alternative multiplier decomposition method. Thus going back to equation (3.6) above,

$$M_{c23} = R \cdot D \tag{3.6·}$$

If m_{ij} is an element of M_{c23}, then it can in turn be decomposed multiplicatively into two components:

$$m_{ij} = r_{ij}d_{ij} \tag{3.8}$$

We have shown that the distributional effects can be decomposed further into distributional transfer effects, direct distributional effects, and distributional effects resulting from intersectoral production linkages (see equation 3.7a).

Therefore, a multiplier m_{ij} can be decomposed as

$$m_{ij} = r_{ij}d_{ij} = r_{ij}\,d_{3ij}d_{2ij}d_{1ij} \tag{3.9}$$

In equation (3.4), $dy_2 = M_{c23}dx_3$, let dy_{2i} be an element of vector dy_2, and dx_{3j} be an element of vector dx_3. Then,

$$dy_{2i} = m_{ij}dx_{3j} = r_{ij}d_{ij}dx_{3j} = r_{ij}d_{3ij}d_{2ij}d_{1ij}dx_{3j} \tag{3.10}$$

d. Incorporating poverty sensitivity effects into the previous multiplier decomposition procedure

Assessing the impact of a given sectoral output change on poverty alleviation requires the adoption of an appropriate poverty measure. One such class of additively decomposable poverty measures that has become popular in empirical applications is the Foster-Greer-Thorbecke (FGT) P_α measure that we adopt here (Foster, Greer, and Thorbecke, 1984). For different values of α, the FGT P_α measure becomes, respectively, the headcount ratio ($\alpha = 0$); the poverty gap ($\alpha = 1$); and the FGT distributionally sensitive measure ($\alpha = 2$). In the preceding section, the impact of change in sectoral output on household groups' mean incomes derived. In this section, the sensitivity of the adopted poverty measure to changes in group mean incomes is derived. Poverty sensitivity is determined by the elasticity of the selected poverty measure with respect to mean incomes for the various household groups and their growth rates.

As a first step in computing the change in a poverty measure caused by a sectoral output change, the impact of income change on a poverty measure needs to be clarified. Kakwani (1993) showed that a change in a poverty measure can be decomposed into two parts: part one is the change in mean per capita income (the effect derived and decomposed in the preceding section); part two is the change in income distribution,

$$dP_{\alpha ij} = \frac{\partial P_{\alpha ij}}{\partial \bar{y}_i} d\bar{y}_i + \sum_{k=1}^{l} \frac{\partial P_{\alpha ij}}{\partial \theta_{ijk}} d\theta_{ijk} \qquad (3.11)$$

where $P_{\alpha ij}$ is the FGT P_α measure linking sector j to household group i, $\bar{y}_i$ is the mean per capita income of household group i, and θ_{ijk} reflects the income distribution parameters. Let us assume that the change in the output of production activity j is distributionally neutral so that[10]

$$\frac{dP_{\alpha ij}}{P_{\alpha ij}} = \eta_{\alpha i} \left(\frac{d\bar{y}_i}{\bar{y}_i} \right) \qquad (3.12)$$

where $\eta_{\alpha i}$ is the elasticity $P_{\alpha ij}$ with respect to the mean per capita income of each household group i resulting from an increase in the output of sector j.[11]

The next step is to link the increase in mean income ($d\bar{y}_i$) to the previously derived fixed price multiplier (m_{ij}). From equation (3.4) it follows that:

---

10. Although the assumption of distribution neutrality is common in this type of modeling, this cannot be taken for granted. A very detailed comparison of income distribution by sector of employment in Indonesia between 1984 and 1987 revealed significant changes in intragroup distributions for the same sector between these two years (see Huppie and Ravallion, 1991).

11. In order for poverty alleviation to occur, $\eta_{\alpha i}$ has to be negative. In what follows, this is the convention adopted.

$$d = dx_j \qquad (3.13)$$

where dx_j is the change in the output of sector j defined on a per capita basis for group i. Therefore, equation (3.14) becomes

$$\frac{dP_{\alpha ij}}{P_{\alpha ij}} = \eta_{\alpha i} m_{ij} \left(\frac{dx_j}{\bar{y}_i} \right) \qquad (3.14)$$

Poverty tends to be pervasive in developing countries and to be spread among the different household groups. In order to obtain the aggregate poverty alleviation effects, these effects have to be totaled across the household groups. Thorbecke and Jung (1996) derived the following relationship, where j stands for production sector, i stands for household group, and alpha stands for 0, 1, and 2 respectively.

$$\frac{dP_{\alpha j}}{P_{\alpha j}} = \sum_{i=1}^{m} r_{\alpha ij} d_{3\alpha ij} d'_{2\alpha ij} d_{1\alpha ij} q_{\alpha ij} \qquad (3.15)$$

In other words, the total poverty alleviation effects of an increase in the output of sector j $(-dP_{\alpha j}/P_{\alpha j})$ can be decomposed into (i) mean income change of the poor across all household groups, further decomposed into interdependency effects and three types of distributional effects (transfer effects, direct distributional effects, and intersectoral production linkages effects); and (ii) sensitivity of the selected poverty measure to the mean income change $(q_{\alpha j})$.

An application of the above methodology to the case study of Indonesia revealed that the agricultural and service sectors contribute significantly more to overall poverty alleviation than do the industrial sectors. The case study also revealed that differences in the contribution of different sectors to poverty alleviation were primarily accounted for by two types of distributional effects: direct distributional effects and intersectoral production activity linkages (Thorbecke and Jung, 1996).

As countries develop and undergo a process of industrialization, it becomes increasingly important to strengthen the distributional and interdependency effects. In this context, the decomposition analysis in Thorbecke and Jung (1996) provides potentially important insights about how socioeconomic groups with a high incidence of poverty can participate in, and benefit from, industrialization. It was shown that the low poverty alleviation effects of manufacturing activities are mostly due to low distributional effects (especially direct linkages). These direct linkages depend on the factor endowment of the groups of poor households and the prevailing technology in the production sectors. Since the factor endowment of the poor household groups consists mainly, if not exclusively, of unskilled labor, while manufacturing activities tend to rely on skilled rather than unskilled labor, the decomposition analysis suggests strongly that the human capital of the poor must be enhanced through education and vocational training if the poor are not to be sealed off from participating in modern production activities. Likewise, in the transition period toward full-scale industrialization, certain production activities (such as food processing and textiles) relying on relatively traditional technologies and relatively unskilled labor should not be prematurely and inappropriately displaced by modern capital-intensive technologies.

e. Budgetary rules to minimize societal poverty in a general equilibrium framework

Suppose that a government of a developing country is intent on allocating an exogenously given budget, B (e.g., from a foreign aid grant), to minimize societal poverty. Society is made up of k mutually exclusive socioeconomic groups whose intragroup income distributions are known. For practical and administrative reasons, the government can only target groups rather than individual households. Assume further that the societal measure of poverty to be minimized is P_α. If reducing P_α is society's goal, the increment should be given to the group whose receipt of the increment will reduce P_α the most (i.e., it should be given to the group i for which $\partial P_\alpha / \partial B^i$ is the most negative, where B^i is the incremental poverty budget provided to group i).

Thorbecke and Berrian (1992) have derived budgetary rules to maximize the reduction in societal poverty from a given budget dedicated to poverty alleviation, with and without interaction in the economy. What is relevant in the present context is that they have shown that failure to incorporate interactive (indirect) effects leads to misallocation of a poverty alleviation budget among groups, leading to a welfare loss. Interactive effects can account for a not insignificant part of the reduction in societal poverty. More specifically, the sequence of allocation of benefits and the choice of groups under the budgetary rules—assuming interaction in the economy—are different from those under budgetary rules assuming no interaction.

3. Poverty Analysis and Measurement within Computable General Equilibrium Modeling

The preceding SAM multiplier analysis rests on some limiting assumptions, namely that excess capacity prevails and unused resources are available. In this type of

Keynesian world, any exogenous increase in demand can be satisfied by a corresponding increase in supply, while maintaining constant prices. The comparatively static nature of the SAM multiplier analysis, as such, precludes capturing and estimating dynamic effects. For example, whereas investment demand (the intermediate inputs, labor, and capital required in the construction phase of a project) is explicitly incorporated in the SAM, the future effects of investment on productivity are ruled out by the fact that a SAM is only a one-year snapshot of the economy. Furthermore, when an economy is affected by an exogenous shock or a policy change, a new set of prices obtains, which, in turn, determines production, consumption, employment, and income.

The SAM provides the underlying taxonomy of the CGE. Each account and subaccount of a given SAM appears as a corresponding endogenous or exogenous variable in the CGE based on that SAM. Not only does a CGE take as its initial conditions the values appearing in the base-year SAM, but in addition, the parameters and coefficients of the various equations of the CGE are calibrated on the base-year SAM. In this sense, it can be said that a SAM provides the "navigation table" for a CGE. All the mechanisms and transformations inherent in the SAM and described in detail in Section 2a are an intrinsic part of the CGE's architecture, as well. The SAM structure predetermines the channels (transformations) by which influence is transmitted throughout the socioeconomic system; the CGE formalizes the relationships underlying these channels through a set of behavioral and technical equations and equilibrium conditions.

The specification of a CGE should not only reflect the prevailing socioeconomic structure of the economy (i.e., the classification scheme in the base-year SAM should be consistent with that structure), but also the behavior of the actors and the constraints they face. Hence, a typical CGE starts with a set of neoclassical rules and modifies them to reflect the idiosyncratic environment specific to the setting that is described.

CGE models have traditionally been used to simulate the impact of exogenous shocks, such as changes in international terms of trade or a recession in importing countries, and of changes in policies, on the socioeconomic system and, in particular, on income distribution. Good examples of such models are those that were built in connection with the research program of the Organization for Economic Cooperation and Development to explore the impact of structural adjustment on equity (Thorbecke, 1991, for Indonesia; de Janvry, Sadoulet, and Fargeix, 1991, for Ecuador; and Morrisson, 1991, for Morocco). Since CGE models are fully calibrated on the basis of an initial-year SAM that provides a set of consistent initial conditions, and the SAM, as such, does not contain information on income distribution within a socioeconomic household group, it follows that conventional CGEs can only simulate the impact of a shock on the representative household in each group. This amounts to the implicit assumption that the variance of income within a group is zero. To the extent that poverty is pervasive and is likely to affect many socioeconomic groups (albeit to different degrees), it appears essential in any analysis of the impact of a shock on poverty levels to start with information on intragroup income distribution. Increasingly, as more income and expenditure surveys become available, it is possible to generate the intragroup income distributions prevailing in the same base year as that of the SAM used to calibrate the general equilibrium model.

Decaluwe et al. (1999) built a CGE model of an archetype African economy incorporating the poverty dimension. The major additional features of this model compared to a conventional CGE model are as follows: first, it proposes a more flexible income distribution function. Second, it specifies the intragroup distributions so as to conform to the different socioeconomic characteristics of the groups. Thus, as will be seen subsequently, the characteristics displayed by rural landless households contrast markedly with those of large landowner households and yield significantly different distributions. Third, it postulates a unique and constant basket of basic needs commodities. Since commodity prices are endogenously determined within the model, the monetary value of the poverty line is also endogenously determined. These three innovations help shed more light into the black box pertaining to the behavior of poverty following a shock.

Table 3.3 presents an illustrative example of a SAM for an archetype African developing economy that provided the foundation of the above model. Although it was calibrated to reflect approximately the socioeconomic structure of the Ivory Coast, it should be considered as a demonstration SAM reflecting many of the characteristics of a prototype African economy. The SAM is disaggregated in terms of four factors, namely unskilled labor, skilled labor, capital, and agricultural capital (land); six categories of households, namely rural landless workers, rural small landowners, rural large landowners, urban low-education (and hence relatively low-income) workers, urban high-education (high income) workers, and capitalists; and enterprises. The geographical location of households, the origin of their income or occupation, and other socioeconomic characteristics define the groups. For example, a rural household has the characteristics of living in rural areas and being endowed exclusively with unskilled labor (and thus being landless). Six production activities are identified: domestic agriculture, export agriculture, mining, industry, services, and public services. Finally, five different commodities are specified: domestic agriculture, export agriculture, mining, industries, and services.

The import-competing sectors are industry and traditional agriculture. The export sectors are represented by mining and export crops. Land/agricultural capital, capital, unskilled labor, and skilled labor are the four primary factors of production employed by the activities, as described above.

Except for the incorporation of a poverty module, the specification of the

Table 3.3. Social Accounting Matrix for Archetype African Developing Country

			Factors				Households						
			1	2	3	4	5	6	7	8	9	10	11
Factors	Unskilled labor	1											
	Skilled labor	2											
	Capital	3											
	Land	4											
Households	Rural workers	5	228.0	0.0	0.0	0.0							
	Rural land-owners (small)	6	790.5	0.0	255.9	156.3							
	Rural land-owners (large)	7	76.0	141.7	511.8	290.3							
	Urban low education	8	425.7	0.0	85.3	0.0							
	Urban high education	9	0.0	226.7	341.2	0.0							
	Capitalists	10	0.0	198.4	511.8	0.0							
	Enterprise	11			222.7								
Activities	Agriculture	12											
	Export Agriculture	13											
	Mining	14											
	Industries	15											
	Services	16											
	Public Services	17											
Commodities	Agriculture	18					95.0	412.7	271.9	171.6	97.1	32.4	
	Exp. Agr.	19					0.0	0.0	0.0	0.0	0.0	0.0	
	Mining	20					0.0	0.0	0.0	0.0	0.0	0.0	
	Industries	21					83.1	402.8	384.2	191.7	242.4	153.1	
	Services	22					57.5	291.0	271.9	141.2	146.1	98.6	
	Government	23					12.4	60.1	51.0	26.5	28.4	71.0	
	Accumulation	24					0.0	36.1	40.8	0.0	53.9	355.1	222.7
ROW	ROW	25											
	Total		1 520.2	566.8	1 928.7	446.6	248	1 202.7	1 019.8	531	567.9	710.2	222.7

64

Table 3.3 (cont.)

	Activities					Commodities									
12	13	14	15	16	17	18	19	20	21	22	23	24	25	
365.5	81.0	38.5	474.2	293.2	267.8									1,520.2
4.5	10.0	144.6	107.8	97.7	202.2									566.8
72.0	30.0	292.4	955.3	567.1	11.9									1,928.7
361.6	85.0	0.0	0.0	0.0	0.0									446.6
											20			248
											0			1,202.7
											0			1,019.8
											20			531
											0			567.9
											0			710.2
						1 038.3		0.0	0.0	0.0			181.2	1,219.5
							50.0						231.0	281.0
						0.0		507.4	0.0	0.0			535.0	1,042.4
						0.0		0.0	2 135.1	0.0			195.0	2,330.1
						0.0		0.0	0.0	1 325.0			110.0	1,435.0
						0.0		0.0	0.0	594.0			0.0	594.0
204.8		0.0	323.3	0.0	0.0						0	274.9		1,883.7
	40.0											10		50
0.0		19.3	43.1	0.0	0.0						0	445		507.4
186.1	30.0	337.5	301.7	143.3	0.0						0	50		2,505.9
0.0		173.6	43.1	247.6	76.5						471.9	0		2,019.0
25.0	5.0	36.5	81.6	86.1	35.6	85.6			74.2					679
1.0	281.0	1.0	2.0	1.0	594.0	759.8	50.0	0.0	296.6	100.0	167.1		-95.8	779.9
219.5		42.4	330.1	435.0		1 883.7		507.4	2 505.9	2 019.0	679.0	779.9	156.4	1,156.4

Source: Decaluwe et al. (1999).

65

CGE model is standard, reflecting the structure of a small open economy that has no influence on international markets. The model consists of different blocs: production, employment incomes and savings demand, and foreign trade, in addition to the poverty module. (The full model is given in the Appendix to Decaluwe et al. [1999].)

The way in which income distribution and poverty analysis is incorporated into this model is described in the next subsection, as its methodology is applicable and transferable to other countries.

In this illustrative case and consistent with the SAM (Table 3.3), the households are aggregated into six groups representative of those living in an archetypal African country. To each of these groups income and demographic characteristics typical of an African economy are attributed. These descriptive data are presented in Table 3.4. As can be observed, the mean income varies from 13.57 for the rural households to 117.72 for the capitalist households. As for the population shares, small landowners are the largest group, with 36.1 percent of the total population. In this example, the rural households have the highest initial poverty headcount ratio with 93.3 percent of the population below the poverty line, followed by the urban low-income category with 57.7 percent of the population below the poverty line. It should be noted that in the great majority of developing countries, detailed income and expenditure survey data exist from which the actual intragroup income distributions can be derived.

Table 3.4. Income and Demographic Characteristics

	Rural households	Small landowner households	Large landowner households	Urban low-education households	Urban high-education households	Capitalist households
Mean Income	13.57	27.75	29.91	23.27	41.49	117.72
Maximum Income	40.00	50.00	55.00	40.00	60.00	140.00
Minimum Income	5.00	10.00	15.00	15.00	20.00	25.00
Population Share	0.13	0.31	0.25	0.17	0.10	0.04
% Below the Poverty Line	93.30%	36.10%	19.40%	57.70%	0.50%	0.00%

In order to analyze and derive poverty by household group, an income distribution formulation corresponding to the characteristics of each household group is postulated. This distribution will depend on the minimum and maximum incomes and on the skewing of the income distribution.[12] To represent these characteristics in the income distributions, we use the Beta distribution function (equation 3.16). Parameters mx and mn are, respectively, the maximum and minimum incomes within a group. As for the parameters p and q, they influence the shape and the skewing of the distribution.

---

12. A left-skewed distribution (skewness < 0, long tail in the negative direction) is defined by mode > median > mean and a right-skewed distribution (skewness < 0, long tail in the positive direction) is defined by mode < median < mean. A right-skewed distribution occurs when the mode is superior to the median.

$$I(y; p, q) = \frac{1}{B(p,q)} \frac{(y - mn)^{p-1} (mx - y)^{q-1}}{(mx - mn)^{p+q-1}}$$

where

$$B(p,q) = \int_{mn}^{mx} \frac{(y - mn)^{p-1} (mx - y)^{q-1}}{(mx - mn)^{p+q-1}} dy \qquad (3.16)$$

Unlike the lognormal, the Beta function is much more flexible when it comes to the asymmetric forms it can adopt (Decaluwe et al., 1999). The parameters assigned to each household category are selected so that the income distribution accords with the characteristics of the household groups described in Table 3.4.

These distributions are used to evaluate the incidence of poverty within each group in a general equilibrium framework. Following an external shock to the economy, it is assumed, albeit arbitrarily, that the intragroup distributions shift with the change in the mean income, without changing the shape or the variance of each distribution (see Figures 3.3a–3.3f). Although there are recorded cases of significant changes in intragroup distributions following a shock, as in the case of Indonesia's adjustment process between 1984 and 1987 (Huppie and Ravallion, 1991), more recent work by Ravallion and Chen (1997) finds that inequality increases as often as it falls during spells of growth in developing countries, and that neutrality is actually a defensible first-order approximation. However, it is unlikely that distribution neutrality can be assumed to prevail following shocks leading to negative growth (such as the Asian financial crisis), and it is unclear even in spells of growth whether distribution neutrality would be a good first-order approximation in estimating poverty as opposed to inequality. As stressed by Dervis, De Melo, and Robinson (1982), the complete endogenization of intragroup income distributions following shocks still remains the biggest challenge in studying income distribution in a general equilibrium context. This question is treated subsequently.

The procedure described above allows us to compare the poverty levels obtaining in the post-simulation case with those prevailing in the pre-simulation case using the FGT P_α measures. The FGT P_α class of additively decomposable poverty measures allows us to measure not only the proportion of poor in the population (the headcount ratio), but also the depth and severity of poverty. The P_α measure expressed in terms of the Beta given distribution in equation (3.16) becomes

$$P_\alpha = \int_{mn}^{z} \left(\frac{z - y}{z} \right)^{\alpha} I(y, p, q) d \qquad (3.17)$$

where α is a poverty-aversion parameter, z is the poverty line, *mn* is the mini-

Figure 3.3. Effect of a 30 Percent Reduction in World Export Price of Export Agriculture Crop on Income Distribution

a. Rural Households

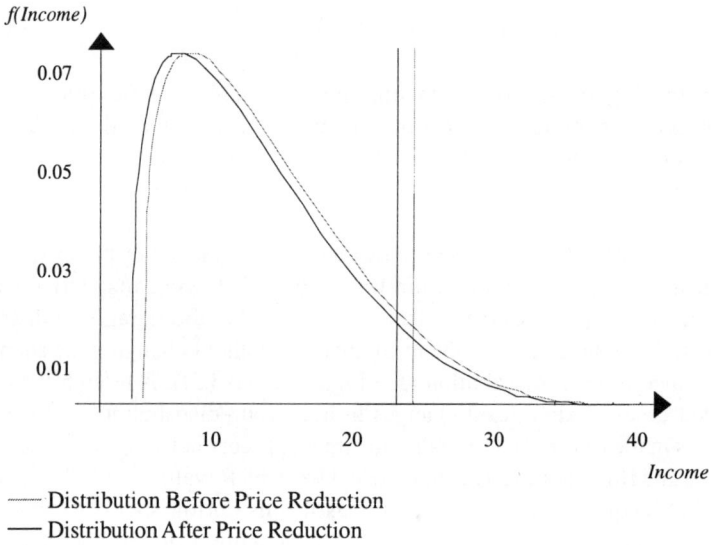

------- Distribution Before Price Reduction
——— Distribution After Price Reduction

b. Small Landowner Households

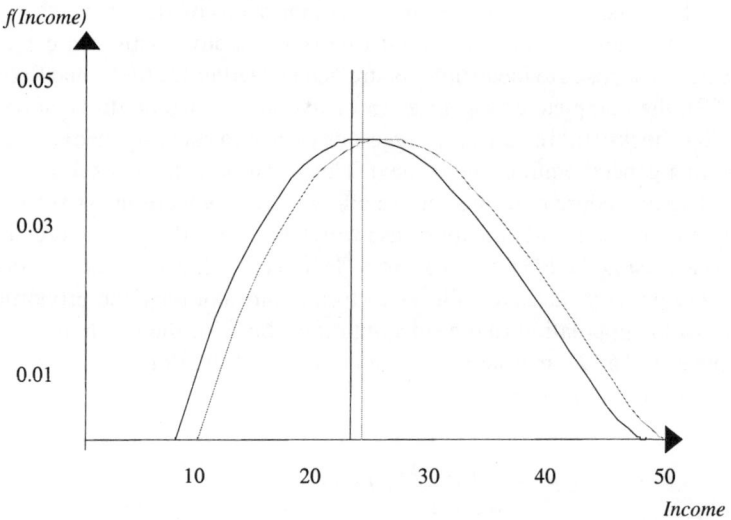

Figure 3.3 (cont.)

c. Large Landowner Households

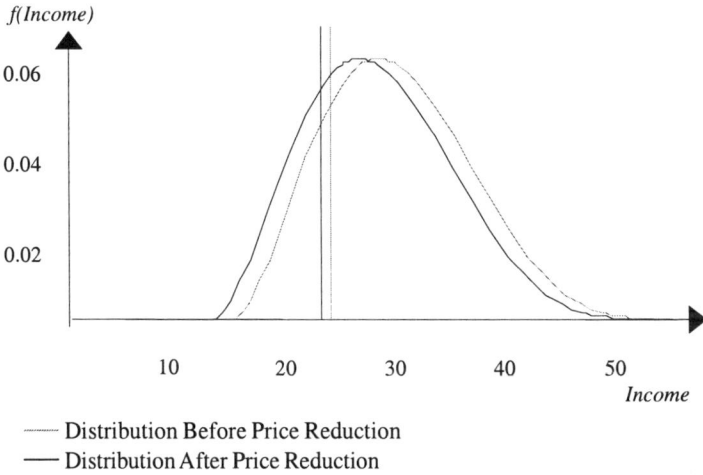

------ Distribution Before Price Reduction
—— Distribution After Price Reduction

d. Urban Low Income Households

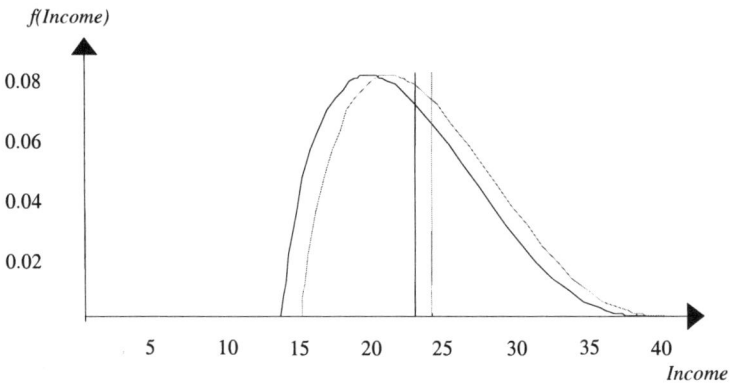

Figure 3.3 (cont.)

e. Urban High Income Households

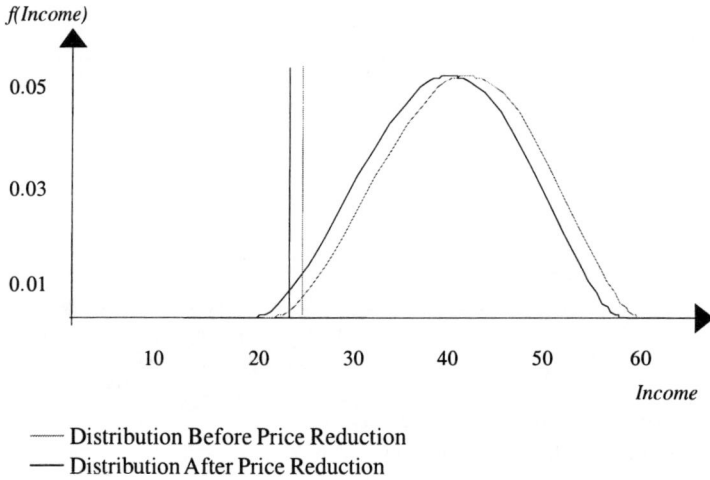

—— Distribution Before Price Reduction
—— Distribution After Price Reduction

f. Capitalist Households

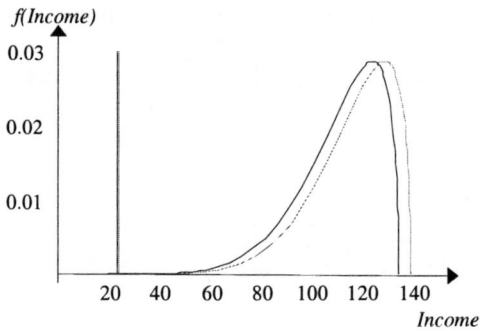

mum (intragroup) income, and p and q are parameters of the Beta function as defined earlier.

The poverty line itself (z in equation 3.17) is determined endogenously within the CGE model. It is postulated that the poverty line is determined by a basket of quantities of commodities reflecting basic needs consistent with Ravallion's (1994) approach to estimating absolute poverty. We denote this basket as ϖ^p_{com}. This basket remains invariant from one simulation to another and applies to all households regardless of group membership. In turn, the monetary poverty line is obtained by multiplying the basic needs commodity basket by the commodities' respective prices (Pq_{com}) and aggregating across commodities:

$$\text{Monetary Poverty Line: } \sum_{com} \varpi^p_{com} Pq_{com}$$

Since commodity prices are endogenously determined within the model, so is the nominal value of this basket, i.e., the poverty line. If commodity prices rise following an external shock, the poverty line will increase (shift to the right) and poverty will rise, all other things being equal.

The demand system specified in the model is based on the Linear Expenditure System (LES):

$$C_{h,com} = \frac{Pq_{com}\varpi_{h,com} + \beta^C_{h,com}\left(CH_h - \sum_{com}\varpi_{com}Pq_{com}\right)}{Pq_{com}} \qquad (3.18)$$

where $C_{h,com}$ is the demand for commodity com by household group h; C_h is disposable income of household group h; $\varpi_{h,com}$ is the basket of committed (minimal) consumption in volume terms for the commodities specific to household group h; Pq_{com} is the price of com; and $\sum_{com}\varpi_{h,com}Pq_{com}$ is the monetary value of the committed (minimum) consumption specific to household group h.

This demand system implies that each socioeconomic group has its own perception of the minimal commodity basket that it needs to be satisfied, consistent with the socioeconomic characteristics and the overall standard of living of the group. Clearly, this minimum basket is bound to be different for the high-income capitalist group and for the low-income rural households. Hence, the first term on the right-hand side in the numerator of equation (3.18) represents the amount needed to satisfy this household-specific minimum consumption requirement of commodity com. In turn, the second term in the numerator represents the proportions or marginal expenditure propensities ($\beta_{h,com}$) of discretionary income ($CH_h - \sum_{com}\varpi_{h,com}Pq_{com}$) to be spent on each respective commodity. It can be seen that if this last term is zero (i.e., if there is no discretionary income), then each household group consumes a quantity of each commodity corresponding exactly to its household-specific postulated minimum.

It is essential to grasp clearly the distinction between the poverty BN basket that applies to all households, regardless of group membership, and is defined at the level of the society; and the LES demand system that specifies a group-specific consumption level for each commodity that is intractable downward. Each group is assumed to behave lexicographically in such a way that it first satisfies its minimum consumption of the respective commodities.

Two simulations were performed on the model's base-year equilibrium; the first is a reduction in the world price of the agricultural export crop on the international market and the second is an import tariff reform. The effects of these simulations on the whole socioeconomic system and how they ultimately affect the household income distribution and poverty based on the P_α measures are derived. The results of the first simulation are shown graphically in Figures 3.3a–f, where the decline in each household category's nominal mean income is presented by a horizontal shift of the income distribution to the left.

Since the prices of the commodities are endogenously determined, so is the new monetary poverty line:

$$\sum_{com} \varpi^P_{com} \ Pq_{com}$$

Hence in Figures 3.3a–f the new post-simulation poverty line is drawn next to the pre-simulation line. For the first simulation the poverty line decreases by 4.4 percent. This reduction is the consequence of a fall in the consumption prices of the basic needs basket, which determines the poverty line. With the post-simulation distribution and a new poverty line, we can use the P_α class to estimate the effects on poverty.

The headcount ratio P_0 increases for all household groups—except the rural households. Rural households display, by far, the highest headcount ratio, with 92.9 percent of the population below the poverty line. Compared with the base year, this represents a 0.4 percent improvement in the headcount ratio. Rural households constitute the only group enjoying a reduction in poverty. This is explained by the poverty line reduction that dominates the reduction in nominal income of this specific household group. We find the highest relative increase in P_0 among the urban high-education households; this ratio increases from 0.5 percent to 0.8 percent following the fall in price of the export crop.

In an ongoing project, Azis and Thorbecke (2001) have built a CGE model of the Indonesian economy to simulate the effects on it of the Asian financial crisis. The model contains a detailed financial sector and a poverty module similar to the one described above in the CGE of an archetype African economy. In addition, the model attempts to endogenize the urban-to-rural migration that occurred between the onset of the crisis (1997) and 1999.

As part of this project, the post-crisis (1999) actual intragroup income distributions of eight socioeconomic household groups are obtained from the large-scale SUSENAS National Socioeconomic Survey (covering some 205,000 households) and compared to the pre-crisis (1996) intragroup distributions. An attempt is being made to identify and replicate the exogenous events and endogenous mechanisms yielding the post-crisis observed income distributions and poverty estimates.

Under the auspices of the World Bank, this project also attempts to link a microsimulation model of the Indonesian economy (under the leadership of Francois Bourguignon and Anne-Sophie Robillard) with the Azis–Thorbecke financial CGE. It is hoped that this project will throw more light on the process of endogenizing the intragroup income distributions that obtain following an exogenous shock or policy change.

It is interesting to note that the intragroup income distributions for seven Indonesian socioeconomic household categories were extremely similar after the crisis (1999) to those obtaining before the crisis (1996). Figure 3.4 presents the pre-crisis and post-crisis distributions for each group. These distributions are the actual distributions derived from the SUSENAS survey.

The fact that the shape and variable of each group distribution remained more or less the same in 1999 as in 1996 provides a rationalization for the arbitrary assumption, made in the model described above, that the intragroup distributions remained constant and shifted horizontally to the left or to the right, depending on group mean income.

It is hoped that the combination of a financial CGE model and a microsimulation approach may prove fruitful in understanding better the mechanisms and channels through which the financial crisis affected poverty in Indonesia.

Figure 3.4. Nonparametric Income Distribution for Indonesian Household Groups, 1996 vs. 1999 (at constant 1996 prices based on GDP Deflator)

a. Agricultural Workers

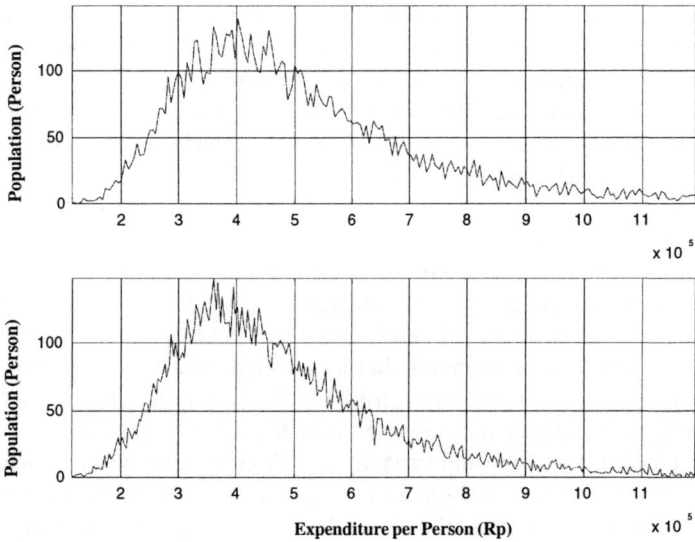

Source: Central Statistical Bureau: SUSENAS Survey (1996 and 1999).

b. Farmers with Land

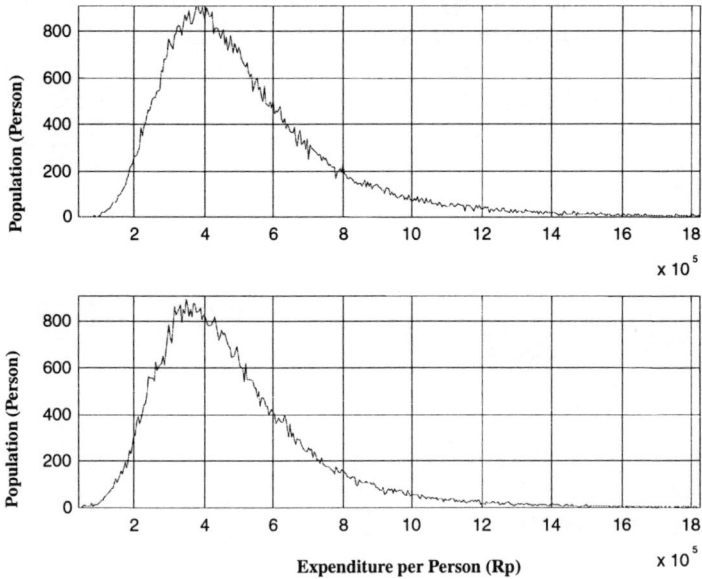

Figure 3.4 (cont.)

c. Rural Low Education

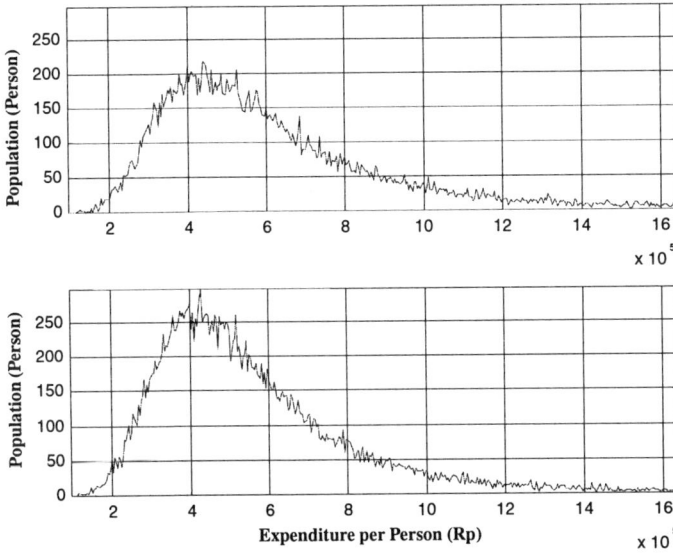

Note: Top figure (1996), Bottom figure (1999).

d. Rural High Education

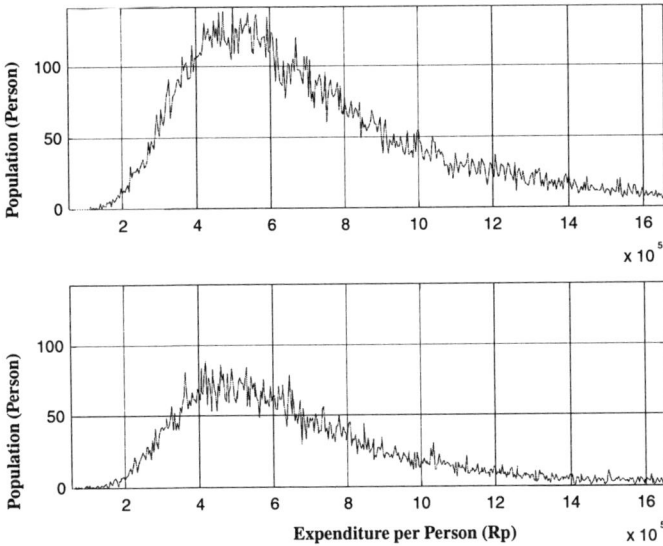

Note: Top figure (1996), Bottom figure (1999).
Source: GDP Deflator with different horizontal scale.

Figure 3.4 (cont.)

e. Rural Non-LbF

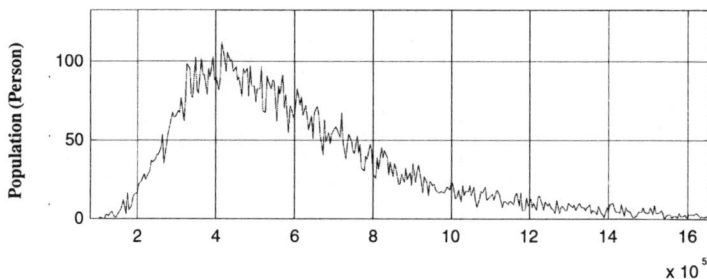

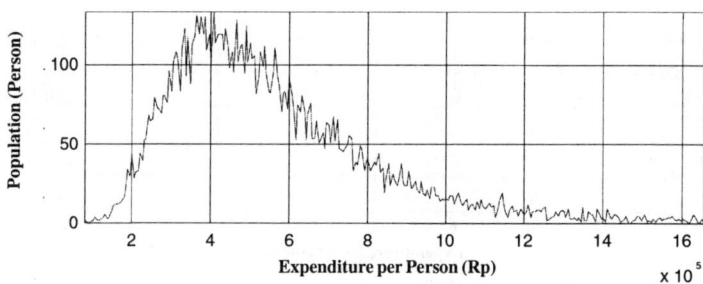

Note: Top figure (1996), Bottom figure (1999).

f. Urban Low Education

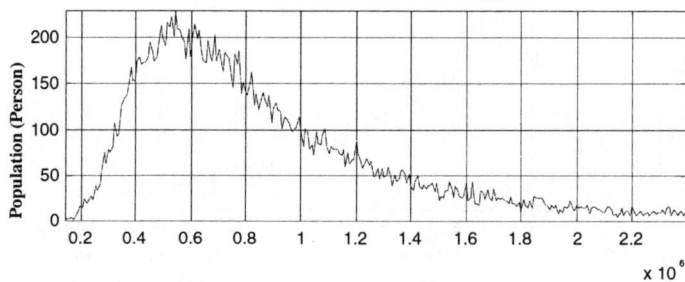

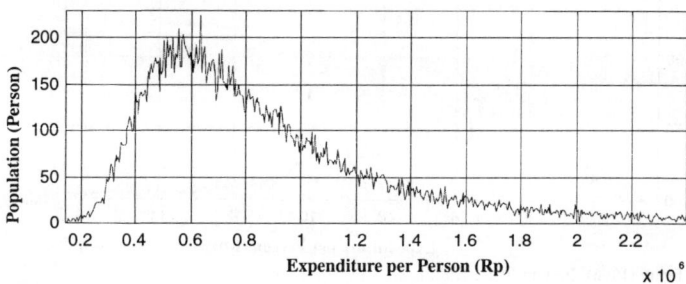

Note: Top figure (1996), Bottom figure (1999).

Figure 3.4 (cont.)

g. Urban Non-LbF

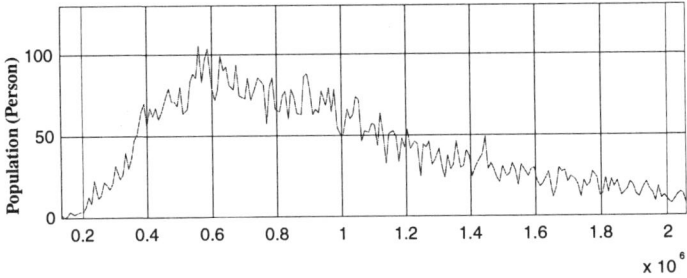

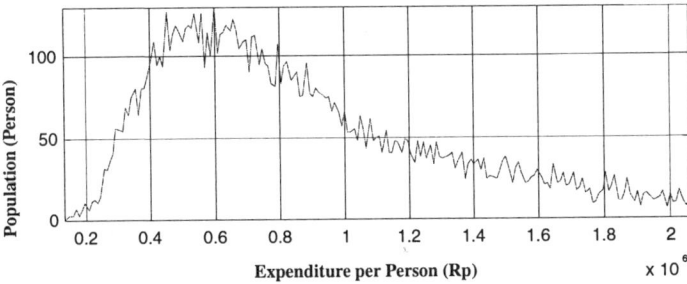

Note: Top figure (1996), Bottom figure (1999).

h. Urban High Education

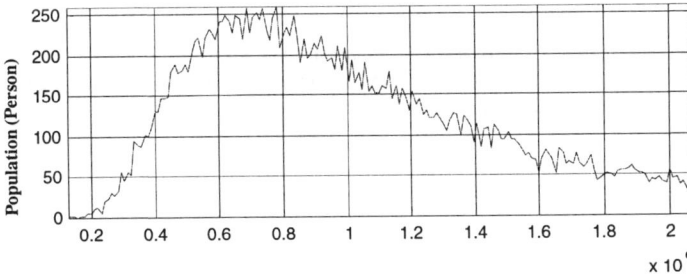

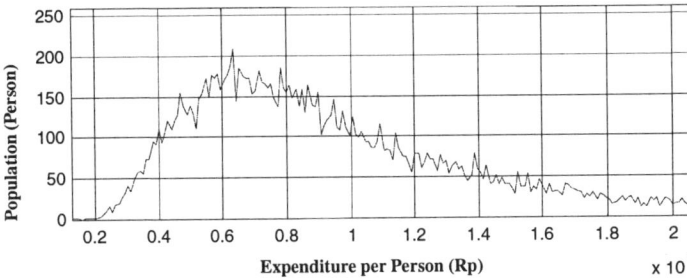

Note: Top figure (1996), Bottom figure (1999).

References

Azis, I., and E. Thorbecke. 2001. Modeling the Socio-economic Impacts of the Financial Crisis: The Case of Indonesia. Mimeo. Ithaca, NY: Cornell University.

Decaluwe, B., A. Patry, L. Savard, and E. Thorbecke. 1999. General Equilibrium Approach for Poverty Analysis. Mimeo. Ithaca NY: Cornell University.

de Janvry, A., E. Sadoulet, and A. Fargeix. 1991. *Adjustment and Equity in Ecuador.* Paris: Organisation for Economic Cooperation and Development, Development Center.

Dervis, K., J. De Melo, and S. Robinson. 1982. *General Equilibrium Models for Development Policy.* London: Cambridge University Press.

Foster, J., J. Greer, and E. Thorbecke. 1984. A Class of Decomposable Poverty Measures. *Econometrica* 52(3): 761–766.

Government of Indonesia. 1996, 1999. *SUSENAS* (National Socioeconomic Survey). Jakarta: Central Statistical Bureau.

Huppie, M., and M. Ravallion. 1991. The Sectoral Structure of Poverty During an Adjustment Period: Evidence for Indonesia in the Mid-1980s. *World Development* 19(12).

Kakwani, N. 1993. Poverty and Economic Growth with Application to Côte D'Ivoire. *Review of Income and Wealth* 39(2): 121–139.

Morrisson, C. 1991. *Adjustment and Equity in Morocco.* Paris: Organisation for Economic Cooperation and Development, Development Center.

Pyatt, G., and J. I. Round. 1979. Accounting and Fixed-Price Multipliers in a Social Accounting Matrix Framework. *Economic Journal* 89: 850–873.

Ravallion, M. 1994. *Poverty Comparisons.* Harwood Academic Publisher.

Ravallion, M., and S. Chen. 1997. What Can New Survey Data Tell Us About Recent Changes in Distribution and Poverty? *World Bank Economic Review* 11.

Thorbecke, E. 1991. Adjustment, Growth and Income Distribution in Indonesia. *World Development* 19(11): 1595–1614.

———, and D. Berrian. 1992. Budgetary Rules to Minimize Societal Poverty in a General Equilibrium Context. *Journal of Development Economics* 39: 189–205.

———, and H. S. Jung. 1996. A Multiplier Decomposition Method to Analyze Poverty Alleviation. *Journal of Development Economics* 48: 279–300.

4.　Macroeconomic Policies and Poverty Reduction: Stylized Facts and an Overview of Research

Ratna Sahay, Paul Cashin, Paolo Mauro, and Catherine Pattillo

1. Introduction

While poverty reduction is the key challenge facing the world community, an important debate is taking place on the policies that may help attain that objective, and on how international financial institutions can contribute toward that goal. This chapter provides a brief and selective review of ongoing research efforts aimed at identifying the policies that can help reduce poverty. The focus is on issues that relate to the interaction between macroeconomic policies—which are at the core of the International Monetary Fund's (IMF's) mandate—and poverty.

　　The links between macroeconomic policies and poverty are complex, and the vast literature on poverty does not yet fully specify how one should think about the direct impact of macroeconomic polices on the poor. Likewise, empirical research on these topics remains at a somewhat preliminary stage. Lack of data, particularly in poor countries, often hinders high-quality research. More recently, attempts at cross-country work have been made but are subject to various criticisms, as highlighted in Srinivasan (2000). The only systematic evidence that exists concerns the poverty-reducing effects of economic growth and, to some extent, the beneficial impact of lowering inflation and, not uncontroversially, freeing trade regimes. But in all these areas, the magnitude of the estimated effects on the incidence of poverty has varied widely across countries and across time in the same countries. While poverty reduction has become a new global mantra, the challenge facing the world community looms large, with the specifics of how to spread the fruits of economic progress leaving room for a wide research agenda.

　　Recognizing the complexity of the relationships and the political economy aspects of reform programs, the world community is redefining the role of the State. The new consensus is that public policy will now be formulated with active participation from different sections of society.

Participatory policymaking not only ensures popular support for each country's economic programs, but also provides a more level playing field for the poorest sections of society, by removing the structural and cultural impediments to pro-poor economic development. According to this new consensus, a one-for-one response from growth to poverty reduction cannot be taken for granted. Rather, appropriate conditions, such as ensuring that exchange rates are not overvalued, easing constraints on domestic credit markets, reducing labor market distortions, building human capital, and increasing access to trade markets, need to be created so that the poor benefit from growth and so that growth rates rise and are sustained.

This chapter is organized as follows: Section 2 conducts a survey of the literature on macroeconomic policies, macroeconomic adjustment, and poverty in the run-up to the new emphasis on participatory processes that emerged toward the end of the 1990s. Section 3 gives a preliminary look at the data, focusing on a United Nations Development Programme (UNDP)-developed measure of well-being, the Human Development Index (HDI). This section examines changes in the HDI of individual countries between 1975 and 1998, and explores the association between macroeconomic policies and improvements in well-being. Section 4 concludes with comments and suggestions for future research.

2. Research on Macroeconomic Policies, Macroeconomic Adjustment and Poverty

The consequences of macroeconomic policies for the welfare of the poor and on the distribution of income are issues that attract increasing interest from both economists and policymakers. While most analyses of poverty and inequality have been microeconomic in nature, there is an increasing recognition that macroeconomic policies and macroeconomic stabilization programs can have important effects on both the distribution and level of incomes.

The literature on the relationship between macroeconomic policies and poverty is gradually evolving away from an emphasis on the strong link between economic growth and poverty reduction toward an exploration of policies, beyond growth itself, that contribute to both poverty reduction and improvements in the distribution of income. This line of research explores whether macroeconomic imbalances, such as excessive fiscal and balance of payments deficits, large debt and debt servicing costs, and high inflation, have implications for poverty beyond those they exert on economic growth.

Of interest are the consequences that IMF- and World Bank-supported adjustment programs for income distribution have had on the poor, particularly in the wake of the severe economic crises experienced by many countries in the 1990s. In examining the effects of macroeconomic adjustment on real incomes, the main theoretical model utilized has been the dependent economy model. In addition, several analyses of the actual effects of macroeconomic adjustment programs on income distribution and poverty complement the large literature that examines the relative economic performance of countries undertaking macroeconomic adjustment programs.

Macroeconomic instability (characterized by rising debt-servicing costs, shocks from adverse terms of trade, high inflation, and large fiscal and external imbalances) generates an unsustainable excess of aggregate demand over aggregate supply. To restore macroeconomic balance, countries undertake (in conjunction with the IMF and/or the World Bank) macroeconomic adjustment programs. As noted by Lipton and Ravallion (1995), the case for adjustment programs depends on demonstrating that the present social value of the future sequence of consumptions is greater with adjustment than without.

In this context, the workhorse-dependent economy model (which assumes constant terms of trade) is a useful means to highlight the likely effects of structural adjustment on real incomes, particularly the incomes of the poor. In response to excess aggregate demand, restoring internal and external balance means that the price of nontraded goods must decrease relative to that of traded goods (a real devaluation), and domestic absorption needs to fall (typically through lower domestic consumption and net public expenditures). Given that the poor typically possess labor in abundance, and that labor is mobile across the traded and nontraded goods sectors, the Stolper-Samuelson theorem would predict that returns to the abundant factor (labor) will rise. Returns to labor will increase only if the traded goods sector is more labor-intensive than the nontraded goods sector. This seems a plausible assumption for most developing countries, which have a comparative advantage in the production of labor-intensive products. Accordingly, the poor should gain, as their real wage (in terms of nontraded goods) will rise with structural adjustment, though this may take a long time.

In the short run, however, the impact of the depreciation on the poor may be mixed. The impact effect is to increase the profitability of traded goods production and decrease that of nontraded goods production. This could have adverse distributional effects in some countries. For example, the gains of poor producers in the traded goods sector will be limited if the government does not pass on much of the export price increase to smallholder farmers. The lower profitability of nontraded goods could also worsen poverty, where incomes are already very low for households producing nontraded food crops. Other important caveats to this beneficial effect of adjustment on the poor concern the pattern of fiscal consolidation, particularly if spending cuts target programs that benefit the poor; and the rise in traded goods prices (particularly for food staples), which may adversely affect the urban poor (as net consumers) even as they benefit the rural poor (as net producers). Despite an apparent rejection of the view that structural adjustment (relative to nonadjustment) is uniformly bad for the poor, it is true that the speed of supply-side response to adjustment (as embodied in the dependent economy model) may also have been overestimated for many developing countries.

a. Poverty, income inequality, and economic growth

One possible link between macroeconomic policies and poverty may well be indirect. Good macroeconomic policies are generally considered to lead to higher growth, and higher growth in turn to poverty reduction. Considerable evidence supports the former premise, particularly over the long run: good macroeconomic polices, if sustained, lead to higher growth rates for countries at the same level of economic development. We do not report on this strand of literature here, as it is vast and would detract from the issue at hand.[1]

The theoretical literature on poverty and growth has explored the relationship between relative concepts of poverty (income distribution) and growth. Interestingly, researchers have not yet fully developed a theoretical framework for thinking about the links between absolute poverty levels and income growth.[2] Several empirical studies, however, have been undertaken to understand this link, including country studies and, more recently, cross-country studies. These studies have generally found a strong positive association between income growth and income measures of poverty.[3] An important question is the elasticity of this relationship, or the extent to which the poor benefit from growth. One approach is that of Ravallion and Chen (1997), which uses data from developing and transition countries where at least two household surveys are available, and finds an elasticity of poverty reduction (proportion of population living on less than 50 percent of the mean) to growth in average consumption of 2.6. Similarly, Roemer and Gugerty (1997) and Dollar and Kraay (2000) use aggregate data, and find that a 1 percent rise in per capita income is correlated with a 1 percent increase in the income of the poorest quintile.

---

1. See, for example, Fischer (1993).
2. One mechanism examined in the literature is the relationship between inequality, education, capital markets, and growth (see Banerjee and Newman [1993] and Galor and Zeira [1993]).
3. See Srinivasan (2000) for an assessment of the links between growth, poverty alleviation, and income inequality.

However, the estimated relationship between economic growth and poverty reduction varies substantially across studies (Timmer, 1997; Hamner and Naschold, 1999; Bruno, Ravallion, and Squire, 1998). Many of these studies also employ different types of data; methods; and definitions of poverty, income, or consumption growth variables, making comparison difficult. For example, Lipton and Ravallion (1995) reference individual country studies where elasticities of the poverty gap (a measure of poverty intensity) with respect to growth in mean consumption range from 1.5 to 4.1. They note that since poverty headcount (as compared to poverty gap) elasticities tend to be lower, this suggests that the growth-induced benefits of poverty reduction are felt well below the poverty line. Ravallion (1997) also finds higher elasticities for lower poverty lines.[4]

The *World Development Report 2000-01* (World Bank, 2000) points out several qualifications and extensions to the growth-poverty nexus. First, there is large variation in the statistical relationship between national per capita income growth and poverty measures. Given this wide variance in outcomes, many authors point out that the interesting policy question is not the connection of the poor to economic growth on average, but rather the role of policy and economic structure in turning growth into poverty reduction. In other words, both growth and poverty are possibly affected by a third set of factors that we do not yet fully understand.

What explains some of these different cross-country patterns in the relationship between growth and poverty? One important factor is the sectoral pattern of growth, as the poor are typically located in rural areas to a greater extent than in urban areas. There is some evidence from individual country studies that agricultural sector growth has the largest effect on poverty reduction (Datt and Ravallion, 1998, on India; Thorbecke and Jung, 1996, on Indonesia). While Lipton and Ravallion (1995) agree that the balance of evidence supports a correlation between high and growing farm output and falling rural poverty (Bourguignon, Berry, and Morrison, 1998), they note that an empirical debate on this issue continues, both for particular country cases and in general.

Most recent research has found no systematic global relationship between growth and inequality, either when specifically testing the Kuznets hypothesis (Anand and Kanbur, 1993; Deininger and Squire, 1998; Barro, 2000) or in other analyses (Perotti, 1996; Ravallion and Chen, 1997; Kanbur and Lustig, 1999; Li, Squire, and Zou, 1998; and Bruno, Ravallion, and Squire, 1998). If the distribution of income does not change during the growth

---

4.   There seems to be little systematic work on the differences in the elasticities of the headcount, poverty gap, and squared poverty gap measures with respect to economic growth.

process, the extent of poverty reduction during growth will depend on the extent of initial inequality. A number of studies (Ravallion, 1997; Timmer, 1997) have shown higher growth elasticities of poverty reduction in countries with lower Gini indices (that is, a more equitable income distribution). Clearly, the nature of the growth-poverty relationship becomes more complex if inequality changes during the growth process.

While there may be no significant relationship, on average, between income inequality and growth, there appears to be large variation in experience across countries. The same growth rate is associated with very different patterns of inequality change in different countries, which could explain some of the variation in poverty reduction for given growth rates, although this feature has not been systematically explored. Using survey data, Bruno, Ravallion, and Squire (1998) find that rates of poverty reduction respond even more elastically to rates of change in the Gini index than they do to the level of the index, indicating that even modest changes in inequality can lead to sizable changes in the incidence of poverty.

The poor are also hurt by high initial income inequality if countries with a more unequal distribution of income grow more slowly. Deininger and Squire (1998) find a strong negative relationship between initial distribution of real assets (such as land) and long-term growth: inequality reduces income growth for the poor but not the rich. Most other studies use data on income inequality, and currently there is no consensus on whether empirically there is a positive or negative link between initial income inequality and growth (Banerjee and Duflo, 1999; Forbes, 2000).

b. Inflation and the poor

The literature on the relation between inflation and poverty has generally found a significant association between improvements in the well-being of the poor and lower inflation (Easterly and Fischer, 2001). Using panel data on a range of developed and developing countries, Romer and Romer (1998) also find the income share of the poorest quintile to be inversely related to inflation. Bulír (1998) shows that past inflation worsens income inequality. He finds that the effects are nonlinear: reductions in inflation from hyperinflationary levels lower income inequality much more than further reductions to low inflation levels. Earlier research by Cardoso (1992) found that the poor of Latin America were adversely affected by higher inflation, primarily through a decline in real wages (given the rigidity of nominal wages), as their holdings of cash were very small.

c. Trade liberalization and poverty

While there is extensive research on the impact of trade liberalization on income distribution, the direct links between absolute poverty and trade reform are only beginning to be explored.[5]

Winters (2000) sets out an analytical framework for tracing the impact of trade liberalization on individuals and households through changes affecting enterprises (including wages and employment), distribution (price changes and markets), and government (taxes and spending). Viewing trade reform broadly as including any accompanying domestic market liberalization, Winters suggests that the following factors matter: creation or destruction of markets where the poor participate; intrahousehold effects; intensity of factors of production in most affected sectors and their elasticity of supply; the effect on taxes paid by the poor and government revenue; and whether transitional unemployment will be concentrated on the poor. In addition, trade liberalization can affect poverty through incentives for investment, innovation, and growth, as well as by influencing the economy's vulnerability to negative external shocks that could affect the poor.

As to empirical work, Winters (1999) summarizes field studies on trade liberalization and poverty in Africa (Zambia and Zimbabwe) and South Asia (Bangladesh and India). The Zambian study found that following domestic deregulation of cash crop purchasing, the poor suffered as functioning markets disappeared and private markets did not develop in some areas, while contrasting effects were found for Zimbabwe. In the two South Asian countries, labor market segmentation prevented the benefits of liberalization from spreading widely, and trade liberalization had uneven effects within households. In addition, a study of the first-round effects of trade liberalization in Nicaragua finds that while the fall in the price of agricultural products negatively affects poor producers, this is offset by the income effect of a decline in consumer goods prices (Kruger, 2000).

Another recent strand of research uses computable general equilibrium models to estimate the sectoral price effects of trade liberalization, and traces them to consumption and factor price changes for various types of households. Some preliminary findings are available for South Africa (Devarajan and Van der Mensbrugghe, 2000) and for Indonesia (Friedman, 2000).

---

5.   Greater trade openness in a number of developing countries has been associated with relative increases in the wages of skilled workers relative to unskilled workers, contrary to what might be expected from the Stolper-Samuelson theory (see, for example, Harrison and Hanson [1999] on Mexico and Beyer, Roxas, and Vergara [1999] on Chile). On trade liberalization and income inequality, see Wood (1997), Morley (1999), and Spilimbergo, Londoño, and Székely (1999).

d. Poverty and external debt

Both in the development of, and modifications to, the HIPC (heavily indebted poor countries) initiative, much has been written by the IMF, World Bank, and nongovernment organizations on strengthening the link between debt relief and poverty reduction. The focus has been on developing comprehensive poverty reduction strategies, and in designing adjustment programs to effectively use resources freed up from debt service for the task of poverty reduction. A key point recognized is that the extent to which increased education and health care spending improves social indicators is dependent on how efficiently the funds are spent and how well they are targeted to the poor (IMF, 2000: Box 4.3; Gupta et al., 1998). However, an important caveat emerges: to the extent that HIPCs were not servicing some of their debts, debt relief will not provide additional fiscal resources. While lower debt-service payments on existing borrowings should contribute to spending on poverty reduction, new loans and grants are expected to provide the bulk of total resources for that purpose. Despite the importance of the issue, there is still little research on helping policymakers decide how to prioritize the allocation of available resources in accordance with poverty reduction targets.

There appears to be little work on answering the following questions about the direct relationship between external debt and poverty:

- Does high debt increase poverty, and if so, how?
- What is the incidence of poverty in heavily indebted countries—is there a positive correlation between poverty incidence and debt burdens?
- How would an aid allocation geared to meet some poverty reduction criterion differ from an allocation aimed at achieving debt sustainability?
- Have countries that have improved debt sustainability without debt relief been more successful than other countries at reducing poverty?
- What do we know about the relationship between sustainable fiscal deficits, debt sustainability, and poverty?

e. Macroeconomic crises and poverty

World Bank (2000) summarizes country case studies showing that macroeconomic crises tend to be associated with increases in income poverty, and often with increases in inequality (see also Lustig [1999] and Baldacci, De Mello, and Inchauste [2001]).[6] An important question raised in

---

6.   See Eble and Koeva (2001) for an interesting study of the distributional effects of the Russian crisis.

this context is whether poverty that arises during the transition would lead to chronic poverty even after the economic crisis has passed. It is argued that since crises are often associated with increases in inequality, such crises reverse previous poverty reduction gains proportionally more. In contrast, in a cross-country context, Dollar and Kraay (2000) find no difference in the growth-poverty relationship during periods of negative growth (crisis episodes) and periods of positive growth, and so conclude that crises do not affect the income of the poor disproportionately.

Further, there appears to be little or no research so far exploring how or why the extent of worsening poverty differs across crisis-hit countries. Key questions are just beginning to be asked, though not necessarily examined:

- Do certain types of macroeconomic policies associated with crises have a more negative impact on the poor than others?
- Do macroeconomic responses that are optimal for the poor differ from responses that are optimal for the economy as a whole?
- What are the most important elements of a pro-poor crisis response?
- What types of safety nets set up before a crisis hits are the most effective in protecting the poor during a crisis? (Ferreira, Prennushi, and Ravallion [1998], Lustig [1999].)

f. International Monetary Fund programs and poverty

The debate regarding the effects of IMF programs on the welfare of low-income groups has recently been rekindled by the IMF's high-profile involvement in economic crises affecting Brazil, Indonesia, Republic of Korea, Pakistan, and Russia. Programs aimed at restoring internal and external balance through fiscal consolidation, cuts in domestic absorption, and real devaluation are viewed by critics of the IMF as having adverse effects on the poor. Supporters of IMF activities respond that the Fund's programs assist in macroeconomic stabilization and the restoration of international capital flows, which boost both economic growth and the welfare of the poor.

While studies of the macroeconomic effects of IMF programs (on growth, inflation, and the balance of payments, for example) are abundant,[7] studies of the distributional effects of such programs have been rare, with

---

7. Work by Conway (1994), for example, finds evidence that IMF programs are associated with real depreciation, smaller fiscal imbalances, lower economic growth, and lower public investment. Later work by Dicks-Mireaux, Mecagni, and Schadler (2000) finds that IMF lending to low-income countries has raised output growth and improved debt sustainability, yet with no significant effects on inflation. For a more skeptical view, see Przeworski and Vreeland (2000).

the exception of recent work by Garuda (2000).[8] In examining 58 IMF programs over the period 1975–1991, he finds evidence of a significant deterioration in the distribution of income (as measured by Gini coefficients) and in the income of the poor (as measured by the income share of the lowest quintile), in the two years following the initiation of an IMF program. This deterioration is most marked in countries with large external imbalances in the preprogram period. However, when preprogram external imbalances are not large, income distribution improves to a greater extent in countries participating in IMF programs than in nonprogram countries.

Of the four main channels by which IMF programs could beneficially affect poverty reduction and the distribution of income—currency devaluation (lowering the price of nontradables relative to tradables), shrinking of fiscal imbalances, increases in growth rates, and decreases in inflation rates—Garuda (2000) finds that real depreciation of the currency is the most plausible mechanism by which IMF programs assist the poor. Easterly (2000) also finds that World Bank and IMF adjustment lending is closely associated with a more depreciated real exchange rate. Real devaluation assists the rural, farm-based poor by raising the domestic-currency value of agricultural goods (the reverse effect would occur for the food-consuming urban poor). To the extent that the bulk of poverty is rurally based, and that the labor intensity of production is greater for the tradables sector than for the nontradables sector, then overall poverty can be reduced through the exchange rate channel.

Using data from household consumption surveys for a group of African countries, Demery and Squire (1996) find that those countries that implemented effective World Bank and IMF reform programs have generated declines in overall poverty; those that implemented ineffective reform programs have generated increases in overall poverty.[9] Like Garuda (2000), they find that real exchange rate depreciation is a key component of a successful, poverty-reducing adjustment strategy, through its beneficial effect on export-led economic growth, its changing of the structure of

---

8. Earlier work by Pastor (1987) found that the initiation of an IMF program reduced the income share of labor relative to both its preprogram level and in comparison with nonprogram countries. This is indicative of a worsening distribution of income, given that the poor typically possess much labor and little capital.

9. See also the findings of Sahn, Dorosh, and Younger (1996), derived using household survey data on 10 African countries during the 1980s. They find that real devaluation, fiscal policy reform, and agricultural market liberalization, which are commonly part of IMF and World Bank adjustment programs, have improved the distribution of income and have not adversely affected the poor. However, these policies did not result in rapid economic growth, which might have further aided poverty alleviation, due to the poor implementation of adjustment policies.

production in favor of labor-intensive agriculture (which employs the majority of the poor), and the reduction of rents earned (through import quotas and exchange controls) by urban households. The important message is that the maintenance of overvalued exchange rates hurts the poor.[10]

These results are broadly consistent with analyses conducted by IMF itself as to the consequences for poverty and income inequality of IMF-supported programs. In IMF (1986), the experience of programs in 94 countries in the 1980s indicated that the effect on poverty and income distribution varied with the composition of programs. Poverty-reducing and distribution-improving measures included real devaluation, elimination of exchange controls, expanded access to credit markets, the widening of the tax base to property and income taxes, and the switching of expenditures to basic health care and education. Measures that had the reverse effect included increases in indirect taxes (such as customs duties and value-added taxes), and the erosion of expenditures on social safety nets.

3. A Preliminary Look at the Data

Indicators of well-being have improved in the vast majority of countries over the past few decades, though with major variations both within countries and across countries. A well-known composite indicator of well-being is the UNDP's HDI, which UNDP has defined as the arithmetic average of a country's achievements in three basic dimensions of human development.[11] These include longevity (measured by life expectancy at birth), educational attainment (measured by a combination of the adult literacy rate and the enrollment ratio in primary, secondary, and tertiary education), and living standards (measured by GDP per capita in United States dollars at purchasing power parity).

The HDI has a number of advantages: it moves beyond per capita income alone as a measure of well-being, it is compiled with uniform data sources and methodology over time and across countries, and it is available

---

10. Two points should be noted. First, studies examining reforms and poverty in Africa during the 1980s and early 1990s were limited in scope due to the lack of household survey data. Improvements in data availability for the 1990s are starting to allow more comprehensive analyses (Christiaensen, Demery, and Paternostro, 2000). Second, looking forward, since many African countries have already eliminated large overvaluations of the real exchange rate, it is not clear whether further real depreciation would have a positive impact on their levels of poverty.

11. The HDI ranges between zero (low human development) and one (high human development), and its distribution is non-normal: it is skewed with a relatively long left-sided tail, that is, with the cross-country median HDI exceeding the mean HDI.

for 100 countries on a consistent basis over the period 1975–98.[12] The HDI does not capture income inequality directly. However, for a given per capita income, countries where income is distributed more evenly will tend to display greater average longevity and educational attainment, and therefore a higher HDI, because of the obvious limits to longevity and educational attainment faced by individual people.

Both the HDI and per capita income are highly correlated with other widely used measures of poverty, such as the Human Poverty Index (HPI) used by UNDP;[13] the share of the population with income less than $1 per day (a World Bank measure); the share of the population that is undernourished (a Food and Agriculture Organization measure); and measures of well-being, such as life expectancy, infant mortality, and educational attainment.[14] Figures 4.1a and 4.1b show the close association among some of these variables. Figure 4.2 reports the association between the HDI and a measure of income distribution—the Gini coefficient.

Table 4.1 provides a complete list of the 174 countries for which 1998 HDI data are available, categorized by regions, and in descending order of their HDI. In general, the African and Asian countries had relatively low HDI, while industrial, transition, and Latin American countries had relatively high HDI. The HDI improved in almost all countries between 1975 and 1998, and, as set out in Figure 4.3, the median value of the HDI in 1998 (0.73) was significantly higher than in 1975 (0.62). At the same time, there was little change in the ranking of countries by HDI over this period: the cross-country rank correlation between the observations for the HDI in 1975 and in 1998 is 0.98.

Despite the basically unchanged ranking of countries, there is some evidence that low-HDI countries have been "catching up," albeit slowly, with the high-HDI countries. Considering those countries for which HDI data are available for both 1975 and 1998, Table 4.2 shows that countries that

---

12. A potential drawback of the HDI is that it may be positively related to urbanization, as there seems to be an urban bias in the provision of social services. While this is beyond the scope of our study, it may be an interesting avenue for further research.

13. While the HDI measures the overall progress of a country in achieving human development, the HPI focuses on the distribution of that progress. Introduced in the *Human Development Report 1997* (UNDP, 1997), the HPI captures deprivation in three key areas: deprivation in a long and healthy life (as measured by the percentage of people alive today not expected to reach age 40), deprivation in knowledge (measured by the adult illiteracy rate), and deprivation in economic provisioning (measured by a combination of the percentage of people lacking access to safe water and health services, and the percentage of children under five years who are underweight). The HPI is the simple average of these three component indexes; see UNDP (2000).

14. The rank correlation (for the 80 developing countries where both indexes exist) between the HDI and the HPI for 1998 was extremely high at 0.94.

commenced in 1975 in groups with relatively low HDI tended to display a greater improvement in HDI (in absolute terms) over the next two decades.[15]

a. Macroeconomic policies, human development, and income inequality

Poverty in a given country can be reduced by fostering per capita GDP growth,[16] that is, by raising the total resources available to the population, and by increasing the share of those resources going to the poorer segments of that population. A widely held view is that economic growth can be fostered through a set of policies aimed at promoting macroeconomic stability (low and stable inflation, low budget deficits, and sustainable external debt), openness to international trade, education, and the rule of law. A large number of studies based upon cross-country evidence are consistent with that view, although the evidence on whether each individual policy among those listed above raises economic growth is typically not very robust.[17]

Casual observation is also broadly suggestive of an association between sound macroeconomic policies and rapid improvement in HDI. Table 4.3 shows that, within "low HDI," "medium HDI," and "high HDI" groups of countries, lower inflation, lower variability of inflation, lower external debt, better rule of law, a lower black market premium, and a lower frequency of financial crisis were associated with greater improvement in HDI. At the same time, as in the economic growth literature, it is difficult to show conclusively whether individual policies cause countries to experience more rapid improvements in well-being.

There is also a debate regarding the policies that improve the well-being of the poorer segments of the population for a given growth rate of GDP per capita,[18] and an even more fervent debate about whether certain policies imply a trade-off between increasing total available resources (raising growth rates) and improving their distribution (reducing poverty). In the latter respect, there seems to be broad agreement that policies aimed at improving basic education and health care can both raise economic growth and improve distribution, but

---

15. The countries that displayed the greatest improvement in HDI from 1975 to 1998 are from Africa and Asia: Nepal (by 63 percent), Mali (53 percent), Pakistan (48 percent), The Gambia (47 percent), and Chad (45 percent). The countries with the least improvement were Guyana (5 percent), Democratic Republic of the Congo (3 percent), Romania (3 percent), and Zambia (–5 percent).
16. As expected, improvements in HDI are found to be strongly and positively correlated with per capita income growth, though this is largely the result of the inclusion of per capita income as one of the components of the HDI.
17. Robust evidence is obtained when a variable is significant in a battery of regressions that include several combinations of other potential explanatory variables.
18. See Agénor (1999) for cross-country regressions linking macroeconomic variables and poverty rates, while controlling for GDP growth.

Figure 4.1a. Human Development Index (HDI), Human Poverty Index (HPI) and Poverty Line: 1998

Scatter plot of HDI and HPI
(All countries)

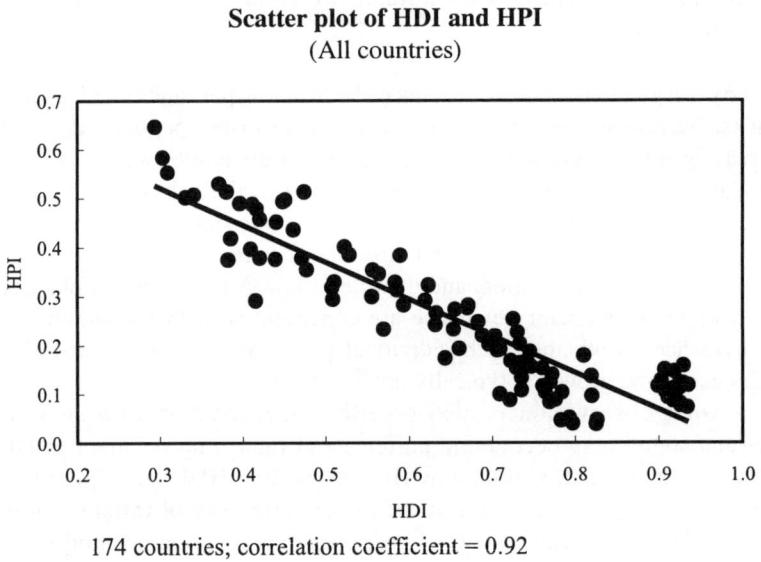

174 countries; correlation coefficient = 0.92

Scatter plot of HDI and HPI
(Low- and medium-HDI countries)

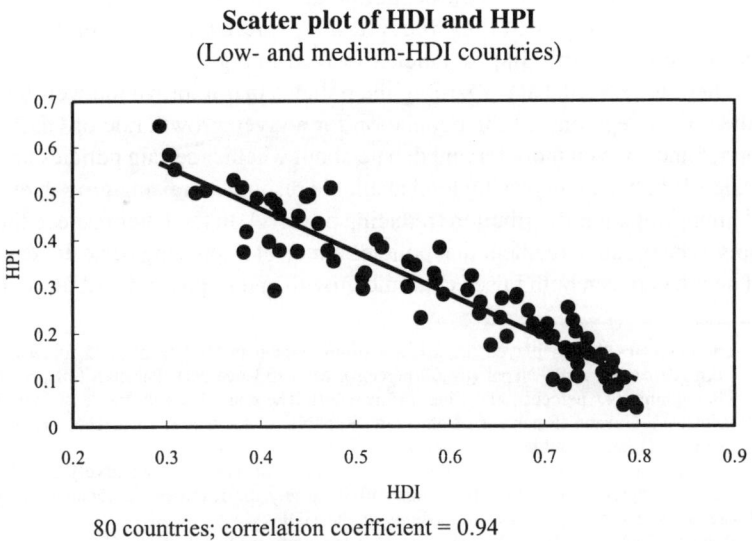

80 countries; correlation coefficient = 0.94

Source: UNDP (2000); World Bank (2000).

Figure 4.1b. Human Development Index (HDI), Human Poverty Index (HPI) and Poverty Line: 1998

Scatter plot of HDI and Poverty Line ($1 a day)

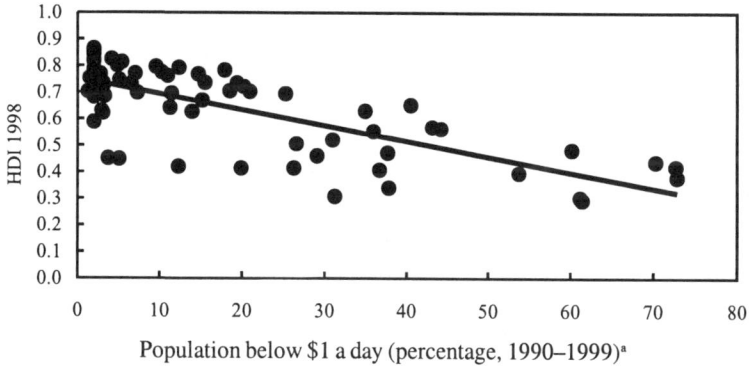

71 countries; correlation coefficient = 0.74

Scatter plot of HDI and Poverty Line ($2 a day)

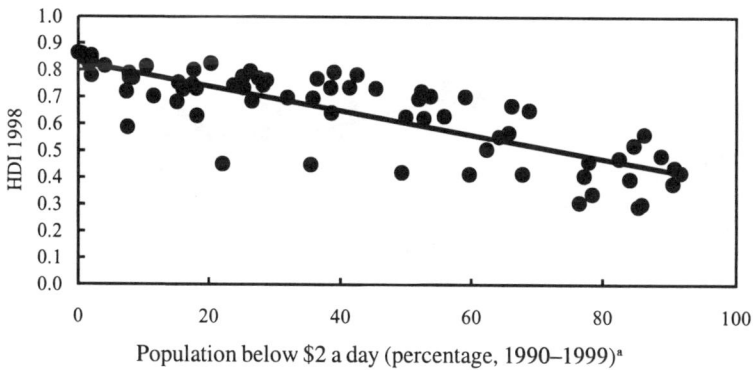

49 countries; correlation coefficient = 0.80

Note: [a] Most recent available observation.

Source: UNDP, *Human Development Report* (2000); World Bank (2000).

Figure 4.2. Human Development Index (HDI) and Gini Coefficient

Scatter plot of HDI and Gini Coefficient: 1990

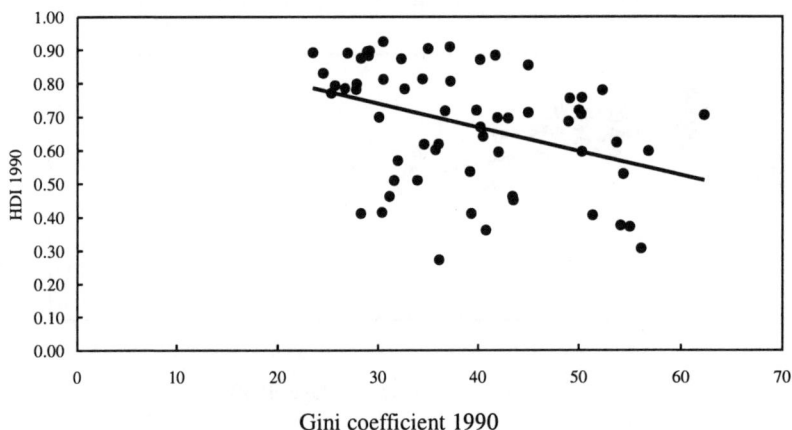

63 countries; correlation coefficient = 0.39

Scatter plot of HDI and Gini Coefficient: 1980

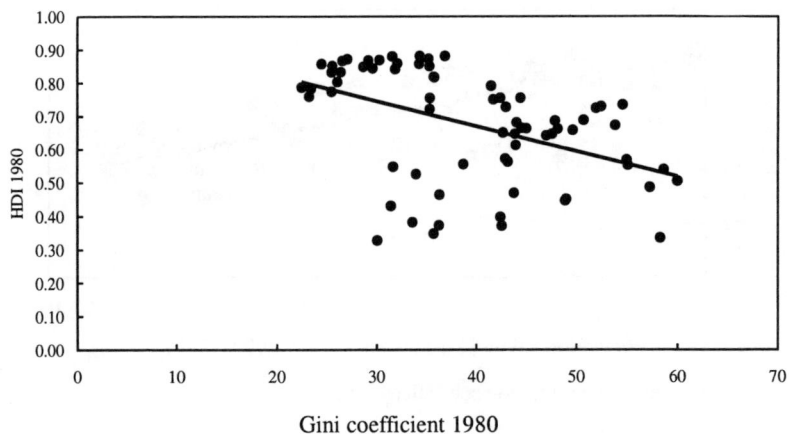

70 countries; correlation coefficient = 0.46

Source: UNDP (2000); World Bank, *World Development Indicators* (2000).

Table 4.1. Human Development Index (HDI), 1998

HDI	0.22 – 0.50	0.51 – 0.70
	Africa	Africa
	Madagascar (0.48)	South Africa (0.7)
	Sudan (0.48)	Cape Verde (0.69)
	Togo (0.47)	Algeria (0.68)
	Mauritania (0.45)	Swaziland (0.66)
	Djibouti (0.45)	Namibia (0.63)
	Nigeria (0.44)	Botswana (0.59)
	Congo, Dem. Rep. of the (0.43)	Gabon (0.59)
	Zambia (0.42)	Morocco (0.59)
	Côte d'Ivoire (0.42)	Lesotho (0.57)
	Senegal (0.42)	Ghana (0.56)
	Tanzania,U. Rep. of (0.41)	Zimbabwe (0.56)
	Benin (0.41)	Equatorial Guinea (0.55)
	Uganda (0.41)	São Tomé and Principe (0.55)
	Eritrea (0.41)	Cameroon (0.53)
	Angola (0.4)	Comoros (0.51)
	Gambia (0.4)	Kenya (0.51)
	Guinea (0.39)	Congo (0.51)
	Malawi (0.38)	
	Rwanda (0.38)	Asia
	Mali (0.38)	Vietnam (0.67)
	Central African Republic (0.37)	Indonesia (0.67)
	Chad (0.37)	Mongolia (0.63)
	Mozambique (0.34)	Vanuatu (0.62)
	Guinea-Bissau (0.33)	Solomon Islands (0.61)
	Burundi (0.32)	Myanmar (0.58)
	Ethiopia (0.31)	India (0.56)
	Burkina Faso (0.3)	Papua New Guinea (0.54)
	Niger (0.29)	Pakistan (0.52)
	Sierra Leone (0.25)	Combodia (0.51)
	Asia	Transition Economies
	Lao People's Dem. Rep. (0.48)	Moldova, Rep. of (0.7)
	Bhutan (0.48)	Uzbekistan (0.69)
	Nepal (0.47)	Tajikistan (0.66)
	Bangladesh (0.46)	
		Middle East
	Middle East	Syrian Arab Republic (0.66)
	Yemen (0.45)	Egypt (0.62)
		Iraq (0.58)
	Western Hemisphere	
	Haiti (0.44)	Western Hemisphere
		El Salvador (0.7)
		Honduras (0.65)
		Bolivia (0.64)
		Nicaragua (0.63)
		Guatemala (0.62)
Number of countries	35	38

Table 4.1 (cont.)

HDI	0.71 – 0.80	> 0.80
	Europe/Industrial Countries Turkey (0.73)	Europe/Industrial Countries Canada (0.93) Norway (0.93)
	Africa Seychelles (0.79) Mauritius (0.76) Tunisia (0.7)	United States (0.93) Australia (0.93) Iceland (0.93) Sweden (0.93) Belgium (0.92)
	Asia Malaysia (0.77) Fiji (0.77) Thailand (0.74) Philippines (0.74) Sri Lanka (0.73) Maldives (0.73) Samoa (Western) (0.73) China (0.71)	Netherlands (0.92) Japan (0.92) United Kingdom (0.92) Finland (0.92) France (0.92) Switzerland (0.92) Germany (0.91) Denmark (0.91) Austria (0.91) Luxembourg (0.91)
	Transition Economies Croatia (0.79) Lithuania (0.79) Belarus (0.78) Bulgaria (0.77) Russian Federation (0.77) Latvia (0.77) Romania (0.77) Macedonia, TFYR (0.76) Georgia (0.76) Kazakhstan (0.75) Ukraine (0.74) Azerbaijan (0.72) Armenia (0.72) Albania (0.71) Kyrgyzstan (0.71) Turkmenistan (0.7)	Ireland (0.91) Italy (0.9) New Zealand (0.9) Spain (0.9) Greece (0.88) Portugal (0.86) Cyprus (0.89) Malta (0.87) Asia Singapore (0.88) Hong Kong, China (SAR) (0.87) Korea, Rep. of (0.85) Brunei Darussalam (0.85)
	Middle East Libyan Arab Jamahiriya (0.76) Saudi Arabia (0.75) Lebanon (0.74) Oman (0.73) Jordan (0.72) Iran, Islamic Rep. of (0.71)	Transition Economies Slovenia (0.86) Czech Republic (0.84) Slovakia (0.82) Hungary (0.82) Poland (0.81) Estonia (0.8)
Number of countries	34	35

Table 4.1 (cont.)

HDI	0.71 – 0.80	> 0.80
	Western Hemisphere	Middle East
	Saint Kitts and Nevis (0.8)	Israel (0.88)
	Costa Rica (0.8)	Kuwait (0.84)
	Trinidad and Tobago (0.79)	Bahrain (0.892)
	Dominica (0.79)	Qatar (0.82)
	Grenada (0.78)	United Arab Emirates (0.81)
	Mexico (0.78)	
	Cuba (0.78)	Western Hemishpere
	Belize (0.78)	Barbados (0.86)
	Panama (0.78)	Bahamas (0.84)
	Venezuela (0.77)	Argentina (0.84)
	Suriname (0.77)	Antigua and Barbuda (0.83)
	Colombia (0.76)	Chile (0.83)
	Brazil (0.75)	Uruguay (0.82)
	Saint Vincent and the Grenadines (0.74)	
	Peru (0.74)	
	Paraguay (0.74)	
	Jamaica (0.73)	
	Dominican Republic (0.73)	
	Saint Lucia (0.73)	
	Ecuador (0.72)	
	Guyana (0.71)	
Number of countries	21	11

Source: UNDP (2000).

of course there certainly is no consensus regarding the most effective policies that will raise levels of education and health care.

To examine whether macroeconomic policies have a direct impact on poverty, in a cross-country framework we attempted to estimate the relationship between economic policies and improvements in the HDI (or other indicators of well-being such as life expectancy), for a given rate of growth of GDP per capita. The rationale is that when policies bring about greater improvement in the HDI than would be expected on the basis of the observed rate of economic growth, they are likely to be of particular benefit to the poorer segments of the population. This makes it possible, in principle, to estimate the relationship between economic policies and that component of the improvement in well-being that is unrelated to economic growth.[19]

---

19. Therefore, our approach was to regress the improvement in the HDI on initial HDI, per capital GDP growth, and average economic policies during the period; and to repeat the exercise using infant mortality and life expectancy instead of the HDI.

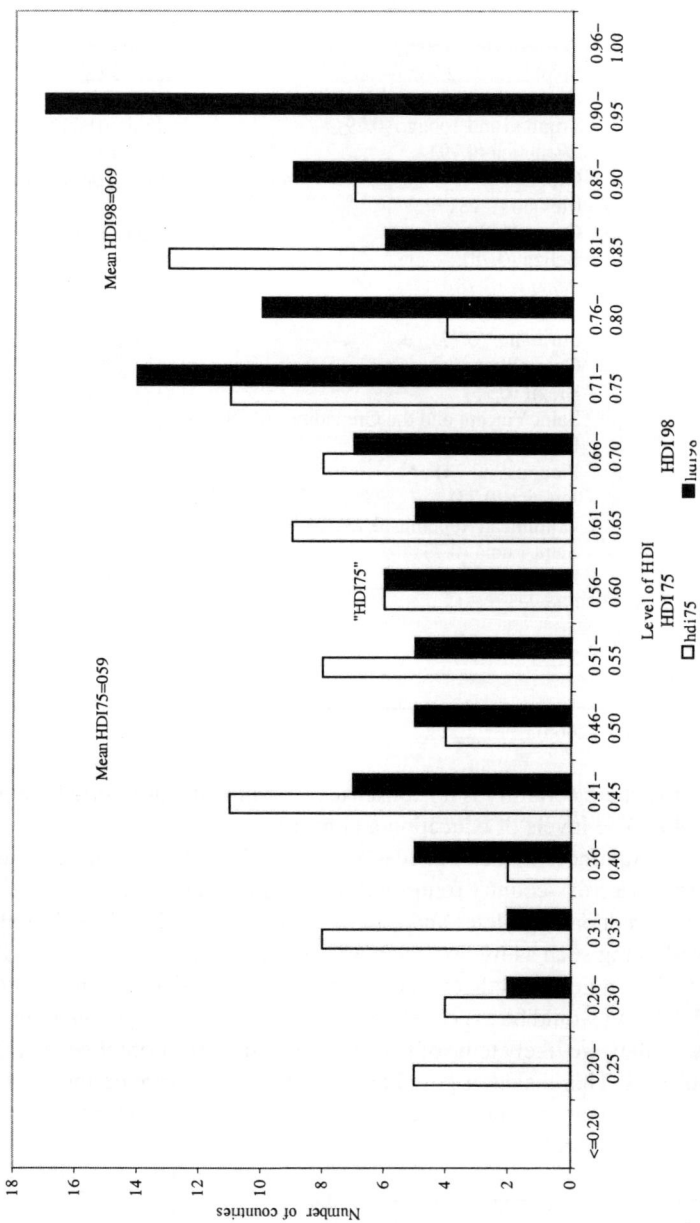

Figure 4.3. Histogram of Human Development Index (HDI): 1975 and 1998

Source: UNDP (2000).

Table 4.2. HDI Transition Matrix [a]

	Absolute Changes in HDI 1998		
HDI in 1975	< 0.10	0.10 – 0.15	0.16 – 0.20
Low (0 – 0.5)	Burkina Faso, Burundi, Central African Republic, Dem. Rep. of the Congo, Congo, Côte d'Ivoire, Guinea-Bissau, Kenya, Madagascar, Malawi, Niger, Togo, Zambia	Bangladesh, Benin, Botswana, Cameroon, Chad, The Gambia, Ghana, Lesotho, Mali, Mauritania, Nigeria, Papua New Guinea, Senegal, Sudan	Egypt, India, Indonesia, Morocco, Nepal, Pakistan
Medium (0.5 – 0.7)	Fiji, Guyana, Jamaica, Mexico, Nicaragua, Paraguay, Philippines, South Africa, Zimbabwe,	Bolivia, Brazil, Colombia, Dominican Republic, Ecuador, El Salvador, Guatemala, Honduras, Islamic Rep. of Iran, Mauritius, Peru, Sri Lanka, Swaziland, Syrian Arab Republic, Thailand, Turkey	Algeria, Peoples Rep. of China, Rep. of Korea, Malaysia, Saudi Arabia, Tunisia
High (0.7 – 0.8)	Argentina, Costa Rica, Hungary, Panama, Romania, Trinidad and Tobago, United Arab Emirates, Uruguay, Venezuela	Chile, Hong Kong (SAR), Malta	Singapore

Note: [a] Twenty-three industrial countries were excluded from the table because they almost invariably began with very high HDIs in 1975 and tended to have rather small improvements over the following two decades.

Source: UNDP (2000).

We examined a large set of potential explanatory variables related to economic policies. The set included many of the variables that previous researchers have used to analyze the determinants of economic growth: inflation and its variance; budget deficits, government spending, and foreign aid as a share of gross domestic product (GDP); indicators of openness, such as the ratio of foreign trade to GDP and the black market foreign exchange premium; and indexes of the rule of law). It also included others that have received less attention in previous work, such as the presence and length of exchange-rate or banking crises; and initial external debt as a share of GDP; see Table 4.3 for a partial list of variables.

When this cross-country regression approach is used, no significant and robust evidence is found that any of these variables are individually associated with pro-poor (or anti-poor) economic growth. Of course, by no means does this constitute proof that these policies do not matter. On the contrary, it suggests that alternative research approaches are needed to find significant and robust evidence of the direction and strength of the effects of these variables on the poor. Other studies have relied on panel regressions, which use the information contained in the variation both over time and across countries. These studies have generally also not found significant evidence of links between policy variables and improvements in the relative well-being of the poor, with the possible exception of a significant association with lower inflation (see, for example, Easterly and Fischer [2001]).

b. Governments' actual behavior

Although simple cross-country regressions do not provide conclusive evidence on the policies that help reduce poverty, it is useful to analyze how governments behave in practice with respect to the policies that are widely believed to help in that regard, especially when they are faced with macroeconomic shocks.

The conventional wisdom is that certain policies, such as fiscal spending on education and health, tend to help the poor.[20] In fact, the international financial institutions have often encouraged countries not to reduce spending on health care and education (at least as a share of total spending, and often also in real per capita terms) at times when fiscal adjustment was needed, and to increase spending on health and education as a share of total spending at times when countries were able to afford increases in overall spending.[21]

This section provides a more detailed, systematic analysis of the composition of large government expenditure cuts (or increases), as an illustration of governments' actual behavior with respect to policies that are believed to affect the poor. Considering 179 countries during 1985–1998,[22] there are about 60 (nonoverlapping) instances in which governments cut total spending by more than 5 percentage points over three years. The share of education spending in total spending and the share of healthcare spending in total spending rose in three-quarters of those instances. On average, the share of education spending in total spending increased by 2 percentage points and the share of healthcare spending in total spending increased by 1.5 percentage points. By comparison, the average level of education spending and healthcare spending amounted to 13 percent and 7 percent, respectively, of total spending

---

20. See, for example, Gupta et al. (1998).
21. While the international institutions have typically encouraged countries to preserve the share of spending on health and education, this has not been a condition for IMF loans. Consistent with this absence of conditionality, the results presented in this paper are similar if the sample is restricted to those instances involving IMF-supported programs.
22. The data were drawn from the Expenditure Policy Division in the IMF's Fiscal Affairs Department.

Table 4.3. Macroeconomic Performance, 1975–1998 (Averages during Period)

	Growth in real GDP per capita[7]	Inflation[8]	Deficit[9] (% of GDP)	Government consumption[10]	Standard deviation in inflation[11]	Log difference in terms of trade[12]	External debt[13] (% of GDP)
Low HDI							
Slow change in HDI[1]	-0.22	91.50	-4.89	16.17	259.83	-0.33	87.49
Rapid change in HDI[2]	1.42	13.69	-4.43	12.14	10.81	-0.25	60.74
Middle HDI							
Slow change in HDI[3]	0.63	151.85	-6.22	13.34	311.63	-0.48	77.18
Rapid change in HDI[4]	1.85	54.81	-2.56	14.69	179.01	-0.11	45.36
High HDI							
Slow change in HDI[5]	0.34	82.67	-0.92	13.16	114.53	-0.21	48.77
Rapid change in HDI[6]	5.34	14.77	1.51	12.04	22.82	-0.51	42.00

Notes: 1. Countries in this category include Botswana, Burkina Faso, Burundi, Cameroon, Central African Republic, Congo, Congo, Dem. Rep., Côte d'Ivoire, Ghana, Guinea-Bissau, Kenya, Lesotho, Madagascar, Malawi, Mauritania, Niger, Papua New Guinea, Senegal, Togo. 2. Countries include Bangladesh, Benin, Chad, Egypt, Gambia, India, Indonesia, Mali, Morocco, Nepal, Nigeria, Pakistan, and Sudan. 3. Countries include Brazil, Colombia, Dominican Republic, Ecuador, El Salvador, Rep. of Fiji, Guyana, Jamaica, Mauritius, Mexico, Nicaragua, Paraguay, Peru, Philippines, South Africa, Sri Lanka, and Zimbabwe. 4. Countries include Algeria, Bolivia, People's Rep. of China, Guatemala, Honduras, Iran, Korea, Malaysia, Saudi Arabia, Swaziland, Syrian Arab Republic, Thailand, Tunisia, and Turkey. 5. Countries include Argentina, Costa Rica, Hungary, Panama, Romania, Trinidad and Tobago, United Arab Emirates, Uruguay, and Venezuela. 6. Countries include Chile, Hong Kong, China, Malta, Singapore, and Israel. 7. Log difference of real output. 8. Percentage change in consumer prices per annum. 9. Overall fiscal deficit as a percent of GDP. 10. Government consumption spending as a percent of GDP. 11. Standard deviation of inflation between 1975 and 1998. 12. Log difference in terms of trade between 1975 and 1998. 13. External debt as percent of GDP in 1975.

Table 4.3 (cont.)

	Private capital flow[14] (% of GDP)	Exports and imports (% of GDP)	Openness* GDP[15]	Aid[16] (% of GNP)	Rule of law[17]	Black market premium[18]	Percent of years country had crisis[19]
Low HDI							
Slow change in HDI[1]	2.03	68.21	3.47	13.49	28.80	48.62	44.00
Rapid change in HDI[2]	1.53	47.48	13.07	7.94	34.69	35.35	35.64
Middle HDI							
Slow change in HDI[3]	2.27	66.20	10.73	4.20	40.82	236.99	37.45
Rapid change in HDI[4]	2.92	67.48	28.89	2.56	49.31	103.87	20.24
High HDI							
Slow change in HDI[5]	3.29	63.72	1.66	0.66	59.93	50.98	37.78
Rapid change in HDI[6]	6.58	205.77	271.07	0.61	88.64	4.17	7.50

14. Private capital flow as a percent of GDP. 15. Imports and exports in share of GDP weighted by GDP growth between 1975 and 1998. 16. Aid as a percent of GNP. 17. Rule of law as defined by Kaufmann et al. (1999). 18. Defined as (parallel exchange rate/official exchange–1)*100. 19. Percent of years the country had a financial crisis, during 1970–1999.

Source: UNDP (2000); *World Development Indicators* (various years); and *International Financial Statistics* (various years).

during the sample period. Conversely, the share of education spending in total spending and the share of healthcare spending in total spending declined in about two-thirds of the roughly 30 (nonoverlapping) instances in which governments increased total spending by more than 5 percentage points over three years; in those instances, both education spending and health care spending declined, on average, by 1 percentage point of total spending.

These results suggest that spending on health care and education is typically more stable than spending on the remaining items in governments' budgets. Therefore, when governments are faced with the need to cut overall spending, the share of education and health spending is far more likely to rise than to decline. In this light, an unchanged share for education and health does not appear to be an especially ambitious target at a time when overall government spending is being cut. Conversely, a decline in the share of education and health spending at a time when overall spending is increasing may partly reflect the more stable nature of these expenditures.

As this simple example illustrates, there seems to be much scope for research on how governments behave in practice with respect to policies that are widely believed to affect the poor, and this line of research may help establish more useful benchmarks in assessing the impact of governments' efforts in reducing poverty.

4. Conclusion

On the basis of systematic cross-country studies, the current state of knowledge is that economic growth is associated with improvements in indicators of well-being. However, little has been conclusively proven regarding individual macroeconomic policies that help increase economic growth (given questions about the robustness of many findings), and even less is known about the individual policies that help reduce poverty for a given rate of economic growth. Of course, a wide range of country experiences has made it possible for policymakers to accumulate a certain degree of expertise regarding these issues, the validity of which nevertheless still needs to be confirmed by systematic empirical studies.

This leaves an important and comprehensive research agenda. Further cross-country studies of the types conducted so far appear less likely to yield much value added regarding the effects of macroeconomic policies on poverty. Other issues to be further explored include lags between policy actions and their effects on poverty, and better methods to identify relevant endogenous and exogenous variables. Perhaps the greatest payoff for future research is likely to be obtained through studies based on survey data regarding households or firms for one or a few individual countries, around the time of clearly identifiable macroeconomic shocks. However, while there has been significant progress in recent years, the number of countries for which such reliable surveys are currently available is relatively limited, and continued data collection efforts in this direction may greatly contribute to our knowledge about the links between macroeconomic policies and poverty reduction.

References

Agénor, Pierre-Richard. 1999. Stabilization Policies, Poverty and the Labor Market-Analytical Issues and Empirical Evidence. Mimeo.Washington, D.C.: World Bank, September.

Anand, S. and R. Kanbur. 1993. Inequality and Development: A Critique. *Journal of Development Economics* 41: 19–43.

Baldacci, Emanuele, Luiz de Mello, and Gabriela Inchauste. 2001. *Financial Crises, Poverty, and Income Distribution.* Paper presented at the IMF Workshop on Macroeconomic Policies and Poverty Reduction. April.

Banerjee, Abhijit, and Esther Duflo. 1999. Inequality and Growth: What Can the Data Say? Mimeo. Cambridge, MA: Massachusetts Institute of Technology.

———, and Andrew Newman. 1993. Occupational Choice and the Process of Development. *Journal of Political Economy* 101: 274–298.

Barro, Robert. 2000. Inequality and Growth in a Panel of Countries. *Journal of Economic Growth* 5: 5–32.

Beyer, Harald, Patricio Rojas, and Rodrigo Vergara. 1999. Trade Liberalization and Wage Inequality. *Journal of Development Economics* 59: 103–123.

Bourguignon, François, Albert R. Berry, and Christian Morrison. 1981. *The World Distribution of Incomes Between 1950 and 1977.* Paris: Ecole Normale Supérieure.

Bruno, Michael, Martin Ravallion, and Lyn Squire. 1998. Equity and Growth in Developing Countries: Old and New Perspectives on the Policy Issues. In *Income Distribution and High-Quality Growth*, edited by Vito Tanzi and Ke-young Chu. Cambridge, MA: Massachusetts Institute of Technology.

Bulír, Alec. 1998. *Income Inequality: Does Inflation Matter?* IMF Working Paper No. 98/7. Washington, D.C.: International Monetary Fund.

Cardoso, Eliana. 1992. *Inflation and Poverty.* NBER Working Paper No. 4006. Cambridge, MA: National Bureau of Economic Research.

Christiaensen, Luc, Lionel Demery, and Stefano Paternostro. 2000. Reforms, Recovery and Poverty Reduction in Africa: Messages from the 1990s. Washington, D.C.: World Bank, December. Mimeo.

Conway, Patrick. 1994. IMF Lending Programs: Participation and Impact. *Journal of Development Economics* 45: 365–391.

Datt, Gaurav, and Martin Ravallion. 1998. Farm Productivity and Rural Poverty in India. *Journal of Development Studies* 34: 62–85.

Deaton, Angus. 2000. Counting the World's Poor: Problems and Possible Solutions. Mimeo. Research Program in Development Studies. Princeton: Princeton University Press.

Deininger, Klaus and Lyn Squire. 1998. New Ways of Looking at Old Issues: Inequality and Growth. *Journal of Development Economics*, 57: 259–287.

Demery, Lionel, and Lyn Squire. 1996. Macroeconomic Adjustment and Poverty in Africa: An Emerging Picture. *World Bank Research Observer* 11.

Devarajan, Shantayanan, and Dominique van der Mensbrugghe. 2000. *Trade Reform in South Africa: Impacts on Households*. Paper presented at the conference on Poverty and the International Economy, sponsored by the World Bank and the Parliamentary Commission on Swedish Policy for Global Development, Stockholm. October.

Dicks-Mireaux, Louis, Mauro Mecagni, and Susan Schadler. 2000. Evaluating the Effect of IMF Lending to Low-Income Countries. *Journal of Development Economics* 61: 495–526.

Dollar, David, and Aart Kraay. 2000. *Growth Is Good for the Poor*. Working Paper. Washington, D.C.: World Bank.

Easterly, William. 2000. The Effects of IMF and World Bank Programs on Poverty. Mimeo. Washington, D.C.: World Bank.

———, and Stanley Fischer. 2001. Inflation and the Poor. *Journal of Money, Credit and Banking*.

Eble, Stephanie, and Petya Koeva. 2001. *The Distributional Effects of Macroeconomic Crises: Microeconomic Evidence from Russia*. Paper presented at the IMF Workshop on Macroeconomic Policies and Poverty Reduction. April.

Ferreira, Francisco, Giovanna Prennushi, and Martin Ravallion. 1999. Protecting the Poor from Macroeconomic Shocks: An Agenda for Action in a Crisis and Beyond. Unpublished. Washington, D.C.: World Bank.

Fischer, Stanley. 1993. Role of Macroeconomic Factors in Growth. *Journal of Monetary Economics* 32: 485–512.

Forbes, Kristin. 2000. A Reassessment of the Relationship between Inequality and Economic Growth. *American Economic Review* 90(4): 869–887.

Friedman, Jed. 2000. Differential Impacts of Trade Liberalization on Indonesia's Poor and Non-Poor. Paper presented at the conference on Poverty and the International Economy, sponsored by the World Bank and the Parliamentary Commission on Swedish Policy for Global Development. Stockholm. October.

Galor, Oded, and Joseph Zeira. 1993. Income Distribution and Macroeconomics. *Review of Economic Studies* 60 (January): 35–52.

Garuda, Gopal. 2000. The Distributional Effects of IMF Programs: A Cross-Country Analysis. *World Development* 28: 1031–1051.

Gupta, Sanjeev, Benedict Clements, Calvin McDonald, and Christian Schiller. 1998. The IMF and the Poor 52. Pamphlet Series. Washington, D.C.: International Monetary Fund.

Hamner, Lucia, and Felix Naschold. 1999. Are the International Development Targets Attainable? Unpublished.

Harrison, Ann, and Gordon Hanson. 1999. Who Gains from Trade Reform? Some Remaining Puzzles. *Journal of Development Economics* 59: 125–154.

IMF (International Monetary Fund).1986. *Fund-Supported Programs, Fiscal Policy and Income Distribution*. IMF Occasional Paper 46. Washington, D.C.

———. 2000. *World Economic Outlook*, May 2000. Washington.

Kanbur, Ravi, and Nora Lustig. 1999. Why is Inequality Back on the Agenda? Paper prepared for the Annual Bank Conference on Development Economics. Unpublished. Washington, D.C.: World Bank.

Kruger, D. 2000. *Redistribution Effects of Agricultural Incentives Policies in Nicaragua*. Background paper for the Nicaragua Poverty Assessment 2000. College Park: University of Maryland.

Li, H., L. Squire, and H. F. Zou. 1998. Explaining International Inequality and Intertemporal Variations in Income Inequality. *Economic Journal* 108: 26–43.

Lipton, Michael, and Martin Ravallion. 1995. Poverty and Policy. In *Handbook of Development Economics*, Volume II, edited by J. Behrman and T. N. Srinivasan. Amsterdam: Elsevier Science.

Lustig, Nora. 1999. *Crises and the Poor: Socially Responsible Macroeconomics*. Presidential Address, Fourth Annual Meeting of the Latin American and Caribbean Economic Association. Santiago, Chile.

Morley, S. 1999. Impact of Reforms on Equity in Latin America. Background Paper for the *World Development Report, 2000/2001*. Washington, D.C.: World Bank.

Pastor, M. 1987. The Effects of IMF Programs in the Third World: Debate and Evidence from Latin America. *World Development* 15: 249–262.

Perotti, Roberto. 1996. Growth, Income Distribution, and Democracy: What the Data Say? *Journal of Economic Growth*, 1(2): 149–187.

Przeworski, Adam, and James Raymond Vreeland. 2000. The Effect of IMF Programs on Economic Growth. *Journal of Development Economics*, 62(2): 385–421.

———, 1997. Can High-Inequality Developing Countries Escape Absolute Poverty? *Economics Letters* 56: 51–57.

———, and Shaohua Chen. 1997. What Can New Survey Data Tell us about Recent Changes in Distribution and Poverty? *Economic Review* 11(2): 357–382. Washington, D.C.: World Bank.

Roemer, Michael, and Mary Kay Gugerty. 1997. *Does Economic Growth Reduce Poverty?* Technical Paper. Cambridge: Harvard Institute for International Development.

Romer, Christina D., and David H. Romer. 1998. *Monetary Policy and the Well-Being of the Poor*. NBER Working Paper 6793. Cambridge, MA: National Bureau of Economic Research.

Sahn, David, Paul Dorosh, and Stephen Younger. 1996. Exchange Rate, Fiscal and Agricultural Policies in Africa: Does Adjustment Hurt the Poor. *World Development* 24: 719–747.

Spilimbergo, Antonio, Juan Luis Londoño, and Miguel Székely. 1999. Income Distribution, Factor Endowments, and Trade Openness. *Journal of Development Economics* 59: 77–101.

Srinivasan, T.N. 2000. Growth and Poverty Alleviation: Lessons from Development Experience. New Haven: Yale University. Mimeo.

Thorbecke, Erik, and Hong-Sang Jung. 1996. A Multiplier Decomposition Method to Analyze Poverty Alleviation. *Journal of Development Economics* 48: 279–300.

Timmer, C. Peter. 1997. How Well Do the Poor Connect to the Growth Process? Unpublished. Harvard Institute for International Development.

UNDP (United Nations Development Programme). 1997. *Human Development Report1997*. New York: Oxford University Press.

———. 2000. *Human Development Report 2000*. New York: Oxford University Press.

Winters, Allan L. 1999. Trade Liberalization and Poverty. Unpublished.

———. 2000. Trade, Trade Policy and Poverty: What are the Links? Prepared for the World Bank's World Development Report 2000/2001. Unpublished.

Wood, A. 1997. Openness and Wage Inequality in Developing Countries: The Latin American Challenge to East Asian Conventional Wisdom. *The World Bank Economic Review* 11(1): 33–57.

World Bank. 2000. *World Development Report 2000/2001*. Washington, D.C.

PART II

Targeting Urban or Industrial Sectors

5. New Technologies, Competitiveness, and Poverty Reduction

Sanjaya Lall

1. Introduction

This chapter considers poverty reduction from the perspective of manufacturing competitiveness. Its premise is that industrial growth has been and will continue to be one of the prime drivers of income, employment, and skill generation—the main forces behind poverty alleviation. In the Asian region, even more than elsewhere, the countries that tackled poverty most successfully did so by *growing*, and by using rising incomes to support other economic and social policies to alleviate poverty. Growth, in turn, relied mainly on manufacturing to lead investment, exports, and structural change. The most successful economies were those that oriented their manufacturing sectors to exports. Their initial expansion was in labor-intensive products, but this accompanied rapid upgrading into more complex technologies, products, and activities that were capital-, skill-, and technology-intensive. The growing absorption of labor, in other words, went hand in hand with rising skill levels, greater abilities to use new technology, and a move up the value chain. Industrial competitiveness was the key.

The combination of attaining export competitiveness and upgrading its technical structure was necessary for *sustained* income and employment growth. Realizing export competitiveness was essential to switching from inefficient import substitution, reaping scale economies, integrating into the global economy, and building technical competence. This was a demanding task even in simple labor-intensive products, and a large part of the developing world, such as Sub-Saharan Africa, has failed to achieve it. However, this was not enough: without constant technical upgrading (of products, technologies, and activities), even successful exporters would lose their competitive edge and stagnate in low-value-added activities. Only with upgrading could they cope with intensifying competition, rising wages, rapidly changing technologies, new skill needs, and the spread of global production systems. All these factors are stronger now than they were then, and the lessons from the early leaders apply today with even greater force.

This chapter reviews briefly the technological nature of manufacturing competitiveness in recent years and the strategies adopted by leading East Asian countries.

2. Technical Change and Competitiveness

Technical change is evidently so rapid and pervasive that there is little need to dwell on it in general terms. It is, however, useful to stress some factors of particular relevance to developing countries and their growth strategies.

To start with, no activity, regardless of its nature and location, is immune to new technologies. Exposure to world markets means that every producer has to become competitive, i.e., to use techniques, skills, and organizational forms that allow it to match international levels of cost, quality, flexibility, and delivery. The range of technical choice that used to exist—say, for intermediate technologies—is narrowing rapidly. The cushion against prolonged learning periods and high costs and inefficiencies that firms in developing countries once had is far more limited. The needs that efficient technologies impose are also very different. They call for new skills, logistical systems, specialized infrastructure, and organizational forms, with a heavy emphasis on information and communications. Engaging in technological effort now entails much more networking and collaboration with other firms, universities, and research institutes than before.

Learning to use a technology's "best practice" may sound easy; it is not. It often involves long, complex, risky, and costly processes of building new skills, information, linkages, and supply networks. As a result, firms do not travel along predictable learning curves. Many are even unaware of what the curve looks like and what the process involves. As a result, the same technology is often used at very different levels of efficiency in different countries, and within a country, in different plants. The secret of industrial success lies in reducing these disparities and moving the local frontier closer to international frontiers.

In the developing world, this requires strategies to foster and deepen technological learning. Note that technological learning does not mean "innovation" in the normal sense, but efficiently mastering foreign technologies and keeping up with technical progress. The countries that industrialized fastest and most competitively were those that learned faster and more efficiently, and diffused their learning most widely within the economy. They were able to create systems of learning and diffusion that involved sets of interacting firms, institutions, and government agencies. The learning system had to become more complex and sophisticated as the industrial structure upgraded. With growing industrial maturity, it involved launching into formal research and development (R&D), not so much to innovate at the frontier but to monitor, select, and adapt complex new technologies.

Rapid technological progress has another interesting aspect. Activities with different degrees of "technological intensity"—those with higher than average expenditures on R&D—tend to grow faster than less technology-intensive activities. While every activity makes use of new technologies, differences in innovative potential and the speed of application of new innovations affect growth rates. The data in Table 5.1 show that "high technology" activities the world over are expanding in both production and trade much faster than other manufacturing activities. Note also that trade is growing much faster than production, showing the globalization of world economies. This holds for the most advanced as well as the newly industrializing economies. The 68 countries together account for over 95 percent of total world industrial production.

Not only do technology-intensive industrial activities lead in dynamism, they also generally offer greater learning potential and greater spillover benefits

Table 5.1. Rates of Growth of High-Technology and Other Manufacturing, 1985–1997
(percent)

	All Production	All Exports	High-Tech Production	High-Tech Exports
China, People's Rep. of	11.70	20.50	14.90	30.20
Korea, Rep. of	10.20	10.60	15.40	18.70
Singapore	8.00	15.00	13.10	21.70
68 Adv. or NIE countries	7.30	5.90	10.80	2.70
Taipei,China	4.70	12.00	11.60	18.90
United States	2.90	8.80	4.70	10.10
Canada	2.70	7.30	8.10	10.40
Germany	2.20	4.10	3.80	5.80
Italy	2.00	5.60	0.60	6.20
UK	1.70	6.30	3.30	8.00
Japan	1.70	2.40	5.20	4.40
France	1.20	5.80	3.60	10.80
Hong Kong, China	– 0.20	13.50	3.50	18.10

Source: National Science Foundation, US Senate (1999).

for other activities. Such activities have become the most active field for international investment. This has important implications for developing countries. First comes the "market positioning" argument. A country that wants to locate its production and exports in the fastest-growing markets has to move into technology-intensive activities and upgrade its technology structure. Second, countries that want to deepen technological development and gain from the spillover effects of learning in lead sectors again have to focus on technology-intensive activities. Third, those that wish to share in the most dynamic segments of world trade—the international production systems of transnational companies—have to build the capabilities for technology-intensive activities. They can enter the assembly stage, but later have to upgrade within the system, moving up into manufacturing, design, development, and regional service activities.

Consider now some results of my work on technological patterns of exports. This provides a useful perspective on efficient industrial activity more generally, in that the ability to compete in export markets shows how countries are doing in industrial development per se. The exports are broken down into four categories of manufactured products. Primary products are eliminated because the main concern is with industry. There are four categories of manufactured products: resource-based; low-technology (such as textiles, clothing, footwear, simple engineering products); medium-technology (industrial machinery, automobiles, chemicals, and so on); and high-technology. The medium-technology group is the largest—the heartland of heavy industry—but the high-technology group, with only 18 products at the 3-digit Standard Industrial Trade Classification (SITC) level, is driving world trade and may soon be the single largest category.

Figure 5.1 shows growth rates for the period 1985–1998. Primary products were growing the slowest, followed by resource-based manufactures. Low- and medium-technology products grew at more or less the same rate, but the pattern changed over time, as medium-technology products pulled ahead. The fastest-growing group in every subperiod (including the relatively stagnant one after 1995) was high-technology products. At the start of this period in 1985, the 18 high-technology products comprised about 10 percent of world trade; by 1998, they accounted for nearly a quarter.

Figure 5.1. Rates of World Export Growth by Technological Categories, 1985–1998

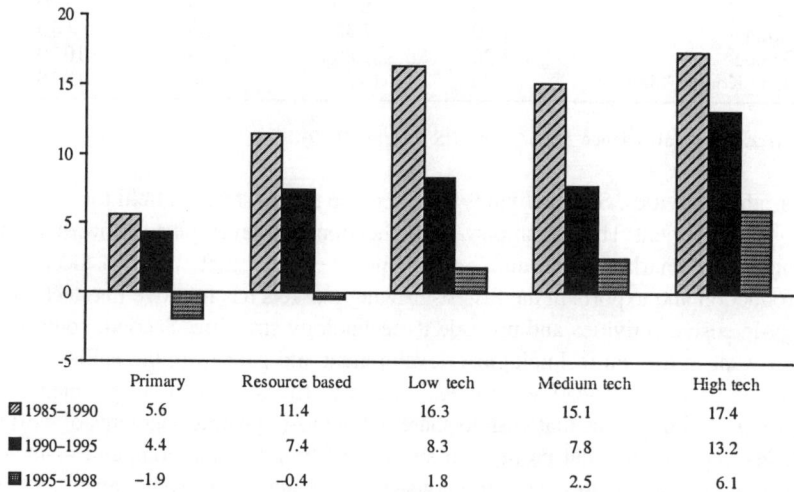

	Primary	Resource based	Low tech	Medium tech	High tech
1985–1990	5.6	11.4	16.3	15.1	17.4
1990–1995	4.4	7.4	8.3	7.8	13.2
1995–1998	–1.9	–0.4	1.8	2.5	6.1

Source: S. Lall (2001).

What were the "drivers" of export growth by technology? High-technology growth was driven by innovation (introduction of new products and substitution of old products), high income elasticity of demand, and relocation (shifting labor-intensive operations to low-wage areas) within integrated global production systems. Medium-technology exports grew because of technical progress and rising demand, but not so much because of relocation in search of low wages: heavy industries need strong local suppliers and capabilities and so do not lend themselves easily to such shifts. Low-technology products, facing stable demand and slow technical progress, were driven largely by relocation from high- to low-wage areas. Over the longer term, we may expect that technology will be the dominant force in relative export growth. High-technology products will continue to lead (the composition of products may, of course, change) and medium-technology products will grow faster than low-technology products, as the restructuring of location in the latter matures. Given the dynamic forces at work, in other words, there will be a continued structural shift up the technology scale, with positioning in the technology-intensive segments being the best for sustained growth.

3. Role of Developing Countries

Developing countries' exports overall are growing faster than those of developed countries; this is expected, since they started from a lower base. However, the technological patterns of their growth are interesting and unexpected. Developing countries grew more slowly than developed countries in primary products and resource-based manufactures (Figure 5.2), presumably because of the faster application of new technology or because of trade barriers and subsidies in the industrial world.

Figure 5.2. Growth Rates of Manufactured Exports by Industrial and Developing Countries, 1985–1998

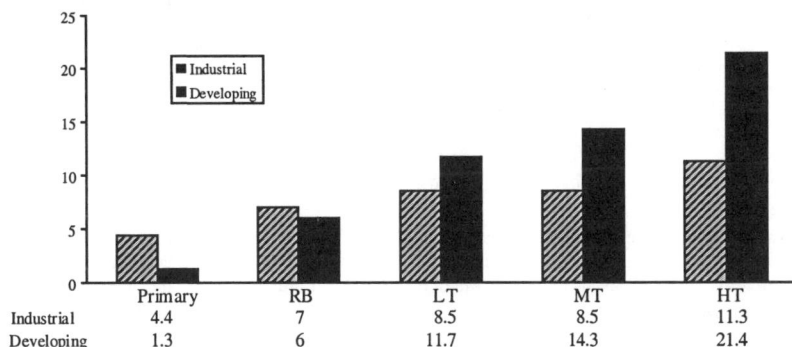

	Primary	RB	LT	MT	HT
Industrial	4.4	7	8.5	8.5	11.3
Developing	1.3	6	11.7	14.3	21.4

Source: Lall (2001).

As far as manufacturers that are not resource-based are concerned, however, the patterns are counterintuitive. Theory would lead us to expect that developing countries would grow fastest relative to developed countries in low technology, less in medium technology, and least in high technology. The data show the reverse. The lead of developing countries rises with technology intensity. Moreover, high-technology exports are now the largest single component of developing country manufactured exports. The value of electronic exports by developing countries in 1998 was nearly $100 billion larger than its exports of textile, clothing, and footwear products (their traditional stronghold).

This pattern suggests that developing countries have made great technological progress and are set to benefit from global competitive trends. Unfortunately this is only partially true. Export dynamism and success in technology-intensive exports are very highly concentrated, both by region and by country. Moreover, the local depth and "rooting" of high-technology activity vary greatly among the successful exporters, raising doubts about the sustainability of competitive performance by those with shallow roots. Consider first the concentration at the regional level (Figure 5.3).

Figure 5.3. Regional Shares of Developing Country Manufactured Exports, 1998

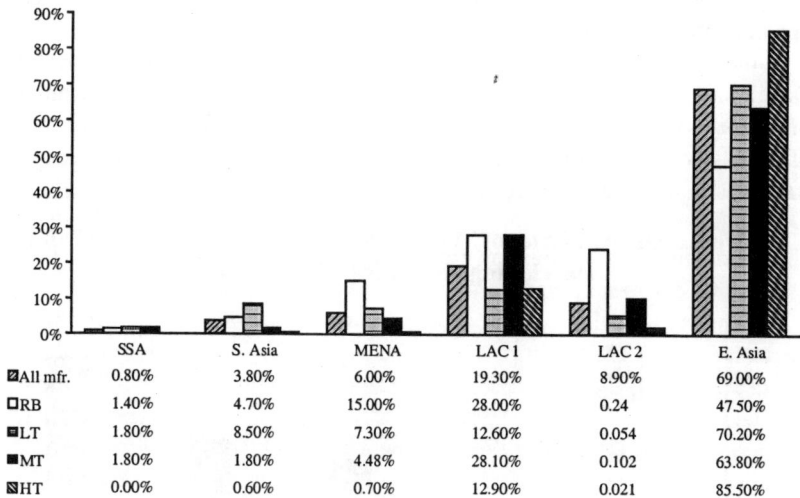

	SSA	S. Asia	MENA	LAC 1	LAC 2	E. Asia
All mfr.	0.80%	3.80%	6.00%	19.30%	8.90%	69.00%
RB	1.40%	4.70%	15.00%	28.00%	0.24	47.50%
LT	1.80%	8.50%	7.30%	12.60%	0.054	70.20%
MT	1.80%	1.80%	4.48%	28.10%	0.102	63.80%
HT	0.00%	0.60%	0.70%	12.90%	0.021	85.50%

Notes: RB = resource-based; LT = low technology; MT = medium technology; HT = high technology; SSA = Sub-Saharan Africa; MENA = Middle East/North Africa; LAC 1 = Latin America and the Caribbean including Mexico; LAC 2 = Latin American and the Caribbean excluding Mexico.

Source: Lall (2001).

East Asia now accounts for about 75 percent of developing country total manufactured exports, and about 90 percent of high-technology exports. At the other end, Sub-Saharan Africa (even including South Africa) is very weak in manufactured exports and practically off the map in high-technology exports—a clear sign of its marginalization in the dynamics of world trade and all that this offers. South Asia does well in low-technology products, basically clothing, but greatly underperforms other categories. South Asia's export structure has remained relatively static over time and is concentrated in slow-growing products (the figures exclude software exports by India). The smaller countries in the region (Bangladesh and Sri Lanka) face particular threats from the impending abolition of the Multi-Fibre Agreement that gave them a sheltered market niche.

Latin America and the Caribbean (LAC) is shown twice. LAC 1 includes Mexico and LAC 2 excludes it. The reason for this distinction is the massive trade "distortion" caused by the North American Free Trade Agreement, which gives Mexico privileged access to the United States (US) and Canadian markets over its neighbors (and over competitive exporters in Southeast Asia). Without this distortion, LAC 2 is doing poorly in dynamic products in world trade—surprising in view of the size and industrial traditions of Argentina, Brazil, and Chile. In Mexico, by contrast, assembly activity in *maquiladoras* (factories located near the US border) and elsewhere aimed at the US market are driving medium-technology exports like automobiles and high-technology exports like electronics.

Now take concentration at the country level. Figure 5.4 shows the 12 largest developing world exporters of manufactures in 1985 and 1998. These countries now account for about 90 percent of developing country exports and their dominance has been rising over time. Levels of concentration rise by technology levels, being highest for technology-intensive products. Thus, liberalization and globalization are leading to higher rather than lower barriers to entry for new competitors in advanced activities.

Consider now the technology composition of exports by the leading exporters, to see how they differ among themselves (Figure 5.5). The results are again surprising: the largest segment of high-technology composition is for the Philippines, with almost 80 percent of manufactured exports coming from semiconductors. Then come Singapore and Malaysia, followed by other Asian newly industrialized economies (NIEs). The laggards in the group are India and Brazil.

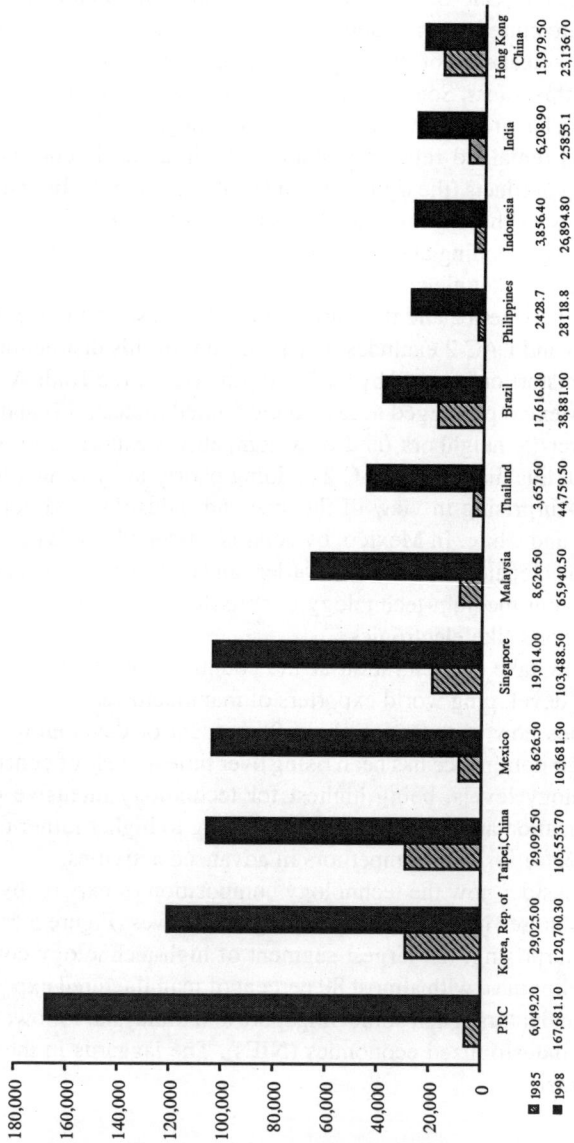

Figure 5.4. Values of Manufactured Exports by Leading Developing Countries, 1985 and 1998 ($ million)

	PRC	Korea, Rep. of	Taipei,China	Mexico	Singapore	Malaysia	Thailand	Brazil	Philippines	Indonesia	India	Hong Kong China
1985	6,049.20	29,025.00	29,092.50	8,626.50	19,014.00	8,626.50	3,657.60	17,616.80	2428.7	3,856.40	6,208.90	15,979.50
1998	167,681.10	120,700.30	105,553.70	103,681.30	103,488.50	65,940.50	44,759.50	38,881.60	28118.8	26,894.80	25855.1	23,136.70

Source: Lall (2001).

116

Figure 5.5. High-Technology Products in Manufactured Exports, 1998

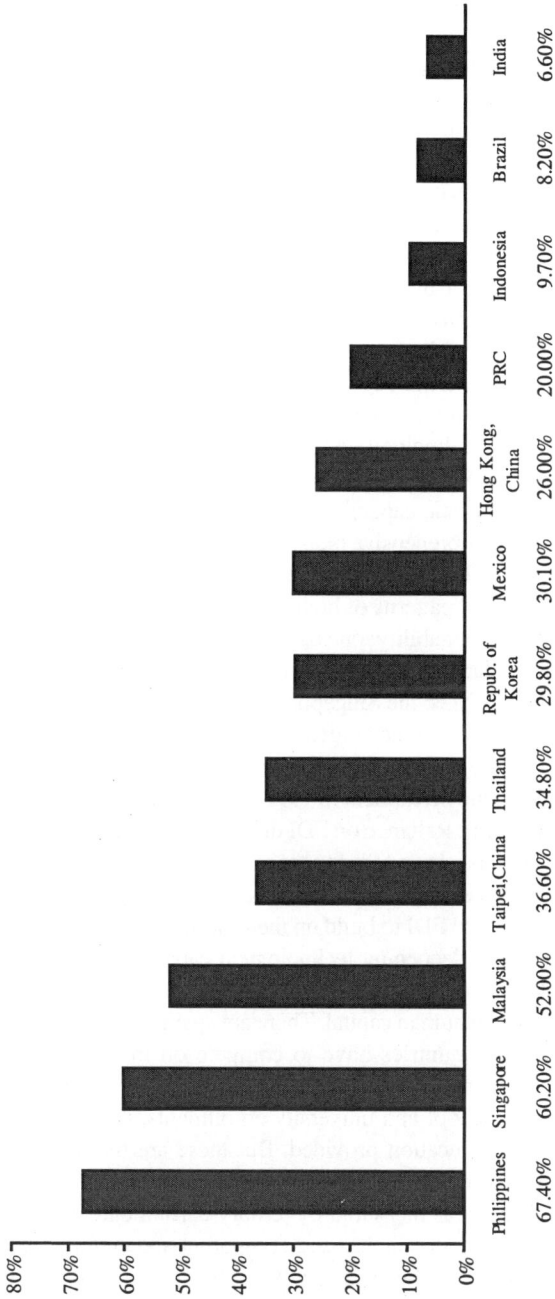

Philippines	Singapore	Malaysia	Taipei,China	Thailand	Repub. of Korea	Mexico	Hong Kong, China	PRC	Indonesia	Brazil	India
67.40%	60.20%	52.00%	36.60%	34.80%	29.80%	30.10%	26.00%	20.00%	9.70%	8.20%	6.60%

Source: Lall (2001).

4. Drivers of Competitive Success Among Newly Industrialized Economies

The drivers of technological success in export activity differ by country. In all countries except the Republic of Korea and Taipei,China, high-technology exports are driven by transnational corporations (TNCs) relocating the final labor-intensive stages of production to low-wage countries. As noted, the rapid growth of high-technology exports reflects not just their innovative content and rising final demand, but the separation and relocation of labor-intensive processes to low-wage areas. Such assembly operations have various beneficial learning and spillover effects (labor-intensive activities in high-technology activities seem to have more positive effects for host countries than low-technology activities), but they do not—at least initially—need strong local technological capabilities. The risk is that when the initial edge provided by low wages runs out, countries may not be able to move up the value chain ladder because they have not built their skills, information, technology, and supplier base to the demanding levels needed.

Only the Republic of Korea and Taipei,China in East Asia have managed to build up strong domestic capabilities in these high-technology activities, by dint of assiduous and comprehensive industrial policy (the People's Republic of China [PRC] is doing well in emulating them, but at a much lower level). Thus, we observe two different patterns of high-technology competitiveness with different implications for sustainability: one based on TNC assembly activity and the other on building local capabilities. A third pattern is industrial policy combined with heavy reliance on TNCs: the Singapore case, to which we return below.

Let us look now at some evidence on these different drivers of competitiveness. The first is foreign direct investment (FDI). Figure 5.6 shows FDI as a percentage of gross domestic investment in 1997 (but the picture is more or less the same over the longer term). Reliance on FDI differs sharply among the NIEs, with very high reliance in Malaysia and Singapore in East Asia and in most of Latin America. There is low reliance in the Republic of Korea and Taipei,China, which deliberately restricted inward FDI to build up their innovative capabilities. This suggests a trade-off between deepening technological capabilities and relying on ready-made technology from TNCs.

Now, let us take human capital. There are again sharp disparities affecting the base of skills that countries have to compete on in technology-based global markets. The figures are only a rough guide to skill formation, since they deal only with formal school and university enrollments, ignoring quality and other differences in the education provided. But these are the only comparable data available, and do show the main form of skill formation. The focus here is on high-level technical skills, as measured by tertiary enrollments in core technical subjects (pure science, mathematics, and computing and engineering) as a percentage of the population. Statistical analysis shows that this measure is the best variable for human capital in explaining export dynamism (Figure 5.7).

Figure 5.6. Foreign Direct Investment as a Percentage of Gross Domestic Investment, 1997

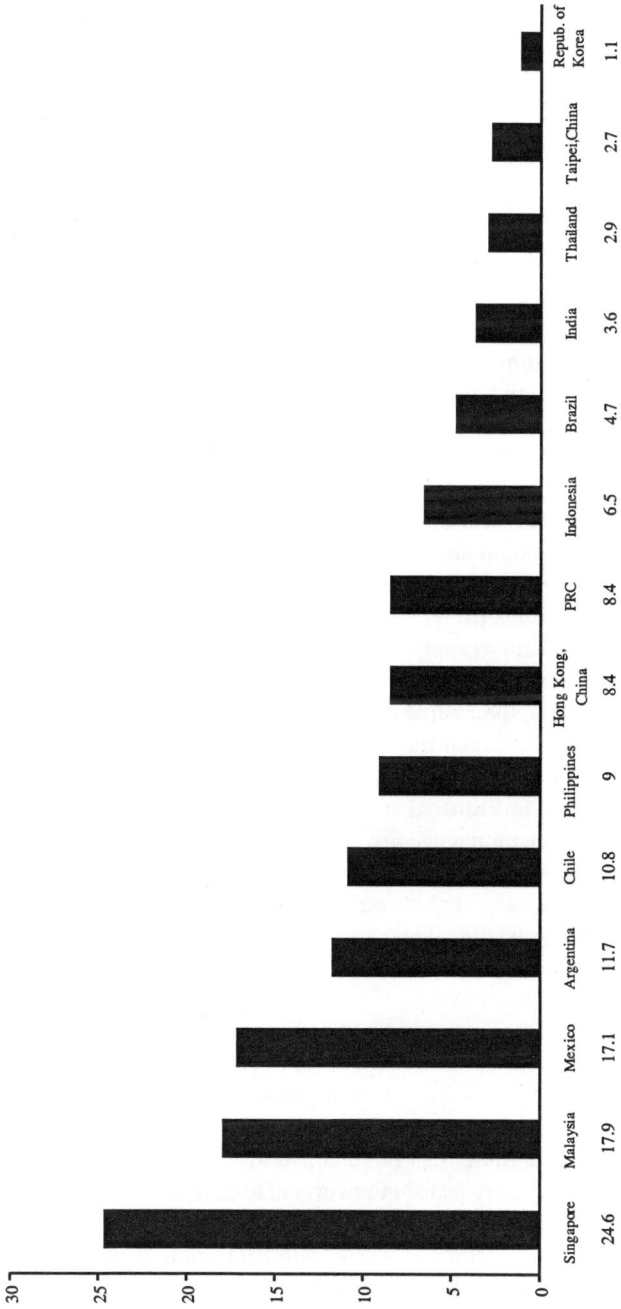

Singapore	Malaysia	Mexico	Argentina	Chile	Philippines	Hong Kong, China	PRC	Indonesia	Brazil	India	Thailand	Taipei,China	Repub. of Korea
24.6	17.9	17.1	11.7	10.8	9	8.4	8.4	6.5	4.7	3.6	2.9	2.7	1.1

Source: Lall (2001).

119

The most striking fact about the chart is the enormous lead established by the four mature Asian Tigers (Hong Kong, China; Japan; Republic of Korea; and Taipei,China), far outpacing even the industrialized countries. They lead the "New Tigers" (Malaysia, Philippines, Thailand) and the main industrial powers in Latin America (Argentina, Brazil, Chile, Mexico) by an even higher margin. Sub-Saharan Africa lags the most in skill creation, reinforcing the picture of marginalization given by the export data above.

Let us now look at R&D spending, taking not total R&D (which can be misleading for analyzing industrial technological activity) but that financed by productive enterprises (Figure 5.8). The leaders in the world in this activity as a percentage of gross domestic product are Japan and the Republic of Korea. Yet only some 20 years ago, the Republic of Korea was a typical developing country, with 0.2 percent of gross national product going into research and development and 80 percent of that coming from the public sector. Today, total R&D is over 3 percent of gross domestic product, with over 80 percent coming from the private sector. Singapore and Taipei,China come next in the developing world, with other countries lagging well behind.

These data again show the highly differentiated response to globalization and technical change among developing countries. The three mature Asian Tigers (Hong Kong, China and the PRC excluded) lead the rest, with other industrializing countries in Latin American and Asia lagging. While the New Tigers like Malaysia, the Philippines, or Thailand do well in technology-intensive exports, their capability base remains weak and shallow. The striking discrepancy between the technology intensity of their exports and their domestic skills and technological capabilities made up by TNC assembly activities has to be rectified if they are to maintain their past performance. Otherwise, technical change and the entry of rivals with stronger skill bases will lead future dynamic activities to locate elsewhere. The PRC is in an intermediate position, with a combination of capabilities and strategies from each of the three leading Tigers. Its size and established capabilities suggest that it will continue to catch up with the leaders and possibly do better.

5. Conclusion

This overview of technological trends in manufactured exports and their drivers provides a useful lens through which to view growth. It is not suggested that growth is the only factor in poverty alleviation, but it clearly is an important one. Without boosting growth, it is difficult to reduce poverty on a sustained basis. In a liberalized world with inexorable technical progress, it is even more difficult for most countries to have growth without building industrial competitiveness.

Figure 5.7. Tertiary Enrollments in Technical Subjects as a Percentage of Population, 1995

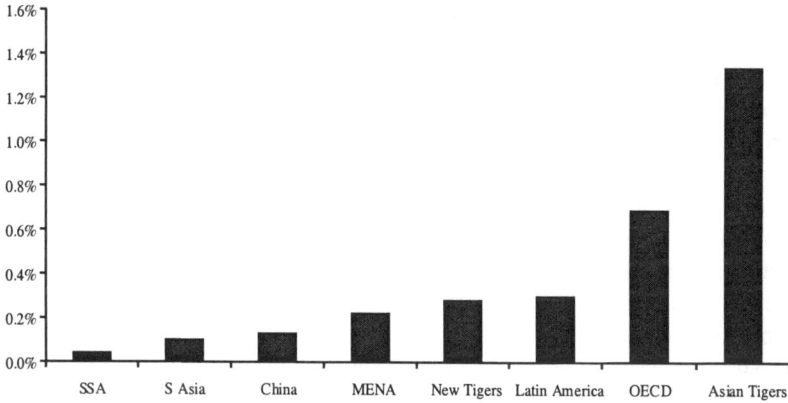

Notes: Asian Tigers = Hong Kong, China, Japan, Republic of Korea, Taipei,China; Latin America = Argentina, Brazil, Chile, Mexico; MENA = Middle East/North Africa; New Tigers = Malaysia, Philippines, Thailand; OECD = Organization for European Cooperation and Development (industrialized countries); SSA = Sub-Saharan Africa.

Source: Lall (2001).

Figure 5.8. R&D by Productive Enterprises as a Percentage of Gross Domestic Product, 1995

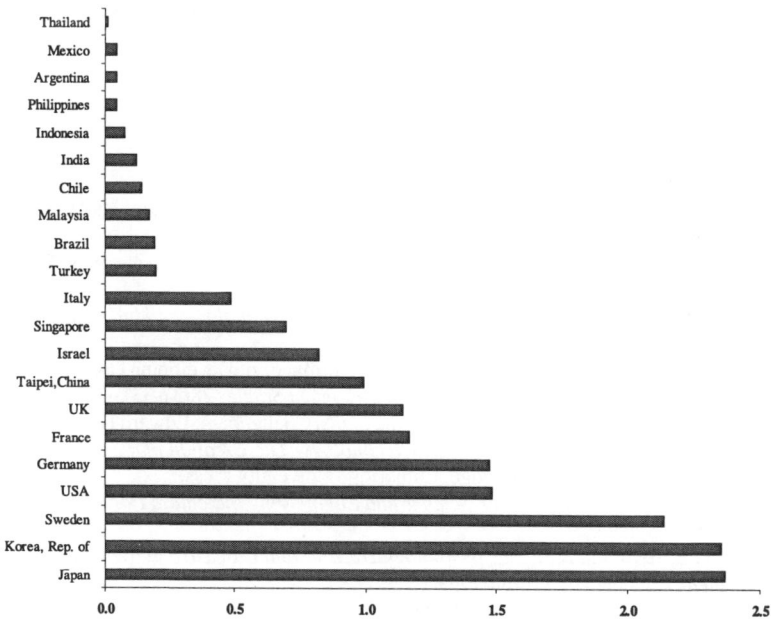

Source: Lall (2001).

The picture has an optimistic and a pessimistic side. The optimistic side is that it is shown to be possible for developing countries to grow and compete effectively in the emerging setting, entering competitive markets for manufactures and moving up the technology scale quickly. The pessimistic side is that the trend is toward increasing divergence rather than convergence. The globalization process is drawing apart the "insiders" and the "outsiders" to technological dynamism. A few countries on the "inside" are participating in integrated international production systems. Of these, the truly dynamic ones are those that have developed strong local technological capabilities; the other insiders need to follow their example by investing in human and technological capital. Other developing countries are "on the outside" to different extents, from some about to join the insiders at one end to those risking long-term marginalization on the other.

Globalization moves productive resources and knowledge around the world at an accelerating pace. It does not, however, reduce the need for *local* capabilities and institutions; quite the contrary, the strength of the local learning system becomes more and more important to attract and "root" the mobile resources available externally. Simply because capital and technologies are more available (and more footloose), countries have to offer stronger skills, capabilities, supply networks, institutions, and infrastructure if they are to attract high-quality resources. Simply opening up economies to global market forces without upgrading skills and capabilities may serve to exploit existing capabilities, but over the longer term may be a recipe for stagnation at the bottom of the technological and income ladder.

References

Dicken, P. 1998. *Global Shift: Transforming the World Economy*. London: Paul Chapman Publishing Company. Third edition.

Hobday, M.G. 1995. *Innovation in East Asia: The Challenge to Japan*, Cheltenham: Edward Elgar.

Lall, S. 1996. *Learning from the Asian Tigers: Studies in Technology and Industrial Policy*. London: Macmillan.

Lall, S. 2000. The Technological Structure and Performance of Developing Country Manufactured Exports, 1985–1998. *Oxford Development Studies* 28(3): 337–369.

Lall, S. 2001. *Competitiveness, Technology and Skills*. Cheltenham: Edward Elgar.

Mathews, J. A. and Cho, D. S. 1999. *Tiger Technology: The Creation of a Semiconductor Industry in East Asia*. Cambridge: Cambridge University Press.

National Science Foundation. 1999. *Science and Engineering Indicators 1999*. Washington DC: U.S. Senate.

Radosevic, S. 1999. *International Technology Transfer and Catch-Up in Economic Development*. Cheltenham: Edward Elgar.

Rodrigo, C. G. 2001. *Technology, Economic Growth and Crises in East Asia*. Cheltenham: Edward Elgar.

Stiglitz, J. E. 1996. Some Lessons from the East Asian Miracle. *The World Bank Research Observer* 11(2): 151–177.

UNCTAD (United Nations Conference on Trade and Development). 1999. *World Investment Report 1999*. Geneva.

———. 2000. *The Competitiveness Challenge: Transnational Corporations and Industrial Restructuring in Developing Countries*. Geneva.

6. Use of Information Technology for Poverty Reduction: A Case Study of Efforts in the Indian State of Andhra Pradesh

Randeep Sudan

1. Introduction

Poverty is a complex and multidimensional phenomenon. Its attributes can be captured in a myriad of characteristics ranging from malnutrition, disease, lack of education, and inadequate shelter to vulnerability, an absence of voice, and powerlessness in society. In view of its complexity, any strategy to tackle poverty needs to encompass a wide range of interventions and policies.

There are today widely divergent views on the relevance of information technology (IT) for tackling poverty. On the one hand, information and communication technologies (ICTs) are thought to have the potential for enabling Third World countries to achieve rapid development. On the other hand, existing inequalities seriously constrain the use of ICTs by the poor. These technologies require "a lot of overt resources including a telecommunications infrastructure to provide network access, an electrical infrastructure to make the ICTs work, a skills infrastructure to keep all the technology working, money to buy or access the ICTs, usage skills to use the ICTs, and literacy skills to read the content" (Heeks, 1999). While recognizing the scarcity of these resources in poor countries, this chapter will argue that IT holds immense potential for poverty reduction.

We will look at the specific example of Andhra Pradesh, one of India's southern states, which has launched a number of initiatives that use information technology to accelerate development. Andhra Pradesh is one of the larger states in India, with an area of 275,000 square kilometers (sq km) (slightly bigger than the United Kingdom, 245,000 sq km). Its 2001 population of 75.7 million accounts for 7.37 percent of India's total population. The annual per capita income was about $320 in 1999–2000. Estimates of poverty incidence in the state range between 22.2 and 27.8 percent for the year 1993–1994. Seventy three percent of the total population resides in rural areas and agricultural activities contribute about 30 percent of the gross state domestic product (GSDP).

2. Information Technology and Poverty Reduction

In its efforts to use IT as a tool for poverty reduction, the Andhra Pradesh government committed itself to "... use information technology to improve the quality of life of its residents and help them achieve higher incomes and employment. Aggressively promote the pervasive use of IT to achieve higher levels of efficiency and competitiveness in both public and private enterprises" (Government of Andhra Pradesh, 1999: 276). The state has selected the following areas where information technology can potentially make a perceptible difference in the lives of the poor:

- Emerging opportunities in IT and IT-enabled services can open up significant possibilities for generating incomes and employment in the state, which in turn can have trickle-down effects, thereby expanding opportunities for the poor. IT-enabled services can potentially become the lead sector, providing momentum to the economy through high rates of growth.
- The delivery of education and health care can be enhanced in a cost-effective manner to improve the quality of human resources.
- IT can contribute significantly to capacity building among the poor.
- Since most poor people live in rural areas, the use of IT to boost agricultural production and productivity can jumpstart poverty alleviation efforts.
- The improved access to information facilitated by IT can translate into higher earnings for the poor and thus facilitate their empowerment.
- The effective use of IT can help in more accurately identifying the poor who ought to benefit from the various programs of poverty alleviation being implemented by the state.
- IT can improve accountability and transparency in government, thereby helping utilize government funds more efficiently for poverty reduction, and also addressing the problem of corruption in a systematic and effective manner.
- Improved efficiency within government resulting from IT use can enhance revenues and cut down on leakage and waste, thereby releasing more funds for infrastructure development and programs for the poor.
- The use of IT can help to speed up decision making and reduce red tape, making the state more attractive to investors and thus improving the overall economy.

These areas for IT applications are discussed below to spell out the state's perspective on using IT to achieve a better life for the poor.

3. Emerging Opportunities in IT and IT-Enabled Services

The state considers IT and IT-enabled services as providing an unprecedented opportunity for leapfrogging into the future. New developments such as the rapid expansion of the Internet are causing a step change in the software and services market. Companies the world over are spending huge sums on software and services to achieve the productivity gains and the competitive edge that IT provides. In pursuit of those gains, they are increasingly outsourcing services to lower-cost parts of the world. Even the current world slowdown in IT growth is likely only to accelerate this process, as existing companies try to cut costs to survive the slump and become more competitive.

According to Prof. Michael Dertouzos, Director of the MIT Laboratory for Computer Sciences, India could boost its gross domestic product (GDP) by a trillion dollars in the next few years by performing backroom white-collar tasks for Western companies (*Time Asia*, 2000). While this estimate may be overly optimistic, the fact remains that IT-enabled services offer a huge opportunity for tapping India's vast reservoir of well-educated, unemployed manpower.[1] Such services typically do not require advanced infrastructure, can easily be standardized, require simple interfaces, and most importantly, can be sited in remote places.

Because of the wage-cost differentials between India and a country like the United States (US), net savings of 50 to 60 percent can be achieved by offshoring services to India, even after taking into account higher telecom costs. Thus, employment of Indians in IT-enabled services could increase from 23,000 in 1998–1999 to 1.1 million in 2008, with a corresponding increase in revenues from $225 million to nearly $19 billion.[2]

This gives states like Andhra Pradesh a huge advantage in rapidly developing their IT sectors. If this huge pool of educated manpower were to be harnessed through the establishment in the state of world-class communication infrastructure, training, and marketing support, the economy would undergo a major reorientation.[3] A number of companies have already set up major facilities

---

1. The country has the second largest pool of English-speaking scientific manpower in the world and graduates 70,000 computer professionals every year, in addition to graduates from the prestigious Indian Institute of Technology. See Bajpai and Sachs (2000).
2. Projections by the National Association of Software and Service Companies (NASSCOM), an apex industry organization focusing on the interests of software and service companies, and McKinsey & Co. for India.
3. Based on a conservative estimate, the number of educated unemployed would easily exceed a half million persons in Andhra Pradesh, while a large number (340,000) are added to the pool of educated manpower every year. A survey conducted by NASSCOM in May 1998 indicates that 23 percent of India's software professionals were from Andhra Pradesh.

in Andhra Pradesh to provide back-office services.[4] As many as 24 Indian companies in Hyderabad are providing medical transcription services for US-based and other foreign clients. There will be enormous space for more players in this area. It is expected that human relations services, customer interaction services, finance and accounting, data search, integration and analysis, and remote education will have a very high potential for being outlocated.

Apart from its impact on direct employment, IT also contributes to indirect employment by creating numerous jobs in support services. For example, in the case of Hyderabad Information Technology and Engineering Consultancy (HITEC) City,[5] the ratio between technical and support staff was 2:1. This ratio captures only the immediate employment in support activities; higher spending by IT professionals can in turn have further downstream effects on employment. Though no immediate estimates for such employment are readily available, there is every reason to believe that each high-salaried technical job is likely to create a number of downstream semiskilled and low-skilled jobs.

The various detailed initiatives the state has undertaken to broaden the use of IT in different sectors are discussed further below. Since most of these initiatives are either recent or are in the process of being implemented, it may be difficult at this stage to quantify exactly their impact on poverty reduction. It is hoped, however, that the initiatives will begin to yield tangible results in the medium to long term.

4. Delivery of Education and Health Care

a. Education

i. Literacy

With the limited availability in the state of computers and computer-literate teaching staff, the literacy program has depended on more conventional approaches to imparting literacy through volunteers. TCS,[6] a leading IT player in India, has initiated a project that aims to propagate functional literacy through computer-based training. About 80 centers have been set up and 1,500 people are undergoing computer-aided literacy training. Using the multimedia capabilities of computers, the method involves a

---

4.   Including GE Capital, the Hong Kong and Shanghai Banking Corporation, and Deloitte & Touche.
5.   Set up as a joint venture between the Government of Andhra Pradesh and Larsen & Toubro.
6.   Tata Consultancy Services.

faster method of teaching people. The project has demonstrated that the use of computers and multimedia can significantly speed up the process of acquiring literacy.

The state government is also developing content for literacy programs over the electronic media. Through an arrangement with the Indian Space Research Organization, the government has secured "Ku" band capacity on the INSAT 3-B for beaming literacy-related content to all parts of the state. A memorandum of agreement has also been signed for the use of the Malaysian MEASAT 1 and 2 satellites having a footprint over the state. Transmission of literacy messages and lessons through cable networks, and using both the "C" and "Ku" bands, offers the possibility of reaching learners even in remote parts of the state.

ii. School education

Recognizing the importance of training teachers to impart computer literacy, the state made computer education compulsory in the Diploma in Education and Bachelor of Education curricula, starting from the school year 1999–2000. Facilities are being set up in various institutions for computer training and for upgrading teacher training through distance-learning technologies.

The state is working with leading IT education companies[7] to use IT to improve education. It reached an arrangement with the private sector whereby the latter will provide the computer and connectivity infrastructure and teaching activities during school hours, but will be allowed to use the equipment and infrastructure after school hours for commercial purposes. This model could minimize initial investments by the government, while providing a commercially sustainable means of channeling private sector investments into education. In addition, geographical information systems (GIS) tools for school mapping and micro-area planning are being used to determine the location of new primary schools in all habitations without schools and for upgrading all primary schools to upper primary schools in phases.[8]

iii. Technical and professional education

In an effort to develop a large pool of technically skilled IT manpower, the state has increased the number of engineering colleges from 32 in 1995 to 180 at present. A new Bachelor of Computer Applications degree program has been introduced in 469 colleges, while 163 colleges offer a Master's degree in

---

7. NIIT, SchoolNet, and Zee Education.
8. There are 7,189 habitations (12 percent of the total) in the state without primary schools within one km, and 21,762 habitations (34 percent of the total) without an upper primary school within a three-km radius.

Computer Applications. At present, about 18,000 engineering students graduate from IT programs in the state every year.

In addition to increasing the number of institutions for technical education, the government has facilitated the setting up of an International Institute of Information Technology (IIIT) in Hyderabad.[9] The state also joined Carnegie Mellon University to initiate a Master of Science in Information Technology (MSIT) program to be delivered over computer networks. The MSIT degree will be a multi-university degree and will be cosigned by Carnegie Mellon University, IIIT, and an affiliating local university. The program combines the best of conventional teaching methods, using trained mentors, with the power of distance learning technology.

b. Health care

The health care infrastructure in the state essentially consists of 1,386 primary health centers and 10,568 subcenters, with a network of district, area, and speciality hospitals at the referral level. There is a significant disparity in the provision of infrastructure between urban and rural areas.

Information technology can help improve the quality of health care in the following ways:

- using telemedicine to make medical expertise available in remote locations;
- helping doctors to upgrade their knowledge and skills through better availability of medical research and information;
- maintaining health records and patient histories in order to avoid repetitive tests and expensive visits by patients;
- procuring drugs and medicines using e-procurement to improve availability and cut down on waste; and
- using analytical tools to determine patterns and trends in diseases for remedial action.

i. Telemedicine

A substantial portion of the state Medical and Health Department budget goes to staff salaries and overhead. In the year 2000–2001, this accounted for Rs8.07

---

9.   IIIT, affiliated with Carnegie Mellon University in the US, has schools that have been set up by leading IT companies, including IBM's School for Enterprise-Wide Computing, Oracle's School for Software Technology, Signaltree's School for Advanced Software Technology, and Motorola's School for Communications. Microsoft recently donated US$250,000 to establish a faculty chair at IIIT. A leading local software company, Satyam, has set up a School for Applied Information Systems at the Institute.

billion out of the total department budget of Rs14.64 billion. Telemedicine may prove to be a highly cost-effective method for efficiently utilizing existing manpower. One of the major corporate hospitals in the state has established a pilot telemedicine project at Aragonda in Chittoor district. The project provides for remote consultation, along with support for obtaining second opinions and interpretations. Another corporate hospital has developed an innovative IT solution for remote diagnostics, using computer-based, web-enabled diagnostic equipment. Such equipment includes electro-cardiography, electro-encephalography, electro-myelography, color Doppler, direct digital radiography, and digitizers with teleradiology. The company intends to offer computer-based diagnostic equipment to healthcare providers, using a pay-per-use system to recoup its investment.

ii. Education and training of health staff

The state intends to use the Internet to provide continuing education and training to medical and paramedical personnel and update their knowledge and skills. One study found that only 12.6 percent of doctors in the private sector subscribed to periodicals other than those published by drug companies. Even the periodic training of doctors in the public sector has been centered around the implementation of national programs and not on keeping their knowledge and skills current.

iii. Health records

It would be extremely useful to maintain online access to health records and patient histories. Not infrequently, patients have to repeat tests at considerable expense for want of proper documentation and records. Such expenses could be avoided and test results submitted immediately over computer networks in all referral cases. The state government plans to equip all primary health care centers with computers in order to streamline health information and improve the referral system.

iv. Procurement of medical supplies

A computerized system of inventory control using e-procurement as a tool is being worked out so as to bring down costs significantly, on the one hand, and improve availability of medicines and drugs, on the other.

v. Analytical tools

The Medical and Health Department has also started using GIS tools to map the incidence of diseases like malaria and Japanese encephalitis. Such mapping is being utilized to formulate measures to prevent the spread of these diseases.

5. Capacity Building

The government of Andhra Pradesh has taken up a reform agenda focused on improving governance and promoting stakeholders' participation in all decisions that affect them. The strategy of the state government for tackling poverty also depends critically on self-help groups, some examples of which are given below.

a. Women's self-help groups

Some 5.4 million poor rural women have been organized into thrift groups and are being provided with microcredit, technology, and marketing inputs. At present, women's groups produce 450 products that are marketed locally. The state government is facilitating the marketing of these products over the Internet. Together with improved quality control and packaging, it should be possible for members of these groups to augment their incomes through the online sale of their products. Already, some of the women's groups have begun to use computers to maintain their accounts and to acquire skills for manufacturing superior products. For instance, recipes for different types of pickles are being accessed by some of the women's groups using CD-ROMs.

b. Water users' associations

Another important self-help initiative taken up in the state is the formation of water users' associations to involve farmers in the management and maintenance of irrigation systems.[10] Videoconferences have been extensively used to raise the awareness level of both government officials and water users' association presidents about the new regime for the management of irrigation systems in the state.

---

10. The Andhra Pradesh Farmers' Management of Irrigation Systems Act 1997 was especially enacted for this purpose.

c. Joint forest management committees

Stakeholders' involvement has also been introduced in the management of forests. In order to involve the poor in the management of forests, 6,616 Joint Forest Management (JFM) Committees have been formed in the state. More than 1.3 million people, including 0.6 million women, are now jointly managing 1.632 million hectares of forest area. Monitoring of the increase in vegetative cover under each JFM, using remote sensing technologies, has provided an objective means of appraising the performance of both the forest officials and the individual JFMs.[11]

d. Training

Since training is a key element for capacity building among self-help groups, the state government has set up Training and Technology Development Centers in all districts. These centers are being connected using satellite communications to facilitate the transmission of high-quality content and training to the self-help groups across the state.

6. Agriculture

Agriculture's direct impact on rural poverty results from its being the most important source of employment and income generation in rural areas. Thus, accelerating agricultural growth through the use of information technology is an important component of any rural poverty reduction strategy, especially in the short term.

a. Irrigation

The provision and management of irrigation is the most critical element in agricultural development in the state. The most important single source of irrigation in Andhra Pradesh is canal irrigation. A pilot project is currently underway to design a comprehensive irrigation management information system for the Krishna river basin. The system would combine satellite-derived crop condition and soil moisture readings with meteorological information and real-time gauge data for the efficient use of irrigation water. Farmers would thus have access to information they need to make the best use of the irrigation resources and services available to them.

---

11. Some of the JFMs evaluated in Adilabad district that used remote sensing technologies reported an increase in vegetative cover of 14.27 percent.

The same system would also be extremely useful for optimizing hydropower generation in the state. At present, the state can generate 2,673 megawatts (mw) of installed hydropower and 2,952.5 mw of thermal power.[12] In 2000, the average cost for each unit of thermal power generated was 157.4 paise, while the cost of hydropower was only 26.7 paise. Correct forecasting of inflows into reservoirs and an accurate estimate of irrigation needs can therefore help in augmenting power availability through hydrogeneration, thus helping minimize the cost of generating power.

b. Watershed development

The selection of watersheds to be developed is being done using land degradation mapping, based on inputs from the National Remote Sensing Agency and the All-India Soil and Land Use Survey. Remote sensing and satellite imagery are also being used to evaluate wasteland projects. Evaluation of these projects has reported increases in water levels in 90.7 percent of the watersheds.

c. Water harvesting

Stimulating groundwater development is crucial to improving agricultural yields in many of the state's backward areas. It is here that a scientific program of augmenting groundwater through water harvesting structures and techniques becomes especially important. The planning and design of these structures can significantly benefit from the use of IT. In addition, a hydrology project to automate data collection, transmission, and analysis of groundwater data over computer networks covering the entire state is currently being implemented.[13]

d. Weather information

Weather forecasting information can play a pivotal role in precision farming and in the adoption of information-based response-farming strategies. In order to provide farmers with accurate weather information, the state government is in the process of initially establishing six automatic weather forecasting stations in existing research establishments. In the next phase, it proposes to set up one automatic weather forecasting station in each district (Department of Agriculture, 2001).

---

12. A total of 21,499 million units were generated in the state by thermal power in 1999–2000, while 8,131 million units were generated by hydropower.
13. It involves the construction of 625 purpose-built peizometers and the procurement of 366 automatic water level recorders and data retrieval systems.

e. Market information

The state has taken the first step in providing market information to farmers by equipping market yards with networked computers: 87 yards have been provided with computers and market information is regularly sent from the yards to the Directorate of Marketing using modems and telephone lines. The directorate in turn feeds market information to all market yards. The system is proposed to be upgraded with the setting up of a unified portal that will service a wide range of information needs of farmers, including information on prices and markets. Eventually, farmers should be able to use the Internet for managing most of their market transactions, both for procurement of inputs and for sale of their produce.

f. The application service provider model for farmers

A majority of the farm holdings (59.1 percent) in the state, covering 20.20 percent of the area under cultivation, are worked by small and marginal farmers. This category is on the bottom rung of the ladder in terms of purchasing power and the capacity to benefit from technology. While individual farmers may lack purchasing power, however, together they can command the resources to use IT. The state government intends to mobilize this collective clout by using the network of 4,610 Primary Agricultural Credit Societies (PACSs) in the state as an entry point. The PACSs in 1999–2000 contributed 33.3 percent of the total credit provided to the farm sector by institutional lending agencies.

Recently a company called Cooptions has come forward to equip PACSs with hardware, software, and content, together with operating and maintenance support, in return for a monthly fee. The computers would be used to facilitate the provision of timely credit to farmers; the purchasing of fertilizer, seeds and pesticides; the availability of information on procurement prices and markets; and the dissemination of best practices in agriculture.[14]

g. Natural disasters

Natural disasters tend to impact hardest on the lives and livelihood of the poor. While loss of life, disability, and injuries affect the main asset of the poor, which is their ability to perform labor, the damage inflicted by disasters on their natural, physical, and social assets can trap poor families in chronic poverty. In 1996–1997, for example, heavy rains, floods, and cyclones cost the state an estimate Rs30 billion.

---

14. Data from a pilot project implemented by the company in Bibinagar showed that using the system facilitated the timely disbursement of credit, reduced the PACSs' nonperforming assets, speeded up the rate of recovery, and markedly improved their service, as reflected in higher satisfaction levels.

Under a World Bank-assisted project, cyclone and flood management studies have been undertaken, along with the installation of a cyclone warning, communication, and response system. Coastal (topographic and bathymetric) mapping of land and near-shore areas to 0.5 m contour is being used to design and develop adaptive Decision Support Systems to achieve effective flood forecasting, flood control, and land and water management in the deltas for protecting human lives and crops. Equipment such as gauges, computers, data collection platforms, and telemetry will be used in conjunction with a rainfall, wind, and storm surge model interfaced with a flood forecasting model for decision support. The installation of state-of-the-art Doppler radars along the coast has been proposed, to provide information on cyclonic wind speeds, which is not available with the existing conventional reflectivity radars. The Forest Department has been utilizing satellite imagery to ascertain the gaps available along the coast on which to situate shelterbelt plantations consisting of mangroves and casuarina.

Along with flood forecasting models, crop modeling and pest forecasting techniques can also prove extremely useful for farmers. For example, cotton, which is one of the most important crops in the state, has frequently suffered from pest attacks. Crop modeling and pest forecasting techniques would tremendously improve integrated pest management.

7. Targeting the Poor

Very often, many of the benefits meant for the poor never reach them, because they are siphoned off by those who are otherwise not eligible. Political influence and corrupt practices often deny the benefits of these schemes to the deserving poor. It is important, therefore, that objective and transparent methods be used for determining the eligible poor. The Andhra Pradesh government is addressing this problem by building up a comprehensive database on citizens, with a view to making the identification of beneficiaries under poverty programs a more objective exercise.

Data, including such information as date of birth, incomes, occupation, type of shelter, landholdings, etc., have been digitized on each of the state's 75.7 million citizens. The data, which will ensure the linking of different databases for any given individual, will be extremely useful in identifying those eligible for assistance under various poverty reduction programs, ensuring that benefits are not cornered by ineligible individuals, but are provided to the most deserving. The availability of these data would also greatly streamline the administration of safety nets for the poor.

8. Better Governance

a. Corruption

One of the serious maladies besetting the government has been the phenomenon of corruption, which unfortunately inflicts its worst consequences on the poor. Interacting with the government can be both an unpleasant and demeaning experience for the poor. Lacking influence and voice, they are likely to suffer harassment in their transactions with government offices. Corruption arises essentially from the monopoly by government functionaries of the dispensation of certain services, as well as from the inherent features of the governmental system that allow it to cause interminable delays and harass the common citizen. A number of IT projects—discussed later in this chapter—have been designed to remove monopoly in dispensing services and also provide cross-departmental linkages through the sharing of data and information, thus making the whole system less prone to corruption.

b. Accountability

The state has introduced objectivity in evaluating the performance of government functionaries and reduced political discretion in matters of postings and transfers of officers. For example, in the forest department, one of the parameters for assessing the performance of officers is the increase in forest cover. For this purpose, remote sensing data on forest density are being acquired right down to the beat level, which is the smallest unit of forest administration. Similarly, in the case of schoolteachers, an objective computerized system has been devised for effecting postings and transfers and assessing performance, thus insulating the whole process from extraneous influences. In the case of the Roads and Buildings Department, a GIS-based system that is linked to data obtained from axle-mounted road quality measurement devices called roughometers has been found extremely useful for identifying poor-quality maintenance work. The system has made it possible to pinpoint responsibility for the lack of proper quality control in the execution of road maintenance work.

c. Coordination with field level functionaries

A statewide videoconferencing facility has been set up over, the Andhra Pradesh State-Wide Area Network (APSWAN[15]), for greater coordination in the day-to-

---

15. The Department of Telecommunications initially provided a bandwidth of two megabyets per second free of cost to the state government to provide connectivity for data, voice, and video communications between the state headquarters and the districts.

day functioning of different tiers of government. Previously, the communication of policy decisions passed through an elaborate hierarchy, causing delays and slow responses to emerging situations. Videoconferencing, in sharp contrast, has brought the policy echelons of government into close touch with field level functionaries, precluding procedural delays and weak coordination. When a problem is articulated, all concerned decision makers are available on the spot to respond to the problem. Though it is difficult to quantify the impact of videoconferencing on the implementation of government programs, it is widely recognized that videoconferences have contributed to better coordination, closer supervision, and higher levels of accountability. The government machinery has, as a result, responded faster on a number of issues concerning the poor, including price support operations for farmers, solutions for drinking water problems, and health problems like Japanese encephalitis and gastroenteritis.

9. Information Technology Strategy

The IT strategy adopted by Andhra Pradesh consists of five key elements:

- focusing on development of human resources,
- creating bandwidth,
- taking up SMART government applications,
- forging public-private partnerships, and
- providing a regulatory framework to facilitate the pervasive spread of information technology.

Each element individually is critical to the success of IT initiatives, but they also form a closely interconnected group.

a. Human resource development

The strategy and initiatives for developing human resources have largely been detailed in the education section. Action has also been taken to create a cadre of IT-savvy functionaries within the state government.[16] Computer awareness training programs are also being conducted for ministers, secretaries and heads of departments.

Large-scale training programs for government staff have been strengthened using distance learning technologies to widen the reach and improve the

---

16. A core team designated as chief information officers has been identified from different departments and provided with training at the prestigious Indian Institute of Management, Ahmedabad, and at the IIIT at Hyderabad.

quality of training programs. As part of this effort, the HRD Institute of Andhra Pradesh is establishing a district training center in each of the state's 23 districts and is setting up five regional training centers. A Centre for Good Governance is being established under the aegis of the HRD Institute of Andhra Pradesh.[17] The Centre will focus on improving the quality of governance in the state through training, consultancy, and research programs.

b. Bandwidth

In an increasingly interconnected world, high-quality telecommunications infrastructure is critical for development. Bandwidth per capita has already emerged as an important measure, in addition to the more conventional parameters of development (Friedman, 1999: 169). In the absence of legacy systems, modern telecommunications infrastructure affords the opportunity for developing countries to leapfrog in terms of technology. Some 25,000 km of fiber-optic networks have already been established in Andhra Pradesh by Bharat Sanchar Nigam Ltd. (BSNL), formerly the Department of Telecommunications. This is one of the most extensive networks available in any state in the country.

The state has announced a liberal right-of-way policy, which allows private sector companies royalty-free access to establish fiber-optic networks in the state. In pursuit of this policy, Reliance Infocom, part of the huge Bombay-based, $12.9 billion Reliance Industries conglomerate, is establishing a high-speed digital backbone in the state to support data speeds ranging from one terabit to one petabit per second. The company has already completed a fiber-optic backbone extending 2,500 km in the first phase, and intends adding another 5,500 km in subsequent phases. The entire investment for the project is being made by Reliance Infocom itself, with no financial commitment on the part of the government. Other companies are also establishing high-speed fiber-optic networks in the state.[18]

The government strongly encourages various technologies to achieve universal access to telecommunications. Both Reliance and BSNL plan to set up code division multiple access-based wireless in local loop connectivity to reach out to all parts of the state. As mentioned above in the section on education, the state government has also taken steps to utilize satellite communications to provide communications access to all parts of the state. The government is also encouraging the rapid expansion of cable networks: as

---

17. The center was established with assistance from the Department for International Development (DFID) of the United Kingdom.
18. These companies include Bharati Telecom (covering 2,500 km) and Tata Teleservices (1,750 km).

of now, 2.5 million households are connected to cable networks.[19] Digital subscriber line technologies are also being used wherever feasible. For instance, APSWAN uses high data rate digital subscriber lines for last-mile connectivity. The government has also been proactive in encouraging the establishment of international gateways connecting domestic networks to international circuits.[20]

c. SMART[21] government

The state has launched a number of applications in different departments as part of its SMART government initiative. The Computer-aided Administration of Registration Department (CARD) project has cut down on the time for registration of property sales from 10 days to less than one hour. The project has been implemented in 214 sub-registrars' offices across the state.

A pilot project, the Twin Cities Integrated Network Services (TWINS) has been successfully implemented in Hyderabad, duly integrating into a one-stop facility 25 services pertaining to six departments. Services range from accepting utility bill and tax payments to issuing certificates and providing information to the public. Recently TWINS has been expanded and eSeva (e-service) centers have been set up in different parts of Hyderabad/Secunderabad offering more than 30 services online to citizens.

Under the Fully Automated System for Transport (FAST) project, services like the granting of learner's and driver's licenses and the registration of vehicles have been computerized and 37 regional transport offices in the state are currently being networked.

A sophisticated web-based GIS application has been initiated to provide decision support over the governmental Intranet. Maps of the State on 1:50,000 scale have been digitized for this purpose.

The state government has set up a unified portal to provide information and services to citizens in a convenient manner. The portal will provide a single point interface for obtaining government information and services electronically. A joint venture with a leading private sector player has been finalized for designing, implementing, and maintaining the portal. Since a large number of financial transactions are likely to take place through the portal, it is potentially a viable commercial proposition.

---

19. It is estimated that there are 2.1 million cable connections in urban areas and 0.4 million in rural areas of Andhra Pradesh.
20. A memorandum of understanding with Malaysia's Satcom Holdings envisages establishing an undersea cable link connecting the state with Malaysia. The possibility of an undersea link between Visakhapatnam and Penang, together with a terrestrial link to Kuala Lumpur, is currently being explored. Reliance has also filed an application to set up a landing at Visakhapatnam to provide international connectivity.
21. SMART is the acronym for "simple, moral, accountable, responsive, and transparent" and captures the attributes of good government.

A private sector partner has been tasked to design and implement a knowledge management and workflow automation system for use in the state secretariat. The Secretariat Knowledge and Information Management System (SKIMS) will help to cut down on delays and introduce greater accountability within the secretariat.

To ensure interoperability of databases within and across departments, as well as consistency in the development of applications for the delivery of public services, the state has engaged the services of an internationally reputed consultant to design a uniform IT architecture.

d. Public-private partnership

Given the limited resources of government, investments in IT effectively divert precious resources from other development areas like the provision of water, sanitation, health care, shelter, production technology, and skills development. It is for this reason that many governments have strategically enlisted the support of the private sector to invest in information technology.

The state has focused its energies on the creation of content and the digitization of databases so that transaction-based services can attract private sector players. For example, the success of the TWINS pilot project has led to greater involvement of private sector partners in providing services to the public through eSeva counters. In the case of infrastructure creation, the government has leveraged assets like land to attract private sector investments in the setting up of facilities such as HITEC City. Similarly, the government has used the provision of a royalty-free right of way as an incentive for setting up high-speed fiber-optic networks. The possible use of such networks for e-government applications in the future has in turn enhanced their commercial viability.

e. Electricity regulatory framework

A state that aspires to use IT as a strategic tool for development must give due attention to planning the availability of quality electric power into the future. The state has taken steps to reform the power sector by unbundling generation, transmission, and distribution, and by setting up an Electricity Regulatory Authority to ensure adequate availability of power to meet future needs.

10. Lessons of Experience

It has been the experience of Andhra Pradesh that the use of IT for poverty reduction has less to do with technology per se and more to do with the management of change (Kotter, 1996). Introducing IT in government demands a sense of urgency in order to achieve success. Further, it is important to create a core of IT champions both within and outside the government, who can guide the use of technology and provide the necessary leadership and sense of direction in grappling with issues emerging along the way. Political vision and commitment have always been important, but are even more so in the context of IT. Without an overarching vision for the future, it is difficult to inspire people and organizations to adopt IT. The state has been fortunate in having a leadership that has recognized the importance of IT and has given it top priority.

A well-targeted public education and promotion campaign is necessary to educate the public about the benefits of IT. The Chief Minister in the state has skillfully used the electronic and print media to create widespread public awareness about the importance of IT for the state's future. This has been part of a sustained communication exercise to gain public acceptability for the government's various IT initiatives.

It is also important to demonstrate quick wins for sustaining the momentum and consolidating the gains from the use of IT. Projects like CARD, TWINS, e-Seva and APSWAN have visibly demonstrated the usefulness of IT for improving the quality of services delivered to citizens.

To ensure that IT becomes part of the organizational and cultural ethos that there are no reverses along the way, the state has made efforts to institutionalize IT through major training programs and develop a cadre of technology-savvy professionals.

While implementing IT projects, it has been the state's experience that all stakeholders should be actively involved in the planning, design, prototyping, and implementation process. The lack of such involvement can lead to project failure, as was the case in 1998 with the AP Value Added Network Services (APVAN) project.[22] Poised to become India's first value-added network for delivery of online services, APVAN was to enable citizens, businesses, and the government to transact with one another online and realize the vision of taking the benefits of IT to the masses. However, some of the elements of the business plan relating to job redundancies and the reengineering of certain processes led to a major agitation by the employees; the project had to be abandoned midstream. This failed undertaking illustrates the importance of ensuring constant communication with all stakeholders, including the employees, while implementing major IT projects.

Another important lesson is involving the private sector to create sustainable models for e-government applications. The government should

22. Armed with a business plan drawn up by a leading international consultant, the government had decided to launch APVAN in 1998 in collaboration with a consortium of government companies from Singapore.

concentrate its efforts on its own core competencies and focus on the management and delivery of information and services to the public, while largely leaving to the private sector the task of developing applications and establishing and managing infrastructure, such as high-speed networks.

11. Conclusion

This paper has attempted to present the range of initiatives taken up by the state of Andhra Pradesh in the use of IT to improve governance and leapfrog toward progress. Past approaches have tended to focus on the primacy of the agricultural sector for escaping from the poverty trap. However, the state views IT as offering a new paradigm of development very different from conventional approaches. In today's fast-changing world, the transition from the past to the future is not a smooth continuum. Consequently, traditional approaches for dealing with issues like poverty may have to be abandoned. It pays to think outside the box, to look at new opportunities emerging in a networked world, and to create a radically different model of development based on these opportunities. While the traditional sectors like agriculture cannot be ignored, the new opportunities driven by IT must not be missed.

References

Bajpai, Nirupam, and Jeffrey D. Sachs. 2000. India's Decade of Development. *Economic and Political Weekly* (15 April).

Friedman, Thomas L. 1999. *The Lexus and the Olive Tree*. New York: Farrar Straus & Giroux.

Government of Andhra Pradesh. 1999. *Vision 2020*. Hyderabad. January.

———. 2001a. *Strategy Paper on Agriculture*. Hyderabad: Department of Agriculture. January.

———. 2001b. *Strategy Paper on Employment Generation*. Hyderabad: Employment Generation Mission. January.

Heeks, Richard. 1999. *Information and Communication Technologies, Poverty and Development*. Development Informatics Working Paper Series: Working Paper No.5. Manchester: Institute for Development Policy and Management. Also available at http://idpm.man.ac.uk/idpm/diwpf5.htm.

Kotter, John P. 1996. *Leading Change*. Boston: Harvard Business School Press.

Time Asia. 2000. What Will We Do for Work. 155 (May 22). Available at http://www.time.com/time/asia/magazine/2000/0522/cover1.html.

7. Small and Medium Enterprise Development in Equitable Growth and Poverty Alleviation

Dipak Mazumdar

1. Introduction

The role of small and medium enterprises in aiding an equitable development process comprises three different topics in the literature. The first is the role of off-farm employment in agricultural growth in peasant economies. As popularized by Mellor (1976), among others, a decentralized labor-intensive growth in agriculture based on the seed-fertilizer revolution creates new demands and linkages—which tend to stimulate the growth of off-farm activities in village industry, trade, and services. These developments provide new income-earning opportunities for members of the rural labor force, providing further sources of savings for investment in the farm sector. Thus a virtuous circle of interdependent growth is established in the economy of small farmers, such as has been witnessed in Java and parts of India in recent decades.

Second, the development of small and medium enterprise promotes equitable rural growth through nonagricultural household enterprises that are largely based on family labor, although sometimes supplemented by one or two hired hands. In rural areas, such enterprises concentrate on traditional crafts, using nonmechanized techniques, and they spill over into the urban areas in a variety of activities, mostly in the trade and service sector, but also extending to low-grade manufacturing and repair activities. Such enterprises generally use small amounts of fixed capital, but can be expensive in the use. of working capital. Typically, the period of production (defined as the time taken to transform inputs into outputs) in such enterprises is long, compared to mechanized processes, but since only family labor is used, the implicit valuation of the waiting period is low, given the supply of plentiful labor. If the labor time used in the waiting period were valued at market wages, the cost of working capital would be substantial, but under surplus-labor conditions the enterprises tend to value family labor at a very low rate.

Support for household enterprises is an important component of poverty alleviation. The subsidies provided to handloom weavers in India are a case in point, and are best viewed as an income maintenance program in the absence of other schemes like unemployment insurance. The role of household enterprises in the economic growth process is small. They tend to disappear with sufficient development of alternative sources of employment, as surplus-labor conditions diminish in intensity. At one time, all manufacturing activity took place in such establishments. Their share in manufacturing employment is reduced with economic growth, as modern technology makes inroads into the traditional methods of production. Household manufacturing is, for technical reasons, confined to a very few industries. In India in the early 1980s, three quarters of total employment in household manufacturing was accounted for within five two-digit industries (as per the Standard International Industrial Classification): food, cotton textiles, textile products, wood furniture, and nonmetallic minerals (Mazumdar, 1983: Table 5). Detailed evidence available from enterprise surveys in Africa and elsewhere suggests that microenterprises, even in the urban economy, show little upward mobility (Liedholm and Mead, 1992; Biggs, Ramchandaran, and Shah, 1998).

Third, there is the varying importance of nonhousehold small enterprises in the modern sector of the economy, making use of hired labor, even if some of them are managed by working proprietors. Since such enterprises are expected to exhibit substantial growth potential, they are referred to in the literature as small and medium enterprises (SMEs). The boundary between such enterprises and large ones is statistical, not conceptual. It cannot be drawn exactly, since statistical offices in different countries have different criteria, and sometimes the boundaries change in response to changes in national economic policies. But as a rule of thumb, the lower limit is given by five workers, and the upper boundary rarely exceeds 300, and is more likely to be 100. In this chapter, the concentration will be on this third category of enterprises. Moreover, since policies can affect manufacturing enterprises more directly than service sector units, attention is confined to manufacturing.

2. The Development of SMEs and Equitable Growth

Why is the healthy growth of SMEs expected to encourage a desirable growth path for developing countries?

a. The factor proportion argument

SMEs are expected to be more labor-intensive than large enterprises and, thus, to lead to a choice of technology that more closely resembles the factor markets in developing economies—with scarcity of capital and more plentiful supply of labor. Distortions in factor markets, accentuated by government policies, have often allegedly affected the SME sector adversely, hence the need for policy intervention in favor of this sector. It is well known that capital market distortions produce a situation in which the price of capital for large enterprises is below its true opportunity cost in the economy. But it is equally well known that wage levels are higher for larger firms for a variety of reasons, including institutional factors like government legislation and trade union activities. Why does the labor market distortion favoring the SMEs not offset the capital market distortion going the other way? The answer to this question may turn on the different characteristics of the two factors, labor and capital.

The supply of labor has two dimensions, quantity and quality, whereas capital as a financial magnitude is a one-dimensional factor: a dollar is a dollar, and an increase in the unit price of capital in dollars fully represents an increase in its cost to the firm. On the other hand, a higher wage per worker facing the large firm could be, and is generally, compensated for at least in part by the higher efficiency of the work force, so that the difference in wage cost per unit of standard efficiency of labor between firms of different size-groups is much smaller than the difference in workers' wage.[1] The lower unit price of capital for the large firm is thus offset only to a small extent, if at all, by a higher cost of an efficiency unit of labor.

If this reasoning is correct, and the hypothesis is supported by evidence, two conclusions follow. First, the small-scale sector in the economy would be smaller than it would have been otherwise in the absence of factor market segmentation. Secondly, the capital intensity, defined as the ratio of capital per worker (measured in numbers, not efficiency units) would be larger than otherwise. Both factors would be welfare-reducing in terms of efficiency and equity.

b. The growth rate argument

SMEs are generally thought to be instrumental in developing a wide base of entrepreneurship. While the development of large enterprises does promote modern business practices and might be important in research and development, their growth is often associated with excessive concentration in the major metropolitan areas. Sooner rather than later, this type of concentration drives up public and private costs, threatening to choke off the growth potential of urban areas. By contrast, widespread SME growth could create many growth poles in small towns and rural areas, which could serve as the basis for renewed sources of growth.

---

1. A particularly pertinent example comes from Puerto Rico, when the minimum wage covering the mainland of the United States was extended to Puerto Rico in the early 1950s. The response of employers to the increase in wages was to augment labor productivity through a large increase in the capital-labor ratio. But this increase in capital intensity was not due to a change in technology embodying new labor-saving machines. The time period involved was too short for this type of basic adjustment. In any case, in many of the plants, which were branches of mainland companies, the equipment was relatively new. Rather, the reduction of labor per unit of capital came through changes in the selection, management, and deployment of labor. In other words, the labor flow needed was effectively supplied by a smaller stock of labor per machine. See Reynolds and Gregory (1965).

There is a theme in the literature that suggests that even if SMEs are efficient in reflecting more closely the factor price ratio appropriate to developing countries, it is the large enterprises that show dynamism and growth. Thus, even if SMEs create more employment per unit of capital in a static sense, in a growth context large enterprises have the potential for growing faster and thus creating more jobs over a period of time. Such arguments probably rest on some notion of increasing returns to scale, although a higher savings and investment rate has been stressed in some earlier versions of this theme. There are several arguments against pushing this hypothesis too far.

First, of course, we have the empirical evidence that the economic growth of post-1960 Taipei,China, with its greater reliance on SMEs, was as fast as that of the Republic of Korea, which stressed large-scale enterprises in its early phase of industrialization.

Second, there have been several developments in recent decades that might have reversed the trend toward an increasing optimum size of plants, an important feature of the manufacturing industry since the industrial revolution. First, although the optimum plant size continues to be large in heavy industries, some durables like automobiles and newer industries based on information technology clearly have a much smaller optimum size as far as production technology is concerned. Second, it is increasingly understood that the very large optimum size observed in some periods of manufacturing development in OECD countries has been the result of the production process consciously chosen rather than anything inherent in the production of the items concerned. In particular, the development of "Fordist" industries of mass production had a large optimum size, because they were based on "batch processes" employed in the organization of the factory. An argument advanced more frequently in the last few years is that small firms are better able to adapt to changing—and sometimes disruptive—economic circumstances. The 1970s and 1980s have produced several shocks demanding a flexible response from industrial firms. According to some authors, traditional mass production units have been less successful in responding to these shocks than have small establishments that use the flexibility of the craftsman to produce more varied products.[2]

Third, the economies of scale are often more relevant to the marketing economies of firms, rather than to the production economies of plants. Levy (1991) has drawn attention to the possibility that higher transaction costs facing industrial firms in the Republic of Korea compared to those in Taipei,China might have been responsible for the larger presence of vertically integrated large firms in the former in the first phases of industrial growth in these countries. The recent history of multinational corporations, with their growing use of subsidiaries in developing countries, also suggests that the scope for vertical disintegration increases

---

2.   See also Piore and Sabel (1984) and the literature on "flexible specialization."

with the growth of market-oriented institutions. The optimum size of firms is accordingly reduced.

c. The distribution of income argument

It is widely, but often implicitly, assumed that an economy with a larger share of production in SMEs will have a more equal income distribution. It seems fairly clear that the capital share of manufacturing value added will increase with a shift towards large-scale enterprises (LSEs), both because LSEs tend to be capital-intensive and because they often operate under oligopolistic market conditions, permitting a higher "mark-up" above costs. The expectation of a more equal distribution of entrepreneurial income is also straightforward. And the typically large wage difference between SMEs and LSEs implies that a larger share of output produced by the former leads to more of the wage bill going to workers in the lower wage groups. This favorable effect on the distribution of labor earnings may indeed be a more compelling argument for policies to promote the growth of SMEs than the efficiency arguments based on distortions in the labor market, since, as noted above, the efficiency wage difference between SMEs and LSEs may not be very large—and in any case may be much less than the difference in the wage per worker.

For simplification, we have so far distinguished between two groups—SMEs and LSEs. But what really matters is the entire distribution by size-groups. Distribution by size-groups in manufacturing could be considered with respect either to value added or to employment. In fact, the former is the more basic of the two and is the product of two separate variables: first, the distribution of employment by size-groups; and second, the differences in productivity or value added per worker as between size-groups. In what follows, working with these two variables will shed more light on the economic processes involved. A comparative picture for several Asian economies is presented. The Census or Survey of Manufacturing, on which this analysis has to be based, is confined to the "formal" or "registered" sector (with a low cut-off point of around five workers).

Wages generally increase proportionately with labor productivity (Berry and Mazumdar, 1991). Thus, the extent of productivity differentials between small and large units would reflect differences in wage levels between them. Insofar as informal sector undertakings would have wage and productivity levels near to those found in the smallest size-group in the formal sector, the large-small productivity differential in the formal sector would also be a measure of the economic distance between the informal and the formal sector firms in the economy concerned.

Both variables affect the distribution of labor earnings. Given the size distribution of employment, the larger the productivity (and hence wage) differential between the size-groups, the more unequal would be the distribution of wage earnings. For a given productivity differential, the worst scenario for unequal distribution of earnings would be the concentration of employment in the small and very large size-groups, with the medium-size groups conspicuous by their virtual absence.

3. The Objective of Government Policy for Equitable Growth

The point just made has implications for the role of government policies affecting the size distribution in the industrial sector. The argument for the promotion of SMEs given above has now to be modified to take account of an additional policy goal. It is not enough to simply aim at increasing the share of employment in SMEs. Policies must also aim at reducing the economic distance between SMEs and LSEs in terms of the productivity (and wage) differentials between them. In the discussion below, the contrasting cases of India and the Republic of Korea in achieving this goal with their respective policies for encouraging SMEs are examined. But before coming to this topic, an overview is presented of the comparative picture of Asian economies in terms of both the size distribution in manufacturing and the economic distance between the size-groups.

4. Size Distribution and Labor Productivity Differentials by Size-Group in Selected Asian Countries

Data could be assembled for only a few Asian countries, for various years in the 1980s. Table 7.1 presents data on the distribution of employment by size groups, while Table 7.2 sets out the data on relative labor productivity for the various size groups.

Three basic "types" can be distinguished within this small sample:

- A fairly even size distribution in which small, medium, and large firms play more or less equally important roles and the productivity difference between the size-groups is small.
- A distribution in which employment by size-groups is distinctly skewed to the large firms. Typically, in this pattern the productivity difference between large and small firms tends to be substantial.
- The "dualistic" type, in which there is a strong mode at both ends of the distribution, i.e., a relatively large proportion of employment both in the small and the large size-groups. Within this type, two subtypes can be distinguished depending on the extent of the productivity differential between small and large firms.

Table 7.1. Percentage Distribution of Employment by Size-Groups in Manufacturing, Selected Asian Countries (various years in the 1980s)

Size-groups	India 1987	Korea 1986	Japan 1987	Hong-Kong, China 1982	Malaysia 1981	Philippines 1988	Taipei, China 1986
5–9[a]	41.8	3.8	13.2	12.2[b]	4.3	21.5	10.4
10–49	10.1	20.6	29.2	27.4	20.5	13.6	24.0
50–99	5.9	12.9	12.9	15.6	13.5	6.5	13.5
100–199	6.2	12.7	11.6	14.5	15.4	8.9	28.1
200–499	7.7	14.8	12.4	13.8	16.6	49.5	
500 & over	28.0	35.0	20.8	16.5	29.7		24.1

Size-groups	Indonesia 1985	Size-groups	Thailand 1989
5–19	29.5	1–4	3.7 (0.7)[c]
20–49	9.3	5–9	4.9 (1.2)
50–199	13.3	10–49	17.3 (8.4)
200–995	25.2	50–99	9.3 (9.1)
1000 & over	22.8	100–299	17.9 (20.7)
		300–499	10.2 (16.1)
		500 & over	36.6 (43.7)

Notes: [a] 6–9 for India; [b] 1–9 for Hong Kong, China; [c] The sources for India are fully documented in Mazumdar (1997). The figures in parentheses are for the provinces surrounding Bangkok, which saw the fastest growth of manufacturing in the last two decades. The use of ( ) means that the groups enclosed by the brackets are merged together for this country.

Sources: India: *National Directory of Medium Enterprises* and *Annual Survey of Industry* data (author's calculations); Korea: *Statistical Yearbook*; Japan: *Statistical Yearbook*; Hong Kong, China: *Annual Digest of Statistics*; Malaysia: Fong (1990): 161; Indonesia: Hal Hill (1990): Table 19; Taipei,China: Abe and Kawakami (1997: Table 1); Philippines: National Statistical Office; Thailand: *Yearbook of Labor Statistics*.

Table 7.2. Relative Productivity (Value Added per Worker) by Enterprise Size-Groups in Manufacturing, Selected Asian Countries (various years in the 1980s)

Size-groups	India 1987	Korea 1986	Japan 1987	Hong Kong, China 1982	Malaysia 1981	Philippines 1988	Taipei, China 1986
5–9	12[a]	31	32	54[b]	54	9[c]	34
10–49	39	42	39	61	58	30	35
50–99	45	59	50	66	73	56	38
100–199	60	56	59	71	94	74	49
200–499	74	81	76	82	93		
500 & over	100	100	100	100	100	100	100

Size-groups	Indonesia 1985
5–19	21
20–49	44
50–199	84
200–999	95
1000 & over	100

Notes: [a] 6–9 for India; [b] 9 for Hong Kong, China; [c] 1–9 for Hong Kong, China.

Sources: Same as for Table 7.1.

The first group is classically represented by the case of Hong Kong, China. As can be seen in Table 7.1, employment was fairly evenly distributed among the various size groups, with the small enterprises playing as large a role in the island's manufacturing structure as medium and large enterprises. At the same time, the difference in labor productivity between the largest and the smallest size-group is the smallest in the sample (Table 7.2).

The pattern of distribution in Hong Kong, China may be usefully compared with that in the Japanese economy, which has been characterized by the strong role of small establishments. It will be seen from Table 7.1 that although the modal size-group for both Hong Kong, China and Japan is 10–49 workers, the proportion of employment in large enterprises of 500-plus workers is significantly larger in Japan. Further, the data in Table 7.2 show that productivity differences between small and large firms were much smaller in Hong Kong, China. The wage differential between small and large units was accordingly much smaller. Average earnings in Hong Kong, China in 1982 were only 55 per cent higher in establishments with more than 1,000 workers than in those with 1–9 workers. In Japan, the wage differential was twice as large.[3]

Hong Kong, China comes closest to a free market model of development in Asia. Beng (1988: 88) observes that "within the proclaimed *laissez faire* environment in Hong Kong the government does not seem to have a policy towards manufacturing not to mention any policy towards the small medium enterprises (SMEs)." An obvious hypothesis emerging from the Hong Kong case is that left to itself modern industry makes efficient use of small enterprises in a striking way. Further, in the absence of the usual set of policy biases that protect both capital and labor in large firms, labor productivity and wage differentials are kept within fairly narrow bounds.

Of the other countries represented in the sample, Taipei,China comes close to the Hong Kong, China pattern. The size distribution is very similar. While the productivity difference in Taipei,China would seem to be larger if we compare the lowest and the highest size-groups, closer examination shows that this appearance is largely due to the high relative productivity of the largest (500-plus*)* size-group in Taipei,China. Value added per worker rises very gently up to the level of the large firms of 500-plus workers, and then seems to take a big jump. Differences in wage levels, as measured by average earnings of the workers between the smallest and the largest size groups, are almost the same for Taipei,China and Hong Kong, China.[4]

The second pattern in the sample is a size distribution of employment that is skewed to the right, with the modal size-group employing 500-plus employees. The countries in the sample that show this distribution are the

---

3.   Data on average earnings for the two countries can be found in the same national sources as are cited for Table 7.1.
4.   It is apparent that the reason that the difference in value added per worker between the

Republic of Korea and Thailand, although, as of 1986, the Republic of Korea had a larger presence of smaller firms than Thailand, particularly in the 20–50-employee size-group. But the Republic of the Republic of Korea had been consciously trying to develop its small and medium sectors since about a decade earlier. In 1976, when the proportion of employment in the largest size-group peaked at 45 percent, the Korean distribution was much more skewed, almost at par with Thailand's (see Table 7.3).

Malaysia is another country that, in 1981, showed a pattern of distribution skewed to the large size-group. But it can be seen from Table 7.2 that the productivity differential between small and large firms is much smaller than in the case of

Table 7.3. Classification of Republic of Korea Workers in Small-Scale Enterprises, 1971

Percentage of Workers in Units of <100 Workers	Number of Industries	Percentage of Employment In SSEs
75–100	114	17
50–74	61	24
25–49	86	39
1–24	112	20
Total	373	100

Source: Little, Mazumdar, and Page (1987: Table 6-4).

The Republic of Korea. Thus, we would expect different economic forces operating on the size distribution in the case of these two countries.

Finally, the dualistic pattern is characterized by, first, the strong presence of both small establishments and large firms, and second, the substantial economic distance between small and large firms.

The classic case of this type is Japan. The dualistic pattern of Japanese industrialization has a long history. It has its roots in the initial surplus-labor conditions prevailing in Japan during its initial industrialization (which contributed to labor market segmentation) and the simultaneous development of a complex tying large industry, the State, and financial conglomerates that accentuated capital market dualism.

The other less developed countries in Asia—India, the Philippines, and Indonesia—all share with Japan the dualistic pattern in their modern (formal) manufacturing sector.[5] There is, however, a big difference between them and

---

largest and the smallest size groups in Taipei,China is larger than that in wages per worker is because Taipei,China has a fair presence of large conglomerates, with a large share of capital, along with the small and medium-scale firms. Such conglomerates play a smaller role in the manufacturing economy of Hong Kong, China.

5. It should be emphasized once again that the sets of data considered here exclude the very

Japan, which is brought out in Table 7.2. The productivity difference between the small and the large size-groups of firms is much larger in these Asian countries than in Japan. Thus while the surplus labor situation in Asian countries causes the dualistic pattern to emerge in a wide variety of Asian economies, Japan had, by the middle 1980s, succeeded in narrowing the gap in productivity between small and large firms that typically characterizes the dualistic development. We will return to this point later.

In South Asia, the extreme peculiarity of the Indian structure is immediately apparent. India has an exceptionally large proportion of employment in the lowest size-group of 6–9 workers and an exceptionally low relative value added per worker in this group. Furthermore, the size distribution is characterized by a large presence of the 500-plus group of firms, with a conspicuous "missing middle." This pattern resembles that of Japan in terms of a dualistic development, but in the Indian case it is wildly exaggerated. There can be little doubt that this outcome is basically due to the protectionist policy adopted by the Government since 1950, which favored the small scale.

a. Hypotheses to explain the different patterns of size structure in manufacturing

It can be hypothesized that the dualistic pattern has typically emerged in Asian economies with the coming of new technology to an economy characterized by surplus labor in the large peasant sector, and substantial segmentation in the capital market. Underemployment in agriculture creates an ample supply of low-skilled labor—often nonpermanent migrants to the urban sector with limited commitment to the modern technologically advanced firms, at a supply price much lower than what is needed to attract labor committed to the type of work performed in large factories.[6] At the same time, efficiency wage and profit-sharing considerations induce employers in the large firms to offer wages even in excess of the supply price of stable, committed labor.

The impact of labor market conditions is accentuated by capital market segmentation, which makes the supply price of capital cheap to large firms, and also by product market and technological differentiation. What India, Indonesia, and the Philippines have in common is a large labor force in household manufacturing units, which is slowly shifting to the nonhousehold manufacturing sector. The lack of technical dynamism of the small-scale sector explains its

---

large household and other parts of the informal sector in establishments employing less than five workers.

6.   In economic terms, the gap arises because the marginal contribution of a worker in a family farm with "surplus labor" is much lower than the wage needed to attract a stable migrant with family to settle in town and be committed to work in large factories. This and the subsequent point have been much discussed in the literature. For a summary see Mazumdar (1983) and Little, Mazumdar, and Page (1987: Chapter 10).

limited upward mobility, even when it is not reinforced by government policies—leading to the phenomenon of depressed relative labor productivity in
the small enterprises and the phenomenon of the "missing middle." All three
countries had their share of import-substituting industrialization, and it is
arguable that the rent creation and the generally noncompetitive environment
are not particularly conducive to the dynamic growth of SMEs. As far as factor
markets are concerned, trade unions and state intervention in the labor market
were considerably weaker in Indonesia and the Philippines until very recent
years. But there is evidence to suggest that industrial and financial policies in
both contributed to a marked degree of capital market segmentation—which
favored the use of capital-intensive techniques in the large-scale sector.[7]

More direct government policies impacting on the industrial structure have
sometimes increased the distance between small and large enterprises in terms
of their capital intensities, and hence labor productivity. India is a prime and
rather extreme example of this point. The Indian case is discussed in detail in
Section 5b below.

What explains the case of the other countries—the two cases, Hong Kong,
China and Taipei,China, where we find an even size distribution of employment
with a limited productivity difference between small and large firms; and the other
three, with a distribution skewed to the right? Hong Kong, China is, of course, a
city-state, which did not have a large agricultural surplus labor sector. It can be
hypothesized that factor markets, both labor and capital, were less segmented than
in the less developed Asian economies cited above. It has already been noted that
government policies were not strong enough to have had much impact on the
industrial structure. Taipei,China is frequently contrasted with the Republic of
Korea with respect to the size structure. Capital markets, quite definitely, and labor
markets, most probably, are less segmented in Taipei,China. At the same time, a
lower level of transaction costs and a wider distribution of capital among native
entrepreneurs in Taipei,China meant there was differentiation between small and
large firms in terms of resource costs.

The case of Thailand has attracted much notice since it experienced spectacular growth in manufacturing in the 1980s and the first half of the 1990s; unfortunately, it was the first country to have experienced the recent economic crisis in the
region. The distribution of employment in Thai manufacturing has been very much
tilted toward the large size-group. In fact if we look specifically at the provinces
surrounding Bangkok, where the recent growth in manufacturing has been concentrated, the tilt to large units is even more pronounced. This size distribution of
manufacturing employment, resembling more the pattern of Indonesia, the Philippines, and the Republic of Korea in its earlier decades, and away from the

---

7. Hill's detailed study of the Indonesian textile industry showed that the prevalent
    factor-price ratio, particularly the relative factor price ratio, led to a less than socially
    optimal choice of techniques in the large textile firms (Hill, 1983).

Taipei,China-Hong Kong, China model, is more likely one of the reasons for the rising cost of labor and the deteriorating labor market situation of the Thai economy that led to the crisis.[8] This pattern traces its roots both to the labor supply problems besetting Thai industry and the peculiarities of entrepreneurial and financial development in Thailand's modern sector. Although Thailand has been a land-abundant economy with much less population pressure than Indonesia (or Java), for example, labor seems to have been "locked up" in the agricultural sector of the North and the Northeast. The incidence of low income per worker in these areas has been responsible for Thailand showing one of the worst cases of interregional disparities in Asia. At the same time, the tie-up between large industrial enterprises and financial institutions has produced a lopsided development of manufacturing enterprises in terms of the size distribution, very much like Indonesia and Korea.

The case of Malaysia is similar to that of Hong Kong, China, in that it has a low level of labor differential between small and large firms. The 1981 data, however, show a more limited role for small-scale enterprises (SSEs). A logical interpretation, both of the small dimensions of SSEs and the low productivity gap is that Malaysia is not a labor-surplus economy. Land has been relatively accessible, and the government has, over the last few decades, invested heavily in adding to the supply of good quality land. One hint that the SSE sector has not become a sponge for masses of people seeking a modest level of income—as might be true of India or Indonesia, and Japan in the early years of industrialization—lies in the high earnings of the self-employed production workers relative to those of employees (Mazumdar, 1981: 108).

5. Evaluation of Government Policies for SMEs

a. Should the government intervene at all?

The review of the empirical picture in Asian economies might raise some questions about the necessity for government policies towards SMEs aimed at increasing its importance in the industrial structure and of reducing the economic distance between SMEs and LSEs. The example of Hong Kong, China, and to a lesser extent Taipei,China, might suggest to some that, left to itself, industrial development could produce a scenario in which SMEs are an important part of the development process with a limited productivity (and wage) gap with respect to LSEs. Others might argue that a dualistic industrial structure, such as that which evolved in Japan and has persisted to the present, might not be inimical to equitable growth. Japan's manufacturing growth over many decades did, in fact, successfully absorb sur-

8.   See Mazumdar (1997) for a detailed discussion of this point.

plus labor from its farm sector and led to an economy of full employment and rising wages after World War II. Furthermore, at the end of this period of sustained growth, the productivity and wage differential between the small and large sectors was no higher than in the early periods.[9]

It is, however, possible to point to special conditions or institutions in all three examples. As mentioned, Hong Kong, China is a city-state, without surplus labor, and with an easy supply of capital in fairly open financial markets. Taipei,China's pattern of industrial growth was heavily influenced by new skilled immigrants from the mainland, which served to reduce the ransaction costs of interfirm contracts (Levy, 1991). A basic condition of the relatively successful dualistic system in Japan seems to have been the constantly evolving, and ultimately competitive, "subcontracting" system, which other Asian countries have found difficult to reproduce. Against these examples, we have the cases of India, Indonesia, and Thailand, where the dualistic system in manufacturing has opened up huge economic distances between the small and large sectors. It is plausible to argue that inadequate SME support policies, or even policies with the wrong emphasis, have contributed to industrial development in these countries that is inimical to poverty alleviation and equitable growth.

India, in fact, has adopted an active policy of supporting small enterprises ever since the Second Five-Year Plan of 1956, but it can be argued that basic problems in the conception and application of these policies have produced the inequitable outcomes that can be observed. The deficiency in these policies can best be appreciated by contrasting them with the approach of the Republic of Korea, which also initiated a pro-SME package of policies, starting in the latter half of the 1970s. In the early stages of industrialization, Korean policies clearly favored LSEs, but after the failure of the drive to target heavy industries in the late 1970s, the emphasis was redirected toward SMEs. In what follows, the results of the Korean package are contrasted with the Indian case, and the key differences in the contents of the two types of pro-SME policies are indicated.

b. Indian policies to promote small-scale enterprises

A dual system of protection has been in effect in India since the beginning of post-independence industrial policy. On the one hand, the policy has been to protect the small-scale from the competition of the large by the policy of "reservation," under which a long list of items has been designated as the exclusive preserve of the small-scale (defined in terms of the value of capital assets). The production capacity of these items by large-scale units has been frozen at the level at the time of the legislation. At the same time, import-substituting indus-

9.   The literature on Japan's dualistic sector is huge.

trialization has protected all domestic units, small and large, from the competition of foreign firms. The result has been that small and large firms have developed their own market niches in different lines of production without too much competition between them or from foreign firms.

This method of fostering the growth of SSEs was first introduced in 1967 and the list of items "reserved" for the small-scale has been progressively increased, until today it comprises a total of around 830. The value of the limit in plant and machinery has been increased over time in nominal terms, but the increase in value of this limit after allowing for inflation has been small.

Initially, this approach encouraged the establishment of large numbers of new SSE units, which were protected from competition from the large-scale sector. But the problem with the continuation of such policies is two-fold: (i) in attempting to select labor-intensive products or industries, it misses the point that labor-intensive enterprises are found in many, nearly all, industries, not just a limited set that can be easily identified; and (ii) it is not sufficiently biased toward small enterprises that show potential for growth.[10]

Industry-based policies of reservation overlook the fact that small enterprises are not confined to specific product lines, and that their importance in different product groups is constantly changing. What is needed is for policies to have a pervasive effect, so that all small enterprises, in no matter which product groups, could potentially take advantage of the assistance measures available.

Small enterprises are generally more labor-intensive than large ones, specially if size is defined in terms of fixed investment rather than employment (see section 5c below). But it does not mean that they are concentrated in industries where the mean capital-labor ratio is particularly low. SMEs are found in many industries. There is no reason that in any economy the number employed (or the proportion of total output or investment) in SMEs would be larger in those industries that have a less than average capital-labor ratio than in those in which the ratio is above the average. This is because there is a spectrum of techniques within each industry, and enterprises of different sizes and capital intensities will be found in most of them.

Little, Mazumdar, and Page (1987) analyzed the Korean Industrial Census of 1971 at the five-digit level, and classified the industries by the percentage of workers in SSEs, defined as those employing fewer than 50 workers. The distribution of employment in SSEs among the different industry groups is shown in Table 7.3.

The conclusion is that the correct and generally meaningful way of encouraging SSEs (and labor intensity) is to adopt policies that will correct bi-

---

10. For a more detailed examination of the origins and consequences of the Indian industrial policy affecting the small-scale sector, see Mazumdar (1991) and Little, Mazumdar, and Page (1987).

ases against such units in all industries, not just in the few that appear at a certain level of disaggregation to be labor-intensive.

Turning to the second point of criticism, it is important that SSE support policies not discourage the growth of small enterprises into medium enterprises. Here the approach of the Indian package of polices has been the opposite of what is desired. Along with the reservation policy, there have been a number of fiscal subsidy programs and other forms of support that provide benefits to enterprises below a certain size. Thus there is a built-in disincentive for enterprises to grow beyond this size limit. Labor laws on wages, benefits, and job security are applied to units above the critical size. Enterprises graduating out of the protected small sector are thus faced with extra costs, even as they are denied the benefits of fiscal subsidies and other programs.

The effect has been a polarization of the industrial structure. The small-scale and large enterprises have increasingly occupied different niches of the market in the same industry. Even when industries are defined narrowly in terms of specific product lines, there is generally a great deal of difference in the quality of the product. Small enterprises with low wages and fewer mechanized techniques occupy the lower end of the spectrum, catering to the demand of low-income consumers, while larger mechanized firms serve the high-priced segment of the market. The classic example is the textile industry. Small units with nonautomatic, often reconditioned, looms ("power looms," as they are called in India) produce cheap cloth, while the large factories with automatic looms produce more durable cloth for the upper-class domestic and export markets. This type of polarization accentuates dualism and increases the productivity and wage gap between the small and large sectors.

A useful field study by Guhathakurta (1993) of the metal manufacturing industry can be used as an example to elucidate the major points involved. Guhathakurta found large, medium, and small units in this rapidly expanding industry in the course of his survey.

- The LSE sector clearly has a market leader that is generally perceived to have a superior product and enjoys a special status among consumers. Along with this leading producer, there are about half a dozen large-scale manufacturers that were issued "carry on business" licenses when the reservation for the small-scale went into effect. In spite of the limitation on their capacities, these large-scale units have been able to increase sales by increasing capacity utilization. Because of the strong demand for their products, which are widely perceived to be of higher quality, they have long waiting lists, and are able to charge high prices bolstered by expensive sales campaigns.

The existing reservation policy favors an oligopolistic market structure for these large producers, since no other competitor is able to join their ranks.

- At the other end of the spectrum are small-scale enterprises run by artisans and part-time entrepreneurs who switched from previous jobs in industry; many of them continue to hold on to their industrial jobs while managing their business on a part-time basis. These producers face an intensely competitive, albeit expanding, market: they turn out lower-quality products owing to the dismal conditions of production, and they are also dependent for their profits on middlemen who are often dealers from medium and large units. These small units often survive because of the various government subsidies they enjoy, the payment of very low wages, the use of child labor (dubbed "apprentices"), and their ability to match their labor use to the fluctuations of demand because of the high turnover rate. Not all the provisions of the SSE policy help them, however. Substantial costs are imposed by inspectors who have to be paid off regularly for looking the other way when production and labor conditions are below standard, and by their dependence on the open market for their raw materials, where prices are 20–30 percent higher than the regulated price.

- A few of the smaller units started in the 1960s and 1970s have managed to graduate to medium-scale status, largely aided by government subsidies and mandatory government purchases from the small-scale sector. They are reported to be growing slowly, targeting the lower end of the consumer or niche markets, such as hospital furniture. They are slow to commit major investments or undertake product improvement through more mechanized processes, because the required capital investment would push them over the investment ceiling.

In sum, the reservation policy has created a small segment of large units with high productivity, and a competitive low-productivity sector from whose ranks very few are able to grow sufficiently to challenge the market dominance of the large-scale sector. Secondly, huge wage differentials, reflecting the wide gap in productivity levels, separate the large and the small sectors, with the medium units paying widely varying rates.

Guhathakurta also analyzed trends in productivity, capital investment, and value added from a number of secondary sources. The registered large-scale sector (called the ASI sector, since it reports information to the Annual Survey of Industry) showed a high rate of growth of 3.1 percent per year of value added at constant prices, in spite of a 1.6 percent rate of decline in the number of units. There was a substantial growth rate of fixed capital per factory (5.7

percent), employment actually declined (at a rate of 1.4 percent), while wages per worker increased at a staggering rate of 9.8 percent per year. Evidently, economic forces, reacting to the reservation policies, have accentuated the polarization in the industry. A select group of workers has benefited from the large increase in productivity in the large-scale sector. The driving force behind this has been the striking growth in capital intensity, as the large units sought to beat the limits on expansion of capacity by upgrading equipment quality and productivity. The loss of jobs in the well-paid sector has, unfortunately, been traded off with jobs in the low-wage sector, with adverse effects on the distribution of labor earnings.

c. The Korean case

In the early stages of its industrialization, the Republic of Korea's economic policies favored LSEs. Prior to the 1980s, the Korean Government was consistently engaged in a process of targeting favored industries and individual firms with fiscal, tax, and tariff incentives. The large conglomerates, called *chaebol*, were the major beneficiaries of these targeted policies (Amsden, 1989). The result was a rapid growth of large enterprises in the Republic of Korea. The Korean experience contrasted dramatically with that of Taipei,China—the other East Asian "tiger" pursuing a policy of rapid manufacturing growth. As of the mid-1960s, Taipei,China had a larger share (35 percent) of manufacturing employment in LSEs with more than 500 workers than the Republic of Korea, with 26 per cent. But by 1976, when the Republic of Korea's LSE share peaked at 45 percent, the figure in Taipei,China was down to 26 percent (Levy, 1991).

Abe and Kawakami (1997: 398) provide evidence to show that differences in export experience had little to do with the different experiences of the Republic of Korea and Taipei,China. Their summary of the evidence is that "both economies represent successful cases of export-oriented industrialization, but the export drive in the Republic of Korea has been borne mainly by non-SMEs, while in Taipei,China it has been carried out by SMEs." In the Republic of Korea, the export-sales ratio of firms hovered in the region of 22–25 percent for most of the period 1977–1993. In Taipei,China, SMEs contributed a little over 50 percent of total sales in the 1970s, and increased that total to 70 percent or more in the first half of the 1980s, before it fell to 35–40 percent in the period 1988–92 (Abe and Kawakami, 1997: Table VI).[11]

While factor market differences, and particularly differences in transaction costs (as described in Levy [1991]), might have played some role in the

---

11. In Taipei,China, the definition of SMEs was based on capitalization, while in the Republic of Korea it was defined as those employing less than 300 workers. Abe and Kawakani (1997) found that as of 1990, 99.9 percent of the Taiwanese SMEs employed fewer than 300 workers. Thus the two definitions were comparable.

predominance of SMEs in Taipei,China and that of LSEs in the Republic of Korea, there can be no doubt that the differences in the bias of government policies were the major cause of the disparity. In contrast to Korean policies favoring large firms, Taipei,China was much less interventionist, at least at the level of targeting individual firms. The importance of this factor can be seen in the in the pattern of size distribution, which changed dramatically in the Republic of Korea after the late 1970s. The share of LSEs in Korean manufacturing peaked in 1976. Since then the Government has introduced a number of measures designed to counteract the previous tilt in favor of LSEs.

The tilt toward SMEs in government policies was not driven by the desire to promote employment or increase the employment elasticity of output growth in manufacturing. Quite the contrary: the labor market motivation seems to have been the shortage of labor and the rising wages affecting profitability in large firms. At the time in the mid-1970s when the policies to help SMEs were moved into high gear, the Republic of Korea was in the midst of the push toward heavy industry, unemployment levels had fallen to historically low figures, and the large-small wage differential was being squeezed (Mazumdar, 1994: 562). In recent years, the government measures have derived added strength from the high wage increases starting in the mid-1980s.

The change in the size distribution of manufacturing enterprises in the Republic of Korea since the LSE share peaked in 1976 is shown in Table 7.4. Comparable data for Taipei,China are presented in Table 7.5. Table 7.4 shows that in the Republic of Korea there was some decline in the LSEs' share by 1986, but then it declined in a major way in the next six or seven years. Small enterprises in the less-than-50-workers category more than doubled their share of employment (from 16 percent to 39 percent), while the largest enterprises in the 500-plus group shrank from 45 percent to 25.5 percent of total employment between 1976 and 1993. Taipei,China also reduced its share of employment in such firms, but the rate of reduction was faster in Korea. By 1993, the pattern of size distribution in the Republic of Korea was not all that different from that of Taipei,China.

This is a dramatic change in a country that had favored industrialization through the encouragement of large firms in its early industrial policies. It is also revealed in the data of Table 7.5 that this dramatic change in the distribution of employment by size group produced only modest change in relative labor productivity. The relative productivity of small firms, in particular, in the size groups of fewer than 100 workers, did fall in the decade 1976–1986, but the magnitude of decline is not spectacular, and seems to have stabilized by 1986.

As indicated in Section 2, the change in the size structure in favor of SMEs in the Republic of Korea could be expected to be associated with a reduction in the degree of inequality—and this is exactly what we find. Nugent (1989) notes that a reversal in the trend of income distribution toward increasing inequality

Table 7.4. Republic of Korea: Distribution of Employment in Manufacturing by Size-Groups and Relative Labor Productivity

Distribution of Employment (percent)				Relative Labor Productivity			
Size-groups	1976	1986	1993	Size-groups	1976	1986	1993
5–9	3.8	3.8	8.3	5–9	31	27	29
10–19	4.2	6.6	11.8	10–19	37	31	32
20–49	8.1	14.0	14.2	20–49	42	37	38
50–99	8.6	12.9	12.9	50–99	59	45	53
100–199	12.9	12.7	10.7	100–199	56	55	68
200–299	6.5	7.4	6.0	200–299	75	67	75
300–499	10.8	7.4	5.6	300–499	85	77	82
500 -plus	45.1	35.0	25.5	500 -plus	100	100	100

Source: Korea Statistical Yearbook (various years).

Table 7.5. Taipei, China: Distribution of Employment in Manufacturing by Size-Groups and Relative Labor Productivity

Percentage Distribution of Employment

Size-Groups	1966	1971	1976	1986	1991
1–9	12.8	9.4	10.2	10.4	14.1
10–49	21.2	17.0	17.7	24.0	29.6
50–99	8.7	9.2	11.1	13.5	12.8
100–499	22.5	28.2	30.4	28.1	21.3
500 -plus	34.1	36.1	30.6	24.1	22.2

Relative labor productivity (value added per worker)

Size-Groups	1971	1976	1986	1991
1–9	40	33	34	30
10–49	36	34	35	31
50–99	47	36	38	35
100–499	45	48	49	47
500-plus	100	100	100	100

Note: Blank cells = not available.

Source: Abe and Kawakami (1997: Table 1).

more or less coincided with the shift toward a larger role of SMEs in the size distribution of manufacturing enterprises. Fields and Yoo (2000) have presented data on wage inequality for the years 1971–1993 based on the occupational wage surveys of Korea. Their conclusion is that a trend toward a more equal distribution of wage earnings started to take place after 1976, and the data show successive Lorenz improvements for all the years presented between 1976 and 1993, i.e., each Lorenz curve lies closer to the 45-degree line than the preceding one (Fields and Yoo, 2000: Figure 2, Table 1). While Fields and Yoo consider a wide range of factors like the narrowing of educational, occupational, and gender differentials, the change in the size distribution of employment towards SMEs is surely a significant contributory factor. The authors show that the firm size wage differential is substantial and has probably widened over the period. But the larger proportion of employment in SMEs has reduced the degree of wage inequality emanating from this factor.

d. Factors affecting the change in the size distribution in Korean manufacturing

While the reversal of the government policies favoring LSEs was clearly an important part of the bundle of factors influencing the trend, it was not the only factor. It has already been mentioned that the changing labor market, marked by a growing labor scarcity and upward pressure on wages, influenced enterprises to look to the SME sector, where wages were at a lower level. Capital market segmentation had clearly worked to the advantage of LSEs, and the degree of bias in the financial system seems to have eased after the 1980s. It is relevant to point out, however, that government policies encouraging the tie-up of large-scale finance and the conglomerates were themselves an important cause of the capital market bias favoring large firms.

Nugent (1996) has attempted an econometric analysis of the relative importance of different factors that caused this V-shaped pattern: an increase in the share of employment in large enterprises until 1976 and then a decline in the next two decades. First, he considered and rejected the hypothesis that changes in the composition of industry might have produced this trend reversal. In fact, the pattern remains, even if one holds constant the composition of industry, either in its 1963 mix or its 1973 mix (Nugent, 1996: Table 2). Then, using an econometric model with a variety of explanatory factors, he proceeded to explain the increase in the share of LSEs, both in terms of employment and value added, in the period before 1976, and their decline after 1976. His explanatory variables focused on three broad types: (i) technological and organizational factors, e.g., economies of scale, capital intensity of production, and relative importance of advertising; (ii) financial variables, which include availability of medium-term finance for SMEs, interest rate differentials between large and small firms, etc.; and (iii) trade variables, e.g., relative importance of exports. (For a full list see Nugent [1996: Table 4]).

Nugent concluded that the financial variables, individually and collectively, were the most important in accounting for the divergent trends in the two periods. In particular, the government-mandated minimum credit allocation to SMEs by commercial banks, and the suppression of the curb market for informal finance (which was gradually reduced in intensity after 1973) were quantitatively important factors in the changing share of SMEs between the two periods. The technical-organizational factors, which have been stressed in the literature, contributed little to the observed trends. But the trade-related variables, particularly the declining share of exports and the reduced role of trading firms catering primarily to the large establishments, were also of importance. The latter observation does not imply, though, that SMEs were unimportant in exports. In fact, their share in commodity exports increased from 22.1 percent in 1982 to 42.1 percent in 1990 (Nugent, 1996: 1). Clearly, the fall in the traditionally high export share of large firms has worked in favor of SMEs.

The econometric methodology has not really been able to capture the full impact of government policies, although the financial variables found to be of dominant influence are part of the policy package. We now turn to a more detailed discussion of the elements of the bundle of government policies that was able to turn the size structure in Korean manufacturing around in a very short time.

e. Nature of government policies to support SMEs

The support mechanisms for the SMEs in the Republic of Korea are relatively recent, having been initiated in the 1970s and having gained strength only in the 1980s. But several international agencies have already identified the Republic of Korea as a leader in developing effective SME support programs (e.g., UNIDO [undated]). Four major points about the foundations of Korea's support policies deserve special emphasis.

First, the Korean policies were not directed at merely protecting the existence of small enterprises. They are much more concerned with developing SMEs.

Secondly, in keeping with the concern for dynamism in the growth of SMEs, attention was not focused exclusively on very small units. Along with neighboring Japan, the Republic of Korea defines the SME sector as enterprises employing less than 300 workers. This does not imply that only the larger units in the sector benefited from the program. According to the sample survey carried out by Kim and Nugent (1994), most SMEs began with fewer than 50 workers, but many had grown to more than 200 workers, an indication of the generally high level of success of the support policies.

Third, Korean policies discriminated among SMEs in directing the support schemes. The Government granted "special designation" status to SMEs that would receive priority in the allocation of various forms of support. The Republic of Korea had even established "SME sanctuaries" to reserve certain product lines for SMEs *à la* India, but unlike India, they were limited in number, carefully chosen, and lasted no more than three years. Kim and Nugent's survey showed that over three-quarters of the sample had been designated a "promising SME," 30 percent had been selected as part of a subcontracting network, and 13 percent had been favored in the import substitute sector (Kim and Nugent, 1994: Table II.7).

Fourth, Kim and Nugent (1994) have noted some important features in the administration of the Republic of Korea's support system. The agencies were controlled and audited by several oversight agents or "bureaucratic principals," and the authors emphasize that "Korea is unusual in that competence is about equal in importance to political connections" in the appointment of principals and their subordinate executives (Kim and Nugent, 1994). Most of the support agencies sampled in the study emphasized educational qualifications, experience, and competence in their hiring practices. The average salary level was 50 percent higher than the industry average. Finally, although the state support agencies had some advantage over private ones, such as the ability to offer services at below-market prices, there were very few restrictions on private sector participation in the supply of financial, technical, and marketing support, and the state agencies often had to compete with other private institutions and firms.

The support schemes themselves took several forms. Of these, financial assistance seems to be the most critical. State support came through three major avenues: (i) specialized financial institutions and funds catering to the SMEs; (ii) government-supported venture capital companies that finance technologically-based SMEs; and (iii) credit guarantee facilities. In addition, commercial banks (which were heavily controlled by the Government until the liberalization of 1993) were required to allocate a substantial percentage of their loans to SMEs. Another important source of financial support has been central bank discounting of SMEs' commercial bills and export finance. Government-led funds for SMEs increased their percentage of the net lending by commercial banks from 1–2 percent in the early 1980s to an average of over 10 percent in the second half of the 1980s (Kim and Nugent, 1994: table V.1). All the state financial facilities received a high approval rating from the SME units in Kim and Nugent's sample (a score of over 4 on a 5-point scale).

The next important form of public SME assistance was technological support. The Republic of Korea has an extensive network of agencies providing support in the form of training programs, information services, and joint research opportunities. The network of agencies is headed by the Industrial Advances Administration under the Ministry of Trade and Industry.

The third general area of the support system is marketing. The largest public sector marketing agency is the Korea Trade Promotion Corporation, which was originally founded to help in the export activities of large firms. But as these firms became more self-sufficient, the corporation focused its activities more on SMEs. More than half of the firms in the Kim and Nugent (1994) survey used some form of collective marketing services, more so in the early stages of their export growth. But as with technical services, these agencies received lower approval and usefulness ratings than the large number of private channels of support available to Korean SMEs.

6. Conclusions

This chapter has discussed the role of small and medium enterprises (SMEs) in manufacturing as a tool in the promotion of equitable growth, with particular reference to Asian economies. The development of off-farm employment, and that of household enterprises and microenterprises with very few hired workers, was outside the purview of this discussion. SMEs, as defined here, were viewed as an important feature of the industrializing process. Although the subsidization of LSEs as an aid in the rapid expansion of employment, as witnessed in the first phase of Korean industrialization, has some advocates, there are strong arguments against it based on the need to correct for factor price distortion (particularly in the capital market), and, more importantly, to ensure more equitable distribution of income. Section 3 of this chapter examined the details of these arguments.

It was emphasized, however, that the factors affecting the degree of inequality (as well as overall economic efficiency) were not just the distribution of employment by size, but also the productivity difference between different size-groups. Thus it is not enough to aim at simply increasing the share of employment in SMEs. Policies must also aim at reducing the economic distance between SMEs and LSEs in terms of the productivity (and wage) differentials between them.

Section 4 looked at the pattern of size distribution in manufacturing for a number of Asian countries in the light of the two critical variables mentioned. Three basic patterns of size distribution and productivity differentials were identified in the empirical study. The case of Hong Kong, China represented an extreme and "ideal" prototype from a welfare point of view, with a fairly even size distribution of employment and a relatively small productivity differential between SMEs and LSEs. But Hong Kong, China is an extreme economic example: a city-state that has been peculiarly free from state intervention in factor markets and industrial evolution. Taipei,China would be the closest among the other Asian economies to approximating the situation of Hong Kong, China.

The Republic of Korea presented a striking contrast to Taipei,China in having a distribution of establishments skewed to the large size-groups, at least until the mid-1970s, after which this trend started to reverse itself. Thailand, in its recent period of industrial growth, shared some of the characteristics of the pre-1976 Korean pattern.

The more typical pattern of size distribution in Asian economies was dualistic, with a bipolar distribution of firms. It was argued that this pattern emerged because of the coming of new technology and capital market institutions to a peasant economy characterized by surplus labor in agriculture. While the dualistic pattern was the direct result of segmentation in labor and capital markets, it was strengthened by the differentiation in technology and product markets. The dualistic system yielded the poorest result from a welfare point of view, given the wide difference in productivity between the small and large firms, and the phenomenon of the "missing middle," because of the limited upward mobility of small firms. Indonesia, and more emphatically, India, were examples of this pattern. In the Indian case this phenomenon has been exacerbated by perverse government policies.

The evaluation of government policies to promote SME growth was tackled in Section 5e, which showed the contrast between the policies of India and the Republic of Korea (after the latter sought to reverse its pro-LSE policies in the mid-1970s). The Indian policymakers depended heavily on a policy of protecting SMEs from competition with large-scale producers (even as the latter were protected from foreign competition), through a policy of reservation of a large and growing list of products. These were supplemented by fiscal and other measures, e.g., the administration of labor laws, which provided benefits to SMEs as long as they stayed below a designated size. This made the cost of graduation of small enterprises to a size-group above the line of protection very high. The net effect of this bundle of policies was to create a small segment of large units with high productivity and a competitive low productivity sector from whose ranks very few were able to grow sufficiently to challenge the market dominance of the LSEs. This polarization was also evident in the wide gap between wage levels, reflecting the huge difference in productivity levels between the large- and small-scale sectors, with the medium units paying widely varying rates.

The Korean case discussed next is strikingly different. Results of statistical analysis documented the shift in the size distribution in Korean manufacturing toward SMEs in the 1980s and 1990s and showed that the shift took place without increasing the productivity differential between SMEs and LSEs. The contents of the Korean package to promote SME development contrasted sharply with the Indian situation in terms of the conception of support policies. While the Indian policies were formulated with a rather indiscriminate objective of protecting some lines of production deemed a priori to be capable of being served by SMEs, the Korean policies were geared to encourage the more competitive SMEs to succeed, irrespective of the industry in which they worked. In keeping with this objective, the policies favored discriminatory support to units that showed the capacity to graduate to SME status.

As already emphasized, from a welfare point of view, a size distribution of the Hong Kong, China or Taipei,China type is much closer to the optimum than those found in the other Asian economies. In addition to this static welfare consideration, a productive and vertically mobile SME sector is desirable for the dynamic efficiency and competitiveness of the economy. The development of SMEs not only provides a seedbed for the creation of a body of flexible entrepreneurs, but also helps the development of an elastic supply of labor. This general goal is better served by the Korean model of protection than the Indian model, which seems to have perpetuated a rather extreme form of dualism in the industrial structure.

References

Abe, Makoto, and Momoko Kawakami. 1997. A Distributive Comparison of Enterprise Size in Korea and Taiwan. *Developing Economies* 35(4): 382–400.

Amsden, Alice. 1989. *Asia's Next Giant: South Korea and Late Industrialization*. New York: Oxford University Press.

Beng, Chew Soon. 1988. *Small Firms in Singapore*. Singapore: Oxford University Press.

Berry, Albert, and Dipak Mazumdar. 1991. Small-Scale Industry in the Asian-Pacific Region. *Asian Pacific Economic Literature* 5 (2, Sept.) 35–67.

Biggs, T., V. Ramachandran, and M. Shah. 1998. *Does Greater Competition Improve Firm Performance in Africa?* Regional Program for Enterprise Development, Discussion Papers No. 085. Washington, D.C.: World Bank.

Fields, Gary F., and Gyeongjoon Yoo. 2000. Falling Labor Income Inequality in Korea's Economic Growth: Patterns and Underlying Causes. *Review of Income and Wealth,* 46(2): 139–159.

Fong, Chan Onn. 1990. Small and Medium Enterprises in Malaysia: Economic Efficiency and Entrepreneurship. *Developing Economies* 28(2): 152–179.

Government of Hong Kong. Various years. *Annual Digest of Satistics*. Hong Kong: Census and Statistics Department.

Government of Japan. Various years. *Japan Statistical Yearbook*. Economic Research Institute Statistics Office, Prime Minister's Office. Tokyo.

Government of Korea. Various years. *Korea Satistical Yearbook*. Seoul: National Statistical Office.

Government of Philippines. Various years. *Yearbook of Satistics.* Manila: National Statistical Office.

Government of Thailand. Various years. *Annual Digest of Statistics.* Bangkok: Ministry of Labor.

Guhathakurta, Suubhrajit. 1993. Economic Independence Through Protection? Emerging Contradictions in India's Small-scale Sector Policies. *World Development* 21(12): 2039–2054.

Hill, Hal. 1983. Choice of Techniques in the Indonesian Weaving Industry. *Economic Development and Cultural Change* 31(2).

———. 1990. Indonesia's Industrial Transformation. Part 1. *Bulletin of Indonesian Economic Studies* 26(2).

Kim, Linsu, and Jeffrey B. Nugent. 1994. *The Republic of Korea's Small and Medium-Size Enterprises and their Support Systems.* Policy Research Working Paper No. 1404. Washington, D.C.: World Bank.

Levy, Brian. 1991. Transactions Costs, the Size of Firms and Industrial Policy. *Journal of Development Economics* 34.

Liedholm, Carl, and Donald Mead. (1992). *The Structure and Growth of Microenterprises in Southern and Eastern Africa: Evidence from Recent Surveys.* Ann Arbor: Department of Economics, Michigan State University.

Little, Ian, Dipak Mazumdar, and John Page. 1987. *Small Manufacturing Enterprises.* Washington, D.C.: Oxford University Press.

Mazumdar, Dipak. 1981. *The Urban Labor Market and Income Distribution: A Study of Peninsular Malaysia.* A World Bank Research Study. New York: Oxford University Press.

———. 1983. The Role of Small-scale Enterprises in the Indian Economy. Processed. Washington, D.C.: World Bank Development Research Department.

———. 1991. Import-substituting Industrialization and Protection of the Small-scale. *World Development* 19(9): 1197–1213.

———. 1994. Korea. Chapter 11. In Kanbur, Horton, and Dipak Mazumdar, *Labor Markets in Structural Adjustment.* Vol. 2. Washington, D.C.: EDI Economic Development Studies. World Bank.

———. 1997. *Structure, Growth and Productivity of the Small-scale Manufacturing sector in India: An Overview.* New Delhi: National Council of Applied Economic Research. Processed.

Mellor, John W. 1976. *The New Economics of Growth: A Strategy for India and the Developing World.* Ithaca, NY: Cornell University Press.

Nugent, Jeffrey B. 1989. *Variations in the Size Distribution of Korean Manufacturing Establishments Across Sectors and over Time.* Korea Development Institute Working Paper No. 8932. Seoul, Republic of Korea.

———. 1996. What Explains the Trend Reversal in the Size Distribution of Korean Manufacturing Establishments. *Journal of Development Economics* 48: 225–251.

Piore, Michael, and Charles Sabel. 1984. *The Second Industrial Divide.* New York: Basic Books.

Reynolds, Lloyd, and Peter Gregory. 1965. *Wages, Productivity and Industrialization in Puerto Rico.* Homewood, IL: Richard D. Irwin.

UNIDO (United Nations Industrial Development Organization). Undated. *SMEs in the Evolution of the Italian and Indian Industrial Systems.* Vienna.

PART III

New Developments and Issues in
Poverty Measurement

8. Poverty Lines: Eight Countries' Experiences and the Issue of Specificity and Consistency

Abuzar Asra and Vivian Santos-Francisco

1. Introduction

The poverty line is the starting point of poverty analysis. It serves as an objective standard by which the so-called "poor" are distinguished from the "nonpoor." In many cases, the poverty line is specified as the cost of satisfying the daily basic per capita food and nonfood needs.

Countries estimate poverty lines for a number of purposes, but primarily to monitor and compare poverty across time, regions, and population groups. Relating poverty trends with the corresponding policy regimes can give an indication of the effectiveness of certain policies in reducing poverty. Comparing poverty levels in different areas helps identify those needing more assistance. For targeting purposes, the poverty line often serves, along with other criteria, as a threshold for basic entitlements to various benefits provided by the government.

In the long history of poverty measurement, several issues have been raised. This chapter revives the discussion about two practical issues of poverty line estimation: specificity or relevance, and consistency or comparability. "Specificity or relevance" of a poverty line refers to the extent to which a poverty line reflects the specific characteristics of an area. "Consistency or comparability" concerns itself with the ability of derived poverty lines to indicate a comparable level of "welfare" across space and time. This issue has been examined by various researchers (Bidani and Ravallion, 1993; Wodon, 1997). Wiebe (1994: 2) says, "A poverty measure is said to be consistent if it identifies the same poverty status (poor or not poor) for two households with identical welfare levels." For problems arising due to inconsistent poverty lines, see Ravallion, 1998.

The chapter starts with a discussion of the general principles behind the issue of specificity or relevance and consistency or comparability. A summary of standard approaches in deriving (absolute) poverty lines, and a short description of eight countries' experiences (Bangladesh, People's Republic of China [PRC], India, Indonesia, Nepal, Philippines, Thailand, and Viet Nam) in deriving their poverty lines follows. The issue of specificity or relevance and consistency or comparability is then detailed, together with the countries' examples. An illustration of the need to pay attention to measurement is also given. The chapter concludes that the current practice shows that countries have developed their own poverty lines and measures taking into account their own view of poverty, regardless of the need for comparability across countries. The countries' estimates and internationally comparable estimates need not be contrasted, as they serve different purposes.

2. Specificity or Relevance versus Consistency or Comparability

a. Across space

Specificity or relevance of a poverty line (in a particular area at a given time) arises out of the need for the poverty line to constitute the existing norms or values of a society. The poverty line should therefore reflect the particular characteristics of the area under study, such as life pattern, culture, social condition, and norms. It follows that the poverty line of a certain area is independent of that being used in another. This view leads to the construction of "location-specific" poverty lines. Wodon (1997: 72–75) says, "A poverty profile will be deemed specific if its underlying poverty lines represent local or temporal perceptions as to what constitutes poverty." The Asian Development Bank (ADB) also acknowledges this aspect of specificity, as it says, "This yardstick (the poverty line) varies from country to country, depending on income and cultural values" (ADB, 1999: 3). In fact, the sociocultural specificity of poverty norms goes back to Adam Smith, who in 1776 said that

> By necessaries I understand, not only the commodities that are indispensably necessary for the support of life, but whatever the custom of the country renders it indecent for creditable people even of the lowest order, to be without... (quoted in Srinavasan, 2000: 15).

On the other hand, consistency or comparability proponents argue that to enable comparison across areas, the poverty lines for different areas should indicate the same standard of living (Ravallion and Bidani, 1994; Wodon, 1997). Some sort of "standardization" should then be undertaken to enable strict comparability. Money metric measures, like the poverty line, should therefore be adjusted for price differentials so they maintain a fixed real value to make valid spatial and even intertemporal comparisons of absolute poverty rates. In other words, to enable comparison, the poverty line should be fixed in terms of standard of living across the entire domain of the poverty comparison. This entails using, say, a poverty line in a rich region which may be considered "low" or "not relevant" per its "own standard" for the sake of making it comparable, because the domain of the comparison goes well beyond the borders of that region.

In constructing poverty lines for urban areas, for instance, the derived poverty line can reflect the life pattern, culture, social condition, and norms existing in urban areas. This poverty line may not reflect the same standard of living as the one developed for rural areas; thus comparability or consistency is lost. That is why Ravallion and Bidani (1994: 77) suggest that the measurement choice rests ultimately on the purpose of the poverty profile being constructed.

b. Across time

Similar to spatial specificity or relevance, intertemporal specificity or relevance of a poverty line refers to its ability to reflect the specific condition/ characteristics of a particular region/area at a given time. It has been argued that the derivation of the poverty lines across time should consider changes in the life pattern, culture, social conditions, and norms prevailing in different years. One well-known quotation from 1938 supports this view:

> A standard budget worked out in the 1880s, for example, would have no place for electric appliances, automobiles, spinach, radios, and many other things which found a place on the 1938 comfort model. The budget of 1950 will undoubtedly make the present one look as antiquated as the hobble skirts (cited in Kanbur and Squire, 1999).

Essentially, the proponents of specificity or relevance question whether the poverty line, or some components of it—for example, a food basket that was constructed 10 years ago—would still be relevant to the present situation, due to the changing social and economic environment. This is analogous to the fact that even the weights used for price index construction are updated after a certain period of time. Kanbur and Squire (1999) discuss the normal definition of poverty as "the state of one who lacks a usual or socially acceptable amount of money or material possessions." A "social" or "moral" element of poverty is contingent on time and place. As stated by Kanbur and Squire (1999: 2):

> As technology progresses and the general standard of living rises, three effects have an impact on poverty: new consumption items, changes in the way society is organized [that] may make it more expensive for the poor to accomplish a given goal, and general upgrading of social standards can make things more expensive for the poor.

However, by updating the basket to reflect the current years, the derived poverty lines are likely to lose their inter-temporal consistency or comparability. In sum, the question is whether it is necessary to update at a more or less regular interval the yardstick of the poverty line (e.g., by revising the consumption basket) to take into account changing conditions, consumption/life patterns, and perceptions of poverty. If yes, the next question is how frequently, and how about the comparability of the derived poverty lines over time?

The comparability or consistency of the poverty lines for different years usually requires that they should be kept fixed in terms of standard of living, and in practice only some sort of price (inflation) adjustment is made to update the poverty lines in the base years. This leads to the question of what price index should be used: a general price index that may either cover commodities that are not being consumed by the poor or include prices that are not paid by the poor, or a price index of the commodities consumed by the poor (with the actual prices paid by the poor)? It may be argued that the price index to be used should be the index reflecting the price changes in the consumption basket of the poor. India, for instance, uses the specific cost of living indexes for middle rural and urban populations to update the rural and urban poverty lines separately.

The need for comparability or consistency is in line with the World Bank's stand, as it says, "In measuring absolute poverty in one country, the poverty line should have the same value across all groups or regions, and over time" (World Bank, 1991: 1–2). Fields (1994: 91) says: "In particular, we should not do as some suggest and increase the poverty line by the rate of economic growth. To do this would cause us to lose the notion of poverty as a state of absolute economic deprivation."

Ideally, the two aspects should both be met in poverty line estimation exercises. To be acceptable, the estimated poverty line should reflect the existing conditions in the area or region or in a particular time for which the poverty line is derived, and at the same time it should enable us to compare poverty across regions or areas and across time.

Hence, in practice there is a trade-off between the two and some compromises should be made. The poverty lines being developed may not perfectly reflect existing norms and culture at a particular location and time, so long as they can be used for spatial and intertemporal comparisons.[1]

---

1. In addition, the methodology should be as simple as possible: easy to understand, practical, acceptable, and at the same time logically defensible.

3. Standard Approaches In Deriving (Absolute) Poverty Lines

This section draws heavily from Ravallion (1998). The technology for constructing a (absolute) poverty line is fairly established. The (total) poverty line is often defined for satisfying either calorie consumption or basic food and nonfood needs. To be meaningful and reliable, the poverty line should be explicitly fixed to a specific "welfare" level (fixed "real value") across time and space. By being fixed to a specific welfare level, the poverty line allows a meaningful comparison across time and space. This is because "such a poverty line guarantees that the poverty comparisons made are consistent in the sense that two individuals with the same level of welfare are treated the same way" (Ravallion, 1998: 5). Standard approaches for poverty line estimation could be generally classified as follows:

a. Direct calorie intake method

The direct calorie intake (DCI) method estimates poor households by counting those households with a per capita energy intake that is less than the standard per capita requirement of energy.[2] This method is probably the easiest to apply in estimating poverty lines, given the simplicity and transparency of the standard used. There are several arguments, however, against its continued use. While consistent in reflecting the same nutrient intake, the DCI method measures "undernourishment," and not poverty, which entails deprivation in all aspects of welfare including calorie intake. The DCI method also removes the poverty phenomenon from the income and expenditure nexus of households.

b. Food-energy intake method

The food-energy intake (FEI) method, which is an improvement over the DCI method, measures consumption or income poverty (a household's command over basic food and nonfood items). This is done by finding a monetary value of the poverty line where "basic needs" (in this case a predetermined food energy requirement/calorie intake) are met. Once this consumption or income level is located, it automatically provides the allowance for both food and nonfood consumption. This method avoids the need for price data to value the "basic needs" items.

---

2.   Bangladesh uses a national threshold of 2,122 calories per capita per day in accordance with Food and Agriculture Organization standards for a healthy diet in South Asian countries.

Poverty lines using the FEI method can be derived in two ways: first, by calculating the mean income or expenditure of households whose estimated caloric intake is approximately equal to the stipulated requirements; second, by using the empirical relationship between food energy intake and consumption expenditure.[3]

Poverty line estimates based on the FEI method (with a single calorie requirement) assure consistency in terms of calorie requirements, in the sense that on average, people at the poverty line will have the same food-energy intake. However, by relating the energy intake to consumption expenditure, the method implicitly regards consumption expenditure (of goods and services) as a better welfare indicator.

Ravallion (1998: 11–14) also argues that the FEI method will lead to inconsistent poverty lines in terms of command over basic consumption goods across space (and time). The relationship between food-energy intake and income or expenditure levels at which the required intake is met moves with factors other than cost of living differences. Instead of being consistent, estimated poverty lines using the FEI method are more like revealed preferences of households that are relative to the different market conditions where they operate. It is said that other than prices, such factors as tastes, activity level, availability of substitutes, and publicly provided goods all have an effect on estimating expenditure levels at which a particular level of need is met. For instance, it is possible that because in general, per capita expenditure in richer areas tends to be higher than per capita expenditure in poorer areas, the resulting poverty lines, even when using the same benchmark calorie requirement, will tend to be higher in the former. While the difference may be due to the fact that prices are generally higher in the more progressive areas, the preference for superior or more expensive sources of calories and other items of expenditure also pulls the poverty line upward. This argument is also valid for comparisons over time.

c. Cost of basic needs method

An often-proposed ideal method of deriving a poverty line is the cost-of-basic needs (CBN) method, which stipulates a basket of goods and services that are required by every person (or household) to attain an acceptable standard of living in the society. The CBN method usually sets the poverty line by computing the cost of a food basket enabling households to meet predetermined minimum daily nutritional requirements and adding an allowance for nonfood consumption. There are three steps to implementing this method: (i) defining a basket of food items meeting a defined required

---

3.   Either regressing intake against consumption and inverting the estimated function, or simply regressing consumption expenditure on nutritional intake, can do this.

daily nutrient (usually caloric) intake, (ii) estimating the cost of the food basket, and (iii) computing an allowance for nonfood items.

i. Food component

There are two ways of defining the basic food basket. One is to exogenously determine a commonly consumed and least-cost food basket, which yields a specific calorie requirement, and to evaluate this at current prices. A food basket derived in that manner, however, does not guarantee that people with food expenditure levels equal to the food poverty line are actually consuming the required minimum nutritional intake, because of diverse food preferences.

Another approach is to determine the food basket (satisfying a specific calorie requirement) based on what is actually consumed by "a reference group," as shown by household consumption surveys (in most cases, the food basket is determined with some understanding of local diet and food preferences). There are at least two choices of reference groups: the general population or an "a priori" definition of a poor group. Population belonging to the lower deciles of the distribution is often taken as the reference group. Selecting these households ensures that expensive, luxury food items are not represented in the basket. And when the composition of the basket is based on existing consumption patterns in the study area, the food items included in the basket clearly reflect the tastes, culture, and norms of the area. This method requires detailed consumption data, including the total food expenditure levels and the quantities of the food items actually consumed. There is also an issue of what prices are to be used: the average market prices or the prices actually paid by "the poor."

ii. Nonfood component

There are also a number of ways to estimate the nonfood allowance. A bundle of nonfood items is directly estimated using a nonfood consumption survey and then added to the food poverty line to yield the total poverty line. This method of deriving the nonfood component is analogous to the method of constructing food poverty lines in the CBN method. But even though this method is simple and straightforward, it unavoidably becomes arbitrary, because there is no absolute standard for minimum nonfood requirements similar to that for food, which has a standard calorie intake as a basis. Operationally, the definition of the items to be included in the basic nonfood basket is hard to formulate without being arbitrary and relative to the norms of society.

Another approach is the food-share method attributed to Orshansky (1963), where the poverty line is derived by dividing the minimum cost of a food basket by some estimate of the share of food in total expenditure. There are at least two variations of this approach: the average food share or the food share of the "poor" group. Ravallion (1998) suggests lower and upper poverty lines, based on, respectively, (i) the nonfood expenditure of poor families whose total income or expenditure is just enough to meet its subsistence needs, and (ii) the nonfood expenditure of families whose food expenditure equals the food poverty line.

Determining the food share may be done parametrically, by estimating a functional equation relating food share with total expenditure or food expenditure and other household characteristics that may be used to predict the food share at given expenditure levels. Another possibility is to use a simple nonparametric procedure, where the average nonfood expenditure is calculated from observed survey data for those households with total expenditure or food expenditure in small intervals around the food poverty line. In practice, some sort of spatial price indexes are used to derive the poverty lines for various regions, and inflation rates are applied to update the poverty lines over time. This way, the CBN method can maintain spatial and intertemporal consistency.

In sum, the DCI method, although consistent in terms of reflecting the same nutrient intake, measures undernutrition only. The FEI method, on the other hand, is also consistent insofar as it uses only a single calorie requirement. In addition, it measures consumption or income poverty by considering both food and nonfood needs. But by relating the energy intake, which can either vary or be fixed across areas, to expenditure or income levels, the FEI loses consistency, since the relationship between food-energy intake and income or expenditure moves with factors other than cost of living differences. It is possible that even when using the same benchmark calorie requirement, richer areas have higher poverty lines than poorer areas due to factors other than price differences. In this case, the CBN method is preferable, as it can assure consistency in terms of real expenditure, unlike the FEI method. However, in practice, the CBN method may entail tradeoffs between the "consistency" and "relevance" aspects of poverty measurement. To ensure comparability over time or across groups, consistent CBN-derived poverty lines (using a fixed consumption basket) normally account only for changes in the price level, but not changes in consumption behavior and taste preferences, thereby losing their practical relevance. Regarding the FEI and CBN methods, Wodon (1997: 95) says, "In practice, any method for computing poverty lines is likely to make room for both consistency and specificity."

4. Countries' Experiences: Official Methodologies

This section presents a summary of the procedures by which poverty lines are set in selected developing countries.

a. Bangladesh

The DCI and FEI methods have been used for computing official poverty estimates, while independent researchers use the CBN method more often. However, the FEI method was recently decided on as the official method, whereby the poverty lines are derived through regression of the functional equation relating per capita daily calorie intake to monthly per capita expenditures. For 1999, separate urban and rural poverty lines were computed (with differing per capita-per day calorie requirements: 2,112 for urban areas and 2,122 for rural areas) for 21 regions.

b. People's Republic of China

Estimating the prevalence and extent of poverty in the PRC follows several approaches that are dictated mostly by the need for criteria for allocating poverty alleviation funds. Efforts to assist the poor are concentrated historically in the resource-constrained and remote rural areas where the system for identifying the poor is fairly established. More recently, rising poverty in urban areas that became hosts for rural migrants, and a vast number rendered unemployed by enterprise reforms, has also called for specific interventions requiring the development of a poverty criterion to measure urban poverty.

In 1986, the setting of rural poverty standards became mandatory when the Central Government launched a large-scale poverty reduction program, which needed the identification of poor counties as beneficiaries. The official rural poverty cutoff was "arbitrarily" set at 150 Yuan annual net per capita income. Higher cutoffs of 200 Yuan and 300 Yuan were set for counties in old revolutionary base areas and counties with large minority populations. The number of poor counties was derived based on per capita net income data collected from the Rural Household Survey (RHS) conducted by the State Statistical Bureau in 1984.

Rural poverty calculations were improved in 1993 using RHSs conducted in 1984 and 1990. The food poverty line was set as the total cost of a fixed food basket meeting a 2,100 calories per capita-per day nutritional requirement, and reflected actual consumption patterns. The food basket was then valued, using the average market price for each food item paid by the poor for both own-produced and purchased items. The allowance for the consumption of basic nonfood items was estimated as the residual share after the food share was established at 60 percent of the food poverty line, based on the average share of expenditure on food spent by Chinese rural households.

This estimation procedure was improved in later years by using a regression model to estimate actual nonfood expenditures of households with expenditures just reaching the food poverty line. The rural poverty line is estimated every year when an RHS is available; the most recent poverty line estimate is derived taking account of average price changes.

Urban poverty estimates, on the other hand, are not based on a unique poverty criterion but on officially accepted definitions of what constitutes urban poverty in the PRC. With the deepening economic reforms, the layoff of state-owned enterprise workers has been an important factor leading to urban poverty. The urban poor have therefore been defined collectively as those who are laid off from work, those unemployed due to labor disability or old age, and individuals or households whose per capita income is below minimum living security standards. In the absence of official urban poverty estimates, past poverty assessments made by researchers are largely based on independent calculations made by agencies such as the World Bank and the United Nations Development Programme.

c. India

The Indian official poverty line was defined in 1979 via the FEI method, using calorie norms of 2,400 calories per capita per day for rural areas and 2,100 calories per capita per day for urban areas. By the use of the 1973–1974 National Sample Survey data, an inverse linear interpolation on average per capita monthly expenditure and the associated calorie consumption level was applied separately to rural and urban areas to define all-India urban and rural poverty lines. In short, the poverty line is defined as the per capita expenditure level at which the calorie norms were met on the basis of the all-India consumption basket for 1973–1974, equivalent to Rs49.1 and Rs56.6 per capita per month for rural and urban areas, respectively, at 1973–1974 prices.

Unlike Bangladesh, India applies the FEI method only to estimate all-India urban and rural poverty lines (in 1973–1974 prices), and uses the derived urban and rural spatial price indexes to calculate state-specific urban and rural poverty lines. To monitor poverty trends, the derived state-specific poverty lines in terms of national 1973–1974 prices are updated following the movements of the state-specific CPIs constructed for later years.

d. Indonesia

Indonesia started compiling poverty statistics in 1984, using the same poverty definition through the years, i.e., the inability to meet a predetermined consumption level for both food and nonfood needs. Continuing improvements have been made in computing the poverty benchmark, using primarily the National Household Socio-Economic Survey (SUSENAS) compiled every three years by the Central Agency of Statistics, or Badan Pusat Statistik (BPS). In 1993, the BPS started using additional surveys to derive nonfood items to be used for estimating the nonfood allowance.

The computation of the food poverty line assumes a minimum requirement for food that is equivalent to a per capita daily consumption of 2,100 calories. Before 1993, the food poverty line was derived through linear interpolation given total expenditure and corresponding calorie intake per expenditure group. This was done at the national level for urban and rural areas separately. In 1993, a basket of commonly consumed food items meeting the said calorie requirement was first defined for each province, using the consumption pattern of a reference poor group. Total monthly average per capita expenditure for each item in the basket then became the food poverty line. The commodity baskets were unique to each province (applied to both rural and urban areas within the same province) to take account of the wide variety in consumption patterns among Indonesian provinces. The same method is still used, with updated food baskets to allow for shifts in the consumption pattern.

The procedure for estimating the rupiah equivalent of the basic nonfood allowance has likewise gone through several changes. Recently, a basket of basic nonfood items, based on a special survey on nonfood consumption of a reference poor group, was determined. The basket differs from one province to another, as well as between urban and rural areas. The rupiah value of the selected nonfood commodities was estimated as the average monthly per capita expenditure for each of the selected nonfood items, and then added to the food poverty line to derive the total poverty line.

The modifications in Indonesia's poverty measurement methodology continue to reflect the view that the minimum standard for both food and nonfood needs should take into account local needs and market conditions.

e. Nepal

Official poverty measures in Nepal are based on three nationally representative surveys conducted over the past 20 years: the 1976–1977 Survey of Employment, Income Distribution and Consumption Patterns in Nepal; the 1984–1985 Multipurpose Household Budget Survey, and the 1995–1996 Nepal Living Standards Survey (NLSS).

The country's most recent poverty estimates follow the World Bank's initiative of estimating poverty lines following the CBN method. Specifying a reference food basket based on a nationally representative food consumption pattern meeting the daily 2,124 calories per capita requirement (assumed as similar to that of the Indian population) sets the poverty line. Average quantities of food items, with appropriate adjustments to yield the calorie requirement, consumed by Nepali households in the second to fifth deciles of the per capita consumption distribution, are used as the reference composition of the appropriate food basket. An assumed living standard is fixed by costing the basket on the basis of average prices prevailing in a reference area, which is the Rural Eastern and Central Terai region. The average nonfood expenditure of households whose food expenditure is just enough to meet their minimum nutrition requirements is computed nonparametrically from the NLSS data and is added to the food poverty line to get the (total) poverty line. To assess poverty across regions, a regional cost-of-living index for 1995–1996 using the Rural Eastern and Central Terai prices as a base is constructed. This index is used to express regions' expenditure distributions in terms of Rural Eastern and Central Terai prices, and uses the derived poverty line.

f. Philippines

The Philippines adopts the CBN method in deriving official measures of poverty. Food poverty lines equivalent to the cost of daily per capita food needs are derived by pricing low-cost and nutritionally adequate menus (for breakfast, lunch, supper and snack) for each urban and rural area of the 13 regions, using local average prices. The menus satisfy the nutrient requirements equivalent to 2,000 calories and 80 percent of the per capita Recommended Dietary Allowance for vitamins, minerals, and other nutrients, and reflect the food preferences of the regions.

The average food expenditure share of households within the 10 percentiles around the food poverty line is used to divide the food poverty line to provide allowance for nonfood needs. A national-level poverty line is estimated as the average for all regions disaggregated by urbanity, using population size as weights.

g. Thailand

Poverty measurement in Thailand recognizes that households differ with respect to calorie needs, and that there are price differences between regions and areas (urban and rural) over time.

In determining the food basket that meets the calorie requirement, nine different baskets—separate baskets for rural (sanitary districts and villages) and urban areas (municipal areas) in five regions are examined (Bangkok is urban only). Calories obtained per baht from various baskets in 1992 are estimated. The average calorie figure obtained per baht for a sanitary district basket is chosen as a basis for computing food poverty lines in 1992. Calories obtained per baht for other years are estimated, using price indexes that are comparable across five regions, two areas, and over time; and are computed for 1992 with Bangkok as a base. This information forms the basis for calculating the per-month cost that would meet the calorie requirements of a household, depending on its specific calorie requirement according to the age and sex composition of its household members and its location.

To arrive at the total poverty line, it is assumed that the poor in Bangkok spend 60 percent of their total expenditure on food. Given the food poverty line, the total poverty line is estimated by dividing the food poverty line by the ratio of food to total expenditure. Given the differences in relative prices of food and nonfood items of consumption, this ratio is estimated every year, separately for each area and region, using the spatial price indexes for food and nonfood items of consumption. A household is poor if its per capita income is less than the household-specific poverty line.

h. Viet Nam

The General Statistical Office has defined a (food) poverty benchmark for 1993 as the per capita income necessary to meet essential food needs equivalent to 2,100 calories per capita per day. The method used is the CBN method: choosing 12 food items containing approximately 2,100 calories of the middle group income quintile for two sectors. Similarly, the country's Ministry of Labor, Invalids and Social Affairs defined a (food) poverty line in 1997 based on the quantity of rice per month (expressed in money terms), depending on the region (there are three groups: below 15 kilograms (kg), below 20 kg, and below 25 kg).

A broader view of poverty, however, is adopted in *Viet Nam Development Report 2000* (Viet Nam, 2000), jointly published by the Government of Viet Nam, the aid provider community, and nongovernment organizations. Following the CBN method, the report maintains the nutritional requirement at 2,100 calories per capita per day, but takes per capita expenditure as the welfare indicator instead of income. Poverty estimates are derived using the Viet Nam Living Standard Surveys conducted in 1992–1993 and 1997–1998.

The food poverty line is derived for 1992–1993 using the food consumption of households in the third quintile to derive an appropriate food basket. The cost of this basket is computed based on national average prices for each item in terms of January 1993 prices. For 1997–1998, the cost of the 1992–1993 food basket is recalculated in terms of January 1998 prices. To obtain a total poverty line for 1992–1993, the average nonfood spending of the same reference group is computed and added to the food poverty line. This nonfood allowance is updated to 1998 prices using the inflation rate for nonfood items covering the period in a separate price survey. Spatial poverty rates are estimated using regional adjusted expenditures derived by employing the estimated regional cost of living index.

5. On Specificity and Consistency of Countries' Methodologies

The best example of how the "specificity or relevance" issue is given importance is shown by how poverty lines are constructed in Indonesia and the Philippines.

In Indonesia, different food and nonfood baskets are set for each province, and these are changed every time the poverty rates are estimated. The fact that its poverty lines have been constructed in a way that sacrifices comparability over time and across regions has recently been acknowledged, even in official publications (see Sutanto, Irawan, and Said [1999]; BPS [1999]). By choice, the poverty lines were derived to account for "the dynamic of the society and living standard," and "the poverty line measured by the official method moves with time, the change in tastes, and in the general standard of living" (Sutanto Irawan and Said, 1999: 15). Sutanto (1999: 2) states, for instance, that unlike the previous measurement of poverty in Indonesia, "expenditure for schooling is revised to account not only [for] expenditure for primary school but also for junior high school as it is now become compulsory." Recognizing that what constitutes basic needs or even poverty may change over time, the BPS itself states that the trend in Indonesia's poverty should be analyzed carefully and take this fact into consideration. In sum, Indonesia adopts a "dynamic" view of poverty, as clearly stated:

> The poverty line or standard being used to measure poverty is dynamic in nature. This standard is revised upward every three years to reflect the change in the consumption pattern of [the] low-income class which is still below the normative standard' (BPS, 1999: 1).

The consistency of Indonesia's poverty lines has been questioned. Bidani and Ravallion (1992, 1993), Asra and Virola (1992), Booth (1993), and Asra (1999) argue that the use of a cost-of-calorie method (a variant of the food energy method) used for deriving the poverty lines until 1993 generated noncomparable urban and rural poverty lines. Even after the CBN method was adopted, the ratios of urban to rural poverty lines were still higher than the perceived urban-rural price differential. For instance, the estimated urban-rural food price differential during 1987–1996, based on SUSENAS results, was only 13–16 percent, compared to 28–52 percent as implied by the official food poverty lines (Asra, 1999). Suryahadi et al. (1999), using the iterative method for setting the reference group, found that during 1996 and 1999 the derived urban poverty line was only 12 percent and 9 percent higher than the rural poverty line. The ratios based on the official poverty lines were 39 percent and 30 percent.

In the Philippines, to reflect the existing consumption pattern, nutritionally adequate food menus for breakfast, lunch, supper, and snack for an individual for urban and rural areas of each region were derived based on the Recommended Dietary Allowance for the average healthy Filipino (see Section 3 above). There are 27 one-day sample menus corresponding to 13 regions (urban and rural areas) and the National Capital Region. These menus were developed to closely represent regional differences in, among others, consumer preferences, cultural patterns, climate, and urbanization. The consistency aspect of the Philippines' poverty lines has been questioned by Balisacan (1999) and Kakwani (2000). They argue that official poverty estimates yield a poverty picture that is relative to the living standards of the regions. In Balisacan's words: "By construction, the official approach tends to yield poverty lines that are not consistent, that is, the standard of living implied by the poverty lines varies for each of the regions as well as over time" (Balisacan, 1999: 6). The regional poverty line conforms only to a common nutritional requirement and cross-comparison is valid only in terms of implied food energy intake. Inconsistency results when translating this nutritional requirement to low-cost typical menus, since the process is largely informed by regional living standards. The adjustment of food thresholds to poverty thresholds compounds the problem.

In 1992, the National Statistics Coordination Board of the Philippines approved a new methodology for poverty assessment. One of the differences between the old and new methodologies is the components of the nonfood requirement: the new methodology does not make provision for expenses on alcoholic beverages, tobacco, recreation, durable furniture and equipment, miscellaneous, and other expenditures. Obviously the estimates of poverty incidence based on the new methodology for the three years 1985, 1988, and 1991 are lower than those based on the old methodology.

India's case provides an example of an explicit recognition for the need for comparable poverty lines across states. State-specific rural consumer price indexes (CPIs), derived from the CPI for agricultural laborers for food, the CPI for the whole population for nonfood items, and the rural consumption pattern of people around the poverty line at the national level in 1973–1974, are used to derive state-specific poverty lines for rural areas. State-specific urban price indexes are also constructed to derive state-specific urban poverty lines.

The use of price indexes to derive state-specific poverty lines in the base year, and of state-specific inflation rates to update the base-year poverty lines, ensures comparability across states as well as over time. However, it is also recognized that by keeping the same consumption meeting the calorie norm, the adopted method of updating the poverty line considers only price changes with reference to the base year consumption basket and does not take into account shifting consumption patterns. In terms of "relevance," the implicit consumption basket of the derived poverty lines may already be outdated, considering that the base year is already more than 20 years ago.

Bangladesh's poverty lines, derived using the DCI method, are consistent in terms of calorie intake, but the welfare indicator used is "undernutrition," which may not be widely accepted as a measure of poverty. The FEI method, on the other hand, considers "relevance" (or "location" specificity) as an important aspect, as it captures regional dietary preferences and prices by estimating calorie cost functions for 21 regions (separately for urban and rural areas) using region-specific consumption data. However, this may result in inconsistent regional poverty lines in terms of command over basic consumption goods (Ravallion, 1998: 11–14). Appendix Table 8.A1 provides the ratios of urban to rural poverty lines of 21 regions for 1999. The ratios range from 1.20 in Dinajpur (indicating that the urban poverty line is 20 percent higher than the rural) to 1.95 in Kushtia. In 17 regions, the ratio is at least 1.30, i.e., the urban poverty line is 30 percent higher than the rural. These considerably "higher" ratios may support the view that the derived poverty lines are not comparable across (urban-rural) areas.

Poverty line estimates in the PRC are far from being consistent yardsticks (across space). However, in this case, the efficacy of poverty statistics should be judged by how these are able to serve the purpose for which they are designed, which is for targeting beneficiaries of the country's social relief program. In this case, the main consideration has been the availability of fiscal resources rather than gauging the extent of and meeting basic needs deprivation, which requires that a uniform basic needs standard be adopted nationwide. As the definitions of rural and urban poverty are not all comparable, it could be concluded that the issue of consistency across space has not been paid sufficient attention. Recently rural poverty lines have been made comparable over time.

Recent poverty lines in Viet Nam and Nepal are estimated more or less by the same version of the CBN method (with a fixed food basket), using the results of their living standard surveys. To ensure spatial consistency of estimates, poverty rates in Viet Nam are obtained by comparing the food and total poverty lines (valued at national average prices) with the per capita expenditure of households adjusted for regional price differences relative to the national average. For each household, nominal expenditures are expressed in January 1993 and January 1998 prices, using the cost-of-living index. Spatial and temporal poverty comparison is therefore based on consistent poverty lines, accounting only for price inflation over time and cost-of-living differences across areas, while maintaining the same food and nonfood standards. Similarly, Nepal constructed a regional cost-of-living index for 1995–1996 using the Rural Eastern and Central Terai prices as a base and used this to express nominal per capita expenditure in terms of the base price. This price for adjusted per capita consumption is then used to assess poverty across regions.

However, using a common food basket for the whole country could be considered inadequate, because cultural consumption patterns of households may vary across areas or across time. Thus from the "relevance" aspect, the use of a fixed and common food basket may not reflect the existing consumption pattern of some regions (see Wodon [1997] for other issues regarding the use of a fixed basket). Kakwani (n.d.: 6) says, "It is obvious that the food basket must take into account the consumption pattern of the population living in different regions and areas."

6. Why is Attention to Measurement Important?

In most cases, policy is derived based on the poverty figures, which in turn are dependent upon the methodology used. It is important therefore, that policymakers should understand how poverty estimates are made. Alternative sets of poverty estimates may lead to different policy prescriptions. Below are two examples.

a. Indonesia

Official poverty incidence estimates, which are location-specific, for the years 1987, 1990, and 1993 show that urban poverty was higher than rural poverty, indicating the need for diverting more attention and resources to urban areas. Ravallion (1992), Booth (1993), and Asra and Virola (1992) questioned this finding. The adjustment for cost of living differences, which is much lower than the implicit price differentials shown by the official figures, is argued to have changed the focus of poverty-oriented actions (Ravallion, 1992).

In addition, using a derived "consistent" poverty line, the decomposition analysis indicates that, while it is not the case based on the official poverty lines, rural-urban migration or population shifts were significantly associated with poverty alleviation (Ravallion and Huppi, 1991; Asra, 1999). Thus policy decisions, in this case on migration, will be made differently, depending on which set of poverty measures is accepted.

The implications for regional targeting of different poverty profiles based on alternative (more consistent) poverty lines has been emphasized by Bidani and Ravallion (1992). Recently, Asra and Santos-Francisco (2000) show another consistent set of provincial poverty estimates for 1993 (based on the spatial purchasing power parity indices developed by the BPS, following the approach used by the United Nations International Comparison Project/Gearry-Khamis method; see BPS [1996]). The figures provide a different ordering of provincial priorities for poverty alleviation (see Appendix Table 8.A2). The correlation of the ranking is only 0.24. Suryahadi et al. (1999) produce consistent regional poverty estimates for 1996, leading to a different ranking from that of the official method (although the Spearman rank correlation between the two rankings is reasonably high, 0.62).

The choice of poverty measures to adopt will also affect provincial resource allocation. In fact,

> Indonesia's new government has decreed that allocation of central government funds to provincial governments will reflect poverty incidence at the provincial level, with poorer provinces receiving greater allocations (Warr, 2000, 2).

Thus, whatever the view adopted by the Government, the implications of using different poverty estimates should be clearly understood.

Finally, in its most recent and more complete publication of poverty estimates, the BPS shows the effect of the revised basket on the estimates (see Appendix Table 8.A3). It shows the extent of the effects of revision on the poverty estimates and their trend. Instead of 24.2 million poor in 1999, the revised basket leads to an estimate of 37.5 million poor for the same year—a difference of around 13 million. While the revised basket approach shows that there is a significant rise in the number of the poor, from 22.5 million to 37.5 million, the original basket approach indicates a slight increase of the poor, from 22.5 million to 24.2 million. Again, whatever figures are adopted would lead to a different judgment.

b. Philippines

Balisacan (1999) suggested that food poverty lines in richer areas will tend to be higher because these areas would prefer better quality food items that are naturally more expensive sources of calories. Thus, a person's poverty would depend on his/her location and the prevailing living standard in the area, rather than his command over basic consumption needs wherever he/she happens to live. The spatially consistent poverty estimates for 1994 given by Asra and Santos-Francisco (2000) and by Balisacan (1999) lead to different regional poverty rankings from the ones based on the official estimates (Appendix Table 8.A4). The rank correlation of both estimates with the official ranking is the same, 0.59, implying that there is substantial reranking of provinces, while the rank correlation between the two estimates is high, 0.78.

In sum, the measurement aspect of poverty analysis, in particular the issue of specificity and consistency, cannot be neglected, as it will surely impact on policy decisions. Kanbur and Squire (1999) state, for instance, that

The importance of precise measures of poverty increases when we turn to the design of specific, poverty-reducing actions, because equal treatment of equals is one of the fundamental principles of public policy.

7. Conclusion

The experiences of some countries reviewed in this chapter show that although they all use more or less similar types of household survey data, there are various approaches being applied to construct their poverty lines. With respect to the issue of specificity and consistency, Indonesia and the Philippines (although acknowledging the importance of consistency/comparability) pay more attention to specificity. On the other hand, Viet Nam, India, and Thailand explicitly take more consideration of the consistency or comparability aspect (they may not regard specificity/relevance as one consideration).

In addition to the fact that poverty is multidimensional, as each country has its unique characteristics and specific political, economic, social, and cultural conditions, the poverty measurement methodology that is adopted eventually depends on each country's considerations. The important thing is for the policymakers in each country to be aware of the methodological underpinnings behind the poverty figures being used in the development planning process and their implications.

From the countries' perspective, it is desirable for each to develop its own poverty measurement methodology, taking into account the specific characteristics of the country and of its various regions. However, whenever possible, the consistency principle should be followed to enable spatial and over-time comparisons within a country. With regard to comparability across countries, while the international community needs to have internationally comparable poverty estimates for its own purposes, these could be derived regardless of whether these are the same or different from the countries' figures.

This compromise will serve the need of both the country and the international community. Countries will use their own estimates in making domestic policy decisions, while the internationally comparable estimates will serve the purposes of the international community. Fields (1994: 92), after discussing internationally comparable poverty estimates and countries' estimates, concludes that "as a practical matter in such cases, the national poverty lines have to be respected." And this is what has been happening.[4]

---

4.   The World Bank's regional poverty estimates using $1 and $2 at purchasing power parity per capita, which are theoretically the most consistent or comparable poverty lines cross countries, have been widely used for international comparisons. However, countries have developed their own poverty estimates using the poverty lines that they find more appropriate to their countries' conditions. The two sets of estimates need not be contrasted, as they are derived for different purposes.

Appendix

Table 8.A1. Ratio of Urban to Rural Poverty Lines, Bangladesh

Countries	Year	Poverty Lines (in National Currency Units)		Ratio
		Urban	Rural	
Bangladesh	1999			
Dhaka		956.5	704.4	1.36
Mymensingh		863.3	486.9	1.77
Jamalpur		709.2	501.3	1.41
Kishoregonj		857.0	527.6	1.62
Tangail		800.8	633.0	1.27
Faridpur		829.4	584.5	1.42
Chittagong		878.5	623.9	1.41
Chittagong H.T.		758.5	584.9	1.30
Comilla		1045.3	615.7	1.70
Noakhali		833.7	733.8	1.14
Sylhet		854.7	607.1	1.41
Rajshahi		625.0	496.4	1.26
Rangpur		636.5	477.0	1.33
Dinajpur		608.9	507.5	1.20
Bogra		817.3	520.1	1.57
Pabna		759.5	544.7	1.39
Khulna		716.8	540.6	1.33
Jessore		750.0	571.0	1.31
Kushtia		1016.9	521.5	1.95
Barisal		831.9	596.7	1.39
Patuakhali		783.0	579.1	1.35

Source: Ahmed (2000).

Table 8.A2. Provincial Rankings Based on Headcount Index, Indonesia, 1993

Provinces	Official		PPP-adjusted	
	Incidence [a]	Ranking [b]	Incidence [b]	Ranking [b]
Aceh	13.5	15	47.9	10
North Sumatera	12.3	11	57.8	20
West Sumatera	13.5	16	35.2	6
Riau	11.2	6	15.4	2
Jambi	13.4	14	41.2	8
South Sumatera	14.9	8	56.5	19
Bengkulu	13.1	12	60.4	22
Lampung	11.7	7	68.0	24
Jakarta	5.6	1	6.5	1
West Java	12.2	10	62.4	23
Central Java	15.8	19	68.5	25
Yogyakarta	11.8	8	40.7	7
East Java	13.2	13	54.6	16
Bali	9.5	3	24.6	3
West Nusa Tenggara	19.5	21	53.9	14
East Nusa Tenggara	21.8	23	59.0	21
East Timor	36.2	27	69.5	26
West Kalimantan	25.0	26	56.0	18
Central Kalimantan	20.8	22	51.7	12
South Kalimantan	18.6	20	30.2	4
East Kalimantan	13.8	17	32.0	5
North Sulawesi	11.8	9	53.6	13
Central Sulawesi	10.5	4	80.1	27
South Sulawesi	9.0	2	41.6	9
Southeast Sulawesi	10.8	5	55.8	17
Maluku	23.9	24	54.0	15
Irian Jaya	24.2	25	50.0	11
Correlation coefficient				0.24

Note: The ranking is from lowest (=1) to highest (=27) poverty incidence.

Source: [a] Official poverty incidence estimates are BPS (1998); [b] Author's estimates.

Table 8.A3. Provincial Rankings Based on Headcount Index, Indonesia, 1996–1998

Year	1996 basket		Revised basket	
	Percent poor	No. of poor (million)	Percent poor	No. of poor (million)
1996	11.34	22.5	11.34	22.5
1998	17.86	36.5	24.23	49.5
1999	11.72	24.2	18.17	37.5

Note: Unlike the 1996 figures, the 1998 and 1999 figures are based on a SUSENAS-type survey with only 10,000 sampled households.

Source: BPS (n.d.), Table 5.1

Table 8.A4. Regional Rankings Based on Headcount Index, Philippines, 1994

Region	Official		Authors' Estimates		Balisacan's Estimates	
	Incidence	Rank	Incidence	Rank	Incidence	Rank
National Capital Region	10.5	1	0.7	1	0.7	1
Cordillera Autonomous Region	56.4	12	33.6	5	28.5	9
Ilocos Region	53.6	10	34.3	6	25.8	6
Cagayan Valley	42.1	5	32.5	4	25.3	5
Central Luzon	29.2	2	17.9	2	13.6	2
Southern Luzon	34.9	3	20.2	3	16.8	3
Bicol region	60.8	14	49.7	11	38.5	13
Western Visayas	49.9	8	37.4	8	26.9	8
Central Visayas	37.5	4	52.1	13	31.4	10
Eastern Visayas	44.8	6	55.1	14	41.3	14
Western Mindanao	50.6	9	49.1	9	37.9	12
Northern Mindanao	54.1	11	50.3	12	41.5	15
Southern Mindanao	45.6	7	36.0	7	24.6	4
Central Mindanao	58.7	13	49.1	10	36.2	11
Autonomous Region of Muslim Mindanao	65.3	15	57.1	15	26.8	7
Correlation to official rankings	1.00		0.59		0.59	
Correlation to Balisacan's estimates			0.78		1.00	

Note: The ranking is from lowest to the highest: 1 = the lowest poverty incidence and 15 = the highest poverty incidence.

Source: National Statistical Coordination Board (1999); Authors' estimates using 1994 Family Income and Expenditure Survey; Balisacan et al. (1999).

References

ADB (Asian Development Bank). 1999. *Fighting Poverty in Asia and the Pacific: The Poverty Reduction Strategy*. Manila.

Ahmed, F. 2000. Poverty Incidence in Bangladesh'99: Regional and National Estimates. Regional Seminar on Poverty Monitoring Survey, Dhaka, 21 May.

Asra, A. 1999. Urban-Rural Differences in Costs of Living and Their Impact on Poverty Measures. *Bulletin of Indonesian Economic Studies*, 35(3): 51–69.

————, and R. Virola. 1992. *Comparative Study of Poverty Assessment: Indonesia and the Philippines*. Report to the Asian Development Bank. Manila.

————, and V. Santos-Francisco. 2000. *Philippines and Indonesia: Issues on Regional Poverty*. On-going research.

BPS (Badan Pusat Statistik). 1996. *Human Development Index (HDI) of Indonesia: Provincial Comparison, 1990–1993*. Jakarta.

————. 1998. *Statistical Yearbook*. Jakarta.

————. 1999. *Bahan Laporan Untuk Rapat Koordinasi Bidang Kesra*. October.

————. n.d. *Penpukuan Penjukuran Tingkat Kemiskinandi Indonesia, 1976–1999*. Metode BPS. Jakarta: Seri Publikasi SUSENAS Mini 1999. Buku 1.

Balisacan, A. 1999. What Do We Really Know—or Don't Know—About Economic Inequality and Poverty in the Philippines. In *Causes of Poverty*, edited by A. Balisacan and S. Fujisaki. Diliman: University of the Philippines.

Bidani, B. 1992. *Poverty in Indonesia 1990: A Consistent Regional Profile and its Implication for Regional Targeting*. Washington, D.C.: World Bank.

————, and M. Ravallion. 1993. A Regional Poverty Profile for Indonesia. *Bulletin of Indonesian Economic Studies* 29 (3): 37–68.

Booth, A. 1993. Counting the Poor in Indonesia. *Bulletin of Indonesian Economic Studies* 29 (1, April): 53–58.

Fields, G. 1994. Poverty and Income Distribution: Data for measuring poverty and inequality changes in the developing countries. *Journal of Development Economics* 44: 87–102.

Government-Donor-NGO Working Group. 1999. *Attacking Poverty: Viet Nam Development Report 2000*. Joint Report for the Consultative Meeting for Viet Nam, 14–15 December.

Kakwani, N. 2000. Poverty, Inequality and Well-being in the Philippines with Focus on Mindanao. Unpublished report to Asian Development Bank.

————. n.d. Poverty in Thailand. Sydney School of Economics, University of New South Wales. Unpublished.

Kanbur, R., and Lyn Squire. 1999. *The Evolution of Thinking About Poverty: Exploring the Interaction*. Paper presented at the Symposium on the Future of Development Economics in Perspective, Dubronovik. May.

Orshansky, M. 1963. Children of the Poor. *Social Security Bulletin* 26: 3–29.

Ravallion, M. 1992. *Poverty Comparisons: A Guide to Concepts and Methods*. Living Standards Measurement Study. Working Paper No. 88. Washington, D.C.: World Bank.

————. 1998. *Poverty Lines in Theory and Practice*. Living Standards Measurement Study Working Paper No. 133. Washington, D.C.: World Bank.

————, and B. Bidani. 1994. How Robust is a Poverty Profile? *World Bank Economic Review* 8: 75–102.

————, and M. Huppi. 1991. Measuring Changes in Poverty: A Methodological Case Study of Indonesia During an Adjustment Period. *World Bank Economic Review* 5(1): 57–82.

Smith, A. 1937. *An Inquiry into the Nature and Causes of the Wealth of Nations.* Edited (with an Introduction, Notes, Marginal Summary and an Enlarged Index) by Edwin Cannan. New York: The Modern Library.

Srinivasan, T. N. 2000. *Growth and Poverty Alleviation: Lessons From Development Experience.* High Level Symposium on Alternative Development Paradigms and Poverty Reduction. Tokyo: Asian Development Bank Institute 8 December.

Suryahadi, A. et al. 1999. *Poverty Measurement in Indonesia: Comparison Over Time (1996–1999) and Across Regions.* Paper presented at the International Conference on Methodologies of Poverty Calculations in Indonesia Jakarta, 30 November.

Sutanto, A. 1999. *Poverty in Indonesia: Some Findings and Interpretation.* Paper presented at the round table discussion on the Number of Indonesian Poor People, BAPPENAS (National Development Planning Agency). Jakarta. 21 July.

————, P. B. Irawan, and A. Said. 1999. *Poverty Measurement: Problems and Development.* Paper presented at the International Conference on Methodologies of Poverty Calculation in Indonesia, Jakarta. 30 November.

Warr, P. G. 2000. Targeting Poverty. *Asian-Pacific Economic Literature* 14 (1 May).

Wiebe, F. S. 1994. *Measuring Poverty in Indonesia: Identifying the Under Heterogenous Conditions.* A dissertation submitted to Stanford University. USA.

Wodon, Q. T. 1997. Food Energy Intake and Cost of Basic Needs: Measuring Poverty in Bangladesh. *The Journal of Development Studies* 34: 66–101.

World Bank. 1991. *Indonesia: Stability, Growth and Equity in Repelita VI.* Report No. 12857-IND. Washington, D.C.

9. Poverty Comparison in the Philippines: Is What We Know About the Poor Robust?

Arsenio M. Balisacan

1. Introduction

Efficient targeting of resources to achieve poverty reduction objectives requires information about the poor and their circumstances—who they are, where they live, what social and economic conditions they face, how they respond to programs and projects intended for them, etc. If it is known, for example, that poverty is concentrated in a few geographic pockets of a country, it may be possible to reduce the cost of poverty reduction by focusing poverty alleviation efforts on these areas. Put differently, if the poverty profile is known, it should be possible to exploit this information to maximize the benefits—measured in terms of, say, reduction in national poverty—of poverty budgets through improved design and implementation.

Construction of poverty profiles requires not only good data but also analytically sound procedures for measuring poverty. Perhaps the most controversial aspect of poverty measurement is the construction of the poverty standard that is used to identify the poor in a given population. Often, ambiguity in policy objectives adds to the confusion in poverty measurement. For example, while absolute poverty reduction is the central thrust of development policy in the Philippines, the official approach to constructing poverty lines for spatial and intertemporal comparison falls short of fully capturing this concern (Balisacan, 2001). Poverty profiles based on these lines may thus fail to inform policy and program choices vis-à-vis reduction of absolute poverty. As shown in this chapter, poverty profiles are quite sensitive to poverty norms employed in poverty measurement.

This chapter has two main objectives. The first is to reexamine the official approach to measuring poverty in light of measurement theory and practice in household welfare comparison, especially in relation to the construction of poverty norms for poverty comparison. The second is to reconstruct poverty profiles in the Philippines, both spatial and intertemporal, in an effort to improve understanding of recent development experience vis-à-vis economic growth and poverty reduction. The reconstruction involves developing an alternative approach to poverty measurement, one that addresses the inconsistency in official poverty comparison and, hence, the inadequacy of the current approach for monitoring performance in the reduction of absolute poverty.

The rest of the chapter is organized as follows: Section 2 discusses measurement issues relevant to poverty comparison in the Philippines. Section 3 then describes certain poverty profiles to highlight the difference that the measurement approach makes on what is known about poverty in the Philippines, especially in relation to economic growth and poverty. Finally, Section 4 gives concluding remarks.

2. Poverty Measurement

Long-held measurement practices for poverty measurement partly reflect what we know—or think we know—about inequality and poverty profiles in the Philippines. Some of these practices have been neither well justified nor informed by recent developments in poverty measurement. Yet these are the profiles that often inform policy discussions, including proposals for engendering "growth with equity," fostering "adjustment with a human face," and "empowering the poor." This section briefly discusses two measurement issues: (i) the choice of a broad indicator of economic well-being and (ii) construction of poverty standards, which have important implications for inequality and poverty comparisons, as well as for policy design, in the Philippines.[1]

a. Choosing a welfare indicator

Identification of the poor in the Philippines requires the use of a broad indicator of a household's standard of living. In determining the magnitude of poverty and inequality, the Government uses current household incomes generated from nationally representative household surveys. However, as is well known, income may overestimate or underestimate living standards. If a person can borrow or use his savings, his level of living is not constrained by current income. Moreover, a household that can share in the income of others may have a higher welfare level than its current income would permit.[2]

Using standard arguments in microeconomic theory, it can be claimed that since the welfare level is determined by "life-cycle" or "permanent" in-

---

1. Extensive discussions of the conceptual and measurement issues are available elsewhere (see, in particular, Ravallion [1994, 1998], Deaton [1997], and Foster and Sen [1997]). For a discussion of these and related issues in the Philippine context, see Balisacan (1999 and 2001).
2. Cox and Jimenez (1995) found evidence of substantial interhousehold income transfers in the Philippines, typically from relatively rich households to poor households.

come, and since current consumption is a good approximation of this income, current consumption can be better justified as a measure of current welfare. This does not, of course, suggest that consumption does not vary over time. It does, and the change over the life cycle is sometimes large. This is especially true among the poor who do not have access to capital markets (or to interhousehold transfers) and whose current consumption is constrained by current instead of life-cycle income. But even in this case, current consumption is as good an approximation of life-cycle income as current income.

An even stronger case for preferring consumption over income as a broad indicator of welfare rests on practicality and data. Acquiring accurate information proves to be more difficult for income than for consumption (Deaton, 2001; Ravallion and Chen, 1997). For example, multiple visits and recall are required in obtaining information on a household's annual income, whereas it is necessary only to ascertain consumption over, say, the previous few weeks to get a satisfactory measure of individual welfare. Moreover, households may understate their incomes to avoid future problems with tax agencies (Krugman et al., 1992; Manasan, 1988). Owing partly to cost considerations, the survey instrument used by statistical agencies to acquire information on households is often short of details needed to accurately estimate "net income" from own-production activities, especially farming. In short, measurement errors can be expected to be greater for income than for consumption.

Thus, on both conceptual and practical grounds, consumption is preferred to income as a broad indicator of a person's living standard. For this reason, the alternative approach to poverty measurement proposed in this chapter employs consumption as the relevant welfare measure.

A desirable feature of the chosen indicator of living standards is its ability to capture differences in household needs, as well as scale economies in household consumption. Households may vary in their "needs" depending on their size or composition. Scale economies in household consumption, on the other hand, arise from the fact that certain household expenditures are public goods (e.g., housing or electricity), suggesting that, for reaching a given welfare level, per capita cost decreases as household size increases. While several procedures have been suggested in the literature to estimate so-called equivalence scales to account for household heterogeneity (see, for example, Buhmann et al. [1988] and Deaton [1997: 241–69]), still, no preferred estimation procedure stands out. Thus, the common practice of adjusting the chosen household welfare indicator only for household size, i.e., using per capita expenditure in the welfare comparison, is employed.[3] Traking this track also rests on the assumption

---

3.   Kakwani (1986) argues that, for most practical purposes, this is a valid assumption.

that each individual in a household gets a welfare value equal to the per capita consumption of that household.

b. Setting poverty lines

When the objective of a poverty measurement is to inform policy choices for reducing *absolute* poverty, an appealing property of a poverty line is that it should not depend on the subgroup to which the person with that standard of living belongs (Ravallion, 1994, 1998). Put differently, poverty lines constructed for various subgroups must be fixed in terms of a given living standard. Thus, two persons deemed to have exactly the same standard of living in all relevant aspects but located in different regions would have to be treated as either both poor or both not poor. The poverty lines are then said to be *consistent*; they imply the same command over basic consumption needs.

The Philippine Government's approach to constructing poverty lines starts with the construction of representative food menus for urban and rural areas in each region of the country. The menus, prepared by the Food and Nutrition Research Institute (FNRI), consider local consumption patterns and satisfy a minimum nutritional requirement of 2,000 calories per person per day and 80–100 percent of recommended daily allowances for vitamins and minerals. The menus for 1985 were based on FNRI's 1982 Food Consumption Survey, while those for 1988 were based on the 1987 Food Consumption Survey. Menus for 1991 and 1994 were the same as those for 1988. Evaluated at local prices, the menus form the *food poverty thresholds*.[4] The Family Income and Expenditures Survey (FIES) is then utilized to determine the average expenditure share of households whose incomes fall within a 10 percent band around the food threshold. This share is used to divide the food threshold to come up with the poverty line (food plus nonfood thresholds).

By construction, the official approach tends to yield poverty lines that are not consistent, that is, the standard of living implied by the poverty lines varies for each of the regions as well as over time. It is well known that as household incomes rise, consumption of cheap sources of calories tends to decline as consumers shift to higher-quality and more varied—but not necessarily more nutritious—food sources.[5] The shift is invariably associated with an improvement in standard of living. Hence, since the official approach starts with the local consumption pattern in the construction of a food threshold for the urban/rural area of each region of the country, estimates of food (as well as

---

4. It should be noted that the food menus have not been validated by any of the statistical agencies.
5. Put differently, the income elasticity of demand for calories is typically much lower than that for food as a group. See, for example, Bouis and Haddad (1992) and Subramanian and Deaton (1996).

nonfood) thresholds tend to be higher for the economically more progressive regions/areas than for those that are economically backward. Moreover, since consumption patterns prevailing in various years inform the construction of food thresholds, estimates of food thresholds also tend to rise with improvement in overall living standards (like what may happen during episodes of economic growth). In short, the food poverty lines employed for the various regions and years are not comparable, since they imply different levels of living standards. They cannot therefore be suitable for either monitoring national poverty or assessing comparative performance across regions, provinces, or areas of the country—*if the main policy objective is to reduce absolute poverty.*

For this chapter, an alternative, albeit practical, approach to deriving poverty lines has been followed. The approach respects the consistency feature of an absolute poverty line, i.e., it is assumed that the main purpose of poverty comparison is to inform progress in the reduction of absolute poverty. Its implementation requires

- deciding on a bundle of food in each province that is the average consumption of a reference group fixed *nationally* in terms of their expenditure;
- adjusting this bundle to satisfy the minimum nutritional requirement of 2,000 calories per person per day;
- valuing the adjusted bundle at consumer prices prevailing in each province; and
- estimating the nonfood spending of the reference households in the neighborhood of the point where *total* spending equals the food threshold.

The approach does not require that the same bundle of goods be used in each province; rather it requires that the bundle be typical of those within a predetermined interval of total consumption expenditure nationally. Put differently, the approach fixes the standard of living used for provincial comparison, but not the composition of goods used in each province. Differences in composition may arise as a result of spatial differences in relative prices faced by households. Details of the approach and its implementation, as well as poverty line estimates for the country's 78 provinces, are given in the Appendix.

At the outset, it should be pointed out that the objective of this exercise is not to derive an alternative estimate of the level of national poverty, but rather to come up with a practical approach to constructing poverty lines that can be used for consistently ranking (absolute) poverty status across provinces, regions, or socioeconomic groups, as well as for monitoring performance in reducing absolute poverty over the medium term (say, 5–10 years).

The underlying assumption of the exercise is that the main objective of development policy is to reduce absolute poverty across space and over time. A poverty indicator and monitoring system must therefore be capable of adequately capturing comparative performance in terms of the changes over time, or differences across space, in absolute poverty.

Figure 9.1 shows estimates based on these criteria and estimates made on official criteria of 1997 poverty lines for the country's 15 regions, including the two autonomous regions of the Cordillera (CAR) and Muslim Mindanao (ARMM).[6] The regions are arranged in ascending order of adjusted mean per capita expenditure, where the adjustment takes into account regional cost-of-living differences (see Appendix). Evident from these results, as expected, is the lack of correlation between the estimates derived from total consumption data (hereafter referred to as "absolute" lines) and the official estimates. Moreover, as expected, the absolute lines do not rise with mean living standard. On the other hand, the official lines tend to rise with mean living standard.[7] The elasticity of the official poverty line with respect to mean living standard is 0.31, while that of the absolute line is not significantly different from zero.

The consistency feature of setting poverty lines was likewise adopted by Kakwani (2000) in coming up with poverty estimates for 1998. Kakwani's poverty thresholds implied a fixed standard of living across regions and were adjusted to capture differences in food needs of household members depending on age and sex.

3. Poverty Profile

This section employs the measurement approach discussed above to update what is known about the poverty profile in the Philippines. The data sets employed are the 1994 and 1997 rounds of the FIES. Conducted every three years since 1985 by the National Statistics Office (NSO), the FIES has been the principal data source for the generation of poverty and income distribution statistics on the Philippines. The 1994 and 1997 sur-

---

6. There are no official figures for provincial poverty lines. For comparison, our regional absolute poverty lines shown in Figure 9.1 are weighted averages of provincial lines, where the weights are provincial population shares. Provincial poverty lines are given in the Appendix.

7. Regressing the logarithmic values of official lines with the logarithmic values of mean expenditure gives a slope coefficient estimate (i.e., poverty line elasticity) of 0.31, which is significantly different from zero at a 2 percent significance level. Similar regression for the absolute poverty lines gives a coefficient of 0.14, which is not significantly different from zero. Using real regional gross domestic product per capita as an instrument for regional mean living standard, the elasticity is 0.16 (significant at 2 percent) for the official line regression and not significantly different from zero for the absolute line regression.

Figure 9.1. Mean Expenditure and Poverty Line

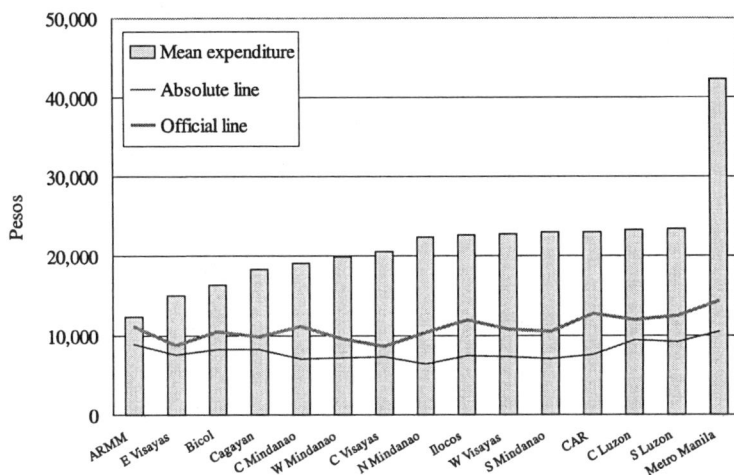

Notes: ARMM = Autonomous Region of Muslim Mindanao; CAR = Cordillera Autonomous Region. All figures pertain to 1997. Mean expenditure is average per capita household expenditure adjusted for regional cost-of-living differences.

Sources: Official poverty lines, National Statistical Coordination Board; all other figures, author's estimates based on the 1997 Family Income and Expenditures Survey of the National Statistics Office.

veys cover a total sample size of 24,797 households and 39,520 households, respectively. Both surveys have the urban and rural areas of each province as their principal domains, thereby permitting the generation of poverty statistics by province.

a. Poverty in 1994 and 1997

Table 9.1 shows estimates of the three dimensions of poverty—incidence, depth, and severity for 1994 and 1997.[8] Estimates based on the official poverty lines are also shown for comparison.[9] Note, however, that the interest here is not on the absolute magnitude of poverty for any particular year, but the *change* in

---

8.   For this chapter, the familiar headcount index, defined simply as the proportion of the population deemed poor, as a measure of the incidence of poverty, is used. For the depth of poverty, the poverty-gap index, defined by the mean distance below the poverty line as a proportion of that line (where the nonpoor are counted as having a zero poverty gap), is employed. Finally, for the severity of poverty, the distribution-sensitive Foster-Greer-Thorbecke (FGT) index, defined as the mean of the squared proportionate poverty gaps, is used. This index incorporates a society's "moderate" aversion to poverty (Foster, Greer, and Thorbecke, 1984).

9.   The official lines applied for 1997 are, in real teams, the same lines as applied for 1994. In this chapter, what are referred to as "official estimates" pertain not to officially

poverty depicted by each of the two approaches in measuring poverty. Recall that the approach adopted in this paper, hereafter referred to simply as the *preferred approach* (PA), differs from the official one in three respects:

- it makes use of current consumption expenditure rather than current income as a broad indicator of household/individual welfare;
- it imposes consistency in the construction of absolute poverty lines; and
- it does not depend on a food consumption survey (for food menu construction) independent of the household expenditure survey used for identifying household welfare levels.

Both sets of estimates show a reduction in national poverty during 1994–1997, regardless of the particular aspect of poverty depicted. However, the percentage-point reduction portrayed by the PA estimates is higher than that shown by the official estimates. The incidence index, for example, falls by about 7 percentage points for the PA estimates, compared with about 3 percentage points for the official estimates. This conclusion holds true for the other two poverty measures. Thus, the overall reduction in absolute poverty during the growth period of 1994–1997 is much greater

Table 9.1. National Poverty Estimates, 1994 and 1997
(in percent, except for income and expenditure, which are in 1997 pesos)

	Mean Real per capita expenditure		Mean Real per capita income		1994			1997		
	1994	1997	1994	1997	Incidence	Depth	Severity	Incidence	Depth	Severity
National	19,600	23,694	24,016	29,214						
Preferred					32.1	8.7	3.4	25.0	6.4	2.3
Approach					(0.35)	(0.13)	(0.07)	(0.29)	(0.10)	(0.05)
Official					40.6	13.5	6.1	37.4	12.5	5.6
Approach					(0.36)	(0.16)	(0.10)	(0.30)	(0.13)	(0.08)
Urban	25,093	31,657	31,082	39,994						
Preferred					18.6	4.4	1.5	11.9	2.6	0.9
Approach					(0.37)	(0.11)	(0.05)	(0.26)	(0.07)	(0.03)
Official					28.0	8.8	3.9	21.9	6.4	2.7
Approach					(0.41)	(0.17)	(0.10)	(0.33)	(0.12)	(0.06)
Rural	14,153	16,475	17,010	19,441						
Preferred					45.4	13.0	5.2	36.9	9.8	3.6
Approach					(0.55)	(0.21)	(0.12)	(0.48)	(0.17)	(0.08)
Official					53.1	18.2	8.3	51.4	18.0	8.3
Approach					(0.54)	(0.26)	(0.16)	(0.48)	(0.22)	(0.13)

Note: Figures in parentheses are robust standard errors.

Source: Author's estimates based on the *Family Income and Expenditures Survey,* 1994 and 1997.

published estimates but to our own estimates using official methodology, i.e., using official lines as the poverty norm and per capita household income as a welfare indicator. All poverty estimates reported in this chapter pertain to total population.

than that reflected in official estimates. This reduction—approximately 2 percentage points per year—is not entirely unexpected, considering that real per capita household expenditure grew by an average of 7 percent per year during this period. This suggests that, contrary to common claims in policy discussions (presumably aided by officially available poverty statistics), poverty responded quite well to income growth.

What could account for the difference in the two sets of estimates? One would expect that the choice of expenditure, as opposed to income, as an indicator of living standard would lead to higher poverty estimates, since, as will be seen below, incomes are usually higher than expenditures, even at the bottom ranges of the consumption expenditure distribution. On the other hand, the use of absolute poverty lines should yield lower poverty

Table 9.2. Sources of the Difference in Estimates of Poverty Change

	Incidence	Depth	Severity
Poverty Change			
Official Approach	–3.2	–1.0	–0.5
Preferred Approach	–7.1	–2.3	–1.1
Difference in Poverty Change	–3.9	–1.3	–0.6
% Contributed by:			
Difference in Welfare Indicator	87.2	84.6	83.3
Difference in Poverty Lines	12.8	15.4	16.7

Source: Author's estimates based on the *Family Income and Expenditure Survey*, 1994 and 1997.

estimates, since, as shown above, these are generally lower than the official lines. These expectations are borne out by the estimates in Table 9.1. Table 9.2 gives the relative contribution of these two influences to the difference in estimates of poverty change. Clearly, the bulk—from 83 to 87 percent, depending on the aspect of poverty being measured—of the difference in the two estimates comes from the difference in the choice of welfare indicator.

Why has the choice of welfare indicator mattered so much to poverty change? The answer has to do with the contrasting evolution of income and expenditure across the income distribution during the period of interest. As shown in Table 9.3, for the bottom 30 percent of the population, the rates of increase in real consumption expenditure (our indicator of living standard) are about twice as high as those for real income (the official indicator) between 1994 and 1997. Moreover, while the Gini ratio for the two indicators both increased during the period, the percentage increase in the income Gini is slightly higher than that in the consumption Gini.

The contrast in the conclusion drawn from the poverty profile of urban and rural areas is also apparent in Table 9.1. Official estimates of incidence suggest

Table 9.3. Mean Expenditure and Income, by Decile, and Gini Index
(in 1997 pesos, except for Gini index)

Decile	1994	1997	Percent Change
By Per Capita Expenditure			
First (Poorest)	5,447	6,087	11.7
Second	7,707	8,567	11.2
Third	9,383	10,570	12.7
Fourth	11,118	12,682	14.1
Fifth	13,129	15,044	14.6
Sixth	15,471	17,859	15.4
Seventh	18,528	21,581	16.5
Eighth	22,935	27,102	18.2
Ninth	30,809	36,670	19.0
Tenth (Richest)	61,478	80,787	31.4
Gini Index	39.7	42.6	7.3
By Per Capita Income			
First (Poorest)	5,580	5,952	6.7
Second	8,323	8,873	6.6
Third	10,410	11,287	8.4
Fourth	12,625	13,826	9.5
Fifth	15,139	16,714	10.4
Sixth	18,106	20,411	12.7
Seventh	22,061	25,367	15.0
Eighth	27,921	32,754	17.3
Ninth	38,173	45,970	20.4
Tenth (Richest)	81,827	110,939	35.6
Gini Index	43.4	47.7	9.9

Note: Mean expenditure and income are adjusted for provincial cost-of-living indexes (see Appendix). The Gini index ranges from 0 (perfect equality) to 100 (perfect inequality).

Source: Author's estimates based on the *Family Income and Expenditures Survey*, 1994 and 1997.

that rural poverty hardly changed between 1994 and 1997, while the PA estimates suggest that it did—and substantially, from 45 percent to 37 percent. The two other poverty measures suggest the same conclusion. On the other hand, in the case of urban areas, the percentage-point reduction in poverty shown by the two estimates is quite similar.

The rather remarkable performance of rural areas, where about three-quarters of the poor live, in poverty reduction during the 1994–1997 period deserves elaboration. Real mean consumption in rural areas rose by 16 percent during this period. If the growth had been distributionally neutral (i.e., if the percentage increases in consumption had been the same for all population subgroups), the reduction in the incidence of poverty would have been 14 percentage points.[10] The actual reduction was 8.5 percentage points, suggesting that inequality in the distribution of consumption increased. Indeed, the

10. Conceptually, a change in poverty measure can be decomposed into growth and

consumption Gini rose by 2.6 percentage points, from 33.6 percent in 1994 to 35.2 percent in 1997. We note, however, that the initial Gini for rural areas was lower than that for urban areas (39.2 in 1994). The increase in the Gini index during this period was also higher for urban areas (3.3 percentage points). Thus, the impact of a given mean consumption growth on a poverty measure is expected to be greater for rural than for urban areas.

b. Regional and provincial poverty profiles

The pictures of regional poverty profiles are also remarkably different between the official approach to poverty measurement and the PA estimates. As shown in Table 9.4, in only four of the 15 regions are the ranks identical for both estimates. In some cases, the two approaches provide substantially different poverty ranks. Arranged in ascending order of poverty incidence, for example, official estimates would show that Central Visayas is the fifth least poor region, but the PA estimates would indicate that this region is the fifth poorest in the country. On the other hand, official estimates show that CAR is ranked 11th (i.e., one of the five poorest regions), but the PA estimates indicate that the region is just one step from being one of the five least poor regions. Overall, the rank correlation between the PA estimates and official estimates is 0.69 for the incidence index and 0.54 for the depth index.

Ranking inconsistency also hounds the provincial profile. This is seen in Table 9.5, which lists the 10 poorest and the 10 richest provinces based on estimates of incidence. Only four of the 10 poorest provinces based on PA estimates appear in the list of the 10 poorest provinces based on official estimates. The match is significantly better for the other end of the poverty spectrum, i.e., the top 10 provinces with the lowest poverty incidence. Here, only three of the 10 provinces characterized as least poor based on official estimates do not also appear on the list based on PA estimates.

The estimates in Table 9.4 thus show that what is known about the spatial profile of poverty is not quite robust. Put differently, given that the policy objective is reduction of absolute poverty, the practice of using official estimates of regional poverty to inform policy decisions vis-à-vis geographic allocation of public investments stands on shaky ground.

---

redistribution components. The growth component is the change in poverty measure due to a change in mean consumption per capita while holding the consumption distribution constant at some reference level. The redistribution component, on the other hand, is simply the change in consumption distribution while keeping the mean consumption constant at some reference level. On this sort of decomposition, see Datt and Ravallion (1992) and Kakwani (2000).

Table 9.4. Regional Profile, 1997

	Preferred Approach	Official	Re-ranking[a]	Preferred Approach	Official	Re-ranking[a]
Metro Manila	3.5 (0.41)	8.7 (0.57)	0	0.6 (0.09)	1.7 (0.15)	0
Ilocos	20.8 (0.13)	44.3 (1.42)	2	4 (0.33)	15 (0.65)	3
Cagayan	30.1 (0.15)	37.9 (1.53)	−5	7.5 (0.48)	10.8 (0.58)	−4
Central Luzon	13.2 (0.79)	19.4 (0.87)	0	2.5 (0.19)	4.8 (0.27)	0
Southern Luzon	19.6 (0.77)	30.2 (0.84)	0	4.5 (0.22)	9.2 (0.33)	−2
Bicol	45.6 (1.35)	57.8 (1.28)	1	12.6 (0.52)	20.4 (0.63)	0
Western Visayas	21.8 (1.0)	47.8 (1.12)	4	4.7 (0.29)	16.1 (0.53)	3
Central Visayas	35.2 (1.28)	39.1 (1.28)	−6	10.3 (0.50)	13.2 (0.58)	−7
Eastern Visayas	50.6 (1.38)	45.4 (1.39)	−5	16 (0.61)	15.8 (0.64)	−5
Western Mindanao	35.2 (1.52)	48.7 (1.52)	−4	8.2 (0.51)	16.6 (0.73)	−3
Northern Mindanao	29.9 (1.05)	54.7 (1.06)	4	7.6 (0.35)	20.8 (0.55)	5
Southern Mindanao	27.8 (1.22)	44.6 (1.26)	0	7.1 (0.41)	16 (0.60)	1
Central Mindanao	33.1 (1.49)	55.9 (1.46)	3	9.2 (0.55)	22.5 (0.80)	4
CAR	22.1 (1.36)	49.7 (1.49)	5	4.4 (0.37)	19.1 (0.74)	7
ARMM	50.5 (1.29)	63.1 (1.23)	1	15.1 (0.51)	19.6 (0.53)	−2

Notes: ARMM = Autonomous Region of Muslim Mindanao; CAR = Cordillera Autonomous Region. [a]Official rank less preferred rank, where rank is from 1 (least poor region) to 15 (poorest region). Values in parentheses are robust standard errors.

Source: 1997 *Family Income and Expenditure Survey*, National Statistics Office.

4. Conclusion

If the main objective of poverty measurement is to inform policy choices for reducing absolute poverty across space and over time, then the present official practice of poverty comparison falls short of adequately informing those choices. This chapter has shown that what is known, based on official poverty data, about spatial poverty profiles (regional, provincial, or rural vs. urban), as well as poverty changes in recent years, is not quite robust. This result is rather disturbing, since it is these profiles that often inform policy discussions, including proposals for engendering "growth with equity," fostering "adjustment with human face," and "empowering

Table 9.5. Provinces with Highest and Lowest Poverty Incidence

Preferred Approach	Rank	Official Approach	Rank in Preferred Approach
10 Provinces With Highest Incidence (Ascending Order)			
Sorsogon	69	Mt. Province	42
Tawi-Tawi	70	North Cotabato	63
N. Samar	71	Lanao del Sur	61
W. Samar	72	E. Samar	77[a]
Biliran	73	Agusan del Sur	54
Siquijor	74	Ifugao	41
Romblon	75	Abra	25
Masbate	76	Sulu	78[a]
E. Samar	77	Masbate	76[a]
Sulu	78	Romblon	75[a]
10 Provinces With Lowest Incidence (Ascending Order)			
Metro Manila	1	Metro Manila	1[a]
Pampanga	2	Cavite	6[a]
Bataan	3	Batanes	24
Laguna	4	Rizal	9[a]
Ilocos Norte	5	Bulacan	7[a]
Cavite	6	Pampanga	2[a]
Bulacan	7	Bataan	3[a]
Nueva Viscaya	8	Laguna	4[a]
Rizal	9	Batangas	15
Ilocos Sur	10	Zambales	11

Note: [a]Also included in the 10-province Preferred Approach list.

Source: Author's estimates based on the 1997 *Family Income and Expenditures Survey.*

the poor." One aspect of the problem has to do with the choice of a broad indicator of living standards. Another aspect has to do with the construction of poverty norms: the official practice is somewhat inconsistent, in the sense that poverty norms applied for various subgroups/areas are not fixed in terms of a given living standard.

The chapter has proposed an alternative, indeed quite practical, approach to measuring poverty for spatial/subgroup comparison, as well as for performance monitoring in the war against absolute poverty. The approach differs from the official practice in the following respects:

- it makes use of current consumption expenditure rather than current income as a broad indicator of household/individual welfare;
- it imposes spatial consistency in the construction of absolute poverty lines; and

- it does not depend on a food consumption survey for the construction of food menus independent of the household expenditure survey used for identifying household welfare levels.

Apart from new poverty profiles, the chapter has generated provincial cost-of-living indexes that could prove useful for spatial comparison of average living standards.

Some important points from the resulting poverty profile should be emphasized. First, contrary to common claims in policy discussions (presumably aided by officially available poverty data), poverty reduction was quite substantial during periods of rapid growth, especially between 1994 and 1997. Second, rural poverty responded strongly to the overall income growth—also contrary to common claims that income growth in rural areas did not benefit the rural poor. Third, poverty in the Philippines is still a largely rural phenomenon despite rapid urbanization in recent years: the rural poor account for about 80 percent of the poor. Other poverty measures tell the same story. Fourth, while the poverty status of a province is inversely related to its mean living standard, the variation in poverty across provinces, even for those with more or less the same living standards, is quite substantial (see Balisacan [2001]), suggesting the importance of factors other than mean living standards in poverty reduction. Finally, poverty in the country is still largely agriculture-driven. While agriculture-dependent households now represent only 40 percent of the Philippine population, the sector accounts for over two-thirds of the poor, simply because the incidence of poverty (as well as its depth and severity) is higher in agriculture than in any other sector of the economy.

At present, the government's poverty monitoring and indicator system falls short of enabling decision makers to assess program performance as well as sharpen the focus of efforts toward the attainment of poverty alleviation objectives. As discussed above, the official approach to poverty measurement cannot be suitable for either national poverty monitoring or assessing comparative performance across regions, provinces, or areas of the country—even more so if the policy objective is to reduce absolute poverty. The approach proposed in this chapter is a modest step toward improving the system.

Appendix

This Appendix outlines a simple, nonparametric approach to constructing poverty lines. The approach respects the principle of consistency for spatial comparison of *absolute* poverty, i.e., poverty lines constructed for various areas or population subgroups are fixed in terms of a given living standard. The intent is not to derive an alternative estimate of the level of national poverty, but rather to come up with a practical approach to constructing poverty lines that can be used for consistently ranking poverty status across provinces, regions, or socioeconomic groups, as well as for monitoring performance in absolute poverty reduction over the medium term (say, 5–10 years). The underlying assumption is that the main objective of poverty measurement is to inform policy choices for reducing absolute poverty across space and over time.[11]

a. Food thresholds

As in the official approach, the estimation of poverty lines proposed in this study starts with specification of a food bundle for each province that would generate the nutritional norm for good health.[12] The differences in the food bundle reflect substitution effects arising from differences in relative prices, not differences in real incomes.[13] The bundle for each province is set as the average consumption of a reference group fixed *nationally* in terms of their expenditure (adjusted for family size). In this chapter, the reference group pertains to the bottom 30 percent of the population fixed nationally; the average consumption bundle is obtained for that reference group in each province. Each bundle is then transformed into calories and adjusted to satisfy the food energy requirement of 2,000 calories per person per day.

The main source of data for fixing the reference group is the 1997 *Family Income and Expenditure Survey* (FIES) of the National Statistics Office (NSO). This survey captures a wide range of market-purchased and implicit expenditures, such as use value of durable goods (including owner-occupied dwelling units), consumption of home-produced goods and services, gifts and assistance or relief goods, and services received by the household from various sources.

The FIES data do not, however, contain information on either average unit values or quantities of goods consumed by the household, which are required to transform the food bundle into calories. In this appendix, average provincial

---

11. The approach closely resembles that suggested by Ravallion (1994: Annex 1).
12. See Balisacan (1999) for a discussion of the official approach.
13. This implies that the food bundles all lie on the same indifference curve. If one knows the demand model, one can easily set the bundle for each price regime (representing a province, say). However, in practice, the demand model is not always known. The approach employed here does not require knowledge of such a model.

prices of commonly purchased commodities, together with calorie conversion ratios obtained from the Food and Nutrition Research Institute (FNRI), were used to "recover" the calorie content of the bundle. The price data, covering 73 provinces and 11 main cities (including Metro Manila) and more than 500 different food items, were obtained from the Prices Division of NSO.[14]

To calculate the food expenditures for each province that will just yield the calorie requirement, the cost of the bundle with price information is multiplied by the ratio of recommended calories to computed calories. This assumes that the average cost per calorie of the items without price information is equal to that of the matched items. Furthermore, it is supposed that, within the relevant income range, the composition of the food basket (in terms of expenditure shares) is fixed. The resulting provincial food thresholds are shown in column 1 of Table 9.A1.

b. Nonfood component

The official approach to estimating the nonfood component of the poverty line utilizes the consumption patterns of households within the 10th percentile of the food threshold in the income distribution. Since the food thresholds reflect the consumption patterns (and hence overall living standards) prevailing in each region, as well as in rural/urban areas within each region, the average food share is expected to be lower in progressive areas or regions of the country than in backward areas or regions. For two households with different food shares, the one with the higher food share tends to have the lower standard of living, regardless of their demographic differences (Deaton and Muellbauer, 1980). Thus, by construction, the nonfood component of the poverty lines in economically progressive regions also implies a higher living standard than that for the economically backward regions.

The procedure that follows to estimate the nonfood component draws from Ravallion (1998). It appeals to the notion that "basic needs" come in hierarchy, beginning with survival food needs, basic nonfood needs, and then basic food needs for economic and social activity. Thus, when a person's total income is just enough to reach the food threshold, anything that this person spends on nonfood items can be considered a minimum allowance for "basic nonfood needs," since she/he is sacrificing basic food intake to purchase such nonfood items. It follows that adding this minimum allowance to the food threshold is a reasonable procedure in setting the poverty line.

In practice, the consumption pattern of those sample households whose expenditures are at or near the food threshold is used in order to estimate this minimum allowance. The estimation takes the weighted average of the households whose per capita expenditures fall within a 10 percent band around the

---

14. These are the same prices used in the computation of the current consumer price index series.

food line. The weights are selected so as to decline linearly, the farther the per capita expenditure is from the food line. The resulting poverty lines for each province and region of the country are summarized in Table 9.A1.

This manner of establishing the poverty line is in essence similar to the official approach, except that the food threshold for each province is set as the average consumption of a reference group fixed *nationally* in terms of their expenditure, not by the FNRI-determined food consumption bundle constructed for each province or region. Note that in the approach suggested here, both the food and nonfood components of the poverty line make use of information generated from the same household survey, i.e., FIES. In contrast, in the official approach, the "food menu" is prepared by FNRI using information from its food consumption survey, while the non-food component of the poverty line is generated from FIES data. Consistency is thus not ensured in the official approach.

c. Real expenditures and cost-of-living indexes

Poverty measurement requires combining poverty lines with information on consumption expenditures. If individual data on money incomes are given, the straightforward way to do this is to simply compare these money incomes with poverty lines constructed for each region, province, or area. Thus, a household located in province j is deemed to be poor if its per capita money income m is less than the poverty line z for province j.

Another way to accomplish the same thing is to deflate each money income m by the "true cost of living index" P, defined for fixed reference prices and reference household characteristics. P is just the ratio of each person's poverty line to the reference poverty line, the latter defining a household with given demographics at a given location and time. The normalized value m/P gives what is often termed "real expenditure" or "real income" (also referred to elsewhere in this paper as "living standard"). Thus, a person is deemed poor if that person's real expenditure is less than the base (reference) poverty line.

The cost-of-living indexes (with Metro Manila as the base) are given in the last column of Table 9.A1. For use in future comparative work on household welfare, Table 9.A2 incorporates price increases over time into the regional cost-of-living indexes. This was done by applying the official consumer price index to the regional cost-of-living index. The resulting indexes for 1985–1998 indicate substantial regional variation in any given year, as well as marked regional differences in rates of price increases during the period.

Table 9.A1. Estimates of Food Thresholds and Poverty Lines:
Absolute Cost-of-Basic-Needs Approach
(1997, pesos per capita)

Province	Food Threshold	Poverty Line	Cost-of-Living Index (Metro Manila = 100)
Metro Manila	7,669	*10,577*	100.0
Ilocos		*7,561*	
Ilocos Norte	4,912	7,084	67.0
Ilocos Sur	5,829	7,906	74.7
La Union	5,702	7,669	72.5
Pangasinan	5,645	7,542	71.3
Cagayan Valley		**8,318**	
Batanes	7,512	10,492	99.2
Cagayan	6,573	8,717	82.4
Isabela	6,337	8,546	80.8
Nueva Viscaya	5,360	7,091	67.0
Quirino	4,871	6,649	62.9
Central Luzon		**9,442**	
Bataan	6,819	9,117	86.2
Bulacan	7,204	9,935	93.9
Nueva Ecija	7,968	10,805	102.2
Pampanga	7,109	9,073	85.8
Tarlac	5,950	7,834	74.1
Zambales	6,116	7,789	73.6
Olongapo City	7,280	10,184	96.3
Southern Luzon		**9,239**	
Aurora	6,382	8,657	81.8
Batangas	6,982	9,928	93.9
Cavite	7,426	10,510	99.4
Laguna	7,057	9,443	89.3
Marinduque	6,404	8,544	80.8
Mindoro Occidental	5,426	7,020	66.4
Mindoro Oriental	5,994	8,123	76.8
Palawan	5,516	7,311	69.1
Quezon	6,077	8,372	79.1
Rizal	7,717	10,804	102.1
Romblon	6,155	8,047	76.1
Bicol Region		**8,256**	
Albay	6,717	9,043	85.5
Camarines Norte	5,422	7,495	70.9
Camarines Sur	5,818	7,654	72.4
Catanduanes	5,676	7,426	70.2
Masbate	6,113	8,117	76.7
Sorsogon	7,046	9,274	87.7

Table 9.A1 (cont.)

Province	Food Threshold	Poverty Line	Cost-of-Living Index (Metro Manila = 100)
Western Visayas		**7,403**	
Aklan	6,000	7,988	75.5
Antique	5,093	6,803	64.3
Capiz	5,407	7,350	69.5
Iloilo	5,325	7,436	70.3
Negros Occidental	5,316	7,131	67.4
Bacolod City	5,884	7,607	71.9
Iloilo City	6,559	9,018	85.3
Central Visayas		**7,392**	
Bohol	4,921	6,433	60.8
Cebu	5,887	7,803	73.8
Negros Orient.	4,949	6,158	58.2
Siquijor	5,188	6,930	65.5
Cebu City	6,711	9,387	88.8
Eastern Visayas		**7,570**	
Eastern Samar	6,036	8,240	77.9
Leyte	5,896	7,746	73.2
Northern Samar	4,920	6,584	62.3
Western Samar	5,758	7,538	71.3
Southern Leyte	5,679	7,595	71.8
Western Mindanao		**7,264**	
Basilan	6,072	8,558	80.9
Zamboanga del Norte	5,138	7,093	67.1
Zamboanga del Sur	4,998	6,738	63.7
Zamboanga City	5,542	8,061	76.2
Central Mindanao		**6,294**	
Bukidnon	4,314	5,699	53.9
Camiguin	5,358	7,300	69.0
Misamis Occidental	4,946	6,593	62.3
Misamis Oriental	4,961	6,659	63.0
Southern Mindanao		**7,079**	
Davao del Norte	4,934	6,605	62.4
Davao del Sur	5,065	6,515	61.6
Davao Oriental	4,627	6,406	60.6
South Cotobato	5,190	7,301	69.0
Davao City	5,942	8,002	75.7
General Santos City	5,712	7,548	71.4

Table 9.A1 (cont.)

Province	Food Threshold	Poverty Line	Cost of Living Index (Metro Manila = 100)
Eastern Mindanao		7,042	
Lanao del Norte	5,264	6,906	65.3
North Cotobato	5,108	7,077	66.9
Sultan Kudarat	5,119	7,024	66.4
Cotabato City	5,366	6,979	66.0
Marawi City	6,374	8,371	79.1
CAR		**7,646**	
Abra	5,053	6,474	61.2
Benguet	6,057	8,708	82.3
Ifugao	4,667	6,447	61.0
Mt. Province	4,827	6,558	62.0
Baguio City	7,680	10,759	101.7
ARMM		**8,990**	
Lanao del Sur	5,452	7,618	72.0
Maguindanao	4,900	6,357	60.1
Sulu	9,274	12,700	120.1
Tawi-Tawi	7,379	10,423	98.5
Caraga		**8,990**	
Agusan del Norte	5,304	7,048	66.6
Agusan del Sur	4,593	6,077	57.5
Surigao del Norte	5,610	7,348	69.5
Surigao del Sur	5,154	6,931	65.5

Notes: ARMM = Autonomous Region of Muslim Mindanao; Caraga = provinces of Agusan del Norte, Agusan del Sur, Surigao del Norte and Surigao del Sur.: CAR = Cordillera Administrative Region;   NCR = National Capital Region (Metro Manila).

Source: Author's estimates.

Table 9.A2. Regional Cost-of-Living Indexes (NCR 1997 = 100)

Region	1985 classification of provinces							1997 classification of provinces	
	1985	1985	1988	1991	1994	1997	1998	1997	1998
NCR		30.5	38.1	58.5	79.9	100.0	110.2	100.0	110.2
1 Ilocos	27.2	30.5		45.5	58.8	72.8	80.3	71.5	78.9
2 Cagayan Valley	30.4	32.7		48.3	61.0	76.0	83.1	78.6	86.0
3 Central Luzon	32.6	38.3		57.5	71.7	89.3	98.4	89.3	98.4
4 Southern Luzon	33.4	36.8		56.4	70.2	87.4	96.0	87.4	96.0
5 Bicol	27.7	31.3		48.4	60.3	78.1	85.1	78.1	85.1
6 Western Visayas	26.5	29.9		46.9	57.8	70.0	75.4	70.0	75.4
7 Central Visayas	24.4	27.3		44.8	55.6	69.9	77.3	69.9	77.3
8 Eastern Visayas	26.8	29.6		44.1	56.2	71.6	77.5	71.6	77.5
9 Western Mindanao	29.6	32.9		50.3	62.7	79.0	86.8	68.7	75.4
10 Northern Mindanao	24.8	26.8		39.0	49.2	61.5	67.8	59.5	65.7
11 Southern Mindanao	28.8	31.3		43.2	53.7	66.8	73.0	66.9	73.2
12 Central Mindanao	25.1	28.3		43.4	54.1	66.0	72.1	66.6	72.7
CAR								72.3	77.8
ARMM								85.0	93.7
Caraga								65.2	71.0

Notes: ARMM = Autonomous Region of Muslim Mindanao; Caraga = provinces of Agusan del Norte, Agusan del Sur, Surigao del Sur, Surigao del Norte and Surigao del Sur.; CAR = Cordillera Administrative Region; NCR = National Capital Region (Metro Manila).

Source: Author's estimates.

References

Balisacan, Arsenio M. 1995. Anatomy of Poverty During Adjustment: The Case of the Philippines. *Economic Development and Cultural Change* 44 (October): 33–62.

———. 1999. What Do We Really Know—or Don't Know—about Economic Inequality and Poverty in the Philippines? In *Causes of Poverty: Myths, Facts and Policies—A Philippine Study*, edited by Arsenio Balisacan and Shigeaki Fujisaki. Quezon City: University of the Philippines Press in cooperation with the Institute of Developing Economies, Tokyo.

———. 2001. Poverty Profile in the Philippines: An Update and Reexamination. *Philippine Review of Economics* 38: 16–51.

Bouis, H. E., and L. J. Haddad. 1992. Are Estimates of Calorie-Income Elasticities Too High? A Recalibration of the Plausible Range. *Journal of Development Economics* 39 (October): 333–362.

Buhmann, Brigitte, Lee Rainwater, Guenter Schmauss, and Timothy Smeeding. 1988. Equivalence Scales, Well-Being, Inequality, and Poverty: Sensitivity Estimates across Ten Countries using the Luxembourg Income Study Database. *Review of Income and Wealth* 34: 115–142.

Cox, Donald, and Emmanuel Jimenez. 1995. Private Transfers and Effectiveness of Public Income Redistribution in the Philippines. In *Public Spending and the Poor: Theory and Evidence*, edited by Dominique van de Walle and Kimberly Nead. Baltimore: Johns Hopkins University Press, for the World Bank.

Datt, Gaurav, and Martin Ravallion. 1992. Growth and Redistribution Components of Changes in Poverty Measures: A Decomposition with Applications to Brazil and India in the 1980s. *Journal of Development Economics* 38: 275–295.

Deaton, Angus. 1997. *The Analysis of Household Surveys: A Microeconometric Approach to Development Policy*. Baltimore: Johns Hopkins University Press, for the World Bank.

———. 2001. Counting the World's Poor: Problems and Possible Solutions. *World Bank Research Observer* 16 (2): 125–147.

———, and John Muellbauer. 1980. *Economics and Consumer Behavior*. Cambridge: Cambridge University Press.

Foster, James, and Amartya Sen. 1997. On Economic Inequality after a Quarter Century. In Amartya Sen, *On Economic Inequality*, expanded edition. Oxford: Clarendon Press.

Foster, James E., Joel Greer, and Erik Thorbecke. 1984. A Class of Decomposable Poverty Measures. *Econometrica* 52: 761–766.

Kakwani, Nanak. 1986. *Analyzing Redistribution Policies: A Study Using Australian Data*. New York: Cambridge University Press.

———. 2000. Poverty, Inequality and Well-being in the Philippines: With Focus on Mindanao. Unpublished Paper.

Krugman, Paul R., James Alm, Susan M. Collins, and Eli M. Remolona. 1992. *Transforming the Philippine Economy*. Pasig: National Economic and Development Authority, and United Nations Development Programme.

Manasan, Rosario G. 1988. Tax Evasion in the Philippines, 1981–85. *Journal of Philippine Development* 15: 167–189.

National Statistics Office, Various years. *Family Income and Expenditure Survey*. Manila.

Ravallion, Martin. 1994. *Poverty Comparisons.* Chur, Switzerland: Harwood Academic Publishers.

———. 1998. *Poverty Lines in Theory and Practice.* LSMS Working Paper Number 133. Washington, D.C.: World Bank.

———, and Shaohua Chen. 1997. What Can New Survey Data Tell Us about Recent Changes in Distribution and Poverty? *World Bank Economic Review,* 11 (May): 357–382.

Subramanian, Shankar, and Angus Deaton. 1996. The Demand for Food and Calories. *Journal of Political Economy* 104: 133–162.

10. Assessing the Poverty Impact of Policy- and Sector-Based Lending

John Weiss

1. Introduction

With the current shift by international agencies into lending to support broad policy change and sectorwide interventions rather than specific projects, an important methodological issue is how feasible it will be to assess such loans by the criteria of their impact on poverty reduction. Although the assessment of the poverty reduction impact of individual projects is empirically challenging, there is a reasonably well-established methodology upon which analysts can draw. Conceptual and practical problems are discussed in Fujimura and Weiss (2000). However, when one considers the impact of loans that support change at the macroeconomic or sector level, the difficulties are magnified considerably. This chapter aims to bring out the key issues. It begins with a conceptual discussion of the links between policy change—that which enhances economic growth—and poverty reduction. It then considers methodologies available to assess the consequences of policy change, both ex post and ex ante. The rigorous approaches that have been used by researchers in this area provide insights for analysts who need to focus on the immediate impact of particular loan-financed reforms, but rarely will these approaches be feasible in an operational context that is constrained by time and resources. Hence the chapter considers a simple framework that distinguishes between the poor in their different roles: consumers, producers, employees, and recipients of public services. It discusses how different types of lending can be assessed in this way, and stresses that analysts need to be explicit about the assumptions underlying particular interventions that must prove valid or justified in order for these interventions to improve the position of the poor.

2. Policy Change and Poverty Reduction

There is now considerable empirical evidence that economic growth is a necessary but not always sufficient condition for significant and sustained reduction of poverty. The widely cited paper by Dollar and Kraay (2000) is only one of several cross-country studies that come to this conclusion. Hence the main link between macro or sector policy change and poverty reduction will be expected to be an indirect one, through the mediation of higher growth. Policy reform is expected to improve economic growth and in turn, growth will reduce poverty. It is desirable, however, to extend the discussion a little further: although by definition growth raises real income, it is not obvious that all or much of this increase will go to the poor. It is clear that the more unequal a society is, the lower the poverty impact of a given rate of growth will be. In addition, however, growth itself may cause increased inequality that weakens its poverty effect. There is evidence of this latter process at work in some of the high-growth economies of East Asia: despite an overall reduction in poverty, rising inequality weakened the impact of economic growth (Ahuja et al., 1997; Kakwani and Pernia, 2000).

Further, the poverty reduction impact of a given rate of economic growth will vary with the form that growth takes. It has been shown that patterns of economic growth in different sectors have different poverty consequences. For example, there is evidence that growth in agriculture tends to have a higher poverty reduction impact than growth in manufacturing, and that rural income growth is generally more poverty-reducing than growth in urban incomes. (Ravallion and Datt, 1996, for India; Thorbecke and Hong-Sang, 1996, for Indonesia).

Given this ambiguity concerning the precise growth-poverty reduction relationship, it is worth considering the possible mechanisms through which poverty reduction may occur in response to reform. The first is the effect of reform on employment creation. If economic activity responds positively to reform, the poor can find their wage employment increasing. It is this link which has led to the focus on labor-intensive growth in discussions of poverty reduction (World Bank, 1990). The East Asian experience is usually held out as an example of how poverty can be reduced greatly through a tightening labor market. (World Bank, 1993). However, it is often not the chronic poor who benefit from such employment creation, but those just below the poverty line with the skills or physical strength to take up these opportunities. In terms of employment creation, it should also be remembered that even successful policy reforms can lead to negative short-run employment effects. The most obvious example is the closure of import substitution activities prior to the emergence of successful export-oriented production. In the short run, the number of people below the poverty line may rise, not fall, and even where successful employment reallocation occurs, this may take a significant period of time, so there will be transitional poverty effects that cannot be disregarded.

The second mechanism is the significance of macroeconomic stabilization. It is often argued that while inflation is a tax on the whole society, it falls most heavily on the poor, whose monetary incomes are not just low but relatively inflexible. A significant source of income for the poorest is likely to be casual employment or the monetary equivalent of government-provided services, both of which may rise sluggishly at a time of accelerating inflation. Hence the implication is that if inflation can be stabilized through fiscal and monetary policy, then this loss of real income can be avoided.

The poor should be disproportionate beneficiaries of government expenditure, in the sense that the monetary value of government-supplied services is a higher proportion of their income than for those above the poverty line. This is despite the fact that recent incidence studies show the relatively rich receiving a share of benefits from government education and health expenditure that is well above their share of population (World Bank, 2000). Thus, any real decline in government expenditure for such services, as part of the fiscal retrenchment required for macrostabilization, may have serious short-run consequences for the poor, as may measures to introduce cost-recovery pricing that do not make adequate exemptions for the poor. However, insofar as rising growth makes it easier to finance public social expenditures in the longer term, the poor should benefit from rising expenditure on these services.

The third and potentially most complex area in which macro reform can interact with poverty is through the relative price shifts that it entails. In most macro adjustment or stabilization programs, two important relative price shifts can be expected. One is a rise in the ratio of traded to nontraded prices, where a real exchange rate depreciation is required to remove internal and external imbalances. The other is within the nontraded sector, where a rise in prices for publicly supplied services relative to privately supplied activities can be expected when government bodies are required to raise prices to meet a cost-recovery objective. How the poor will be affected by such shifts will depend upon their situation as net producers or consumers of the goods concerned. Where the poor are net producers of traded goods (their production of such goods exceeds their consumption), they should benefit from the relative price shift, although exceptions can always occur, since in practice not all traded and nontraded prices will shift uniformly. Similarly, where the poor are net consumers of nontraded goods (their consumption of such goods exceeds their production), they should benefit, again with the caveat for possible shifts within the two categories. Distributional consequences of reform programs in Latin America have been explained from this perspective (Morley, 1995). For price shifts within the nontraded category, as noted above, the poor will unambiguously lose where prices for government-supplied services rise relative to other nontraded activities. However, these relative price shifts will occur at a time when real incomes are also changing, hence the full impact on the poor will be determined by the net effect, which allows for both income and price changes as they affect the poor. In the short run, at least, this can be difficult to predict.

Finally, in recent years reforms have focused on institutional change, since it is recognized that market relations operate with widely different levels of efficiency in different institutional contexts. Such institutional change has been widespread in some economies, covering enterprise restructuring and privatization, financial sector reform, civil service downsizing and reorganization, and changes to social service organization and delivery mechanisms. These so-called "second generation reforms" are intended to strengthen the growth impact of more conventional macroeconomic adjustments—and insofar as they succeed in this, they should have some positive impact on poverty alleviation. However, it is far from clear how such changes will impact the poor in the short run. For example, while financial sector reform is widely seen as essential for sustained economic growth, it is not immediately obvious that the commercialization of development banks and the end of subsidized credit will affect the poor.[1]

a. Methodologies for assessing the impact of reform on the poor

During the 1980s, with the widespread adoption of structural adjustment and IMF stabilization programs, a considerable literature built up in assessing ex post the impact of policy change on growth. The basic approach can be summarized by an equation that makes growth a function of a number of variables: initial income, human capital stock, and growth of factor inputs, plus a variable reflecting policy reform. Hence,

$$G = f(X_i, P) \tag{10.1}$$

where G is the rate of economic growth, X_i is a vector of independent variables, and P is a variable reflecting policy change.

Equations such as (10.1) were estimated normally on a cross-sectional basis across groups of economies and the impact of reform was captured by the sign and significance of variable P. Variable P itself was specified in various ways. In the simplest form it was a dummy taking a value of 1.0 in the presence of policy reform. In more sophisticated analyses, P can refer to specific measures of policy, such as real exchange rate movements (Dollar, 1992) or indicators of openness to trade (Sachs and Warner, 1995). The most theoretically rigorous version of equation (10.1) follows the "generalized evaluation estimator" approach (Goldstein and Montiel, 1986). This is based on the insight that a full assessment of policy change must be a with-without comparison to pick up the incremental impact of policy. This is addressed econometrically by extending equation (10.1) to incorporate both past performance and past policy variables as a guide to what things would have been like without reform. The

---

1. See Aron (2000) for a survey of the literature on institutions and economic growth.

incremental policy impact is captured by a dummy variable. Thus equation (10.1) becomes

$$G = f(X_i, G_{-1}, P_{-1}, D) \tag{10.2}$$

Where D is a dummy variable taking 1.0 when reform is present and $_{-1}$ indicates a lagged value.

Examples of this approach are Khan (1990) and Corbo and Rojas (1992). An alternative method that attempts to address the same problem identifies countries with similar situations prior to introducing reform and compares the performance of those that enter into IMF stabilization agreements with the performance of those that do not (Garuda, 2000).

The difficulty with this type of analysis for assessing lending activity is that, first, it is exclusively ex post. Second, it is rarely able to distinguish precisely between different policies, so that normally one can pick up only the effect of the existence of a reform program or some broad measure like shifts in the real exchange rate. Hence, although lessons from country experiences are clearly useful in designing programs, there is a clear limit to how far this methodology can go in a direct assessment of the poverty reduction consequences of reform.

Some of these problems are overcome by the other methodology that is widely used to assess poverty reduction impacts of policy change. This involves using either a Social Accounting Matrix (SAM) or, in a more dynamic form, a Computable General Equilibrium (CGE) macro model based on a SAM. A SAM model is a square matrix, with columns for expenditure and rows covering income accounts. A SAM combines input-output data with the national accounts to reflect the circular flow of income at a particular point in time. In this context, its key use is as a means of assessing the direct and indirect income effects of a particular exogenous impact, such as a policy change leading to different expenditure patterns (Iqbar and Siddiqui, 1999; Khan, 1999). Since SAMs can be constructed with different groupings of households, they can be used to assess how poorer households are affected. SAMs are typically static systems with fixed coefficients and prices. However, they can be extended to more dynamic models by the incorporation of a number of behavioral equations relating to key markets in an economy. These, combined with key parameters, relating, for example, to various demand and supply elasticities, can be developed into a full macro model. These macro models normally assume optimizing behavior, with flexible prices clearing all markets. The great advantage of these models is that they can be designed to incorporate features of individual economies and can be run for different policy simulations. Such models are conceptually the only rigorous means of assessing the counterfactual situation—what would have taken place in an economy if a particular policy reform had not occurred. Versions of such models have been used in a number of countries to assess the poverty impact of policy change; in Asia these economies include Indonesia (Thorbecke, 1991) and Malaysia (Demery and Demery, 1991).

SAM and CGE models provide a first-best methodology for ex ante assessment of policy change. However, their practical relevance remains a subject of considerable debate. Even relatively sophisticated models based on the data from a large and recent SAM must of necessity be a major simplification of reality. Key parameters will often be assumed, or simply taken from work on other economies. Moreover, the structure used for the models can itself influence their results.[2] In addition, such models can normally cope only with the impact of precise policy change, such as a devaluation, a fall in aggregate government expenditure, a change in interest rates, or the removal of a particular subsidy. The effect of more general measures such as the strengthening of the financial sector, institutional change in the civil service, or a new road-building program, may be difficult to express in exact macro terms, and hence difficult to incorporate into models. Finally, and perhaps critically in the present context, accurate modelling of this type is demanding in data and skills. Without a major research effort, such models cannot be expected to be widely or readily available for individual countries.

A shortcut approach is to establish "generic" models for particular types of economies: a low-income labor-surplus economy, as found in South Asia or the poorer parts of East Asia, or transitional economies. Such models could be based on "typical" data of an assumed nature and used to assess the possible consequences of different interventions for poverty reduction. Their results could be no more than suggestive, since the models themselves are not based on an individual economy, but they could give policymakers an insight into possible poverty outcomes under different scenarios and assumptions.

b. A poverty impact matrix

Operational work at international agencies can draw useful lessons from the data derived from the application of the approaches noted above. However, a simpler, more pragmatic approach is likely to be essential in dealing with ex ante discussions of policy packages. A useful starting point for work in this area is the so-called Papanek matrix, developed in the early 1990s and recently revived.[3]

---

2. Relevant here is the debate on the usefulness and accuracy of CGE models in assessing the relationship between poverty and adjustment in Africa; see De Maio, Stewart, and van der Hoeven (1999) and the reply by Sahn, Dorosh, and Younger (1999).

3. For an illuminating discussion of this matrix and its use in policy assessments at the Asian Development Bank, see Bolt and Fujimura (2000).

The logic of the analysis is that income for a poor household will be determined by three parameters: labor earnings of household members in the workforce, return on the nonlabor assets of the household, and net receipts from public and private transfers. Hence, all policy change can be evaluated in terms of how it affects labor earnings, return on assets, and transfers. This discussion is formalized in Behrman (1993). The importance of these three dimensions will vary among poor groups; any framework for poverty impact assessment must be sufficiently broad to cover a range of possible scenarios.

The matrix itself involves two dimensions or axes: one, the channels or mechanisms through which policy change impacts on the poor and two, the timing and degree of impact. The channels specified on the vertical axis are the obvious ones of the labor market, prices, access to government-provided services, and net transfers. The impacts on the horizontal axis are subdivided into direct effects, indirect effects, macro effects, and impact on the nonpoor. Table 10.1 illustrates this framework.

Table 10.1. Poverty Reduction Impact Matrix

Channel	Impact on the Poor			Impact on the Nonpoor
Labor Market	Direct	Indirect	Macro	
Prices				
Access to Public Services				
Transfers				
	Critical Assumptions			

Source: Bolt and Fujimura (2000).

This basic framework was never intended to be any more than a means of organizing thoughts on how particular policy changes might impact on the poor. It is of critical importance to set out clearly the underlying assumptions required to achieve the forecast outcomes. In this sense, the matrix is similar to the widely used logical framework applied ex ante in project work. The merit of this tool is simply that it sets out objectives that a project is intended to achieve and the assumptions that must be valid in order for these to be met. The realism or validity of the critical assumptions must then be tested and, if necessary, measures must be applied to ensure that, as far as is practicable, reality matches these assumptions. A precisely analogous procedure, useful in poverty analysis, also pertains here: in general, the longer the chain of assumptions required, the more dubious the poverty reduction effect that is being claimed.

Insofar as the poverty reduction impact matrix offers a simple nth-best approach to assessing the poverty reduction consequences of a particular sector and policy loan, it is worth attempting to sharpen up some of the categories it uses. By considering first the mechanisms on the vertical axis, it is possible to make a few simple points of clarification.

First, in relation to labor market and employment consequences, it is sometimes helpful to distinguish between formal (and by implication regular) employment and jobs in the informal sector, since policy change can affect these differently. A major criticism of public sector reform programs, for example, is that they may replace formal sector employment with employment in the informal sector.

Second, in line with the earlier discussion on theoretical expectations of poverty impacts, it may be important in some cases to distinguish between relative price effects that impact the poor differently as producers than they do as consumers. A particular change, such as decontrol of agricultural prices, may benefit poor farmers who are affected as producers, but hurt other groups of the poor who are net consumers of the agricultural goods produced. In addition, some important price effects may arise from a general, not a relative, price change. In other words, the mechanism through which the poor are affected may be the impact of policy on inflation. Hence, as a further refinement, which helps to bring out the potential ambiguity in price changes, one can decompose the price mechanism category into three subgroups: relative price changes for producers, relative price changes for consumers, and general price changes.

Third, the mechanism of access of the poor to publicly provided services such as schools, hospitals, and clinics should strictly cover only nonmarketed services for which a nominal or zero charge is made. This is because if the poor are to be provided with public services on commercial terms, then these will be equivalent to any other commodity and should logically be covered under the prices category.

Fourth, the mechanism of transfers will largely refer to private transfers to the poor, since government programs will rarely provide cash. Transfers are implicit in any subsidized system of supply, but these will be picked up by the previous category of publicly supplied services. An exception will be workfare programs, as used in Maharashtra state in India, for example, where the poor are given work on publicly organized infrastructure and related schemes.

In terms of the impact or horizontal axis of the matrix, it is clear that there will be ambiguity in trying to distinguish among direct, indirect, and macro effects on the poor. The original thinking appears to be that for markets related to a particular policy intervention, it is possible to think of direct and indirect effects. For example, removing a fertilizer subsidy will have a direct effect in raising farm costs, thus directly lowering wage employment among hired farm laborers. However if the removal of the subsidy stimulates higher production because of the greater availability of the fertilizer, there may be positive indirect employment effects. Any employment consequences under the macro heading would arise from the way in which the subsidy had been financed and the use to which the saved funds are put. This direct-indirect-macro distinction may make sense when there is a clearly defined market involved, but if one considers more broadly-based policy interventions and, in particular, various institutional reforms, then the distinction between an indirect and a macro effect becomes highly blurred. Arguably, since all macro effects can be seen as indirect, the justification for maintaining separate categories is weak. Conceptually a more justifiable distinction is between short-term and medium-term effects on the poor—with what have been called direct effects in the first category—and all subsequent effects arising from other related markets and macroeconomic consequences coming under the medium-term heading. Reference to the longer run is deliberately omitted here: so many other factors will be at work that isolating long-run policy impacts in such a simple framework is hardly sensible.

Most policy change will affect those above as well as those below the poverty line, hence the use of a category for the impact on the nonpoor. Where positive effects on the latter can be identified, and where at the same time there are losses for some of the poor, there is the issue of compensatory adjustments in favor of the latter. If any mitigating measures are needed to offset the negative consequences for the poor identified elsewhere in the matrix, then a reference to these can also be added.

The original use of the matrix appears to have been largely qualitative. Responses are given to the question: does a policy impact positively or negatively on the poor, so that cells in the matrix are either completed with a narrative or more simply with positive or negative signs to indicate direction of impact on the income of the poor? This is a starting point. For major interventions, it should be possible to go a little further and quantify their consequences. This need not involve a formal modeling exercise, but rather ad hoc estimates, for example on parameters like job creation, product or service demand, and fiscal cost. This is the type of data that economists might reasonably be expected to derive as part of the overall justification for a particular policy intervention. These figures can be added to the basic narrative in the policy matrix, to sharpen the discussion and projected outcomes that must be assessed in relation to underlying assumptions that are critical for their achievement.

Tables 10.2 and 10.3 illustrate an approach that takes two alternative cases: one a narrowly defined intervention—removal of a fertilizer subsidy— and the other a much broader program of financial sector reform. The former lends itself to approximate quantification, while the assessment of the latter must be much more speculative. In the latter instance, the role of the matrix is to highlight key issues and thus, to require analysts to draw on a combination of a priori theorizing and empirical evidence from recent experience, to assess

Table 10.2. Modified Poverty Reduction Impact Matrix: Removal of Fertilizer Subsidy

Channel	Impact on the Poor		Impact on the Nonpoor
	Short Term	**Medium Term**	
Labor market – Formal			
– Informal	Job losses due to higher cost (thousands)	Job gains with more efficient use (thousands)	Net job change (thousands)
Prices – Producer	Fertilizer prices rise by $x\%$		
– Consumer	Only small direct effect on farm prices		
– Inflation	Lower inflation by $y\%$		
Access to public services			
Transfers – Public			
– Private			

Notes: Blank cells = not applicable. Previously fertilizer was not scarce at subsidized price prior to reform and was sold to benefit of both poor and nonpoor farmers. Removal of subsidy is large enough to allow reduction in budget deficit, which in turn lowers inflation. Higher price of fertilizer stimulates more efficient use and higher output.

Table 10.3. Modified Poverty Reduction Impact Matrix: Financial Sector Reform

Channel	Impact on the Poor		Impact on the Nonpoor
	Short Term	**Medium Term**	
Labor market – Formal			
– Informal	Job losses due to higher cost (thousands)	Job gains with more efficient intermediation (thousands)	Net job gains (thousands)
Prices – Producer	Short term	Higher incomes due to higher savings and investment	Higher incomes
– Consumer		Lower prices due to reduced financial margins	Lower prices
– Inflation			
Access to public services		Medium Term Imporves due to higher government income	
Transfers – Public – Private			

Notes: Blank cells = not applicable. Reform of financial system leads to more efficient intermediation and growth. Benefits of higher government income spent on poor. Poor can gain access to credit in new reformed financial sector.

whether the critical assumptions required for a positive impact on poverty reduction are likely to prove realistic or valid.

5. Conclusions

In the area of poverty assessment, we are a long way from having an agreed operational methodology that links lending in support of policy and sector programs with poverty reduction. Formal modeling and accumulated empirical evidence from individual country cases provide the main sources of information for analysts who seek to assess the ex-ante consequences of particular loans. The poverty reduction impact matrix provides a helpful way of organizing information of both a quantitative and qualitative nature. However, it should be clear that the matrix is only a means of telling a particular story, based on a set of critical assumptions. The story itself will be based on a priori logic and this will always require checking. The accumulated evidence of the past two decades has shown that policy prescriptions based on apparently impeccable economic logic often have not had their expected effects in poor adjusting economies. Sensible policy change requires a serious assessment of program impact on a case-by-case basis. In this context, the matrix can be used to highlight the critical elements in any particular story.

References

Ahuja, V., B. Bidani, F. Ferreira, and M. Walton. 1997. *Everyone's Miracle: Revisiting Poverty and Inequality in East Asia*. Washington, D.C.: World Bank.

Aron, J. 2000. Growth and Institutions: A Review of the Evidence. *World Bank Research Observer* 15 (1).

Behrman, J. 1993. Macroeconomic Policies and Rural Poverty. In *Rural Poverty in Asia*, edited by M. Quibria. New York: Oxford University Press for the Asian Development Bank.

Bolt, R., and M. Fujimura. 2000. Policy-Based Lending and Poverty Reduction: An Introduction to Processes, Options and Assessments. Mimeo. Manila: Asian Development Bank.

Corbo, V. and P. Rojas. 1992. World Bank Supported Adjustment Programs: Country Performance and Effectiveness. In *Adjustment Lending Revisited*, edited by V. Corbo, S. Fischer, and S. Webb. Washington, D.C.: World Bank.

De Maio, L., F. Stewart, and R. van der Hoeven. 1999. Computable General Equilibrium Models, Adjustment and the Poor in Africa. *World Development* 27 (3).

Demery, L., and D. Demery. 1991. Poverty and Macroeconomic Policy in Malaysia. *World Development* 19 (11).

Dollar, D. 1992. Outward-Oriented Developing Economies Really Do Grow More Rapidly: Evidence From 95 LDCs. *Economic Development and Cultural Change* 40 (3).

————, and A. Kraay. 2000. Growth is Good for the Poor. Mimeo. Washington, D.C.: World Bank.

Fujimura, M., and J. Weiss. 2000. *Integration of Poverty Impact in Project Economic Analysis: Issues in Theory and Practice*. EDRC Methodology Series, Number 2. Manila: Asian Development Bank.

Garuda, G. 2000. The Distributional Effects of IMF Programs: A Cross-Country Analysis. *World Development* 28 (6).

Goldstein, M., and P. Monteil. 1986. *Evaluating Fund Stabilisation Programs with Multi-Country Data*. IMF Staff Papers 29 (2). Washington, D.C.: International Monetary Fund.

Iqbar, Z., and R. Siddiqui. 1999. Impact of Fiscal Adjustment on Income Distribution in Pakistan. *Pakistan Development Review* 38 (1).

Kakwani, N., and E. Pernia. 2000. What is Pro-Poor Growth? Mimeo. Manila: Asian Development Bank.

Khan, H. 1999. Sectoral Growth and Poverty Alleviation: A Multiplier Decomposition Technique Applied to South Africa. *World Development* 27 (3).

Khan, M. 1990. *The Macro Economic Effects of Fund-Supported Adjustment Programs*. IMF Staff Papers 37 (2). Washington, D.C.: International Monetary Fund.

Morley, S. 1995. *Poverty and Inequality in Latin America: The Impact of Adjustment and Recovery in the 1980's*. Baltimore: Johns Hopkins.

Ravallion, R., and G. Datt. 1996. How Important to India's Poor is the Sectoral Composition of Economic Growth? *World Bank Economic Review* 10 (1).

Sahn, D., P. Dorosh, and S. Younger. 1999. A Reply to De Maio, Stewart and Van der Hoeven. *World Development* 27 (3).

Sachs, J., and A. Warner. 1995. *Economic Reform and the Process of Global Integration*. Brookings Papers on Economic Activity 118. Washington, D.C.: The Brookings Institution.

Thorbecke, E. 1991. Adjustment, Growth and Income Distribution in Indonesia. *World Development* 19 (11).

————, and J. Hong-Sang. 1996. A Multiplier Decomposition Method to Analyse Poverty Alleviation. *Journal of Development Economics* 48 (2).

World Bank. 1990. *World Development Report 1990*. New York: Oxford University Press.

————. 1993. *East Asian Miracle*. New York: Oxford University Press.

————. 2000. *World Development Report 2000/01—Attacking Poverty*. New York: Oxford University Press.

PART IV

Country Studies

11. Pathways of Poverty Reduction: Rural Development and Transmission Mechanisms in the Philippines

Arsenio M. Balisacan

1. Introduction

The Philippines has lagged behind the major East Asian countries in achieving economic development, particularly in improving the socioeconomic well-being of its people. In the mid-1950s, real per capita Gross Domestic Product (GDP) was higher in the Philippines than in any of these countries (except Japan and Malaysia), while by the turn of the new century, it was one of the lowest among them. In the early 1960s, the Philippines also had the best human development indicators: longest life expectancy, lowest infant mortality rate, highest primary school enrollment ratio, and lowest illiteracy rate. During the subsequent decades, however, major countries not only caught up with, but surpassed, the Philippines in many aspects of human development. By the 1990s, its neighbors had higher income growth, more dynamic structural transformation, and much more impressive poverty reduction.

The development experience of emerging Asian market economies suggests a strong link between agricultural growth and overall economic performance. This is not surprising, given that agriculture and agriculture-dependent manufacturing and service sectors are a relatively large fraction of the economy in the early stages of development. Even more important, the experience shows that rapid growth in agriculture induces rural nonfarm growth and, hence, substantial poverty reduction in rural areas. This has apparently not been the case for the Philippines. At the height of the green revolution (1960s and 1970s), agricultural growth in the Philippines was high by Asian standards. However, rural supply response was weak, resulting in rather poor rural welfare outcomes.

The post-World War II experience of Philippine rural development illustrates how misguided policies and institutional factors could constrain the responses of rural areas to the stimulus provided by agricultural growth, thereby stifling economic development. This chapter reviews this experience, specifically examining the influence of government policies and institutional arrangements on rural welfare outcomes. The next section presents a simple organizing framework for understanding the transmission of agricultural growth to rural welfare outcomes. The chapter then discusses economic and rural performance, focusing on the link between agricultural growth and rural poverty outcomes, as well as the kinds of government policies that could have influenced these outcomes. The chapter moves on to examine the determinants of poverty reduction in rural areas during the 1980s and 1990s, using comparable provincial data. The last section provides concluding remarks.

2. An Organizing Framework

For virtually all the developing Asian economies, the main source of poverty is the rural sector (FAO, 1999; Lipton and Ravallion, 1995; Quibria, 1993). Nearly three-quarters of the poor in these countries come from the rural areas. The large majority depend on agriculture for employment and income. For this reason, agricultural growth and rural development are seen as central to a strategy for sustained poverty reduction in these countries.

In developing economies, where there is a high share of population in rural areas and where urban-rural links are nascent, the rural nonfarm economy is very much linked to agriculture. Increases in agricultural productivity and farm incomes stimulate the growth of nonfarm activities and, hence, employment opportunities. Put differently, while agricultural growth reduces rural poverty and food insecurity directly by increasing agricultural incomes, the indirect effects of this growth on the rural nonfarm economy, through demand and supply linkages, could represent even more important sources of food security and rural poverty reduction in the long term.

The response of the rural nonfarm sector to the stimulus provided by agricultural growth hinges on certain "initial conditions" in rural areas: distribution of assets and incomes, quality of human capital, rural infrastructure, and macroeconomic and political environment (Figure 11.1). The Asian experience shows that a strong response of rural nonfarm areas (as well as urban areas) and, hence, of rural poverty, to the stimulus provided by agricultural growth, as well as to export and/or urban demand growth, requires investment in rural infrastructure to lower transaction costs, remove public-spending biases favoring large farmers and agribusiness enterprises, adopt small-scale enterprises, improve access to land and technology, and maintain macroeconomic and political stability.

In East Asia, where conditions were generally favorable to the emergence of rural nonfarm activities, even agricultural households became increasingly dependent on nonfarm incomes in the course of agricultural modernization (Balisacan, 1996a; Reardon et al., 1998). In Asia and elsewhere, improvements in the living standards of the rural population have been commonly associated with robust rural growth linkages (Ranis and Stewart, 1993; Lipton and Ravallion, 1995; Rosegrant and Hazell, 1999).

Figure 11.1. Rural Growth and Rural Welfare

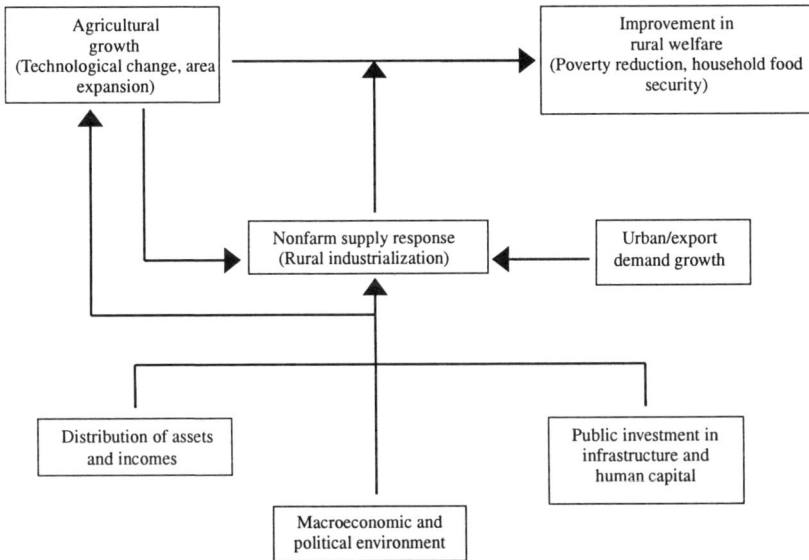

Not surprisingly, given the large differences in initial conditions across countries, experience in rural Asia is quite varied. Some rural areas, such as those of Indonesia and India's Punjab, have responded strongly to agricultural growth, while others, such as those of the Philippines, apparently have not. Even within a country, large disparities in rural performance are evident (Datt and Ravallion, 1992; Rosegrant and Hazell, 1999).

3. Agricultural Growth

The Philippines' agriculture sector continues to account for a sizable proportion of total employment and, to a lesser extent, national income. In accordance with the well-known stylized fact of development, its share in total employment dropped from 59 percent in the mid-1960s to 40 percent in the late 1990s, while its share in GDP declined from about 32 percent to 18 percent (Table 11.1). However, the rather slow decline of agriculture's share in total employment, together with the sluggish absorption of labor in the industrial sector, suggests that the large increments to the labor force over the last three decades were nominally employed in agriculture and in the informal services sector, where self-employment is more common and wages more flexible. This process, however, limited the growth of labor productivity and real income in these sectors.

Table 11.1. Agriculture in the National Economy[a]

	1965	1975	1985	1995	1999
Per capita GDP (1965=100)	100	131	128	143	146
Share of agriculture (%) in:					
GDP	31.5	26.9	28.6	21.8	17.9
Employment	58.6	56.7	48.9	43.5	39.8
Imports	22.2	13.6	12.4	9.8	9.3
Exports	85.6	66.2	35.8	13.6	7.3
Ratio of agricultural imports to agricultural exports (%)	26.8	27.6	38.0	114.0	142.1

Note: [a] Three-year averages centered on the year shown.

Source: NSCB (various issues); Foreign Trade Statistics (various issues).

In recent development experiences, especially in the celebrated newly industrialized economies of East Asia, the development process is also shown to be accompanied by a declining share of agriculture in total exports, an increasing dependence on food imports (at least for countries with relatively low land endowment per worker), and an increasing share of nonfarm income in total income (Oshima, 1987). The development process could also bring about absolute declines in the number of farm workers (Chenery and Syrquin, 1975). In the Philippines, the growth of per capita income, albeit small in relation to those of neighboring countries, was accompanied by a sharp fall in agriculture's share in total foreign trade. Agriculture's share of exports plummeted from 86 percent in the mid-1960s to only 7 percent in the late 1990s. In the case of imports, the fall was from 22 percent to 9 percent.

The agricultural sector performed quite well during the 1960s and the 1970s. The sector's annual growth, averaging 4.6 percent, was then substantially higher than the norm for most Asian developing countries (Table 11.2). Beginning in the mid-1960s, increments to land productivity (i.e., in output per unit of land) increasingly became the major source of growth in food production. At the height of the green revolution, yield increases accounted for much of the growth in agriculture. These gains were brought about mainly by the expansion of irrigation systems, increased application of fertilizers, adoption of high-yielding varieties, and investments in rural infrastructure and education.

In recent decades, less developed countries (LDCs) with relatively high growth rates of agricultural output also tended to have comparatively high GDP growth rates (World Bank, 1986: 79–80). The correlation is clear for the Asian developing countries (Table 11.2). This observation is, of course, not surpris-

Table 11.2. Agricultural Growth in Asian Developing Countries

Country	Average Growth Rate (% per year)				Share of Agriculture in GDP (%)	
	Agriculture		GDP			
	1965–1980	1980–1997	1965–1980	1980–1997	1960	1997
Malaysia		3.0	7.3	6.6	37	13
Thailand	4.6	3.8	7.2	7.6	40	11
Indonesia	4.3	3.2	8.0	6.7	54	16
Philippines	4.6	1.4	5.9	1.9	26	20
Sri Lanka	2.7	1.9	4.0	4.5	32	22
Pakistan	3.3	4.1	5.1	5.5	46	26
India	2.5	3.1	3.6	5.8	50	27
Bangladesh	1.5	2.3	2.4	4.4	58	30
Nepal	1.1	3.3	1.9	4.8		43
China	2.8	5.3	6.4	10.9		20
Vietnam	0.8	4.7	0.8	6.2		

Note: Blank cells = not available.

Source: World Bank, *World Development Report* (various issues); ADB, *Asian Development Outlook* (various issues); FAO (1999).

ing, given that agriculture and agriculture-dependent manufacturing in a typical LDC is a large fraction of the economy. In the Philippine case, the remarkably robust agricultural growth for the period 1965–1980 was accompanied by GDP growth that closely matched the averages for the Asian developing countries (2.3 percent a year) and the middle-income developing countries (3.6 percent a year). Similarly, the dismal growth of agriculture in the 1980s and 1990s paralleled the poor performance of the overall economy.

Growth among the major subsectors, however, was far from uniform (Table 11.3). Fishery registered the highest annual growth rate, averaging 5.2 percent a year, during the 1965–1980 period. Consequently, the share of fishery in the sector's gross value added (GVA) rose from 12 percent in the mid-1960s to roughly 20 percent in the early 1980s. The growth of crop GVA, averaging 3 percent a year during the period, also stood out in historical perspective. Growth was particularly robust for corn, banana, and "other crops." This subsector accounted for about four-fifths of the observed growth of total agricultural output.

However, output growth for virtually all crops decelerated in the 1980s and 1990s. One reason is the slowdown in the conversion of lands for cultivation. While agricultural land expanded (primarily through deforestation) at a rate of 3.6 percent annually in the 1970s, the rate slowed to only 0.8 percent a year in the 1980s and early 1990s.

Table 11.3. Average Growth Rates of Agriculture by Subsector

Sector	1965–1980		1980–1990		1990–1999	
Agriculture	3.7	(100.0)[a]	1.2	(100.0)	1.5	(100.0)
All crops	3.0	(80.5)	0.6	(29.9)	1.5	(50.3)
Rice	4.0	(14.2)	2.6	(24.4)	3.8	(29.3)
Corn	5.7	(8.1)	3.5	(13.6)	0.3	(0.4)
Coconut	3.8	(8.8)	−4.6	(−19.9)	−2.0	(−0.7)
Sugarcane	4.2	(4.7)	−1.6	(−3.0)	4.7	(5.5)
Banana	11.8	(4.8)	−3.5	(−5.1)	2.6	(3.5)
Other crops	7.5	(39.9)	1.5	(20.0)	1.0	(12.3)
Poultry and livestock	2.3	(7.6)	6.0	(53.3)	4.6	(45.0)
Agricultural activities	[b]		4.1	(10.3)	0.0	(1.1)
Fishery	5.2	(20.8)	3.9	(46.1)	1.5	(13.8)
Forestry	−5.2	(−8.8)	−7.8	(−39.6)	−18.5	(−10.1)

Notes: [a] Growth rates pertain to gross value added. Figures in parentheses are contributions to the overall growth of agriculture. The agricultural sector comprises crops, poultry, livestock, fishery, forestry, and agricultural services. [b] Included in "other crops" category.

Source: NSCB (various issues).

Exogenous factors also contributed to the deceleration in the 1980s, including drops in world commodity prices affecting the country's traditional export crops (e.g., sugar and coconut), a series of natural calamities and droughts, and the virtual completion of the green revolution by the early 1980s. In addition, there were policy-related factors, such as the policy uncertainty regarding the Comprehensive Agrarian Reform Program (CARP) and the sharp decline in public investments in agriculture.

The poultry and livestock subsector has emerged as the only consistent performer through the years, growing at an average of 6 percent annually in the 1980s and about 5 percent for most of the succeeding decade. Its strong showing contrasts with the declining performance of the fishery subsector and the diminished role of the forestry subsector. The share of poultry and livestock output in agricultural GVA has steadily climbed, from 14 percent in the mid-1960s to 21 percent by the late 1990s. The macroeconomic difficulties of the 1980s and early 1990s apparently failed to prevent the poultry and livestock subsector from achieving respectable growth rates. It managed to record the highest rate of expansion among all the subsectors of agriculture, contributing about 50 percent of the observed growth of agriculture's GVA in the 1980s and 1990s. Growth in poultry production (mainly chicken) accounted for much of the progress, which could be partially explained by the relatively high nominal protection rate induced by domestic policy.

4. Rural Welfare Outcomes

The rural sector, which comprises half of the total population (52 percent), continues to account for over 70 percent of all the poor nationwide (Table 11.4). The overwhelming majority of the rural poor are in agriculture. Moreover, the incidence of poverty in agriculture (60 percent in 1997) is substantially higher than in either industry or the services sector (Balisacan, 1999).

Table 11.4. Rural Poverty Estimates—Official Methodology

	1985	1988	1991	1994	1997
Rural					
Population share	61.3	62.0	49.9	50.2	52.4
Poverty incidence	56.4	52.3	55.0	53.1	51.4
Share in total poverty	70.2	71.4	60.8	65.7	72.2
No. of poor persons ('000s)	18,744	18,118	17,346	17,988	19,591
Agriculture (urban and rural)					
Population share	47.4	45.5	44.5	43.3	40.1
Poverty incidence	63.7	61.7	63.7	62.0	60.3
Share in total poverty	61.3	61.7	62.7	66.2	64.7
No. of poor persons ('000s)	16,344	15,552	17,910	18,103	17,561

Note: The official approach to poverty measurement uses region-specific poverty lines (i.e., food and nonfood menus), differentiated by urban and rural areas, and current income as a broad measure of household standard of living. A person in a given region is deemed poor if his income is below the poverty line for that region. The incidence of poverty is defined as the proportion of the population deemed poor.

Source: Author's estimates based on the *Family Income and Expenditures Survey* (various issues).

Based on the official approach to poverty estimation, the level of rural poverty hardly changed during the 1960s through the mid-1980s (Table 11.5). The *Family Income and Expenditures Survey* (FIES) data show that poverty incidence in rural areas was 55 percent in the mid-1960s, 57 percent in the early 1970s, and 59 percent in the mid-1980s.[1] Wage income data from the *Labor Force Surveys* (LFS) during the 1970s and early 1980s suggest that the average living standard of rural workers changed only little during the period despite a strong performance in national income growth (Balisacan et al., 2000). The extent of poverty reduction could have been attenuated by

---

1. Conducted every three years since 1985, the FIES provides the only nationally representative surveys for poverty comparison in the Philippines. Unit record data are available for these surveys. Earlier surveys covering 1961, 1965, and 1971 are available only in published form. While surveys covering 1975 and 1979 are also available, these are beset by serious technical problems (Balisacan, 1995).

Table 11.5. Rural Poverty Estimates, 1961–1997

	1961	1965	1971	1985	1988	1991	1994	1997
Official Approach								
Incidence	64.1	55.2	57.3	59.4	50.2	52.4	53.1	51.4
Depth	30.4	26.2	27.1	23.5	18.6	19.0	18.2	18.0
Severity	18.0	16.1	16.4	12.2	9.0	9.0	8.3	8.0
Author's Approach								
Incidence				53.1	45.7	48.6	45.4	36.9
Depth				17.8	14.0	15.6	13.0	9.8
Severity				8.0	5.9	6.8	5.2	3.6

Notes: Blank cells = not available. Official approach uses region-specific poverty lines (i.e., food and nonfood menus), differentiated by urban and rural areas, and current income as a broad measure of household standard of living. This author's approach uses spatially fixed poverty norm and per capita consumption expenditures, adjusted for provincial cost-of-living differences, as a broad measure of standard of living. See Balisacan (1999) for details.

Source: Author's estimates based on the *Family Income and Expenditures Surveys* (various issues).

worsening income inequality, with the poor gaining relatively little from higher average incomes. Furthermore, rural poverty also appeared quite insensitive to agricultural growth itself from the mid-1960s through to the mid-1980s (Ranis and Stewart, 1993; Balisacan, 1993).

In contrast with the relatively stable levels of rural poverty during the 1960s through the early 1980s, poverty incidence during the latter half of the 1980s and through the 1990s appears to follow a declining trend. Based on the FIES data, the incidence of poverty declined from 53 percent in 1985 to 37 percent in 1997 (Table 11.5).[2] The decline is quite impressive, given the fact that, in contrast with the steady aggregate growth during the 1960s and the 1970s (when poverty remained stable at a high level), there were large fluctuations in aggregate economic growth during the mid-1980s through the mid-1990s. Hayami and Kikuchi (2000) argue that the increase in the income of the landless poor during the 1990s came mainly from increased employment opportunities in nonfarm economic activities. The

2.   The official approach to poverty measurement does not capture well the changes in the standard of living of the poor. This is so because the official poverty lines applied for various regions, areas, and years imply different levels of living standards, tending to systematically underestimate (overestimate) the reduction (increase) in absolute poverty in economically more progressive (backward) regions or sectors, or during periods when the overall economy is expanding (contracting). The problem arises because of the use of region-specific (and, within regions, area-specific) poverty lines based on the prevailing consumption pattern of that region (area). See Balisacan (1999).

increase in nonfarm income-earning opportunities for the rural poor, in turn, resulted from both the greater integration of the rural labor markets into the urban and the increase in nonfarm income opportunities within rural areas (such as petty trading and local transportation services).

Thus, despite some fluctuations in the poverty level over relatively short horizons, there has clearly been a consistent trend to reduction in poverty in rural areas after the mid-1980s. Overall, however, the pace of the poverty reduction in the Philippines during the past four decades is nothing but a disappointment compared to the poverty reduction performance in neighboring Asian countries. Using the internationally comparable "$1 a day" poverty line used by the World Bank, for example, the incidence of poverty in the Philippines fell by 10 percentage points, from 36 percent to 26 percent, between 1975 and 1995. In Indonesia during the same period, the result was far more impressive: the incidence of poverty dropped from 64 percent to 11 percent; in Thailand, poverty incidence fell from 8 percent to near zero.

Changes in the welfare level of the rural population cannot be captured solely by the changes in income and consumption expenditure profiles. Equally important are access to resources needed for the opportunity to lead a long and healthy life and the ability to acquire and use knowledge. Considerable improvement in life expectancy, literacy, and child health occurred between the early 1960s and the 1980s, but as with income growth, these achievements paled in comparison with those of neighboring countries (Tables 11.6 and 11.7). The average annual changes in these indicators for the latter group of countries outpaced those for the Philippines, although some improvement occurred in the 1990s.

A little over half the entire rural population in the Philippines had access to safe water and sanitation services in the 1980s, but this situation substantially improved in the next decade (Balisacan, Debuque, and Fuwa, 2000). The same is true with regard to access to sanitation services, although the progress has not been as distinct. Rural-urban disparities in access to services have also somewhat narrowed over time. Access to safe water used to be available to a greater proportion of the rural population than it was for the urban population, while the opposite was true for sanitation services. Despite such developments, however, rural households still have much weaker access to sanitation services. Viewed from an international perspective, a relatively large percentage of the rural population in the Philippines has access to basic services. On average, only about 60 percent of rural populations in developing Asia have access to safe water. For sanitation services, the corresponding figure is even lower at slightly less than 40 percent.[3]

---

3. These figures must be taken with extreme caution, however, given the low quality of available data in many developing countries, including the Philippines.

5. Government Policies Affecting Rural Development[4]

a. Development strategies and economywide policies

There has emerged a consensus among economic researchers that the failure of the Philippines to grow robustly on a sustainable basis and to induce substantial poverty reduction during the last half century stems mainly from the absence of an "effective allocation mechanism" that allows the true comparative advantage of various industries to emerge (Bautista, Power, and Associates, 1979; Bautista and Tecson, 2000). Instead, past governments introduced distortions in economic policies, which, in not a few cases, made socially undesirable investments attractive to private investors and desirable ones (i.e., promising and efficient activities) relatively unprofitable (Power and Sicat, 1971; Medalla et al., 1995). Such policies not only hampered economic growth at the national level, but also produced side effects deleterious to rural development.

From the 1950s to the 1980s, an array of policies meant to push the country onto an import-substituting industrialization track inadvertently stunted the development of the rural sector by creating a bias towards large-scale, capital-intensive manufacturing industries located in urban areas (especially Metro Manila), to the detriment of rural enterprises, which are inherently smaller in size, hire more labor, and make greater use of local materials (Medalla et al., 1995; Ranis and Stewart, 1993). These policies also created an incentive structure that was significantly biased against agriculture, the economic backbone of the rural sector. Trade and exchange rate policies then distorted the relative prices of agricultural inputs and outputs, preventing an efficient allocation of resources, and tended to heavily favor the manufacturing sector over agriculture, nontradable over tradable goods, and import-competing over export products. Under such circumstances, resources move away from agriculture and export sectors; new investments into these sectors are discouraged. Since agricultural production is more labor-intensive, less import-dependent, and more efficient in earning (or saving) foreign exchange than industrial production (especially of import-competing industrial consumer goods), the premature shift of resources away from agriculture dampens the growth of employment opportunities and output in rural areas.

Many authors point out that the bias came largely from measures not aimed directly at agricultural commodities, although government interventions in the form of taxes, customs duties, subsidies, quantitative trade restrictions, import prohibitions, price controls, and monopoly control in international trade had,

---

4.   This section has drawn largely from Balisacan, Debuque, and Fuwa (2000).

Table 11.6. Standard of Living and Human Development in the Philippines, Indonesia, and Thailand

	Real GDP Per Capita (1995 PPP dollar)		Human Development Index	Incidence of Poverty		
	1965	1995	1995	1975	1985	1995
Thailand	1,570	6,723	0.838	8.1	10.0	<1.0
Indonesia	817	3,346	0.679	64.3	32.2	11.4
Philippines	1,736	2,475	0.677	35.7	32.4	25.5

Note: PPP = Purchasing Power Parity.

Source: Real GDP per capita and incidence of poverty, Ahuja et al. (1997); *Human Development Index*, UNDP (1999).

Table 11.7. Indicators of Human Development in the Philippines, Indonesia, and Thailand

	Life Expectancy at Birth (years)				Infant Mortality Rate (per 1,000 live births)				Gross Primary School Enrollment (percent)				Adult Illiteracy Rate (percent)			
	1962	1970	1980	1998	1960	1970	1980	1998	1960	1970	1980	1997	1960	1970	1980	1996
Thailand	54	58	64	72	95	73	49	29	83	83	99	89	32.3	21.4	12.0	6.2
Indonesia	43	48	55	65	133	118	90	43	71	80	107	113	61.0	43.4	32.7	16.2
Philippines	55	57	61	69	76	66	52	32	95	108	112	117	28.1	17.4	16.7	5.4

Source: World Bank, *World Development Report* (various issues).

up until the late 1980s, affected agricultural incentives. It was rather the *indirect* effect of the overall development strategy that accounted for a substantial part of the policy bias in the past (e.g., Intal and Power, 1990; Bautista, 1987; Bautista and Tecson, 2000). The primary channel had been the overvaluation of the domestic currency, which in turn had its roots in the industrial protection system and in fiscal, monetary, and exchange rate policies, specifically those adopted to promote import substitution and accommodate current account imbalances.

Estimates of the overvaluation of the domestic currency in the 1970s and 1980s are on the order of 20–30 percent. Making use of the same methodology, Bautista (1990) showed that these rates are much higher than those derived for Thailand (16–24 percent) and Malaysia (less than 3 percent).

b. Sectoral policies

In the early 1970s, Government interventions in Philippine agriculture started to rise to unprecedented levels. The Government intervened intensively in agricultural production, marketing, and international trade. The intervention in the rice sector was precipitated by a rice crisis in 1971–72 resulting from both local (poor weather, pest infestation and the great flood in Central Luzon) and international (a sharp price hike in the world market) shocks. The Government responded to the crisis by imposing price controls on rice and embarking on a massive program aimed at achieving rice self-sufficiency. Dubbed "Masagana (Prosperous) 99" and launched in 1974, the program called for Government assistance in the form of credit, irrigation, extension services, and fertilizer subsidization.

Furthermore, the National Grains Authority, the Government's rice and corn agency, expanded its control of the food sector to include the effective monopolization of wheat (beginning 1975) and soybean (beginning 1978) imports. Marketing controls included all food commodities by the early 1980s, when the National Grains Authority was transformed into the National Food Authority (NFA) as the Government's food price stabilization arm. The NFA financed its expanded operations partly from price margins on its duty-free imports. In the case of the export crop sector, the Government shifted from its traditional role of allocating domestic sugar quotas, collecting minor export taxes and undertaking research and extension in tandem with the private sector, to that of monopolizing domestic and export marketing.

The economic consequences and cost of Government interventions in the 1970s and 1980s have been well documented in the literature. In most cases, the interventions were either ineffective or yielded results contrary to avowed intentions. In the case of rice, for example, while increased Government intervention during the 1970s reduced seasonal fluctuations in *palay* (paddy) prices, the intervention was inadequate to maintain producer prices at the official floor level. This meant that the opportunities to sell at the official price had to be rationed, often to the disadvantage of small farmers. In addition, because the difference between official ceiling and floor prices was insufficient to cover normal marketing margins, the intervention prevented the development of private trading and storage. Arguably, the Government's objective of reducing marketing margins could have been achieved with nonprice policy interventions such as investment in transport and communications infrastructure.

One other major policy measure that was high on the agenda during the early 1970s was agrarian reform (land reform). Presidential Decree No. 27 (PD27) stipulated that all rice and corn fields of more than seven hectares be transferred to the tenants who tilled them, at a price 2.5 times the value of average annual production; and that all the rice and corn lands of seven hectares or less under share tenancy be converted to fixed-rent leasehold, with the official rental ceiling of 25 percent of average output for the three "normal" years prior to land reform. Compared to earlier land reform legislation, PD27 expanded the potential coverage of the land under the reform program by lowering the retention limit, among other things.

While the 1970s saw an unprecedented rise of Government interventions in agriculture in the form of price and quantitative controls, levies, and taxes, as well as entry into activities for which the public good argument was unjustified, the late 1980s saw an undoing of these policies in the direction of a market-oriented agricultural economy, relieved of the burden of explicit as well as implicit taxation of agriculture. The deregulation that commenced in 1986 took the following forms:

- lifting of the export ban on copra and export taxes on copra (10 percent) and coconut oil (5 percent);
- abolition of monopsonistic agencies and arrangements in sugar and coconut trading and the dismantling of Government monopoly control over international trade in coconut oil, corn, soybeans, soybean meal, and the marketing of sugar;
- liberalization of fertilizer distribution and importation;
- removal of price controls on rice, poultry products, and pork;
- opening up of import trade in wheat, flour, and animal feed to the private sector;
- divestment by the NFA of nongrain activities and the reorientation of its primary function to price stabilization of rice and corn; and
- consolidation of commodity-specific funds into the Comprehensive Agricultural Loan Fund to unify various agricultural lending programs and minimize Government participation in these programs.

Despite these reform measures, however, the deregulation of agriculture was left substantially incomplete. Reforms undertaken did not include the abolition of the remaining restrictions, such as

- the NFA monopoly of international trade and domestic market operations in rice and corn;
- import controls on sugar;
- import prohibitions on onions, potatoes, garlic, cabbage, coffee, and seeds;
- hectarage controls on banana production;
- the centralized importation of ruminants (for breeding and/or slaughter) and beef;
- bans on buntal and ramie planting materials;
- export restrictions on animals and animal products; and
- the licensing and/or registration of production and domestic trade for some agricultural goods.

Rather than expanding the scope of deregulation, which could have had a positive impact on the welfare of the rural population (see Balisacan [1991]), the Government moved instead to strengthen the regulation of agriculture, especially the international trade in agricultural products. In 1992, Congress, with the endorsement of the executive branch, passed Republic Act 7607 (the Magna Carta of Small Farmers), which barred importation of agricultural products produced locally in sufficient quantity.

Another major government program initiated in the late 1980s that had a profound effect on the agriculture sector was CARP. Launched in 1988 under Republic Act 6675, the program, unlike its predecessor PD27, covered all agricultural lands, regardless of commodity produced and type of tenurial arrangement, and included the provision of support services for farmers. CARP was intended to redistribute about 580,000 hectares of rice and corn lands (which were also covered under PD27) and more than 2 million hectares of privately-owned nonrice/corn lands (covered for the first time under CARP) over a period of 10 years. The huge budgetary requirement of the program, together with the limited capacity of the agencies tasked to implement it, stood in the way of swift implementation.

The uncertainty surrounding the program's implementation served to discourage the flow of private investment into agriculture as well as encouraging nonplanting and premature conversion of agricultural lands to nonagricultural uses, a trend exacerbated by weak monitoring by the Government and the absence of a comprehensive land use policy (see, for example, Medalla and Centeno [1994]). Aside from dampening the flow of agricultural investments, CARP also diminished the collateral value of agricultural land by constraining private land sales. This feature of the program has caused the demise of the private market for agricultural land. Indeed, the amount of loans (at constant prices) granted by private and government banks in the early 1990s was only half that in the early 1980s. Loans by private institutions, including private commercial banks, dropped by even more than loans by public institutions. Loans per peso of agricultural value added fell from about 0.42 in 1980–1982 to 0.20 in 1985–1987 and 0.16 in 1991–1992.

As seen in the previous section, production growth rates decelerated during the 1980s and the early 1990s for most crops. The deceleration can be attributed to the combination of some exogenous factors (such as price changes in world markets, natural calamities, and droughts) and government policies. The negative policy impact includes the unintended negative side effects of CARP, as mentioned above, as well as the sharp fall in public investment in agriculture—especially rural roads, irrigation and research—in the 1980s and early 1990s. In particular, investments in agricultural research and development (R&D), the single most important source of long-term output growth, stagnated in the 1970s and then dropped in absolute value in the 1980s; the total spent on R&D in the early 1990s was only 60 percent of that in the early 1970s (David and Roumasset, 2000).

A change in the policy environment had been anticipated with the country's accession to the World Trade Organization (WTO) in 1995, since this required opening up local agricultural markets to competition as well as enacting laws prescribed by the trade treaty.[5] Political negotiations to win public support for this policy direction, in turn, severely weakened the drive toward greater openness in the farm sector. Rice, for instance, has been exempted from the trade commitments for a period of 10 years. In 1996, Congress passed Republic Act 8178, lifting all quantitative restrictions on agricultural imports (except rice), but replacing nontariff barriers with the highest possible tariff protection rate of 100 percent (i.e., the ceiling or binding tariff rates).[6] Clarete (1999) has pointed out that the manner of "tariffication" resulted in tariff levels that exceeded the corresponding equivalent nontariff rates of most products. The tariff rate equivalent of quantitative restrictions on corn, for example, was estimated to be only 60 percent, but government "tariffied" the commodity at the maximum rate of 100 percent.[7] David and Roumasset (2000) similarly showed that binding tariffs were higher than either the nominal protection rates from quantitative

---

5. Commitments of the Philippines with regard to agriculture include a prohibition on the use of (additional) nontariff measures, conversion of all existing quantitative restrictions to tariff measures (except for rice, the tariffication of which has been deferred for 10 years), binding tariffs at ceiling rates, tariff reductions (average cut of 30 percent), and harmonization of sanitary and phytosanitary measures.
6. These binding (tariff) rates are slated to go down to a range of about 40 percent to 50 percent for the various crops in 2004, in accordance with the WTO agreement.
7. Binding rates on corn are scheduled to fall to 50 percent after a 10-year period. High tariff protection of corn, which is used as feed in the livestock industry, in turn spurred high tariff protection of hogs, poultry, and meat products as a compensatory measure.

trade restrictions or the book tariff rates under Executive Order 470 issued in July 1991, which aimed to significantly reduce the number of commodity lines with high tariffs and to increase the number of commodity lines with low tariffs over a five-year period.

As noted in the previous section, after a decade of stagnation in the 1980s, production growth in the agricultural sector recovered in the 1990s. The combination of the sweeping reforms in nonagricultural sectors and the increasing government protection of agriculture led to an apparent rise in relative prices of agricultural products in domestic markets, and thus may partially explain the upturn in agricultural growth in the 1990s.

The Agriculture and Fisheries Modernization Act was enacted in 1997 partly in response to the farm lobbies' opposition to the country's entry to the WTO. The act prescribes a coordinated set of measures aimed at enhancing the competitiveness of domestic agriculture in the global marketplace. These include infrastructure development, devolution of communal irrigation systems to local government units, budgetary allocation for R&D in agriculture, a phase-out of directed credit programs, and provision of post-harvest facilities.

While there have been efforts to liberalize the agriculture sector, crucial restrictions have remained, such as the continued monopoly of the NFA over the rice trade and hectarage controls on banana production. In addition, profitability levels of the sugar and corn sectors were becoming artificially high, due to increased protection afforded by the new tariff regime as well as regulatory barriers, thus reducing the competitiveness of allied industries. Corn is the main input of the livestock sector, while sugar is an essential ingredient in the food processing industry.

The land reform program, meanwhile, could not be completed as scheduled (i.e., by 1997), although relevant local agencies performed relatively well compared to their predecessors in terms of land distribution. Only a little over half the total coverage was redistributed. Implementation had been particularly slow for public alienable and disposable lands and private agricultural lands (other than rice and corn lands), representing about 45 percent and 25 percent, respectively, of the total coverage of the program. For public alienable and disposable lands, the poor performance could be traced mainly to delays in undertaking land surveys, slow reconstitution of land records, and sluggish resolution of land conflicts among competing claimants. For private agricultural lands, the main problems included the time-consuming process involved in land acquisition and distribution, insufficient technical capacity of implementing agencies, legal disputes relating to coverage and land valuation, landowners' resistance, harassment, an unstable peace and order situation, and budget constraints (Balisacan, 1996b). As noted earlier, the negative indirect effects of the slow and incomplete implementation and the uncertainty created as a result (i.e., disincentives for private investment, incentives for nonplanting or premature land conversion, and negative effects on land market transactions) continue to be a serious problem for stimulating agricultural development.

A convenient summary measure of the direct impact of trade and industrial policies is the effective rate of protection (ERP), defined as the percentage excess of protected value added over nonprotected value added by a particular economic activity. This measure takes into account the changes in the domestic prices of both inputs and outputs arising from tariffs and import controls. A positive ERP implies that the sector is accorded protection by the system of tariffs and import controls, while a negative ERP indicates that the system penalizes (i.e., taxes) the activity of the sector.

The primary and agricultural sectors typically had lower ERPs than manufacturing during the period between 1965 and the early 1990s—most of the period under our review. Thus, until the early 1990s, the agricultural sector as a whole was penalized vis-à-vis the manufacturing sector in terms of relative prices (Table 11.8). Through the 1990s, however, this bias against agriculture (at least on aggregate) appears to have finally disappeared; the ERPs for agriculture became roughly equivalent to the ERPs for manufacturing. Such a result can largely be attributed to the substantial changes in the country's tariff structure over the last 10 years. Clarete's (1991) and Medalla's (1992) assessments of Executive Order 470 indicate that the tariff reform program moved the country toward a lower, sector-neutral, and trade-neutral effective protection policy.

With the steady progression of the tariff reform program during the period, the 1990s saw both declining protection rates of manufactured inputs (including agricultural inputs) and increased (tariff) protection of major agricultural commodities for which quantitative restrictions had been removed. Falling input prices (with the obvious exception of yellow corn for the livestock industry) imply that the *effective* protection level of agriculture afforded by domestic policy has outstripped the *nominal* protection level of the sector.

6. Toward an Empirical Examination of the Determinants of Poverty Reduction in Rural Areas

As noted above, rural welfare outcomes vary substantially, not only across regions but also across sectors of the economy. The wide variation also exists across provinces (Figure 11.2). This section assesses the influence of certain time-varying factors, such as policy regime, and *initial* conditions—related to infrastructure, distribution of physical and human assets, income, and institutions—in accounting for the performance of the various provinces of the Philippines in poverty reduction. The analysis focuses on the period from the late

Table 11.8. Effective Rates of Protection by Major Sector (percent)

	1965	1974	1985[a]	1988[a]	1991	1993	1995	1996	1997	1998	1999	2000
Effective rate of protection												
Overall average		36	49	37	28	29	22	25	23	20	19	18
Agriculture and Primary sectors		9	9	5	23	24	22	22	21	19	18	18
Agriculture	17	15	21	15	27	26	26	29	26	26	24	24
Fishery		116	8	5	18	21	16	11	11	6	6	6
Forestry	(26)	(10)	(22)	(22)	12	12	11	5	5	3	3	3
Mining	(17)	(2)	0	(2)	1	1	1	0	0	0	0	0
Manufacturing	51	44	73	56	31	33	23	28	26	22	20	19
Relative protection [b] (Agriculture=100)												
Agriculture and Primary sectors		95	90	91	97	98	97	95	96	94	95	95
Agriculture	100	100	100	100	100	100	100	100	100	100	100	100
Fishery		188	89	91	93	96	92	86	88	84	85	85
Forestry	63	78	64	68	88	89	88	81	83	82	83	83
Mining	71	85	83	85	80	80	80	78	79	79	81	81
Manufacturing	129	125	143	136	103	106	98	99	100	97	97	96

Notes: [a] Estimates were based on price comparisons. [b] $(1 + ERP_j)/(1 + ERP_a)$, where ERP_j is the effective rate of protection of sector j and ERP_a is the effective rate of protection of agriculture. Numbers in parenthesis indicate policies result in negative protection to sector.

Sources: 1965, Power and Sicat (1971); 1974, Tan (1979); 1985 and 1988, Medalla (1990); 1991, 1993, 1995–2000, Manasan and Querubin (1997).

Figure 11.2. Poverty Reduction, 1988–1997: Incidence

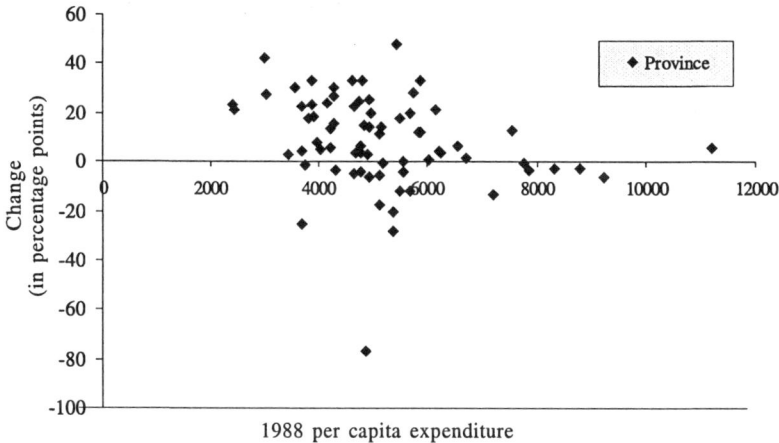

1988 per capita expenditure

1980s to the late 1990s, during which comparable nationwide household survey data disaggregated by province are available.[8]

How important are these factors in explaining provincial differences in poverty reduction? In systematically addressing this issue, we have estimated reduced-form functions relating to changes in the proportion of the rural population deemed poor.[9] The poverty data are estimates based on the comparable provincial poverty lines reported in Balisacan (1999). The household data employed are the 1988 and 1997 FIES rounds. These data are supplemented by provincial indicators obtained from various sources.

In each function, we have included the following initial-condition variables: poverty level at the start of the period; land inequality, given by the landholding Gini ratio which has extreme values of one (perfect inequality) and zero (perfect equality); average farm size; irrigation, expressed as the ratio of irrigated to total farm area; road wealth, defined as quality-adjusted road length per square kilometer of land; and Pinatubo, a dummy variable indicating provinces devastated by the Mount Pinatubo eruption in 1991.

In addition, we have included variables representing the political environment: dynasty, defined as the proportion of local officials related to each other by blood or affinity, with respect to the total number of elective positions; political party, a dummy variable indicating whether the provincial governor

8. The choice of province instead of region as the unit of analysis permits the use of a much larger number of observations (73 as opposed to 13) for econometric work. In this section, "rural areas" pertain to all provinces outside of major cities (Metro Manila, Cebu, and Davao).

9. Results for two other regressions involving the depth and severity of poverty (not reported, for brevity, in this paper) are qualitatively similar to those reported in Table 11.9.

belonged to the political party of the president; and MILF, a dummy variable indicating whether the province had problems with Muslim insurgency.

To capture the effects of time-varying factors on the evolution of poverty, we have added the change in the values of the following regressors: agricultural terms of trade, defined as the ratio of the price of agriculture to nonagriculture; electricity, defined as the proportion of households with access to electricity; functional literacy, defined as the proportion of adult population who can read, write, and execute simple messages; CARP, proportion of cumulative accomplishment under this program to total potential land reform area; and RGDP, defined as regional per capita GDP.

The land-inequality variable reflects access to land and, given imperfections in credit markets, serves as a proxy for household ability to smooth consumption during shocks. This variable is expected to be negatively correlated with performance in poverty reduction. The irrigation variable is a proxy for land quality. It is expected to positively influence poverty reduction. Road wealth is proxy for access to markets and off-farm employment. The functional-literacy variable reflects the quality of human capital. Investment in human capital is expected to improve returns to labor (among other channels) and hence reduce poverty. The terms-of-trade variable reflects the relative price incentives for agriculture. RGDP is a proxy for overall economic climate in the region. The political dummy variables reflect the quality of local governance and access to fiscal resources. The dynasty variable captures the extent of participation (competition) in local politics. One may expect that a political dynasty inhibits economic growth through its negative effect on the efficient operation of markets (e.g., restricting competition in local markets to create rents for the political clan) and, hence, on performance in poverty reduction.[10] The political-party-affiliation variable reflects access to the national coffers for local economic development.

The regression results are given in Table 11.9. The models explain roughly three fourths of the observed differences in poverty reduction across 73 provinces between 1988 and 1997.

As expected, the initial level of poverty influences the speed of poverty reduction. That is, provinces with initially high levels of poverty tend also to be the ones with a relatively rapid rate of poverty reduction, all other factors remaining constant. This has to do partly with the fact that the distribution of living standards is invariably skewed to the left. Thus, for a given growth rate and income distribution, poverty reduction would

---

10. Put differently, local governance by a political dynasty may make feasible the concentration of economic controls in a few hands, thereby leading to (or perpetuating) high income inequality. High income inequality, in turn, may inhibit subsequent growth in the local economy, as suggested by recent development literature.

Table 11.9. Determinants of Poverty Reduction

Explanatory variable	Full Model		Final Model	
	Regression coefficient	t-ratio	Regression coefficient	t-ratio
Initial Conditions: Late 1980s				
Incidence	0.790	8.48	0.820	10.55
Land inequality	0.521	1.01		
Farm size	(0.375)	(0.21)		
Irrigation	9.301	0.97	15.348	1.85
Road wealth	12.700	2.72	12.250	2.90
Dynasty	(7.186)	(1.09)		
Political party	1.206	0.41		
Pinatubo	6.265	0.87		
MILF	1.922	0.33		
Change between 1988 and 1997				
Terms of trade	41.945	1.74	45.590	2.32
RGDP	0.001	3.15	0.002	4.77
Electricity	0.308	2.46	0.277	2.31
Functional literacy	(0.174)	(1.02)		
CARP	4.444	2.31	3.057	2.19
Constant	(85.843)	(2.55)	(61.160)	(5.15)
Adjusted R squared	0.713		0.721	
F-ratio	11.26		22.01	

Note: Dependent variable is change in poverty incidence between 1988 and 1997. Data pertain to 73 provinces.

Source: Author's estimates.

be higher for provinces with initially lower mean income (and hence higher poverty). Put differently, the higher the initial poverty level, the higher the marginal return (in terms of poverty reduction) on an investment raising mean income.

Initial landholding inequality is not significant in all three equations, but the CARP variable is, suggesting that in provinces where the implementation of the agrarian reform program was relatively rapid, poverty reduction likewise tended to be relatively fast, all other things remaining the same. This result supports the finding of Deininger et al. (2000), demonstrating that CARP beneficiaries achieved higher household incomes than comparable households not covered by the program, all else remaining the same.

Farm size and irrigation are also important determinants of poverty reduction, as expected. The positive and significant coefficient of the irrigation variable suggests that improvements in land quality offer an important avenue for speeding up poverty reduction, especially in areas where poverty continues to be a rural phenomenon.

Road wealth is highly significant and positive in all equations. This result suggests that provinces with initially favorable access to markets and off-farm employment tend to have faster poverty reduction, all else remaining the same. The result confirms the common assertion that public investment in rural infrastructure, especially rural transport, generates economic linkages and externalities critical to sustained growth and development of the local economy (ILO, 1974; World Bank, 2000a).

The overall climate for local growth, as indicated by the regional GDP growth variable, likewise proves to be a significant factor influencing the speed of local poverty reduction. This is consistent with the observation made in Balisacan (2000) that overall growth represents the main source of national poverty reduction in recent years.

Surprisingly, functional literacy is insignificant in all regressions. This result appears to contradict the popular story emanating from East Asia's development experience that suggests that substantial improvements in human capital formed part of the building blocks for sustained economic growth and poverty reduction (Ranis, 1995; World Bank, 2000b). Note, however, that the result may have been unduly biased by the rather short interval (five years) chosen for this variable owing to the limitation of available data.

The dynasty variable, as well as the variable representing the political party affiliation of local government executives, is not significant in all regressions. This is interesting, considering the usual claim that dynasties in local politics inhibit economic performance—through their effects on economic efficiency—and hence poverty reduction. It is possible, however, that these variables do not adequately reflect the quality of, and constraints on, local governance. For instance, the dynasty variable falls short of capturing all the possible networks of blood/marriage relationships running from the provincial governor to municipal officials.

7. Concluding Remarks

This chapter has examined the character of rural development in the Philippines and the policy environment influencing the performance of the rural economy during the postwar period. It has attempted to explain why the pace of poverty reduction in the Philippines has been quite disappointing compared to that of its neighbors.

Growth of agricultural production in the Philippines during the 1960s and 1970s was quite substantial. Much of this growth resulted from increases in productivity, specifically from the adoption of high-yielding varieties, increased use of fertilizers, and expansion of public investment (especially irrigation). However, despite this rather impressive growth, the effect on rural poverty was quite weak. While the incidence of rural poverty declined, with some short-term fluctuations, the pace of poverty reduction paled in comparison to that in, say, Thailand or Indonesia.

One of the main reasons for such a weak response could be the historical processes leading to the social structure of the rural Philippines and the growing incidence of landlessness during the period. Additional reasons could be found in policy measures that were "anti-small farmer" and thus "anti-poor." It has been well documented that economy-wide policies making up the import-substituting industrialization strategy (e.g., overvalued domestic currency, industrial protection) during the 1960s and 1970s depressed the relative price of agricultural products and encouraged capital-intensive patterns of industrialization, thereby hampering the labor absorptive capacity of economic growth and industrialization. Furthermore, policy interventions targeted to the agricultural sector appear to have had anti-small farmer biases. For example, small farmers were rationed out of access to credit, due to the subsidized credit program that reached few small farmers; fertilizer subsidies were ineffective; and public investment in research and infrastructure tended to disproportionately benefit larger farmers.

The poor performance of agriculture in the 1980s and early 1990s resulted from a combination of factors, including the decline of world commodity prices, stagnation in public investments (especially in rural roads, irrigation, and research), exhaustion of the potentials of high-yielding varieties, and uncertainty created by the unduly slow implementation of the land reform program. On the policy front, the overvaluation of the domestic currency persisted throughout the 1980s; as a result, the magnitude of the negative (indirect) protection's effect on the agricultural sector remained relatively high.

Policy measures with anti-small farmer biases introduced in the 1970s were reformed in the 1980s, though these are still not complete. Meanwhile, despite the substantial slowdown of agricultural growth in the 1980s and 1990s, rural poverty continued to decline, albeit very slowly. A main factor that contributed to the increased responsiveness of poverty reduction to economic growth during this period appears to be the expansion in the nonfarm income-earning opportunities in rural areas (see, for example, Hayami and Kikuchi, 2000). In addition, the policy reforms of the 1980s and 1990s may have made the impact of aggregate growth more "pro-poor" compared to the earlier period (Balisacan, 2000). In the 1990s, however, there have been both accelerated policy reforms (e.g., liberalization of foreign exchange markets, trade liberalization, privatization in the service sector) and increased protection of the agricultural sector (e.g., high tariffs overcompensating for the removal of import quotas). Consequently, the effective rate of protection of the agricultural sector became roughly equal to that of the manufacturing sector in the 1990s, a major policy shift from the previous several decades, when the effective protection of agriculture was substantially less than that of manufacturing.

Overall, economic reforms in recent years, albeit largely incomplete, have favorably changed the economic environment of the poor. These have meant that recent episodes of economic growth have been beneficial to the poor, even more so than to the nonpoor. The details of the transmission actually involved from policy reforms to improvement in economic well-being of the poor is an interesting area for future research.

Land reform aimed at reducing inequality in the distribution of landholding is a crucial aspect of rural development and poverty reduction. Throughout the past 50 years, efforts aimed at reforming agrarian relations have not been lacking. Yet, results so far have not been encouraging. Indeed, the unduly long period of land reform implementation has bred unintended effects harmful to agriculture and rural areas. (Successful land reform programs elsewhere, especially in East Asia, were invariably implemented swiftly.) As noted earlier, the uncertainty surrounding the program has discouraged the flow of investments into agriculture, as well as encouraging premature conversion of agricultural lands to nonagricultural uses. Moreover, the program has effectively caused the private market for agricultural land to disappear, thereby diminishing the collateral value of agricultural land and hence discouraging lending to agriculture, especially by private financial institutions.

Priority should also be given to rural infrastructure development, agricultural research and technology transfer, and small- and medium-scale industrial development in rural areas. As the East Asian experience demonstrates, investment in land quality and in access to infrastructure, together with sound "fundamentals" (i.e., fiscal and monetary restraint), are critical to the building of initial conditions for broad-based growth and development.

References

ADB (Asian Development Bank). Various years. *Asian Development Outlook*. Manila.

Ahuja, Vinod, Benu Bidani, Francisco Ferreira, and Michael Walton. 1997. *Everyone's Miracle? Revisiting Poverty and Inequality in East Asia.* Washington, D.C.: World Bank.

Balisacan, Arsenio M. 1991. Deregulation in Philippine Agriculture: Has It Benefited the Rural Poor? In *Deregulation and Economic Development in the Philippines*, edited by Joseph Y. Lim and Katsumi Nozawa. Tokyo: Institute of Developing Economies.

———. 1993. Agricultural Growth, Landlessness, Off-farm Employment, and Rural Poverty in the Philippines. *Economic Development and Cultural Change* 41 (April): 533–562.

———. 1995. Anatomy of Poverty During Adjustment: The Case of the Philippines. *Economic Development and Cultural Change* 44 (October): 33–62.

————.1996a. *Rural Growth, Food Security, and Poverty Alleviation in Developing Asian Countries.* UPSE Discussion Paper No. 9610. Quezon City: University of the Philippines School of Economics.

————. 1996b. Investing in Equity: Toward an Alternative Paradigm for Reforming Agricultural Land Relations. In *Financial Sector Issues in the Philippines,* edited by R. Fabella and K. Ito. Tokyo: Institute of Developing Economies.

————. 1998. Policy Reforms and Agricultural Development in the Philippines. *ASEAN Economic Bulletin* 15: 77–89.

————. 1999. *Poverty Profile in the Philippines: An Update and Reexamination of Evidence in the Wake of the Asian Crisis.* Report prepared for the World Bank. Quezon City: University of the Philippines School of Economics.

————. 2000. *Poverty, Inequality, and Welfare.* Paper prepared for the International Conference on The Philippine Economy: On the Way to Sustained Growth?, Canberra, 1–2 November 2000.

————, Margarita H. Debuque, and Nobuhiko Fuwa. 2000. The Political Economy of Rural Development in the Philippines since the 1960s. World Bank, Washington, D.C. Processed.

Bautista, Romeo M. 1987. *Production Incentives in Philippine Agriculture: Effects of Trade and Exchange Rate Policies.* Research Report 59. Washington, D.C.: International Food Policy Research Institute.

————. 1990. *Rapid Agricultural Growth Is Not Enough: The Philippines, 1965–80.* Paper prepared for the Conference on Agriculture on the Road to Industrialization. Taipei, China.

————, and Gwendolyn Tecson. 2000. *International Dimensions.* Paper prepared for the International Conference on The Philippine Economy: On the Way to Sustained Growth?, Canberra, 1–2 November 2000.

————, John H. Power, and Associates. 1979. *Industrial Promotion Policies in the Philippines.* Makati: Philippine Institute for Development Studies.

Chenery, H.B., and M. Syrquin. 1975. *Patterns of Development, 1950–1970.* London: Oxford University Press.

Clarete, Ramon L. 1991. *E.O. 470: The Economic Effects of the 1991 Tariff Policy Reforms.* Prepared for the United States Agency for International Development.

————. 1999. Trade-Related Problems and Policy Issues in Philippine Agriculture. *Philippine Review of Economics and Business* 36: 127–158.

Datt, Gaurav, and Martin Ravallion. 1992. Growth and Redistribution Components of Changes in Poverty Measures: A Decomposition with Applications to Brazil and India in the 1980s. *Journal of Development Economics* 38: 275–295.

David, Cristina C., and James Roumasset. 2000. Agricultural Sector. Paper prepared for the International Conference on The Philippine Economy: On the Way to Sustained Growth?, Canberra, 1–2 November 2000.

Deininger, Klaus, Francisco Lara, Jr., Miet Maertens, and Agnes Quisumbing. 2000. *Agrarian Reform in the Philippines: Past Impact and Future Challenges.* Washington, D.C.: World Bank.

FAO (Food and Agriculture Organization). 1999. *Poverty Alleviation and Food Security in Asia: Lessons and Challenges.* RAP Publication 1999/1. Bangkok: FAO Regional Office for Asia and the Pacific.

Hayami, Yujiro, and Masao Kikuchi. 2000. *A Rice Village Saga: Three Decades of Green Revolution in the Philippines.* New York: Barnes & Noble.

ILO (International Labour Organisation). 1974. *Sharing in Development: A Programme of Employment, Equity and Growth in the Philippines.* Geneva.

Intal, Ponciano S., Jr., and John H. Power. 1990. *Trade, Exchange Rate, and Agricultural Pricing Policies in the Philippines.* Washington, D.C.: The Political Economy of Agricultural Pricing Policy, World Bank Comparative Studies.

Lipton, Michael, and Martin Ravallion. 1995. Poverty and Policy. In *Handbook of Development Economics, Volume III*, edited by J. Behrman and T. N. Srinavasan. Amsterdam: North Holland.

Manasan, R.G., and R.G. Querubin. 1997. *Assessment of Tariff Reform in the 1990s.* Discussion Paper Series 97-10, Philippine Institute for Development Studies.

Medalla, Erlinda M. 1990. An Assessment of Trade and Industrial Policy, 1986–88. Working Paper Series No. 90-07. Makati: Philippine Institute for Development Studies.

———. 1992. An Assessment of Tariff Reform. *Philippine Economic Journal* 31: 25–40.

———, Gwendolyn, R. Tecson, Romeo M. Bautista, and John H. Power. 1995. *PhilippineTrade and Industrial Policies: Catching up with East Asia's Tigers.* Makati: Philippine Institute for Development Studies.

Medalla, Felipe, and Luz Centeno. 1994. Land Use, Urbanization and the Land Conversion Issue. In Arsenio M. Balisacan, Felipe Medalla and Ernesto Pernia, *Spatial Development, Land Use and Urban-Rural Growth Linkages in the Philippines.* Pasig: National Economic and Development Authority.

NSCB (National Statistical Coordination Board). Various. *Philippine Statistical Yearbook.* Manila.

Oshima, Harry T. 1987. *Economic Growth of Monsoon Asia: A Comparative Survey.* Tokyo: University of Tokyo Press.

Power, John H., and Gerardo P. Sicat. 1971. *The Philippines: Industrialization and Trade Policies.* London: Oxford University Press.

Quibria, M.G., ed. 1993. *Rural Poverty in Asia: Priority Issues and Policy Options.* Hong Kong: Oxford University Press.

Ranis, Gustav. 1995. Another Look at the East Asian Miracle. *World Bank Economic Review* 9 (September): 509–534.

———, and Frances Stewart. 1993. Rural Nonagricultural Activities in Development Theory and Application. *Journal of Development Economics* 40: 75–101.

Reardon, T., K. Stamoulis, M. E. Cruz, A. M. Balisacan, and J. Berdeque. 1998. Rural Nonfarm Income in Developing Countries: Importance and Policy Implications. Special Chapter in *State of Food and Agriculture 1998.* Rome: Food and Agriculture Organization of the United Nations.

Rosegrant, Mark, and Peter B. R. Hazell. 1999. *Transforming the Rural Asian Economy: The Unfinished Revolution.* Hong Kong: Oxford University Press.

Tan, N. A. 1979. The Structure of Protection and Resource Flows in the Philippines. In R. M. Bautista, J. H. Power and Associates, *Industrial Promotion Policies in the Philippines.* Manila: Philippine Institute for Development Studies.

UNDP (United Nations Development Programme). 1999. *Human Development Report.* New York: Oxford University Press.

World Bank. 1986. *World Development Report.* Oxford: Oxford University Press.

———. 1990. *World Development Report.* Oxford: Oxford University Press.

———. 2000a. Philippines Rural Development and Natural Resource Management: Trends, Strategy Implementation, and Framework Performance Indicator System. World Bank East Asia and Pacific Region.

———. 2000b. *World Development Report.* Oxford: Oxford University Press.

12. Structural Adjustment, Macroeconomic Policies, and Poverty Trends in Pakistan

Abdul Razzaq Kemal

1. Introduction

The sharp increase in poverty in Pakistan during the 1990s is generally attributed to the slowing of growth rates, from 6 percent in the 1980s to around 4 percent in 1990s. While slowing growth rates could be a factor for the rising poverty in the 1990s, it may not necessarily be so; Pakistan has witnessed periods of high economic growth that were accompanied by an increase in poverty levels, and periods of low growth that were accompanied by reductions in poverty levels (Amjad and Kemal, 1997). Probably the differential impact of economic growth on poverty can be found in the basic structural characteristics of the economy, changes in the structure over time, and economic policies.

Pakistan has implemented structural adjustment and stabilization programs (SAP) since 1987–88 with a view to improving the levels of efficiency and, consequently, higher levels of output and employment. Because the design of these programs has left much to be desired, and successive governments have failed to pursue them with conviction, Pakistan has failed to realize these objectives. GDP growth rates have fallen, unemployment has increased, and poverty incidence has increased. This trend is rather disturbing and the implementation of such programs needs careful examination. However, because SAP entails a broad range of policy changes in a large number of variables, and because a number of other factors also influence the economic development process, it becomes rather difficult to discern its impact.

While the incidence of poverty has already increased at an alarming rate, there is an imminent danger that it may increase even further unless a pro-poor bias is introduced in the macroeconomic policies and/or social safety nets are put in place. The study is based on the firm premise that macroeconomic policies can significantly alter economic performance, not only increasing efficiency and growth trends, but also ensuring a more equitable distribution of the gains of economic development. This can be achieved primarily through ensuring that economic growth has the maximum impact on the creation of remunerative and productive employment opportunities in a labor-surplus economy, as well as through investing in human resource development, especially education and health services.

The main aim of this study is to identify economic policies, especially at the macro level, that can play an important part in ensuring that the process of economic growth and development translates into real improvements in peoples' lives: not just by reducing poverty as measured in meeting minimum nutritional needs, but also by ensuring adequate access to education and health services so as to combat early mortality, high rates of disease, and very high levels of illiteracy. Pakistan's economic performance in fighting poverty cannot be divorced from its so far meager efforts at improving overall human development indicators.

The task of identifying economic policies that impact poverty alleviation is carried out by exploring the key economic variables that explain changes over time in the level and trends in poverty in Pakistan. The plan of the study is as follows: the next section contains a discussion of the availability and nature of data to estimate poverty trends and their determinants; the following section contains an analysis of trends in poverty levels, depth and severity of poverty, income distribution, poverty and child mortality, nutritional status, and functional income distribution. Then follows a review of macroeconomic policies that are pursued under structural adjustment and stabilization, followed by a review of the correlates and determinants of poverty; and the final section presents policy implications and conclusions.

2. Availability and Nature of Data

Data are required to estimate both the levels of poverty and its determinants. Household Income and Expenditure Surveys (HIES) and Pakistan Integrated Household Surveys (conducted by the Federal Bureau of Statistics [FBS]) are the basic sources for estimating poverty trends in Pakistan.[1] Fifteen such surveys have been conducted in selected years between 1963–1964 and 1998–1999, but not at regular intervals. The data are also available separately for rural and urban areas and are broken down by the four provinces of the country. Poverty levels and trends are separately available for the urban and rural areas and the sampling errors are small; however, the same cannot be said about estimates at the provincial level. The coverage of two provinces (Balochistan and North-

---

1.   A number of microstudies at the city level, village level, or slightly larger geographical area are based on field surveys that provide insight into the characteristics of the poor, as well as the changing trends in poverty among different groups living in these areas. Since this study is primarily investigating the relationship between macropolicies and poverty alleviation, these microstudies are not covered in the study that is presented in this chapter. Nevertheless, it uses data collected by the Pakistan Institute of Development Economics for the year 1998–1999.

West Frontier Province [NWFP]) in most years is not fully representative, as it does not cover large areas in these provinces where the incidence of poverty is known to be high.[2]

For the most recent year, 1998–1999, data pertain to the Pakistan Socio-Economic Survey carried out by the Pakistan Institute of Development Economics (PIDE, 1998–1999), which has much smaller samples and covers only one season. While this may not be fully comparable to the earlier data set, the comparison of other characteristics shows that it is not out of line with the HIES data.

The HIES data are the only data to estimate trends in poverty levels, but they suffer from problems such as gross underestimation of income, which has forced researchers to use consumption-based poverty estimates. As to where consumption in excess of income is financed, the studies are generally silent. Moreover, the data are not useful in formulating policies to target those who are poor, as the sample is too small for drawing conclusions, even at provincial levels. Furthermore, poverty-stricken areas sometimes are completely missing. The data are particularly weak for estimating income inequality: the highest income groups are almost excluded and, because of this, the data underestimate the income inequalities. Nevertheless, the trends are not much affected, because these problems exist in almost every year.

3. Trends in Poverty Levels

a. Definition of poverty

Poverty may alternatively be defined as follows: (i) the proportion of the population whose incomes fall below a specified poverty line, generally known as head count; (ii) the income gap, i.e., the income required to bring all the poor above the poverty line; or (iii) income inequality among the poor, known as the Foster, Greer, and Thorbeck (FGT) index or the severity index. Whatever the poverty line, e.g., consumption levels that are essential for meeting the basic needs of common people, the assessment of the basic needs of the poor is subjective. Malik (1988) defined a poverty line with reference to a calorie requirement of 2,550 for an adult,[3] and the revealed expenditure pattern of the poor between food and nonfood expenditures. The poverty line for different years is adjusted by changes in the Consumer Price Index to ensure that the same poverty line in terms of real incomes is used to estimate the poor in each year. Similar methodology is used by the FBS (1995), which defines basic

---

2. Because provincial data involve a large sampling error, such estimates are not included in this study.
3. Malik (1988) used adult equivalence scales to adjust for gender and age considerations.

needs as 2,550 calories for adults, and the average coefficient of nonfood expenditures of the poor is regressed against the food goods. The basic needs of the poor may also be estimated on the basis of educated guesses by knowledgeable persons (Ahmed, 1993). The linear expenditure systems approach may be used to determine the basic needs of the poor and to reflect the norm of society as it relates to the basic needs of people in a particular year (Ali, 1995). The poverty estimates presented in Qureshi and Arif (1999) are based on food energy intake and the cost of basic needs.[4] The requisite food expenditure corresponding to the required calorie intake has been obtained by regressing an equivalent of the daily calorie intake per adult against an equivalent of the monthly food expenditure per adult for both rural and urban areas. The cost of nonfood elements of the basket was determined by assuming that those households whose food expenditures were equal to the food poverty line would also satisfy their other basic needs. They also examine the sensitivity of poverty to increases in nonfood expenditure.

Poverty is not just income (consumption) deprivation; it is a multidimensional concept. The "poverty of opportunity" index, a composite of deprivation in three vital dimensions (health, education, and income) captures more appropriately the real causes of human suffering (MCHD, 1999). Almost one half of the population of Pakistan suffers from serious deprivation of the most basic opportunities of life, compared to the proportion of the population below the poverty line per the head-count definition (Syed, 1999).

b. Incidence of poverty

Because of differences in the methodologies that estimate poverty lines, it is difficult to ascertain the trends in poverty. Even so, studies that are based on different methodologies (or poverty lines) are commonly used to investigate changes in the incidence of poverty. In an effort to mitigate the effects of these different "yardsticks" of poverty, Amjad and Kemal (1997), Jafri and Younis (1999), and the World Bank (2000)[5] have developed a consistent time series on rural, urban, and total poverty.

To establish trends in poverty over different periods of time, we may divide the total period into four broad periods. Naseem (1973) and Alauddin (1975) show that both rural and urban poverty declined between 1963–1964 and 1969–1970; Mujahid (1978), after correcting for a methodological error in these two studies, showed that poverty levels had declined in urban

4.   Poverty lines have been determined on the basis of estimated cost of food, consistent with a calorie intake of 2,550 per adult equivalent per day in rural areas. A daily intake of 2,295 calories per adult equivalent is considered adequate for urban areas of the country.
5.   These studies ignored variations in the size of households that belonged to the same income group, therefore listing nonpoor households as poor, and vice versa.

areas, but had increased in rural areas during this period. Studies that related the poverty line to the absorption of a minimum diet, based on a nutritional requirement of 2,550 calories per day per adult equivalent, also showed an increase in rural poverty during the period (Khan and Khan, 1980; Naseem, 1977; Irfan and Amjad, 1984; and Malik, 1988). Malik (1988) also covered urban areas and concluded that poverty levels in urban areas did decline over the period. It may be pointed out that the 1970s was a period of low growth, yet poverty levels still declined.

All studies unanimously indicate a dramatic decline in poverty in the 1970s overall, as well as in the rural and urban areas, based on caloric norm or monthly household expenditure (Irfan and Amjad, 1984; Malik, 1988; Kruijk and van Leeuwen, 1985). During this period, the growth rate slowed, but the rate of per capita income growth still exceeded 1.8 percent.

During the 1980s, the growth rate increased to 6.5 percent and poverty declined sharply. Malik (1996), Shirazi (1995), and Gazdar, Howes, and Zaidi (1994) show a decline in poverty in both the rural and urban areas between 1984–1985 and 1987–1988. However, while Gazdar, Howes, and Zaidi (1994) show a further decline until 1990–1991, Malik (1996) and Shirazi (1995) show an increase in poverty from 1987–1988 to 1990–1991.

Major differences in the trends in poverty occur between 1987–1988 and 1993–1994. Jafri and Younis (1999) show that the declining trend in poverty in the 1980s continued into the early 1990s, although they show a slight increase in poverty between 1992–1993 and 1993–1994 (Table 12.1). Similar findings by the World Bank (2000) indicate a further decline in poverty in 1996–1997 (Table 12.2). Both Jafri and Younis and the World Bank show that in 1993–1994, about 28 percent of the population was poor. According to the World Bank study, this percentage declined to 24 in 1996–1997. However, Amjad and Kemal (1997) have shown a 5 percent increase in poverty between 1987–1988 and 1992–1993 overall as well as in rural areas (Table 12.3). Several other studies, such as Malik (1992) and Ali and Tahir (1999), support the view that poverty increased in the 1990s. Two more recent studies, Jamal and Ghaus-Pasha (2000) and Qureshi and Arif (2001), show a further increase in poverty in the late 1990s (Table 12.3).

All studies except Jafri and Younis (1999) and World Bank (1995, 2000) show a rise in the incidence of poverty in Pakistan in the 1990s. Moreover, the results reported by Jafri and Younis (1999) and World Bank (1995, 2000) are not very consistent with demographic dynamics that affect the labor force and dependency ratio, employment levels, real wage rates, workers' remittances, ownership and access to assets, and inflationary impact on food availability.

Table 12.1. Incidence of Poverty
(head-count ratios, percentage of poor population)

Year	Pakistan	Rural	Urban
1986–1987	29.1	28.2	29.8
1987–1988	29.2	29.3	30.3
1990–1991	26.1	25.2	26.6
1992–1993	26.8	24.6	28.3
1993–1994	28.7	25.4	26.9

Source: Jafri and Younis (1999).

Table 12.2. Poverty Measures for Pakistan
(head-count ratios, percentage of poor population)

Year	Pakistan	Urban	Rural
1984–1985	46	38	49
1987–1988	37	31	40
1990–1991	34	28	37
1992–1993	25	26	25
1993–1994	28	22	31
1996–1997	24	20	26

Source: World Bank (2000).

Table 12.3. Trends in the Incidence of Poverty
(head-count ratios, percentage of poor population)

Year	Total	Rural	Urban
1963–1964	40.24	38.94	44.53
1966–1967	44.50	45.62	40.96
1969–1970	46.53	49.11	38.76
1979	30.68	32.51	25.94
1984–1985	24.47	25.87	21.17
1987–1988	17.32	18.32	14.99
1990–1991	22.10	23.59	18.64
1992–1993	22.40	23.35	15.50
1996–1997	31.00	32.00	27.00
1998–1999	32.60	34.80	25.90

Source: Amjad and Kemal (1997), Jamal and Ghaus-Pasha (2000), and Qureshi and Arif (2001).

c. Depth and severity of poverty

Changes in the income gap (P_1) and inequality among the poor (P_2) over time are presented in Tables 12.4, 12.5, and 12.6. Two studies by the World Bank (1995, 2000) show a gradual decline in P_1, from 11 percent in 1984–1985 to only 4 percent in 1996–1997 (Table 12.4). Jamal and Ghaus-Pasha (2000) show the value of P_1 to be 7 percent for the 1996–1997 period. Taking the results of these studies into consideration, it seems that the average income of poor households will have to increase by 4 to 7 percent of the average income of the entire sample if the poor have to be pulled out of poverty line. This implies that although poverty is pervasive in Pakistan, it is not very severe, and therefore can be reduced by proper targeting through a comprehensive poverty alleviation program (Jamal and Ghaus-Pasha, 2000). The implications of the low values of P_2 are the same.

Arif, Nazli, and Haq (2000) provide estimates of P_0, P_1, and P_2 using the same poverty line in real terms for three different years. Their estimates show a much sharper increase in the poverty gap (P_1) than do the World Bank estimates: from 5.3 percent in 1993–1994 to 7.6 percent in 1998–1999. Their

Table 12.4. Poverty Trends in the 1990s by Rural and Urban Areas

Year	Rural-urban Areas	Poverty Incidence (P_0)	Poverty Gap (P_1)	Poverty Severity (P_2)
	Total	27.4	5.31	1.6
1993–94	Urban	29.9	6.67	1.8
	Rural	23.1	4.82	1.4
	Total	29.6	5.80	1.7
1996–97	Urban	31.6	6.00	2.1
	Rural	27.4	5.90	1.1
	Total	35.2	7.58	2.5
1998–99	Urban	39.8	8.39	2.6
	Rural	31.7	9.67	3.5

Source: World Bank (1995, 2000).

Table 12.5. World Bank: Poverty Indicator, 1984–1985 to 1996–1997

Year	(P_0)	(P_1)	(P_2)
1984–1985	46	11	4
1987–1988	37	8	2
1990–1991	34	7	2
1992–1993	25	5	1
1993–1994	28	5	2
1996–1997	24	4	1

Source: World Bank (1995, 2000).

estimates indicate that the severity of poverty has also increased, while estimates by the World Bank show a decline.

Data on depth and severity of poverty, as reported by Jafri and Younis (1999) and presented in Table 12.6, show high values for P_1. The average income of poor households was below the poverty line by about 20 percent in 1986–1987, and after a gap of seven years it was still 19 percent in 1992–1993.[6] Jafri and Younis (1999) do not show any change in the value of P_2 over time either. Jafri and Younis's results imply that poverty in Pakistan is severe. Poverty alleviation programs should rigorously address not only the prevalence of poverty, but also its depth and severity.

Table 12.6. Poverty Indicators under Basic-Needs Approach (based on distribution of expenditure)

Year	(P_0)	(P_1)	(P_2)
1986–1987	29.1	19.7	1.7
1987–1988	29.2	19.8	1.7
1990–1991	26.1	19.7	1.5
1992–1993	26.8	18.5	1.4
1993–1994	28.7	19.3	1.6

Source: World Bank (1995, 2000).

Poverty transition is another interesting concept for assessing the nature of poverty. However, only one study (Baulch and McCulloch, 1998) has developed a poverty transition matrix for Pakistan. The data used in this study were taken from a panel data survey; around 800 households in 52 villages in rural Pakistan were surveyed by the International Food Policy Institute (IFPRI) between July 1986 and October 1991.[7]

The IFPRI-Pakistan panel used a relative poverty line that was equal to the bottom quintile of distribution of income or consumption expenditure, each expressed per capita. Simple transition matrices between poverty and nonpoverty were constructed for each sequential pair of years, and between the first and last years of the study. The poverty line (Rs.2,000 per adult equivalent in 1986 constant rupees) represents the lowest quintile of the per adult equivalent income distribution in the first year of the panel and was held

---

6.   Probably Jafri and Younis estimate the percentage gap between incomes and the poverty line, rather than total income. That may explain the difference between their estimates and those of Arif and the World Bank.

7.   Each household in the survey was interviewed a total of 14 times between these dates, although due to the uneven spacing of visits it has only been possible to construct a panel for five annual rounds. Data collection took place in three provinces: Punjab, Sindh, and NWFP. Within each province, surveyors sampled one "least developed district."

fixed for subsequent years. Thus, although the boundary between poverty and nonpoverty is determined relative to the income distribution in 1986–1987, it remains absolute for the duration of the panel. The transition matrix for 1986–1987 to 1987–1988 is shown in Table 12.7 below.

Table 12.7. Poor/Nonpoor Transition Matrix, 1986–1987 to 1987–1988

1986–1987	1987–1988		Total
	Poor	Nonpoor	
Poor	67	71	138
Nonpoor	80	468	548
Total	147	539	686

Source: Baulch and McCulloch (1998).

In 1986–1987, the incidence of poverty on the basis of head-count was 20.1 percent and as much as 51.4 percent of the poor were able to escape poverty. At the same time, 14.6 percent of the nonpoor fell into poverty between these two years. Overall, more than one-fifth of households moved between the two categories in these two years. The dynamic nature of poverty within the panel emphasizes the importance of understanding the factors that influence entries into and exits from poverty.

To calculate the impact of explanatory variables on entry into and exit from poverty, Baulch and McCulloch (1998) constructed a proportional-hazard model. The results show that the district in which a household resides does not affect either its probability of entering poverty or its chances of exit. Education and asset variables also have very little impact on a household's chances of making a poverty transition. Neither the ownership of land nor the value of physical capital affects the entry or exit probabilities. However, ownership of livestock reduces the chances of falling into poverty and helps the poor to escape poverty.

d. Income distribution

Income distribution, measured in terms of Gini coefficient and household income share of the lowest and highest 20 percent for rural and urban areas, is presented in Table 12.8. Since the 1960s, the level of inequality in Pakistan has tended to be moderate, with the Gini coefficient of household income around 0.35 or below. The Gini coefficient reached 0.407 in 1990–1991 and declined slightly to 0.400 in 1996–1997.

In 1990–1991, the income share of the bottom 20 percent of households fell to just 5.7 percent, after being in the range of 7.5 to 8.0 percent during the 1970s and 1980s. With the share of the upper quintile rising, the ratio of the share of the top quintile to that of the bottom quintile rose to an unprecedented 8.6 percent in 1990–1991. The increase in income share of the bottom 20 percent of households increased from 5.7 percent in 1990–1991 to 7.0 percent in 1996–1997 and consequently the ratio declined to 7.1 in 1996–1997 (Table 12.8). Separate data for rural and urban areas, presented in Table 12.9, indicate that the increase in inequality around 1990 occurred in both rural and urban areas. In the former, however, the jump from 1987–1988 was dramatic, while in the latter it was more the continuation of a trend that began in the mid-1980s.

During the more recent period, 1992–1993 to 1996–1997, income distribution has worsened in both rural and urban areas, although there was a slight improvement in income distribution for urban areas between 1992–1993 and 1993–1994. The data on income distribution, particularly for the 1990s, give cause for serious concern about distribution of the fruits of growth in Pakistan. It seems that in Pakistan, growth is weakly associated with distribution of income.

Household income distribution appears to have worsened more in rural areas than in urban areas. The Gini coefficient in rural areas increased from 0.31 to 0.41. While the share of the lowest 20 percent of households has declined, those at the top experienced gains, which resulted in an increase in the highest to lowest income ratio.

e. Functional income distribution

The three main factors that govern personal income distribution are (i) distribution of assets; (ii) functional income distribution; and (iii) transfers from other households, government, the rest of the world, and the tax structure. Industrialization affects the distribution of personal incomes by altering the distribution of assets and by changing functional income distribution. Since wage earners hardly hold any assets, changes in personal income distribution are significantly affected by functional income distribution. Moreover, increases in investment, which embody sophisticated, capital-intensive techniques of production that are imported from capital-abundant countries, tend to increase the share of capital in the output, resulting in the deterioration of functional income distribution. Not only does demand for labor not grow rapidly; real wages remain constant as long as the supply of labor remains relatively larger than the demand for labor, and as a result any increases in productivity tend to increase the rate of profit rather than the wage rates.

Table 12.8. Household Income Distribution in Pakistan

Year	Household Gini Coefficient	Household Lowest 20%	Income Middle 60%	Share Highest 20%	Ratio of Highest 20% to Lowest 20%	GDP Growth Rates
1963–1964	0.355	6.4	48.3	45.3	7.1	6.5
1966–1967	0.336	7.6	49.0	43.4	5.7	3.1
1968–1969	0.336	8.2	49.8	42.0	5.1	6.5
1969–1970	0.330	8.0	50.2	41.8	5.2	9.8
1970–1971	0.345	8.4	50.1	41.5	4.9	1.2
1971–1972	0.373	7.9	49.1	43.0	5.4	2.3
1979	0.369	7.4	47.6	45.0	6.1	5.5
1984–1985	0.335	7.3	47.7	45.0	6.2	8.7
1985–1986	0.346	7.6	48.4	44.0	5.8	6.4
1986–1987	0.348	7.9	48.5	43.6	5.5	5.8
1987–1988	0.407	8.0	45.3	43.7	5.5	6.4
1990–1991	0.410	5.7	45.0	49.3	8.6	5.6
1992–1993	0.400	6.2	45.6	48.2	7.8	2.3
1993–1994	0.400	6.5	46.3	47.2	7.3	4.5
1996–1997		7.0	43.6	49.4	7.1	1.9

Source: Government of Pakistan (2000).

Table 12.9. Household Income Distribution by Rural-Urban Areas

Year	Rural Share		Gini Coefficient	Urban Share		Gini Coefficient
	Lowest 20%	Highest 20%		Lowest 20%	Highest 20%	
1979	8.3	41.3	0.32	6.9	48.0	0.40
1984–1985	7.9	42.8	0.34	7.0	47.7	0.38
1985–1986	7.9	40.0	0.33	7.5	45.0	0.35
1986–1987	8.0	39.0	0.32	7.9	44.0	0.36
1987–1988	8.8	40.0	0.31	6.4	48.1	0.37
1990–1991	6.0	47.4	0.41	5.7	50.5	0.39
1992–1993	7.0	44.8	0.37	6.1	48.9	0.42
1993–1994	7.4	43.1	0.40	6.7	47.1	0.35
1996–1997	7.3	49.3	0.41	7.6	47.0	0.38

Source: Government of Pakistan (2000).

Since green revolution technology is scale neutral, it has reduced poverty and increased the demand for labor (Chaudhry, 1973). Nevertheless, as pointed out by Hussain (1992), the impact of technology on size distribution of farms depends on the prevailing patterns of land ownership and the social organization of agricultural production, perhaps causing an increase in poverty, especially in recent years. Poverty may also have increased in recent years because of increases in input costs, stagnant yields per acre, and marketing problems. While an increase in input prices tends to increase the cost of production, an increase in price of output hardly benefits subsistence farmers, because of their limited marketable surplus.

Functional income distribution in Pakistan indicates an improvement in the share of labor up to 1986–1987: the share of wages in GDP increased from 30.2 percent in 1980–1981 to 33.0 percent in 1986–1987, which is in line with trends in poverty over that period. However, functional income distribution decreased to around 30.0 percent in the 1990s. An increase in capital intensity in recent years, especially in the industrial sector because of fiscal concessions that cheapened the capital, resulted in a worsening of functional income distribution. The increase in poverty in recent years can be at least partly attributed to changes in the functional distribution of income.

f. Poverty and child mortality

Another variant of poverty is high incidence of child mortality. It is higher in rural areas, more commonly experienced by working women than by nonworking women, and more commonly experienced by less educated mothers and poor households in urban areas than by their counterparts in rural areas (Ali, 2001).[8] Housing conditions (persons per room), quality of water, and type of toilet facilities used by households generate differentials in mortality. Nevertheless, there has been a differential impact between rural and urban areas. For instance, although poor urban households are afflicted with a higher incidence of child mortality, the relationship is insignificant in the case of rural areas. Similarly, the relationship between mother's education, sources and cleanliness of water, fecal contamination, and mortality appears to be region-specific.

g. Nutritional status

Three common indicators of nutritional status in preschool children are stunting (height-for-age), being underweight (weight-for-age), and wasting

---

8. The effect of food poverty on the incidence of child mortality in rural areas was insignificant.

(weight-for-height) (Quresh, Nazli, and Soomro, 2001).[9] As much as 38.8 percent of children in 1998–1999 were underweight, 60.1 percent were stunted, and 9.5 percent were wasted (Table 12.10). This indicates that a substantial proportion of children are living in poor socioeconomic conditions at high risk of exposure to disease. While there has been a decline in underweight children from 52 percent in 1985–1987 to 38.8 percent in 1998–1999, stunting increased to 50 percent in 1990–1991 and further to 60.1 percent in 1998–1999. This indicator is associated with poor socioeconomic conditions and the increased risk of frequent exposure to illness. The high incidence of malnutrition can partly be explained by the increasing trend of poverty in the 19290s (Qureshi and Arif, 2001). The increased level of food poverty, coupled with unfavorable socioeconomic conditions and inappropriate feeding practices, has resulted in an increase in the incidence of chronic malnutrition.

Socioeconomic factors significantly affect the growth pattern of children less than five years of age. Using a regression framework, Quresh, Nazli, and Soomro (2001) show that mother's education, breast feeding, and modernization were negatively associated with malnutrition.

4. Macroeconomic Policies under Structural Adjustment and Stabilization Programs

Pakistan has implemented structural adjustment and stabilization programs (SAP): three recent programs relate to the periods 1988–1991, 1993–1996, and 1997–2000. These programs aimed at reducing fiscal and balance-of-payments deficits and creating a market-friendly atmosphere. In particular, they contained rationalization of the tariff structure, import liberalization, broadening of the sales tax net, deregulation of investments and foreign exchange, financial reforms, reduction in subsidies, and divestiture of public assets. While such programs are expected to improve levels of efficiency, their impact on growth rates of output, employment, and poverty is uncertain in the short run. A number of studies, including Corbo and Su (1992); Jain and Bongartz (1994); Banuri, Khan, and Mahmood (1997); Kemal (1994a); Zaman (1995); Zaidi (1995); Killick (1995); McGillivray, White, and Ahmad (1995); Morrissey (1995); Pasha, Stubbs, and Clarke (1995); Cameron (1995); Tetzlaff (1995); and Rieger (1995) provide conflicting evidence on the impact of such

---

9.   In order to examine the status of child malnutrition, a comparison with a reference child of the same age and sex may be made. Z-score is calculated by using the median value and standard deviation (SD) of the reference population. The percentage of children whose Z-score falls below a defined cutoff point, i.e., $-2SD$ from the median of the international reference population, is identified as malnourished children.

Table 12.10. Trends in the Prevalence of Malnutrition (percent)

Data Year	Height-For-Age (Stunted)	Weight-For-Height (Wasted)	Weight-For-Age (Underweight)
1976–1977	42.9	8.6	
1985–1987	41.8	10.8	51.5
1990–1991	50.2	9.2	40.4
1998–1999	60.1	9.5	38.8

Note: Blank cells = not available.

Source: Micronutrient Survey (1977); National Nutrition Survey (1998); Pakistan Demographic and Health Survey (1990–1991); and PIDE (1998–1999).

programs on the economies of developing countries, including Pakistan. In the following subsections, some policies and trends in the strategic economic variables are reviewed.

a. Budgetary deficits, taxation policy, and public expenditures

Deterioration in government revenue, rapidly growing government expenditure, and losses in public sector enterprises are the chronic deficiencies of Pakistan's fiscal system. Despite efforts at reform, the tax structure remains seriously flawed. Government revenues are too narrowly based, inelastic, and subject to individual and sectoral exemptions, whereas government expenditure is dominated by debt servicing. The growing imbalance between government expenditure and government revenue has resulted in the accumulation of public debt, reduction in development expenditure, and further compounding of fiscal problems.

A 1988 agreement focused on controlling the persistently rising budget deficit, which rose to an unsustainable level of 8.5 percent of gross domestic product (GDP) in 1987–1988. Even though the budget deficit did decline to 6.5 percent of GDP in 1989–1990, it increased to 8.7 percent of GDP in 1990–1991, both because of the Government's failure to contain expenditures and because financial reforms increased the debt servicing (Table 12.11). The SAP, initiated in 1992–1993, aimed at reducing the deficit from 8 percent of GDP to 4 percent in three years, but the budgetary deficit never went below 6 percent of GDP. Another program, begun in 1997, also called for a reduction in the fiscal deficit to 4 percent; instead it increased to 7.7 percent in 1997–1998. It declined in subsequent years, but only to 6.3 percent, almost the same level as at the start of the program. Moreover, the already low development expenditure was further reduced. Since private and public sector investments are complementary, as the latter pertain to infrastructure, the implications of the decline in public investment on growth are rather serious.

b. Taxation policy

The tax structure has suffered from several weaknesses: a narrow and distorted base, overreliance on indirect taxes, and weak tax administration. The combined effect of these weaknesses has resulted in a low and stagnant tax-to-GDP ratio, low tax elasticity, and an increase in poverty.

Almost all SAPs call for a reduction in tariff rates; any loss of revenue is to be compensated by imposing a generalized sales tax on manufactures and imports and extending it to the retail stage. Tariff rates have already been reduced from about 125 percent to a maximum of 30 percent. While the sales

Table 12.11. Budgetary Deficit in Pakistan (as percentage of GDP)

	Total Revenues	Tax Revenues	Surplus of Autonomous Bodies	Total	Public Expenditures		Budgetary Deficit
					Nondevelopment	Development	
1980–1981	16.9	14.0	0.7	22.9	13.7	9.3	5.3
1984–1985	16.4	11.9	0.5	24.7	17.9	5.5	7.7
1987–1988	17.3	13.8	0.9	26.7	19.8	6.9	8.5
1989–1990	18.6	14.0	0.8	25.7	19.3	6.5	6.5
1990–1991	16.9	12.7	0.8	25.6	19.2	6.4	8.7
1992–1993	18.0	13.3	1.2	26.0	20.3	5.7	8.0
1996–1997	15.6	13.2		22.0	18.5	3.5	6.4
1997–1998	16.0	13.2		23.7	19.8	3.9	7.7
1998–1999	15.9	13.3		22.0	18.6	3.4	6.1
1999–2000	16.9	12.8		23.4	20.2	3.2	6.5

Note: Blank cells = not available.

Source: Government of Pakistan (2001).

tax net has been widened and efforts are un1derway to extend this to the retail stage, it has failed to compensate fully for the decline in revenue that has resulted from a reduction in import duties. As shown in Table 12.12, tax revenue has decreased from 14.0 percent of GDP in 1989–1990 to 12.8 percent of GDP in 1999–2000. Similarly, total revenue has gone down from 18.6 percent of GDP to 16.9 percent of GDP over the same period.

The share of indirect taxes increased in the 1980s, from 79.9 percent in 1980–1981 to 86.8 percent by 1989–1990, because tariff reductions until 1989–90 were quite redundant and the sales tax net was widened. Direct taxes decreased because concessions were provided to investors. In the 1990s, on the other hand, the share of indirect taxes declined, as tariff revenue fell sharply and increases in sales taxes could not compensate for the decline. By 1999–2000, the share of indirect taxes had declined to 72.3 percent, resulting in a decrease in tax and total revenues.

How has the change in emphasis from import-related taxes to sales taxes affected the poor? Whereas Pakistan's tax structure was progressive in the pre-SAP period (Irfan, 1974; Alauddin and Naqvi, 1976; Jeetun, 1978; Qureshi, 1986; Malik and Saqib, 1989; Kemal, 1994b), by 1997–1998 it had become regressive (Table 12.13). Over the 10-year period from 1987–1988 to 1997–1998, the tax burden on the poorest has increased by 7.4 percent, while for the richest households it has declined by 15.9 percent (Table 12.14).

c. Public expenditures

The extent to which a country's public expenditure is directed toward the goal of poverty alleviation is of central importance. It has the potential to reduce poverty in at least four major ways:

- Creating employment;
- Providing primary education, basic health care, safe water, and sanitation;
- Providing basic infrastructure needed by poor farmers, microentrepreneurs, and labor-intensive manufacturers to provide livelihoods; and
- Providing cash and food transfers to reduce the vulnerability of marginalized segments of society.

Public sector development expenditure as a percentage of GDP has declined from 9.3 percent in 1980–1981 to 6.9 percent in 1987–1988, and further to 3.4 percent by 1999–2000. This decline has had a serious impact on growth and employment, hence the increase in poverty. At the same time, expenditure on social sectors has increased, especially via the SAP,

Table 12.12. Tax Structure of Pakistan (percentage share of tax revenues)

	Direct Taxes	Indirect Taxes			
		Total	Tariffs	Sales	Excise Duties
1980–1981	20.1	79.9	36.7	7.4	27.0
1984–1985	17.4	82.6	41.2	8.4	27.6
1987–1988	13.3	86.7	40.7	9.3	18.8
1989–1990	13.2	86.8	42.4	13.0	19.5
1990–1991	16.0	84.0	39.0	13.0	19.3
1992–1993	21.0	79.0	35.1	13.0	19.8
1996–1997	26.8	73.2	26.5	17.2	17.3
1997–1998	29.8	70.2	21.0	15.2	17.7
1998–1999	27.0	73.0	20.1	17.5	16.0
1999–2000	27.7	72.3	15.7	28.8	13.9

Source: Government of Pakistan (2001 and previous).

Table 12.13. Incidence of Both Direct and Indirect Taxes

Income Groups	Average Income of the Groups (Rs. per month)	1987–88	1988–89	1989–90	1990–91	1991–92	1992–93	1993–94	1994–95	1995–96	1996–97	1997–98	1998–99	1999–2000
GI	489	7.94	8.74	8.95	8.40	8.09	8.97	8.61	8.89	9.58	9.22	8.60	8.38	8.24
GII	656	8.11	8.77	9.01	8.49	8.14	9.13	8.69	9.05	9.65	9.31	8.67	8.36	8.18
GIII	758	8.63	9.13	9.33	8.80	8.28	9.42	8.80	9.42	9.83	9.36	8.63	8.42	8.18
GIV	909	8.18	8.70	8.88	8.36	7.89	8.89	8.33	8.83	9.25	8.86	8.20	8.01	7.81
GV	1,259	8.18	8.62	8.75	8.29	7.78	8.89	8.26	8.95	9.27	8.83	8.10	7.81	7.65
GVI	1,744	8.24	8.63	8.74	8.29	7.75	8.95	8.28	9.10	9.35	8.82	8.00	7.69	7.54
GVII	2,239	8.10	8.46	8.50	8.08	7.50	8.64	7.98	8.85	9.05	8.49	7.67	7.38	7.29
GVIII	2,748	8.29	8.57	8.53	8.14	7.55	8.69	7.97	9.06	9.16	8.54	7.68	7.43	7.33
GIX	3,246	8.03	8.32	8.31	7.93	7.27	8.49	7.77	8.79	8.92	8.31	7.43	7.08	7.13
GX	3,736	8.87	9.17	9.12	8.76	8.00	9.42	8.58	9.85	9.90	9.18	8.14	7.65	7.69
GXI	4,246	8.70	9.05	8.89	8.52	7.68	8.92	8.17	9.40	9.51	8.68	7.65	7.33	7.33
GXII	7,770	10.17	10.41	10.06	9.84	8.74	10.14	9.25	10.70	10.64	9.75	8.59	8.03	8.14

Source: TEPI (2002).

Table 12.14. Percentage Increase in Tax Burden by Income Groups

Income Groups	Percentage Increase in Tax Burden as a Percentage of Income			
	1987–88 to 1990–91	1987–88 to 1995–96	1987–88 to 1997–98	1987–88 to 1999–2000
GI	5.8	12.0	7.4	3.8
GII	4.7	18.7	6.0	0.9
GIII	2.0	13.9	–0.7	–5.2
GIV	2.2	13.0	–0.6	–4.5
GV	1.3	13.2	–1.7	–6.5
GVI	0.6	13.3	3.6	–8.5
GVII	–0.2	11.2	–5.9	10.0
GVIII	–1.2	10.5	–8.0	11.6
GIX	–1.8	11.2	–8.1	–11.8
GX	–1.2	11.6	–8.8	–14.3
GXI	–2.1	9.4	–12.5	–15.7
GXII	–3.3	4.7	–15.9	–20.7

Source: Government of Pakistan (2001 and previous).

which focuses on primary education, primary health care, nutrition, family planning, and rural water supply and sanitation: from 1.96 percent of GDP in 1992–1993 to 2.20 percent of GDP in 1999–2000. However, the increase in public expenditure on social services by one percentage point has had little impact on quality of life. Recent estimates show that the primary school enrollment rate has fallen in recent years, and as may be noted in Table 12.15, social indicators continue to be poor compared to those of other developing economies.

Table 12.15. Social Indicators of Pakistan

Items	Pakistan		All Developing Countries
	1991–1992	2000–2001	
Population Growth rate (%)	3.0	2.1	1.8
Adult Literacy Rate (%)	34.0	49.0	80.0
Primary School Enrollment (%)	66.3	63.2	85.7
Life Expectancy at Birth (years)	55.0	63.0	64.4
Infant Mortality Rate (per 1000)	106.0	90.0	65.0
Total Fertility Rate (%)	6.6	4.9	3.0
Contraceptive Prevalence Rate (%)	8.5	32.1	56.0
Rural Population's Access to Safe Water (% Population)	44.0	50.0	71.0
Rural Sanitation (% Population)	12.0	25.0	42.0

Source: Government of Pakistan (1992, 2001).

d. Subsidies

The SAP also called for elimination of both development subsidies and current subsidies. Elimination of development subsidies tended to increase the price of fertilizer, tubewells, pesticides, etc., but the farmers were compensated through an increase in the prices of agricultural products. While it may have had a positive impact on overall growth, small farmers may have derived very few benefits. As a matter of fact, their output may have fallen. The current subsidies kept down the prices of wheat, vegetable ghee, etc., and a withdrawal of subsidies has led to higher prices for these commodities.

Total per capita subsidies at constant prices increased from Rs. 29.21 in 1980–1981 to Rs. 64.4 in 1987–1988, but fell to Rs. 24.7 in 1996–1997 and increased to Rs. 32.1 by 1999–2000 (Table 12.16). Similarly, as a percentage of GDP, subsidies increased from 0.82 to 1.49 over the period between 1980–1981 and 1987–1988, declined to 0.33 by 1997–1998, then increased to 0.5 percent, mainly due to subsidies that were provided to public enterprises to meet their losses.

Table 12.16. Subsidies in Pakistan (Rs. million)

	At Current Prices			At Constant Prices		
	Total	Current	Development	Total	Current	Development
1980–1981	2,449	1,425	1,024	2,449	1,425	1,024
1984–1985	6,861	5,360	1,501	5,204	3,937	1,139
1987–1988	10,130	7,950	2,180	6,687	5,248	1,439
1990–1991	12,097	10,711	1,386	6,055	6,047	694
1995–1996	10,777	10,730	47	3,188	3,175	13
1996–1997	11,920	11,920		3,153	3,153	
1997–1998	8,840	8,840		2,169	2,169	
1998–1999	15,035	15,035		3,490	3,490	
1999–2000	19,859	19,859		4,410	4,410	

Note: Blank cells = not available.

Source: Government of Pakistan (2000).

e. Safety nets

Safety nets can transfer income at the private level as well as at the state level. That 30 percent of households have received private transfers, which formed 26 percent of their consumption, shows that a wide network exists on a voluntary basis. In the lowest income group, 48 percent of the population was the recipient of transfers and almost half of its consumption was financed this way (World Bank, 1995).

"Zakat" and "ushr" are the major safety nets. Proceeds of this money are used for the most vulnerable groups in the population: the destitute, the sick, and the aged. Zakat is deducted by various financial institutions from deposits. The State Bank of Pakistan keeps a percentage of all proceeds for national welfare and other schemes. The remaining amount is given to zakat committees for distribution: 60 percent for subsistence and rehabilitation of deserving persons and 40 percent for welfare institutions.

Distributed zakat makes up between 1.6 percent and 4.4 percent of GDP, whereas the actual collection is less than 0.25 percent of GDP. Table 12.17 indicates wide variations in zakat as a percentage of GDP collected, and a declining trend over time. Reasons for poor collection include private payment of zakat, absence of legal compulsion, inefficiency of the zakat-collecting administration, and lack of confidence by contributors of zakat in the collecting agency.

Table 12.17. Zakat Receipts (Rs. million)

Years	Total Deduction at Source	Zakat Voluntarily Paid	Other Receipts	Total Zakat	Total Zakat/GDP (percent)
1980–1981	844.25	1.6		845.9	0.31
1984–1985	1,334.80	1.8		1,336.6	0.29
1987–1988	2,069.50	2.4	0.3	2,072.2	0.33
1990–1991	2,792.00	5.6	0.6	2,798.2	0.31
1994–1995	3,073.20	9.9	47.5	3,130.6	0.18
1995–1996	3,260.60	12.5	208.1	3,481.2	0.18
1996–1997	3,805.50	13.0	78.4	3,896.6	0.17
1997–1998	4,088.10	11.2	19.5	4,118.8	0.16
1998–1999	4,061.20	16.0	2,434.8	6,512.0	0.23

Note: Blank cells = not available.

Source: State Bank of Pakistan (various years).

Other safety nets include the Food Stamp Program, which provides income transfers to meet nutritional needs, particularly for children; food, clothing, health services, and income-generating projects run by nongovernment organizations; voluntary private transfers through institutions (including mosques); public sector benevolent funds and group insurance paid through government institutional grants and monthly employee subscriptions; an employees' old age benefit scheme that covers industrial, commercial, and other establishments that employ more than nine workers and provide old-age pensions, invalidity pensions, survivors pensions, and old-age grants to those who are not entitled to a pension; and microcredit to targeted households for poverty alleviation.

f. Monetary expansion

To ensure that sufficient credit for investment is available while the inflation rate is contained in the presence of a high fiscal deficit is a hard act to perform. Supply of credit to the private sector has been significantly lower than demand, though the monetary expansion was rather high during the 1990s. Growth of the money supply has fallen to a single digit during the past two years because of debt rescheduling.

Double-digit growth in monetary assets with an average growth rate of only 4 percent implied double-digit inflation in most years in the 1990s (Table 12.18). Nevertheless, inflation in the past three years has fallen back to the single-digit level. Double-digit monetary expansion financed most budgetary requirements; however, the credit requirements of the private sector were not met. The reduced level of credit for working capital and investments has squeezed credit, especially for labor-intensive, small-scale businesses and microenterprises. As a result, investment, output, and employment growth rates fell and unemployment and underemployment started rising. This led to stagnant or declining real wages and an increase in poverty levels.

Table 12.18. Growth in Monetary Assets

Years	Monetary Assets	Domestic Assets	Inflation Rate
1980–1981	13.2	16.5	10.4
1984–1985	12.6	25.0	5.7
1987–1988	12.3	12.7	6.3
1990–1991	17.4	18.8	12.7
1994–1995	17.2	13.1	13.0
1995–1996	13.8	18.8	10.8
1996–1997	12.2	15.3	11.8
1997–1998	14.5	15.0	7.8
1998–1999	6.2	3.5	5.7
1999–2000	9.4	9.4	3.6

Source: Government of Pakistan (2000).

g. Growth of GDP

In the 1980s, the GDP grew at the rate of 6.5 percent; the agriculture and manufacturing sectors registered growth rates of 5.4 percent and 8.2 percent respectively. However, during the 1990s, the GDP growth rate fell to 4.6 percent and those of the agriculture and manufacturing sectors fell to 4.4 and 4.8 percent respectively (Table 12.19). While inadequacy of infrastructure, especially energy and transport facilities, has always threatened to slow the growth rate, the decline in public investment coupled with the stagnation in private investment has been the major contributing factor to the slowdown. Moreover, stabilization measures to lower domestic demand and the failure of exports to rise led to underutilization of capacity in a number of industries. The slowdown of GDP growth, coupled with a fall in remittances, resulted in very low growth of per capita incomes and that in turn resulted in an increase in poverty.

Since rural incomes did increase by about 4 percent per year, equality in income distribution across sections of the rural population would have resulted in a reduction in poverty. However, the strategy of removing subsidies on agricultural inputs and compensating farmers through an increase in the prices of output had a differential impact on poor and rich farmers. Poor farmers had very little marketable surplus and as such could make little use of the increase in prices of agricultural goods. At the same time, the increase in cost of inputs raised their production costs in excess of the benefits, lowering their income levels.

Table 12.19. Growth of GDP

	GDP	Agriculture	Industry
1980–1981	6.4	3.7	10.6
1984–1985	8.7	10.9	8.1
1989–1990	3.4	3.1	5.3
1994–1995	5.2	6.6	2.6
1999–2000	3.9	6.1	1.4
1980s	6.5	5.4	8.2
1990s	4.6	4.4	4.8

Source: State Bank of Pakistan, *Annual Report* (1999–2000).

In urban areas, poverty increased despite a growth rate of GDP per capita of 2 percent per year, mainly because employment opportunities fell significantly and wages declined for unskilled workers.

h. Employment

Employment generation in the 1990s has been inadequate to provide jobs for the growing work force, resulting in an increase in unemployment and underemployment rates over time (Table 12.20). About 10 percent of the employed had insufficient work, i.e., fewer than 35 hours per week. Unemployment rates are highest among youth and women. Moreover, a quarter of employed persons earn incomes that fall short of the subsistence level, while another quarter is on the borderline of the subsistence level.

Poverty and labor market interlinkage may be investigated through disaggregation of household population and workers by poverty status (Table 12.21). An association between inactivity and poverty, particularly in rural areas, has been witnessed. The labor force that belongs to poor households exhibits a higher level of unemployment and underemployment than its counterparts in nonpoor households. When the poverty status of the households is controlled, the association between employment structure and poverty suggests that workers from poor households are disproportionately absorbed into the informal and farm sectors, whereas the reverse holds for relatively rich households, which are employed in the formal sector.

5. Understanding Poverty: Differentials and Correlates

Who are the poor, and what are the determinants of poverty? These questions are rather important in the formulation of poverty alleviation strategies. The cross-section analysis is used to explore who is poor, and time series analyses explore the determinants of poverty.

Table 12.20. Distribution of Unemployment Rates

Year	Pakistan	Urban	Rural
1989–1990	3.1	4.6	2.6
1992–1993	4.7	5.8	4.3
1993–1994	4.8	6.5	4.2
1994–1995	5.4	6.9	4.8
1996–1997	6.1	7.2	5.7
1998–1999	6.4	8.9	5.0

Source: Government of Pakistan, various years.

a. Cross-section analysis

Multivariate regression, where poverty of food and poverty of basic needs alternate as the dependent variables, has been used to identify the poor (Table 12.22). The dependent variables take the value of one if poor, and zero otherwise.

A head of household who is at a "productive age" reduces the probability that the household is poor, as the experienced worker is expected to earn a higher wage. A larger household is more likely to be poor; households with nine or more members were eight times more likely than households with four or fewer members to be poor. Not surprisingly, a higher number of earners had a significant and negative impact on the probability of poverty. Schooling of

Table 12.21. Percentage Distribution of Workers in Pakistan by Establishment

Establishment	Poor			Nonpoor		
	Overall	Urban	Rural	Overall	Urban	Rural
Farm	43.62	4.45	50.26	37.69	5.09	60.75
NFE <10	37.96	68.42	34.38	25.11	43.37	24.58
NFE = 10	5.78	7.69	4.93	17.44	24.88	3.56
Govt	4.30	6.75	3.14	12.10	16.14	5.47
Other	8.34	12.69	7.30	7.66	10.52	5.64

Note: NFE < 10 = nonfarm enterprises with fewer than 10 employees; NFE = nonfarm enterprises with 10 or more employees.

Source: PIDE (1998–1999).

Table 12.22. Logistic Regression Effects of Predictors on Being Poor

Predictors	Model 1[a] Food Poverty	Model 2[a] Food Poverty
Age of the Head of Household (Years)	0.98*	0.98*
Sex of the Head of Household (Male = 1)	0.97	0.99
Household Size		
1–4	1.00	1.00
5–6	2.78*	2.93*
7–8	4.62*	5.81*
9+	8.34*	10.86*
Education of the Head of Household		
Illiterate	1.00	1.00
Primary (1–5 Years Schooling)	0.74*	0.77*
Middle (6–9 Years Schooling)	0.54*	0.45*
Matriculation & above (10+ Years Schooling)	0.24*	0.22*
Technical Education (Yes = 1)	1.12	0.84
Farm status of households (Farm = 1)	0.55*	0.61*
Duration of Continuous Residence (Head Only)		
Since Birth	1.00	1.00
< 10 Years	1.08	0.99
> 10 Years	0.96	0.85**
Place of Residence (Urban = 1)	0.56	0.31*
Number of Earners in a Household	0.89*	0.96
Remittances (Receiving = 1)	0.69*	0.63*
$-2 \log$Likelihood	3,963	3,852
Sample Size	3,544	3,544

Notes: *Indicates the estimated coefficient is statistically significant at 0.95. [a]The two models are devoted as Model 1 and Model 2. As the dependent variable in both models is binary, logistic regression was used.

Source: Kemal, Irfan, and Arif (2001).

the head of household was very influential on the probability of poverty. If the head of household had at least 10 years of schooling, the household was 0.24 times less likely to be poor than were illiterate households. Primary and middle level education also had a significant negative effect on the probability of poverty. Farm status of the household had an independent effect on the poverty status; farm households are less likely to be poor than are nonfarm households. Residence in urban areas was negatively associated with poverty. Finally, households that received remittances from abroad or within the country were less likely than nonreceiving households to be poor. The sex of the head of household had no significant effect on poverty. Continuous residence, which was insignificant in Model 1, turned out to be significant in Model 2 at a level of 10 percent. Similarly, the number of earners (significant in Model 1) was not significant in Model 2.

b. Time series analysis

Four broad categories of factors that impact the levels and trends of poverty are as follows:

- Structural characteristics of the economy: these include structure of output, sectoral distribution of the labor force, and pattern of ownership of the means of production.
- Output levels: especially important here is the availability of food at stable prices, given the nutritional norms underlying the specification of the poverty line. Levels of per capita income (alternatively GDP or its growth) are expected to be associated with a lower level of poverty; a higher rate of inflation is expected to adversely impact poverty levels.
- Foreign remittances: these flows can impact poverty levels by directly supplementing incomes and consumption levels, increasing the capital stock, and resulting in higher levels of output growth and employment generation in the economy.
- Subsidies: these are provided by the Government to keep prices low for essential commodities and to subsidize key inputs, which would result in increasing the output of key commodities, especially in the agricultural sector.

With respect to the major correlates of poverty, economic indicators are identified that could best capture these characteristics:[10]

- Real per capita GNP, alternatively, GDP and its growth rates;
- Income distribution measured by Gini coefficient (Gini);
- Per capita availability of food grains;
- Inflation rate as percentage change over the previous year; and
- Unemployment rate.

In terms of available output for current consumption we would expect

- the higher the per capita income, the lower would be the level of poverty;
- the higher the per capita availability of food grains, the lower would be the level of poverty;

---

10. The impact of subsidies and real wages could not be examined, as data were not available for some of the years.

- the lower the level of inflation, the lower would be the level of poverty;
- the higher the level of remittances per capita, the lower would be the level of poverty;
- the higher the level of available subsidies, the lower would be the level of poverty; and
- the lower the unemployment rate, the lower would be the level of poverty.

Amjad and Kemal (1997), Ali and Tahir (1999), and Qadir, Kemal, and Mohsin (2001) have used single variables to explain poverty. This does involve specification error, as shown by the results in the single variable case on regression in Table 12.23.

Would the increase in growth rate of GDP or an increase in per capita income help in reducing poverty? This question needs to be analyzed through multivariate analysis. Three variables have alternately been used to capture the impact of growth on poverty: level of GDP, growth rate of GDP, and per capita income. When all variables are introduced in the equation, growth turns out to be an insignificant variable (equations 1, 6, and 11 of Table 12.24). This is because the series is short and a number of variables form a collinear set. As such the impact of each variable is difficult to ascertain. The Gini coefficient has the right sign, but it is insignificant. Cereal production is significant, but it has the wrong sign: an increase in cereal production causes an increase in poverty. Remittances and unemployment are two variables that are significant and have the right sign. Inflation rates also turn out to be insignificant. Cereal production, inflation, and the Gini coefficient are excluded from this specification. Per capita income, employment, and remittances are all significant in explaining poverty. The three factors explain 93 percent of the variations in poverty (see Table 12.25).

Table 12.23. Determinants of Poverty—Single Variable Case (Log-linear)

Explanatory Variable	Coefficient	Standard Error	R^2	Adj. R^2	F-ratio
GDP	−0.422	3.87	0.52	0.48	14.97
Per capita income (x1000)	−0.880	8.80	0.63	0.60	23.73
Growth rate of GDP	−0.188	11.24	0.10	0.03	1.53
Gini coefficient	−2.202	1.81	0.20	0.14	3.28
Remittance	−0.180	7.04	0.78	0.76	49.50
Unemployment	−0.423	1.60	0.15	0.09	2.56
Cereal production	−0.459	2.66	0.34	0.29	7.06
Inflation	−2.541	2.68	0.34	0.29	7.17
Agricultural Productivity	−0.350	5.18	0.66	0.63	26.85
Openness	−0.640	5.88	0.71	0.69	34.57
Exports	−0.487	4.69	0.61	0.58	21.98

Source: Estimates of present study.

Table 12.24. Data on the Variables Used in Regressions

	Per Capita Availability of Food Grains	Consumer Price Index	Gross Domestic Product	GDP Growth Rate	Gini Coefficient	Gross National Product	Trade Openness Index	Export Openness Index	Population	Total Poverty	Rural Poverty	Urban Poverty	Remittances	Unemployment	Wages	Per Capita Income
1963–1964	2.35	9.82	98,902	6.65	0.39	25,157	0.16	0.04	50.31	40.24	44.53	38.94	35.00	0.98	166.48	1,994
1966–1967	2.08	9.80	119,832	3.74	0.36	38,985	0.13	0.03	54.79	44.50	40.96	45.62	39.00	1.13	110.71	2,222
1968–1969	2.76	9.78	135,972	6.15	0.34	41,945	0.11	0.04	58.00	47.59	40.92	49.70	30.00	1.28	125.06	2,385
1969–1970	2.96	9.75	148,342	9.10	0.33	48,298	0.10	0.03	59.70	46.53	38.76	49.11	100.90	1.42	106.81	2,541
1970–1971	2.67	9.73	149,900	1.05	0.35	51,273	0.11	0.04	61.49	49.13	42.55	51.32	48.70	1.57	98.95	2,485
1971–1972	2.68	9.71	153,018	2.08	0.37	55,367	0.12	0.06	63.34	49.85	39.37	53.35	106.90	1.74	99.49	2,695
1979	3.01	10.13	218,258	5.57	0.37	211,004	0.25	0.08	78.94	30.68	25.94	32.51	1,397.00	1.98	108.36	3,353
1984–1985	2.82	10.58	321,751	8.71	0.36	463,375	0.28	0.08	94.13	24.87	21.17	25.87	2,445.92	1.74	80.16	4,127
1985–1986	2.99	10.63	342,224	6.36	0.35	507,678	0.28	0.10	96.84	21.35	19.36	22.20	2,595.31	2.04	81.70	4,248
1986–1987	1.15	10.86	362,110	5.81	0.35	551,809	0.28	0.11	99.60	18.65	16.86	19.43	2,278.56	1.92	97.59	4,336
1987–1988	1.06	10.99	385,416	6.44	0.41	630,120	0.30	0.12	102.41	17.32	14.99	18.32	2,012.60	1.80	86.89	4,433
1990–1991	1.10	11.12	446,005	5.57	0.41	928,406	0.33	0.15	110.79	22.11	18.64	23.59	1,848.29	1.69	79.92	4,639
1992–1993	1.06	11.44	491,325	2.27	0.40	1,201,301	0.36	0.15	116.47	22.40	15.30	23.35	1,562.24	2.16	73.80	4,778
1993–1994	1.08	11.76	513,635	4.54	0.40	1,404,853	0.33	0.15	119.39	27.93	20.89	31.24	1,445.56	2.63		4,813
1996–1997	1.13	12.09	588,191	1.93	0.41	2,207,230	0.36	0.15	128.42	29.60	27.40	31.60	1,489.47	3.10		4,927
1998–1999	1.18	12.43	632,517	3.11		2,685,531	0.32	0.15	134.90	35.20	31.70	39.80	1,055.88	3.55		4,946

Notes:

(i) Real per capita GNP (YPEP). Alternatively GDP and its growth rates (GGDP);

(ii) Income distribution measured by Gini coefficient (Gini);

(iii) Per capita availability of food grains (CPC);

(iv) Inflation rate as percentage change over the previous year (CPI); and

(v) Unemployment rate (UNEMP).

The results regarding the other variables need to be interpreted with extreme caution. The fact that the level of inflation is not significant may have far more to do with the way it has been defined and used in this analysis. The analysis is picking up only the level of inflation in that year and poverty levels are based on observations with widely different time intervals; hence they reflect changes over that time period as well as economic developments in that particular year, and it would be difficult to isolate the impact of inflation in that year unless it were dramatically high. The same is true of changes in the Gini coefficient.

6. Conclusions

The main conclusions are summarized as follows:

- Compared to a significant decline in poverty during the 1980s, the incidence of poverty increased rather significantly in the 1990s. Compared to 17.8 percent of persons falling below the poverty level in 1987–1988 and 22.4 percent in 1992–1993, the incidence of poverty has increased to 32.6 percent according to the calorific poverty line. The incidence of poverty increases to 35.2 percent if poverty lines corresponding to the definition of basic needs are applied.
- The incidence of poverty in rural areas is more widespread than in urban areas. On the basis of poverty lines that correspond to basic needs, the incidence in rural areas was 39.8 percent and in urban areas it was 31.7 percent.
- In rural areas, poverty is more widespread among nonfarm households than among farm households. Similarly, larger households were associated with a higher incidence of poverty. Those having low levels of education and skills form a major proportion of the poor. Remittances have a positive impact on poverty alleviation. Poverty is associated with unemployment, underemployment, and irregular work.
- While per capita income growth did fall, it still increased by roughly 10 percent over the 1990s. However, it has been accompanied by worsening inequality of income distribution.
- Overall unemployment increased from 4.7 percent in 1992–1993 to 6.4 percent in 1998–1999. It is much higher in urban areas, where it increased from 5.8 percent to 8.9 percent; in rural areas it increased from 4.3 percent to 5.0 percent during the period from 1992–1993 to 1998–1999. Teenagers and youth suffer the highest levels of unemployment. Underemployment has also increased, from 11.5 percent to 18.4 percent over the same period.

Table 12.25. Multivariate Regressions of Poverty

	Constant	GDP	GGDP	YPER	REMT	GINI	UNEMP	CPC	CPI	R^2	Adj.R^2	F
1	5.65 (1.65)	0.053 (0.15)			-0.234 (4.61)	0.612 (0.97)	0.616 (2.66)	0.281 (1.85)	-0.58 (0.30)	0.95	0.92	26.40
2	5.083 (2.70)	-0.20 (0.85)			-0.228 (5.17)	0.537 (0.98)	0.611 (2.79)	0.290 (2.06)		0.95	0.92	35.30
3	4.500 (1.15)	0.301 (0.56)			-0.221 (2.84)	-0.193 (0.19)			-1.554 (0.48)	0.83	0.76	11.90
4	8.700 (3.69)	-0.377 (2.04)			-0.178 (4.20)	-0.042 (0.08)	0.837 (3.84)			0.92	0.90	32.50
5	8.77 (5.56)	0.379 (2.61)			-0.180 (5.25)		0.859 (4.77)			0.93	0.91	52.07
6	6.643 (1.86)		0.047 (0.63)		-0.242 (6.87)	0.689 (1.14)	0.762 (2.68)	0.243 (1.68)	-0.72 (0.50)	0.95	0.92	27.74
7	4.897 (9.23)		0.033 (0.60)		-0.243 (7.25)	0.691 (1.08)	0.664 (3.38)	0.295 (3.12)		0.95	0.93	36.28
8	10.64 (3.66)		0.086 (1.12)		-0.244 (6.33)	0.507 (0.77)	0.997 (3.67)		-2.508 (2.30)	0.94	0.90	27.19
9	4.08 (6.44)		0.046 (0.52)		-0.260 (5.73)	-0.508 (0.87)	0.649 (2.41)			0.91	0.86	22.90
10	4.62 (33.47)		0.055 (0.75)		-0.264 (7.69)		0.591 (3.17)			0.89	0.87	33.43
11	5.880 (1.33)			-0.029 (0.05)	-0.225 (3.12)	0.571 (0.91)	0.638 (2.80)	0.269 (1.73)	-0.340 (0.22)	0.95	0.92	26.36
12	5.533 (1.43)			-0.094 (0.17)	-0.221 (3.37)	0.522 (0.94)	0.623 (3.02)	0.281 (2.04)		0.95	0.92	35.40
13	10.79 (3.2)			-0.876 (2.06)	-0.137 (2.33)	-0.148 (0.29)	0.818 (3.88)			0.92	0.90	32.70
14	11.260 (3.28)			-0.501 (-0.79)	-0.167 (-2.37)	0.147 (0.23)	0.842 (3.89)		-1.299 (-0.81)	0.93	0.90	25.38
15	11.32 (4.46)			-0.927 (2.63)	-0.131 (2.64)		0.824 (4.86)			0.93	0.91	52.35

Notes: CPC = per capita availability of food grains; CPI = inflation rate as percentage change over previous year; GDP = gross domestic product; GGDP = gross rate of GDP; Gini = Gini coefficient; REMT = UNEMP = unemployment rate; YPER = real per capita gross national product.

Source: Estimates of present study.

- There is an association between inactivity and poverty, especially in rural areas. Similarly, the labor force from poor households exhibits higher levels of unemployment and underemployment than its counterparts in nonpoor households.
- A rising level of unemployment has also affected wage rates. Real wages of all workers have at best reflected stagnation, and in most cases real wages have fallen. Since the poor form a larger proportion of the working class, both a decline in employment possibilities and a fall in real wages have been responsible for a rise in the level of poverty.
- Child mortality is higher in rural areas than in urban areas. In urban areas the incidence of child mortality is higher among working women than among nonworking women, less educated mothers, and poor households. Housing conditions, quality of water, and type of toilet facilities also are associated with differences in mortality.
- About 38.8 percent of children are underweight, a number very similar to the proportion of poor persons. That as many as 60.1 percent of children are stunted is rather worrisome. About 9.5 percent were wasted. These figures indicate that a substantial proportion of children lives in poor socioeconomic conditions and at a higher risk of exposure to disease. A decline in the mean weight of children aged less than six months is another cause for concern. It not only indicates a high incidence of malnutrition among children of this age group, but also among their mothers. Education and modernization of women have a positive effect on the overall level of nutrition.
- Per capita income, remittances, and employment are the major variables that affect poverty. The export-oriented strategy that is biased toward the generation of employment would help in reducing poverty.

References

Ahmed, M. 1993. Choice of a Norm of Poverty Threshold and Extent of Poverty in Pakistan. *The Journal of Development Studies* 12.

Alauddin, T. 1975. Mass Poverty in Pakistan: A Further Study. *The Pakistan Development Review* 14(4): 431–450.

———, and Bilquees Naqvi. 1976. Tax Progressivity in Pakistan. Islamabad: Pakistan Institute of Development Economics. Unpublished.

Ali, M. Shaukat. 1995. Poverty Assessment: Pakistan's Case. *The Pakistan Development Review* 34(1): 43–54.

Ali, Salman Syed, and Sayyid Tahir. 1999. Dynamics of Growth, Poverty and Inequality in Pakistan. *The Pakistan Development Review* 38(4): 837–856.

Ali, Syed Mubashir. 2001. Poverty and Child Mortality in Pakistan. *MIMAP Technical Paper Series No. 6*. Islamabad: Pakistan Institute of Development Economics.

Amjad, R., and A. R. Kemal. 1997. Macroeconomic Policies and their Impact on Poverty Alleviation in Pakistan. *The Pakistan Development Review* 36: 1.

Arif, G. M., Hina Nazli, and Rashida Haq. 2000. Rural Non-agriculture Employment and Poverty in Pakistan. *The Pakistan Development Review* 39(4): 1089–1108.

Banuri, Tariq J., Shahrukh Rafi Khan, and Moazam Mahmood, eds. 1997. *Just Development—Beyond Adjustment with a Human Face*. Karachi: Oxford University Press.

Baulch, B. and N. McCulloch. 1998. *Being Poor and Becoming Poor: Poverty Status and Poverty Transitions in Rural Pakistan*. Working paper 79. Brighton: Institute of Development Studies, University of Sussex.

Cameron, Johan. 1995. The Impact of IMF and World Bank Policy Stances on the Economic Debates in India. *Pakistan Journal of Applied Economics* XI (1, 2).

Chaudhry, M. Ghaffar. 1973. Rural Income Distribution in Pakistan in the Green Revolution Perspective. *Pakistan Development Review* 12: 3.

Corbo, Vittorio, and Sang-Mok Su, eds. 1992. *Structural Adjustment in a Newly Industrialized Country: The Korean Experience*. Washington, D.C.: World Bank.

FBS (Federal Bureau of Statistics). 1995. *Income Inequality and Poverty in Pakistan*. Islamabad: Government of Pakistan.

Gazdar, Haris, Stephen Howes, and Salman Zaidi. 1994. *Pakistan: Recent Trends in Poverty, Background Paper for the Pakistan Poverty Assessment*. London: STICERD, London School of Economics.

Government of Pakistan. (1988). *National Nutrition Survey 1985–1987*. Islamabad. Nutrition Division, National Institute of Health.

———. 1992. *Social Action Program*. Islamabad: Planning and Development Division.

———. 1999–2000. *Economic Survey: Statistical Supplement*. Islamabad: Ministry of Finance.

———. 2000. *Economic Survey 1999–2000: Statistical Supplement*. Islamabad: Ministry of Finance.

———. 2001. *Economic Survey 2001: Statistical Supplement*. Islamabad: Ministry of Finance.

———. Various years. *Economic Survey*. Islamabad: Ministry of Finance.

Hussain, Akmal. 1992. *Sub-committee on Poverty and Poverty Alleviation, Committee on Social and Economic Well-being for the 8th Five Year Plan*. Islamabad: Pakistan Institute of Development Economics.

Irfan, M. 1974. Shifting and Incidence of Indirect Taxes on Tobacco and Petroleum Products in Pakistan. *Pakistan Development Review* 13: 1.

———, and R. Amjad. 1984. Poverty in Rural Pakistan. In A. R. Khan, and E. Lee, eds. *Poverty in Rural Asia*. Bangkok: International Labour Organisation/Asian Regional Team for Employment Promotions.

Jafri S., and M. Younis. 1999. Assessing Poverty in Pakistan. In *A Profile of Poverty in Pakistan*. Islamabad: Mahbub-ul-Haq Centre for Human Development.

Jain, R.B., and Heinz Bongartz, eds. 1994. *Structural Adjustment Public Policy and Bureaucracy in Developing Societies*. New Dehli: Friedrich Ebert Stiftung.

Jamal, Haroon, and Aisha Ghaus-Pasha. 2000. Alarming Level of Poverty in Pakistan. *The Daily News International*. March 20.

Jeetun, Azad. 1978. Incidence of Taxes in Pakistan. *Discussion Paper No.2*. Karachi: University of Karachi.

Kemal, A. R. 1994a. Structural Adjustment, Employment, Income Distribution and Poverty. *The Pakistan Development Review*. 33(4): 901–911.

————. 1994b. *Recent Tax Structure and Equity*. Bangkok: Economic and Social Council of Asia and the Pacific.

————, M. Irfan, and G.M. Arif. 2001. *MIMAP Synthesis Report: Major Conclusions and Policy Implications*. MIMAP Technical Paper Series No.3. Islamabad: Pakistan Institute of Development Economics.

Khan, M. A., and M. A. Khan. 1980. *Nutritional Standards of Growth for Infants and Young Children and Recommended Dietary Allowances of Pakistani Population*. Islamabad: Planning and Development Division.

Killick, Tony. 1995. Conditionality and the Adjustment-Development Connection. *Pakistan Journal of Applied Economics* XI(1): 2.

Kruijk, H. de, and Myrna van Leeuwen. 1985. Changes in Poverty and Income Inequality in Pakistan during 1970s. *The Pakistan Development Review* 4(3, 4): 407–422.

Malik, M. H. 1988. Some New Dimensions on the Evidence of Poverty in Pakistan. *The Pakistan Development Review* 27(4).

————, and Najam-us-Saqib. 1989. Tax Incidence by Income Classes in Pakistan. *The Pakistan Development Review* 28(1): 13–26.

Malik, S. 1996. Determinants of Rural Poverty in Pakistan: A Micro Study. *The Pakistan Development Review* 35: 171–187.

Malik, Sohail J. 1992. Rural Poverty in Pakistan: Some Recent Evidence. *The Pakistan Development Review* 31(4, Winter).

McGillivray, Mark, Howard White, and Afzal Ahmad. 1995. Evaluating the Effectiveness of Structural Adjustment Polices on Macro-economic Performance: A Review of the Evidence with Special Reference to Pakistan. *Pakistan Journal of Applied Economics* 11(1, 2): 57–75.

MCHD (Mahbub ul Haq Centre for Human Development). 1999. *A Poverty Profile of Pakistan*. Islamabad.

Morissey, Oliver. 1995. The Political Economy of Trade Liberalization: A Framework and Application to Pakistan. *Pakistan Journal of Applied Economics* XI(1, 2).

Mujahid, G.B.S. 1978. A Note on Measurement of Poverty and Income Inequalities in Pakistan: Some Observations on Methodology. *The Pakistan Development Review* 17(3).

Naseem, S. M. 1973. Mass Poverty in Pakistan: Some Preliminary Findings. *The Pakistan Development Review* 12(4): 317–360.

————. 1977. Rural Poverty and Landlessness in Pakistan. In *ILO Report on Poverty and Landlessness in Asia*. Geneva.

National Institute of Population Studies. 1992. *Pakistan Demographic and Health Survey (1990–91)*. Columbia, MD: National Institute of Pakistan Studies, Pakistan, and IRD/Macro International Inc.

Pasha, Hafiz A., Jeffry Stubbs, and Giles Clarke, eds. 1995. Financial Development of Megacities. In *Megacity Management in the Asian and Pacific Region*. Manila: Asian Development Bank.

PIDE (Pakistan Institute of Development Economics). 1998–1999. *Pakistan Socio-Economic Survey*. Islamabad.

Qadir, Usman, Muhammad Ali Kemal, and Hasan Mohammad Mohsin. 2001. Impact of Trade Reforms on Poverty. *The Pakistan Development Review*. 39(4): 1127–1136.

Quresh, Sarfraz Khan, Hina Nazli, and Ghulam Yasin Soomro. 2001. *Nutritional Status in Pakistan*. MIMAP Technical Paper Series No.8. Islamabad: Pakistan Institute of Development Economics.

Qureshi, M. L. 1986. *Incidence of Taxation in Pakistan.* A Report prepared for the National Taxation Reforms Commission. Lahore.

Qureshi, Sarfraz K., and G. M. Arif. 2001. *Profile of Poverty in Pakistan, 1998–99.* MIMAP Technical Paper Series No. 5. Islamabad: Pakistan Institute of Development Economics.

Rieger, Hans Christoph. 1995. Income Distribution, Poverty Alleviation and Human Development: The Structural Adjustment Experience of ASEAN Countries. *Pakistan Journal of Applied Economics* XI(1, 2).

Shirazi, N. S. 1995. Determinants of Poverty in Pakistan. *Pakistan Economic and Social Review* 33(1, 2): 91–101.

State Bank of Pakistan. 1999–2000. *Annual Report.* Islamabad.

———. Various Years. *Annual Report.* Islamabad.

Syed, Murtaza H. 1999. The Human Face of Poverty. In *A Profile of Poverty in Pakistan.* Islamabad: Mahbub ul Haq Centre for Human Development.

TEPI (Social Impact of Trade, Export Promotion and Industry Program). 2002. *Mid-Term Report* submitted to the Asian Development Bank. Islamabad: Pakistan Institute of Development Economics.

Tetzlaff, Rainer. 1995. Good Governance and Structural Adjustment Programmes—The World Bank's Experience in Africa South of Sahara. *Pakistan Journal of Applied Economics* XI(1, 2).

World Bank. 1995. *Pakistan Poverty Assessment.* Country Operations Division Country Department 1, South Asia Region.

———. 2000. *Entering the 21st Century—World Development Report.* Oxford University Press.

Zaidi, S. Akbar. 1995. The Structural Adjustment Programme and Pakistan: External Influence or Internal Acquiescence? *Pakistan Journal of Applied Economics* X(1, 2).

Zaman, A. 1995. The Government's Present Agreement with the IMF: Misgovernment or Folly? *Pakistan Journal of Applied Economics* XI(1, 2).

13. The Poverty Situation and Policy in Sri Lanka

Saman Kelegama

1. Introduction

Since its independence, Sri Lanka has shown impressive progress in reducing the incidence of poverty, reflected in improvements in human development indicators as well as consumption. Two general factors contributed to this progress: (i) a satisfactory long-term growth performance, with real per capita gross domestic product (GDP) growth of about 2.5 percent per year on average during the last five decades; and (ii) satisfactory provision of basic health care and education, together with either food subsidies or income transfers that made possible higher consumption by the poor.

Sri Lanka is well known as an exception among developing countries for its achievements in human development indicators (see, for instance, Table 13.1). However, the country still remains a low-income country. Although Sri Lanka's long-term growth compares favorably with developing countries, it falls short of the growth achieved during the last 50 years by the high-performing East Asian economies such as Republic of Korea, Malaysia, and Thailand. This was partly due to policy mismanagement and the ongoing civil war that has now continued for 17 years. It was also a case of missed opportunities (Kelegama, 2000).

In Sri Lankan policy, it has been a tradition to put efforts to reduce poverty at the top of the government agenda. It was one of the first developing countries, by accident or by design, to understand the multidimensional nature of poverty, and to strongly emphasize policies of free health care and education as early as the 1930s. In addition to its achievements in social indicators, Sri Lanka managed to completely eradicate starvation and destitution. Despite these achievements, between one-fifth and one-third of the population remains poor, depending on the poverty line used (Table 13.2). A much deeper reduction in poverty would have been possible with stronger economic performance.

One reason for the lack of good economic performance was the social welfare programs themselves, which created problems for economic management. Sri Lanka went through all three stages of demographic transition in a relatively short period of 50–70 years, thanks to the social welfare programs. The second stage of demographic transition led to a population explosion

298

Table 13.1. Social Indicators: Sri Lanka and Selected Asian Countries

Indicators	Sri Lanka	Bangladesh	India	Pakistan	Malaysia	Thailand
Populations, mid-year (millions) 1998	18.8	125.6	979.7	131.6	22.2	61.1
Population – average annual growth 1992–1998 (%)	1.3	1.6	1.7	2.5	2.5	1.1
GNP per capita (US$) 1998	810	350	440	480	3,600	2,200
GNP growth rate (1988–1998)	5	4.8	5.6	4.5	7.8	6.9
Life expectancy at birth (years)	73	61	63	62	72	69
Infant mortality (per 1000 live births)	14	57	70	95	11	33
Child malnutrition (% of children under 5)	38	68	53	38	20	Na
Access to safe water (% of population)	70	84	81	62	89	89
Access to sanitation (% of population)	63	48	29	47	94	96
Illiteracy (% of population age 15+)	9	47	44	59	14	5
Gross primary enrolment (% of school age population)	109	96	100	74	102	87
Male	110	93	109	101	101	–
Female	108	100	90	45	103	–
Urban population (% of total population)	23	20	28	36	–	21
Expenditure on health and education	48	3.8	3.8	3.6	–	–
Per capita expenditure on defense (US$, 1997 prices)	31.0	5.0	14.0	28.0	–	–

Notes: GNP = gross national product. Most recent estimate (latest year available, 1992–98) for indicators 5–12.

Sources: Gunatilaka (2000) and World Bank (2000).

that the economic growth process simply could not accommodate and cater to (Sanderatne, 2000). For example, the population below 20 years constituted 50 percent of the population in the early 1970s, and the economy at prevailing rates of growth could not offer employment opportunities to these youth, resulting in sociopolitical disruptions. Some other Asian countries faced such demographic transitions, but of a different nature (ADB, 1997).

After experimenting with an inward-looking strategy for nearly two decades, Sri Lanka embarked on an economic liberalization exercise in 1977. The historical bias in policy that favored social infrastructure at the expense of physical infrastructure underwent a change. There was also a shift in emphasis from universal food subsidies to targeted income transfer programs and interventions aimed at assisting the poor to participate in the growth process. Since the mid-1980s, the relationships between the overall economic perfor-

Table 13.2. Consumption Poverty in Sri Lanka by Sector, 1985–1986, 1990–1991, and 1995–1996

| | Incidence of Poverty (percent) | | | | | |
| | Lower Poverty Line | | | Higher Poverty Line | | |
	1985–1986	1990–1991	1995–1996	1985–1986	1990–1991	1995–1996
Sri Lanka	27	22	21	41	35	33
Rural Sector	32	24	23	45	38	35
Urban Sector	16	18	12	27	28	21
Estate Sector	14	13	12	31	28	27
	Depth of Poverty (percent)					
	Lower Poverty Line			Higher Poverty Line		
	1985–1986	1990–1991	1995–1996	1985–1986	1990–1991	1995–1996
Sri Lanka	7	5	4	11	9	8
Rural Sector	8	5	5	13	10	9
Urban Sector	3	4	2	7	7	5
Estate Sector	4	2	2	8	5	5

Notes: Estimates based on consumption needs. Lower poverty line denotes minimum expenditure necessary to reach minimum nutrition requirements and minimum level of clothing and footwear. This was calculated as Rs.471.20 per person per month in 1985–1986 and 1990 at 1990–1991 Sri Lanka prices, and Rs.717.09 per person per month in 1995–1996. Higher poverty line denotes minimum consumption necessary to achieve a decent standard of living and includes a small amount of discretionary expenditure over essentials such as food, clothing, housing, transport, communications, and health expenses. The higher poverty line was Rs.565.44 per person per month in 1985–1986 and 1990–1991 at 1990–1991 Sri Lanka prices, and Rs.860.51 per person per month in 1995–1996.

Sources: Gunatilaka (2000). All estimates based on data for the first quarter from the Household Income and Expenditure Surveys of 1985–1986 and 1995–1996.

mance and reduction of poverty have preoccupied policymakers. And since the late 1990s, rural poverty alleviation has become a major plank in Sri Lanka's development policy framework.

2. Poverty Profile of Sri Lanka

People fall below the poverty line because stocks of productive assets owned by them, given the prevailing returns to the assets and the availability and cost of publicly provided goods and services, are insufficient to enable them to attain a minimum acceptable standard of living. Thus, it is essential to have a broad look at several areas that influence poverty directly as well as indirectly. As stated, Sri Lanka has been experiencing a tragic civil war in the northeastern provinces for the past 17 years, so much so that its defense expenditure per capita is now higher than in neighboring countries (Table 13.1). Due to the disruption created by the war, the data from these two provinces are highly questionable. Thus, the rest of the chapter excludes these two provinces in the analysis.

Although poverty in Sri Lanka has been subject to debate for many years, there is no clearly defined or officially designated poverty line that is applicable across all sectors (see, for instance, Tudawe [2000]). This is a major problem in obtaining information on changes in poverty status in the country (Dutt and Gunawardena, 1995).

Poverty is observed to be greatest in the rural sector and least in the estate sector (mainly, tea and rubber plantation areas where most of the Indian Tamil community works) with the urban sector in the intermediate position in the early 1990s, but equaling the position of the estate sector in the mid-1990s (according to the lower poverty line; Table 13.2). The shares of the rural, urban, and estate sectors in the total numbers of poor are 79, 17, and 4 percent respectively, compared with their respective population shares of 72, 21, and 7 percent (Dutt and Gunawardena, 1995). The rural sector accounts for approximately four-fifths of aggregate poverty. Rural poverty appears to have declined much more slowly than urban poverty during the early to mid-1990s (Table 13.2). According to Dutt and Gunawardena (1995), this proportion is largely invariant over different poverty measures and poverty lines. A little less than half the poor depend on agriculture for their livelihood, while another 30 percent depend on other rural nonagriculture activity.

Within a region, rural poverty is generally higher than urban poverty. Over the late 1980s, there was a considerable narrowing of rural–urban poverty differentials within regions. Sri Lankan poverty varies on the basis of regions: Western vs. other provinces (Table 13.3); sectors: urban vs. rural (Table 13.2); agriculture vs. nonagriculture, etc. Regional disparity, particularly between the economically dynamic Western province and the rest (Table 13.4), and between urban sectors and rural sectors, continues to concern policymakers (Gunatilaka, 2000).

Despite reducing the poverty level from 27 percent of the population in the mid-1980s to 21 percent by the mid-1990s, the experience during 1990–1995 was not impressive. As Table 13.2 shows, poverty declined very little between 1990–1991 and 1995–1996: from 22 to 21 percent of the population. Some have argued that the year 1995–1996 should be excluded from poverty trend analyses in Sri Lanka because it happened to be a drought year. However, the slow progress in consumption-poverty reduction was striking against the backdrop of relatively faster GDP growth (average 5 percent) during the first half of the 1990s.

Per capita GDP growth was in the range of 3.0 percent per year between 1990 and 1995–1996. According to various surveys, many of the poor experienced an increase in poverty. The slow decline in poverty from 1990–1991 to 1995–1996 is puzzling in the light of these facts: (i) economic growth recorded an average 5 percent; (ii) unemployment declined from 17 percent in 1990 to 11 percent in 1996; (iii) private remittances doubled; and (iv) expenditure on education and health care was maintained despite escalation of defense outlays.

What explains the modest decline in poverty? Poverty is highest (32 percent) in households that derive their income from agriculture: 38 percent of the Sri Lankan labor force is still engaged in the agriculture sector.

Table 13.3. GDP Growth and Poverty Incidence by Region

Province	Annual Average Growth, 1990–1995(%)	Growth Ranking	Poverty Incidence (%)		Poverty Ranking	
			1990–1991	1995–1996	1990–1991	1995–1996
North Central	9.9	1	18.2	31.2	3	4
Western	6.4	2	15.2	13.6	1	1
Southern	6.1	3	23.7	26.5	6	2
Sabaragamuwa	5.3	4	23.1	31.6	4	5
Central	5.0	5	23.5	27.9	5	3
Eastern	5.0	5				
North Western	4.3	6	18.0	33.9	2	6
Uva	3.5	7	23.7	37.0	7	7
Northern	–6.2	8				

Note: Blank cells = not available.

Source: World Bank (2000).

Slow growth in agriculture was perhaps the main determinant of slow poverty reduction during 1990–1996. Agriculture grew by only 1 percent during 1990–1996. The restructuring of estates in the early stages of privatization, low paddy production, and other factors contributed to poverty in estates and rural areas. Availability of two data points calls for caution in interpreting the trends. Even so, the slow decline in poverty during the first five years of the 1990s shows that the poor remain highly vulnerable to income shocks and are unable to take advantage of the opportunities generated by high growth in the early 1990s.

The favorable impact of economic growth on consumption-poverty may be reduced if there is a contemporaneous increase in income inequality. Some rise in inequality in the process of rapid economic growth is, however, unavoidable, as the classic Kuznets income-inequality relationship would imply (inverted-U hypothesis). A sharp rise in inequality in the early 1980s is thus understandable in the context of rapid economic growth and structural change (Kelegama, 1993; and Table 13.5). However, the Sri Lankan experience in the context of 5 percent average growth during the 1990s shows little decline in inequality. Note that the Gini index of income (expenditure) distribution as a measure of relative income (expenditure) inequality did not vary much (Table 13.6). Sri Lanka has not achieved high growth rates like China to compensate for the increase in income inequality. Moreover, as Ravallion (1997) has argued, initial inequality matters, and this could dampen the impact of economic growth on poverty alleviation.

To summarize, first, consumption poverty remains high in Sri Lanka and it is primarily a rural phenomenon. Second, there was slow progress in poverty reduction in the first half of the 1990s and also greater volatility in poverty levels. Third, there are acute regional disparities in poverty.

3. Poverty Strategy in Sri Lanka

a. Poverty alleviation program—Samurdhi

The food subsidy program, centered on free or concessional rice and applied universally across the population, was the main poverty support system in Sri Lanka until 1977. This program was dismantled and a targeted food stamp program was introduced in the late 1970s. However, this program suffered from various shortcomings (Herse et al., 1989) and there were indications of poverty increasing and income inequality worsening by the mid-1980s (UNICEF, 1985). A High Level Poverty Committee that was appointed in 1988 made several recommendations to arrest the situation. Consequent to this report, a targeted safety net program called Janasaviya came into operation. It was an income-transfer program that was designed to supplement the growth process (Lakshman, 1997). The program also had a credit-based entrepreneurial development dimension (see World Bank, 1995). There were various add-ons such as the free midday meal program, free school textbooks, etc., that complemented the Janasaviya program (see Table 13.7).

In 1995, a more ambitious program called Samurdhi replaced the

Table 13.4. Income and Human Poverty by Province (percentage of population)

	Population 1994 (millions)	Population Density 1991 (per sq. km)	Income Poverty Incidence	Deaths before age 40	Adult Illiteracy	No Access to Safe Water	Children not fully Immunized	Births not in Institutions	No Access to Electricity	No Access to Safe Sanitation	No Access to Hygeienic Toilet Facilities (1994)	Rural Road Density 1995 (km/1000 population)
Western	4.7	1174	13.6	0.09	6.2	18.2	14.4	3.0	35.3	11.2	19	1.89
Central	3.9	385	27.9	0.10	15.3	26.1	13.8	21.5	65.0	24.4	40	3.60
Southern	2.6	389	26.5	0.07	11.2	35.0	10.4	8.6	59.2	20.3	37	2.50
N. Western	2.0	51	33.9	0.09	8.1	34.6	3.8	12.8	68.7	30.3	42	5.80
N. Central	1.3	94	31.2	0.15	9.6	48.0	2.1	20.0	72.2	31.7	56	8.84
Uva	1.0	122	37.0	0.10	17.1	44.6	12.3	36.1	73.5	34.1	57	4.58
Sabaragamuwa	1.1	332	31.6	0.07	11.2	32.1	12.0	16.9	74.4	22.7	57	3.5

Sources: World Bank (2000) and Gunatilaka (2000).

Table 13.5. Income Shares Spending Units

Category	1978–1979	1981–1982	1986–1987	1996–1997
Bottom 40	16.6	15.2	14.1	14.6
Top 20	48.9	52.0	52.3	51.6

Source: Based on Dunham and Jayasuriya (1998).

Table 13.6. Gini Coefficient

	1953	1963	1973	1978–1979	1981–1986	1986–1987	1996–1997*
Income Receivers	0.50	0.49	0.41	0.50	0.52	0.52	0.50
Spending Units	0.46	0.45	0.35	0.44	0.45	0.46	0.45

Note: [a] Preliminary Estimates (Round 1).

Source: Central Bank of Sri Lanka, Consumer Finances and Socio-Economic Surveys.

Janasaviya program. There were a number of differences between the two programs as to coverage (Dissanayake, 1995). The program is basically an income transfer to the poor to get out of the poverty trap. It covers 55 percent of the population by targeting 2 million households. The allocation for the program (1998) amounted to 1.3 percent of GDP and 3.6 percent of government expenditure. As can be seen in Table 13.7, the poverty-focused programs accounted for nearly 2 percent of GDP in 1997.

The Samurdhi program has three components. The first is a welfare grant to poor households to purchase essential commodities; the grant acts as both a consumption subsidy and a nutrition supplement. In 1998, 80 percent of the Samurdhi expenditure was allocated for this grant. The grant amounts to Rs.100–Rs.1,000 (US$1.00–$11.80) per household per month, depending on its level of poverty and demographic composition.

The second component is the savings, credit, insurance, and social security schemes that improve access to finance for households. The credit is used for microenterprise launch and income-generating activities. It is basically intended to expand the productive assets available to the poor. The credit is obtained from Samurdhi Banks and Samurdhi Bank Societies holding deposits of Rs. 400 million (US$4.7 million) and Rs. 230 million (US$2.7 million) respectively.

The third component is a community infrastructure development program where irrigation, roads, and water supply projects, among others, are undertaken by the community. Some 11,000 such projects have been implemented at the cost of Rs. 560 million (US$6.6 million) and have generated nearly 37,000 jobs for youth. This increases incomes among households and reduces political unrest.

The Samurdhi program is overseen at the grassroots level by 30,000 Samurdhi animators and managers. The administration cost was 10 percent of the Samurdhi budget in 1998.

b. Employment creation and the labor market

In general, the strategy for poverty reduction is equated by such institutions as the World Bank with employment generation and the economic growth process. The general consensus is that to absorb the annual addition of about 160,000 to the Sri Lankan labor force, the economy should grow by at least 8 percent. The economy has grown at an average rate of 5 percent during the 1990s and is therefore not in a position to absorb all the labor that enters the market. Overseas migration and self-employment have been two major sources of employment generation, and this has helped to decrease unemployment from about 16 percent in 1990 to 11 percent in 1999.

Table 13.7. Welfare and Social Infrastructure Expenditure
(Sri Lankan Rs. Million)

Type of Program	1996 (Actual)	1997 (Provisional)
Poverty-focused Programs		
1. Samurdhi	7,340	9,040
2. NDTF	510	250
3. IRDP	1,092	1,375
4. Public Assistance	240	240
(widows, orphans, etc.)		
5. Food Stamps	831	0
6. Kerosene Stamps	228	0
7. Infant Milk Subsidy	70	132
8. Triposha	250	264
9. Mid-day Meals (school children)	0	0
10. School Textbooks & Season Tickets	816	950
11. School Uniforms	1,157	1,100
12. Emergency Food (refugees)	3,185	3,077
Other Programs		
13. Wheat Flour Subsidy	7,500	0
14. Fertilizer Subsidy	1,500	1,500
15. Public Health Service	12,028	16,338
16. Public Education Services	15,911	17,959
Poverty-focused Programs and Transfers as % of GDP (items 1–12)	2.0	1.9
Poverty-focused Plus other Social Welfare Expenditures as % of GDP (items 1–16)	6.9	5.9

Notes: GDP = gross domestic product; IRDP = Integrated Rural Development Program; NDTF = National Development Trust Fund.

Source: Central Bank of Sri Lanka, Annual Reports (Various Years).

The usual link between poverty and unemployment exists in Sri Lanka (Dutt and Gunawardena, 1995). The unemployment rate declined from about 25 percent for the poorest group (below 80 percent of poverty line) to 5.5 percent for the richest (above 400 percent of the poverty line), (World Bank, 1995: 27). But the link is not obvious and there are unemployed people who are not necessarily poor, while there are employed people who are poor (ADB 1998: 23). Unemployment is to be found sometimes with the better educated and the less poor, mainly in the rural areas. Female unemployment continues to be twice the male rate and there has been an increase in the number of women involved in unpaid work.

The 5 percent growth rate could have absorbed more labor if not for structural problems in the economic system. Based on structural factors, there are three explanations that have been provided to explain the unemployment problem in Sri Lanka: the "skills mismatch" hypothesis, the queuing hypothesis, and the labor market rigidities hypothesis. The skills mismatch hypothesis argues that Sri Lanka's education system produces skills that are not valued by employers, even while they raise the expectations of those who acquire them. As a result, the unemployed are not interested in existing job vacancies, and employers are not willing to fill the vacancies with available candidates. Thus, it is suggested that there should be educational reform, with emphasis on vocational training geared to the needs of the labor market.

The queuing hypothesis is linked to public sector employment and pay policies. At the lower level of the public sector in Sri Lanka, payments and fringe benefits are higher than in the private sector. Hence, new entrants to the labor market have an incentive to wait for such attractive job openings in the public sector, with the majority choosing to remain inactive instead of taking available jobs outside the public sector. Since the Government recruits people to the public sector to reduce unemployment, job seekers wait for their opportunity. The waiting period is facilitated by remittances and income transfers to rural households. It is suggested that the public sector recruitment and pay policies should be reformed to discourage "queuing."

Rigidities in the labor market have prevented the poor from reaping the benefits of the economic growth process. In other words, the rigid laws governing the labor market have been identified as an impediment to employment creation. It is argued that due to these laws, low-quality jobs are created because there is evidence that casual labor, subcontracting, fixed period consultancies, etc., are on the increase (CBSL, 1999). Furthermore, it is argued that these laws discourage firms from restructuring and future expansion. Many youth employed in the informal sector look for jobs in the formal sector. It is suggested that less rigid labor legislation would facilitate labor mobility and reduce the wedge between protected and unprotected jobs.

The Government acknowledges that to reduce the unemployment rate significantly there is a need to create good jobs (such as those in the regulated sector) faster than the labor force grows, by improving the flexibility of the labor market. However, political economy considerations go hand in hand with such good intentions, thus diluting any reform efforts (Section 5).

c. Irrigation and land settlement policies

Since independence in 1948, irrigation and land settlement were used for poverty alleviation purposes. Due to historical reasons, land settlement schemes centered on irrigation schemes were regarded as the best way to restore the country's past prosperity.

The poor living in rural agricultural areas face a scarcity of land, small-sized land holdings, and lack of adequate water. Since independence, various governments have designed policies to make fresh land available for cultivation and to assist farmers to settle in new cultivable areas. Irrigation and land settlement policies may have contributed to poverty alleviation among the rural agrarian poor (Sanderatne, 2000). The land:man ratio worsened, despite a significant decline in forest cover in the country since independence. The agricultural land per family fell to 1.9 acres in 1982. The Accelerated Mahaweli Development Program resulted in the award of slightly larger allotments to assist the poor.

The shortage of new land has had an adverse impact on poverty in the rural sector, with the average land holding falling below commercially viable levels. Roughly 67 percent of land holdings in Sri Lanka are less than two hectares. As the size of agriculture plots decreases, rural farmers become more risk averse, relying more on low-risk, low-yield crops such as paddy. Lately, many rural households have increasingly become more dependent on transfers and remittances from family members working in urban areas or abroad.

Land distributed by the Government under various protected tenure arrangements such as land settlement schemes, colonization schemes, and village expansion schemes do not contain freehold rights. Freehold rights were not granted, on the thinking that if granted free-hold, indebted farmers might sell the land and such sales of land could increase landlessness and poverty. This policy encouraged rural smallholder agriculture and restricted transfer of cultivable land. The World Bank (1995) argues that lack of free-hold decreases investment efforts by farmers, as they do not fully own the properties, and intensifies uneconomical land fragmentation by preventing farmers from selling their land and moving to other activities. The pros and cons of these arguments are currently being analyzed by the Government.

d. Social welfare expenditure

After liberalization in 1977, expenditure on all social services as a percentage of GDP fell from 9 percent during 1970–1977 to 5.5 percent during 1981–1985 and remained at 6 percent of GDP during 1986–1990 (Table 13.8). This reduction in overall expenditure on social welfare was reflected in the performance quality of both the health and education sectors. In the 1990s there was once again an increase in social welfare expenditure to 9.3 percent of GDP (1991–1995 average). The World Bank (1995: 27) estimates that health and personal care account for 3 percent of total expenditure of the poor while education accounts for a little over 1 percent.

i. Public expenditure on health care

As Table 13.8 indicates, total expenditure on health care declined from 1.5 percent of GDP during 1971–1975 to around 1 percent of GDP during 1981–1985, but remained around 1.5 percent of GDP from 1986 to 1995. In the late 1990s, public expenditure on health care remained at 1.5 percent of GDP and 5.7 percent of total government expenditure.

Approximately 3 million in-patient days and 35 million out-patient visits a year are provided by 550 government hospitals with 55,000 beds and 380 central dispensaries in the country. As is well known, the Sri Lankan Government offers universal free health care, which has made a significant contribution to improving health among the poor. However, the overall health environment in the country is relatively weak. Malnutrition, lack of access to safe water, poor sanitary conditions, and disease outbreaks are common (see Table 13.4). Although the number of nurses increased from 9,000 in 1991 to 16,699 in 1997 and doctors from 2,900 to 5,300 during the same period, there are problems of quality—there is a shortage of qualified medical specialists and trained nurses. In rural areas where a high proportion of the poor live, the scarcity is felt more. Moreover, there is congestion in government hospitals; standards of hygiene are low and maintenance of facilities is poor.

Only 30 percent of government health expenditure reaches the poorest 2 percent (Rannan-Eliya and De Mel, 1997). Sri Lanka's health sector needs qualitative improvement. Environmental health also needs improvement. There is a chance to improve the quality of Sri Lankan health services, as explained later in the text.

ii. Public expenditure on education

As Table 13.8 indicates, expenditure on education, which declined from 2.9 percent of GDP during 1970–1975 to 1.9 percent during 1981–1985, once again increased to 2.8 percent during 1990–1995.

Primary education is free. Every village in the country has at least a primary school. Total enrollment in education was 4.1 million, of whom 50 percent were females. It has been estimated that the poor attain approximately seven years of education (Dutt and Gunawardena, 1995). The Government makes special efforts to attract poor children to schools by offering free school textbooks and uniforms (each child is entitled to one set of uniforms a year). The long-term impact of investment in education on poverty reduction depends on its effectiveness on enhancing human capital formation and labor productivity. Here again, the low quality of education has nullified the efficiency impact of educational investment. Rates of return at the primary end of education are low (Athurupana, 1997).

Table 13.8. Social Development Expenditure in Five-Year Periods as a Percentage of GDP

	1951–55	1956–60	1961–65	1966–70	1971–75	1976–80	1981–85	1986–90	1991–95
Social Development Expenditure	7.1	8.1	10.5	9.0	9.9	9.1	5.5	6.0	9.3
Food Security	2.4	2.1	3.7	2.7	4.3	3.4	0.2	1.1	0.9
Education	NS	3.3	4.0	3.6	2.9	2.3	1.9	2.6	2.8
Health Care	NA	2.0	2.0	1.8	1.5	1.2	1.0	1.6	1.5
Other Social Services	0	0	0.1	0.2	0.2	0.2	0.1	1.9	4.1

Note: Blank cells = not available.

Source: Central Bank of Sri Lanka, *Annual Reports* (1950–1995).

Overall government expenditure on education has made an important contribution to enhancing welfare. However, the quality of education is questionable. Athurupana (1997) shows that there is a willingness to pay for high-quality education. But for quite some time, the Government has not provided a favorable environment for the establishment of new private schools and universities. However, there seems to have been a revision of this attitude in 2000, when there were attempts to relax regulations in regard to private sector participation in the education sector (*Sunday Leader*, 2001).

4. Problems in the Poverty Strategy

Several studies have shown that the rate of rural poverty reduction is strongly influenced by the rate of agricultural growth. There has been a general decline in agriculture growth in Sri Lanka. The slow growth was coupled with a decline in real wages in the agriculture sector. According to Dunham and Edwards (1997), the poverty situation in rural areas would have been further aggravated if not for income transfers to the rural areas from Middle East migrants, members of the armed forces engaged in the North and East of Sri Lanka, and rural young females employed in the garment factories located mainly in the Western province. The average per capita inflows of remittances and transfers as a percentage of the World Bank Poverty Line has increased from 31 percent in 1985 to 65 percent in 1997 (Dunham and Jayasuriya, 1998). All these incomes are somewhat unstable. This has become a concern for policymakers, particularly when there is stagnation in the agriculture sector.

The problem of poverty in Sri Lanka is thus multidimensional. The problems in the existing strategies are identified and discussed below.

a. Politicization of targeted poverty programs

All poverty alleviation programs put into operation by the State since 1989 became highly politicized at the implementation stage. This politicization has resulted in two flaws in the programs that in turn have curbed their effectiveness. These are political bias governing the program and poor allocative efficiency (World Bank, 2000).

Genuine poverty alleviation programs have been diluted into vehicles of political patronage at the grassroots level. The current poverty alleviation program, Samurdhi, has utilized an extensive network of administrators for identifying beneficiaries and this process has gained a political dimension. Samurdhi has a network of 20,000 Samurdhi Development Officers and 10,000 *Govi Niyamakas* (Animators of Farmer Organizations) in charge of identifying beneficiaries. Party affiliation influences the allocation of income transfers to the beneficiaries. All new evidence from the international literature on poverty alleviation clearly shows that for poverty programs to be most effective in reaching the poor, the poor themselves should participate actively and freely in the political process.

Poor allocative efficiency is another problem. Several different classes of criteria are being used to target the poor. These are: (i) indicators of household income; (ii) indicators derived from correlates of poverty (such as landlessness, lack of regular employment, poor nutrition, impermanent or semipermanent housing); (iii) special groups-based criteria (such as women-headed or single-headed households); and (iv) criteria that are area- or region-based, considering a geographic area's weak infrastructure facilities and large concentration of poor people. These indicators have been used either singly or in combination with each other to varying degrees of effectiveness in terms of the "E" and "F" errors that have occurred (Gunatilaka, 1997: 15).

The Household Expenditure and Income Survey (HEIS) 1995–1996 shows that transfers from poverty programs reached 66 percent of households in the poorest decile and 14 percent of households in the top three deciles. The Sri Lanka Integrated Survey reveals that only 60 percent of households in the lowest expenditure quintile receive Samurdhi transfers. Gunatilaka and Salih (1999) have argued that Samurdhi's group savings and intragroup credit component and the Samurdhi Bank program are functioning as vital sources of emergency credit for Samurdhi beneficiaries. However, program sustainability is heavily reliant on the income transfer component. Gunatilaka and Salih also find that the microenterprise credit component has failed in its objective of promoting the poor to a higher income growth path. The high rate of default makes the microenterprise development credit program completely unsustainable in the long run.

b. Problems of the rural development programs

The pattern of distribution of growth is crucial in fathoming whether economic growth translates into an equivalent reduction in poverty (UNDP, 1997). The regional imbalance in growth is also visible. Compared to the Western Province, the other provinces did not show any decline in poverty between 1990 and 1996 (Gunawardena, 2000; see also Table 13.3). Current poverty analysis is looking into the role of several structural factors such as assets, human capital, credit and financial markets, existence of income-earning opportunities, etc., that could explain persistent poverty in some regions (GOSL, 2000). Preliminary surveys show that the regional imbalance in growth and poverty reduction are due to both the dependence on agriculture and the inadequate availability of infrastructure facilities in rural areas.

The promotion of off-farm employment for poverty reduction is also an issue in Sri Lanka. The current state of agricultural growth and the lack of technological modernization in the sector imply that the poor have to be absorbed by off-farm activities. The major impediment to creating off-farm employment in rural areas is the lack of proper infrastructure. Some statistics to reveal this situation may prove useful. Only 44 percent of households had access to electricity in 1994, and in some areas only 30 percent benefited from it. Less than 15 percent of the rural population has access to telecommunication services or subpost offices (GOSL, 2000). Capital grants provided to the provinces for the purpose of alleviating regional disparities have remained at less than 0.2 percent of GDP over the years. This partly explains why growth has not trickled down to the countryside, while urban poverty levels, by contrast, have fallen.

The question could be posed whether rural development programs could be effective in poverty alleviation. Take, for instance, Integrated Rural Development Programs (IRDPs). Gunatilaka and Williams (1999) argue that these programs typically benefited the nonpoor who had other inputs, such as irrigable land, that could benefit from such projects. The study further shows that access to infrastructural facilities are most often denied due to the quasi-public nature of many such assets.

> Given the unequal power relations that typify rural communities, the local elite is usually well-placed to capture decision making about development projects, frequently working through decentralized structures of Government themselves, and the poor are often unable to challenge the established social organization and hierarchy (Gunatilaka, 2000).

Poverty alleviation strategies that try to encourage the development of micoenterprises in rural areas may actually spawn only survival strategies, as rural producers are unable to access larger, higher-income markets due to high transport costs (Gunatilaka and Williams, 2000).

Under the 13th Amendment to the Sri Lankan Constitution in 1987, decentralization of finance was supposed to come into operation and poverty programs were supposed to be decentralized. But delivery of poverty programs remained under the central Government's control. Policymakers and aid providers have become increasingly convinced that local governments may be better able to develop rural areas, increase interregional equity, and reduce poverty. Reducing poverty through fiscal decentralization and thereby promoting rural infrastructure development and other development has received emphasis in recent years.

Gunatilaka (2000) argues that whether local governments provide efficient public services depends on both their capacities and the extent to which they are accountable and transparent in their activities. Whether financial resources really reach or benefit the poor depends on factors such as the initial endowment of complementary resources among the poor themselves, the quasi-public nature of assets, and the ability of the nonpoor to capture the decision-making process.

Gunatilaka (2000) also argues that rural development policies, with or without fiscal decentralization, can reduce rural poverty and urban-rural differences only marginally, when implemented alongside macroeconomic policies that favor the dynamic forces of urban agglomeration. Contrary to conventional wisdom, rural poverty reduction may actually need policies that favor planned urbanization in line with centripetal forces, and higher rates of rural-urban migration that ease the pressure on agricultural holdings, making them more viable for those who remain in rural areas. The rural development paradigm as currently conceived is fundamentally flawed.

Agglomeration forces unleashed by economic liberalization policies alongside equity-oriented rural development policies may have reinforced urban-rural differentials in Sri Lanka, perpetuated dualism, encouraged low agricultural productivity, and helped transform the rural economy into a remittance and transfer economy. This happens even when the overall policy framework does not contain an overt urban bias, and may in fact be tilted favorably toward the rural sector.

c. The social sector and poverty

Poverty in Sri Lanka is highly correlated with levels of human development that reflect gaps in the provision of publicly provided goods and services. HEIS 1995–1996 shows that the poverty incidence by education level of household head is highest among those with no schooling (38 percent) and with only primary schooling (34 percent). Similarly, from a health perspective, in both rural and estate sectors, malnutrition reflected in low birth weights, stunting, wasting, and anemia is high. The poor suffer from low-quality social services, with disparities especially prominent in rural and estate areas where the quality of health, education, housing, safe water, and sanitation services is far below the national average.

The ongoing war in Sri Lanka and the high defense expenditure has prevented the Government from allocating more funds for health and education expenditure to improve quality. However, irrespective of the war expenditures, Sri Lanka now has an opportunity to improve the quality of both health and education, due to the rapid demographic transition that has taken place. The proportion of children in the population rapidly declined in the late 1990s, due to low population growth combined with effective family planning.

Since the proportion of children in the population is declining, there is less need to increase the number of schools and teachers, and less need for expanding pre- and postnatal health services. This has provided an opportunity to improve the quality of both education services and health services. This opportunity has to be grabbed now, because after 2006, the reduction in the child dependency ratio will be gradually offset by an increase in old-age dependency. Beyond 2036, the advantage would be completely offset by the increase in old-age dependants (Sanderatne, 2000).

The danger, however, is that a Government faced with fiscal difficulties may use the opportunity to reduce expenditure on education and health. This should be avoided and both education and health planning should be geared to qualitative improvement, taking into account the demographic changes.

5. Unemployment and the Labor Market

The World Bank (1999) took a fresh look at the three main hypotheses that purport to explain Sri Lanka's unemployment situation and highlighted their shortcomings. Basically, the study finds little evidence for the skills mismatch hypothesis, but finds evidence for both the queuing and the labor market legislative framework hypotheses. Thus the suggested solution is reform in public sector recruitment strategy and labor market liberalization.

The need for labor market reform is accepted, but little political consensus exists for increasing employment flexibility or eliminating expectations that the Government will somehow create large numbers of positions in the civil service for educated youth. Given the sociopolitical setup in Sri Lanka, the Government's regular resort to ad hoc creation of jobs in the public sector to satisfy the educated youth is quite understandable, particularly when private sector expansion is inadequate due to the uncertainty created by the war. It is not practical in a highly politicized economy such as Sri Lanka's to wait till the private sector generates employment.

The direct effect of labor legislation on poverty among employed workers can be favorable because of minimum wage stipulations by the Wages Boards and by the Employees' Provident Fund and Employees' Trust Fund, which guarantee retirement funds. The sharp decline in poverty in the estate sector between 1985–1986 and 1990–1991 can be attributed inter alia to the application of minimum wage regulations through organized union activity.

The total employed labor force was estimated at 5.3 million in 1994. The number employed by the formal sector covered by labor laws was estimated to be 2.9 million (1.6 million in the private sector and 1.3 million in government institutions). Thus, labor laws do not cover 45 percent of the employed labor force. Evasion of labor laws is also on the increase (CBSL, 1999). To the extent that coverage by labor legislation is reduced by these factors, the positive impact on poverty reduction is reduced.

The net impact of relaxation of labor laws on poverty depends on the extent to which flexibility in the labor market is translated into economic growth, and the strength of the trickle-down mechanism to the poor, in comparison to the potential loss of worker welfare due to weakening of employee protection in the formal sector. The Sri Lankan Government is of the view that labor market reform should be easy when the economy is growing fast. However, due to the war, Sri Lanka has not been able to achieve high growth rates.

HEIS 1995–1996 data show the significant effect of fluctuating income growth on poverty trends. A significant proportion of the population is clustered around the poverty line and is vulnerable to small changes in income. This is reflected by the fact that a 20-percent increase in the income poverty line raised the incidence of poverty in 1995–1996 from 25 percent to 39 percent. Such a rise in the poverty line represents only a slight increase in consumption expenditure. As the World Bank (2000) argues,

> [The] insufficient mechanism for risk management in agriculture, the large increase in casual and temporary employment in recent years, [and] the poor targeting of beneficiaries through poverty programs contribute to the vulnerability and insecurity of Sri Lanka's poor.

Such vulnerability could also be due to the high dependence by rural households on remittances in recent years.

Increasingly, aid providers have highlighted the politicization of the poverty strategy in the context of the broader issue of "good governance." Over the last two to three years, the Government has made an effort to understand the nature of poverty in order to formulate an effective policy framework for poverty reduction. This framework was presented to the aid providers' meeting in Paris in December 2000 and the Government was commended for its efforts in preparing the document.

6. Conclusion

Since the mid-1980s, there has been a decline in poverty in Sri Lanka. Economic growth that averaged about 5 percent during 1985–2000 has certainly contributed to reducing poverty. Simulation studies on the impact of growth on future poverty alleviation (assuming that relative inequalities remain unchanged at the observed 1990–1991 levels) estimated that a 2 percent annual rate of growth of real consumption per capita would, by the turn of the century, reduce the proportion of ultrapoor from 22 percent to 12 percent, and the proportion of poor from 35 percent to 21 percent.

Economic growth of 5 percent annually has not been broad-based enough to realize a breakthrough in poverty reduction. In other words, economic growth has not automatically trickled down to the poor. Links between growth and poverty reduction are weak in some provinces; this situation calls for new policy measures to maintain outreach to the poor.

Liberalization of the factor markets needs serious attention. Market liberalization has not gone far enough in the labor and land markets, due to political economy factors. The rigidities in the land market have acted as a constraint to agricultural growth, while rigidities in the labor market have reduced the labor absorption capacity of the economy. Gradual liberalization could somewhat offset high short-run adjustment costs. A start has to be made while promoting dialogue with the stakeholders.

While liberalization is essential for growth, it will underuse the resources of the poor if their specific problems are not addressed directly. Sri Lanka recognized this long before many other developing countries, but the existing programs for directly addressing the problems of the poor suffer from various deficiencies. Specific poverty policies need fine-tuning to meet the current issues. The problem of targeting Samurdhi recipients has received attention in the Government's poverty framework document: "[C]ategorical measures of impoverishment should be used to determine eligibility instead of ... income-based criteria" (GOSL, 2000: 53). In some regions, the combination of private remittances and Samurdhi payments has raised the reservation wage and discouraged the poor from seeking employment. The report argues for exit procedures and incentives for households to graduate from Samurdhi and prevent welfare dependency.

Both the education and health sectors require urgent reform. Notwithstanding the comparative edge that Sri Lanka commands over other developing countries in these two areas, their performance record during the last two decades has not improved in consonance with earlier achievements, especially when taking into account the quality of services provided and new indicators of sector performance. This is mainly due to the slow adjustment of policies to the emerging needs of society and an open economy. For example, the existing financial and managerial systems for the health and education sectors established over the years are no longer adequate to meet the new challenges. It is commendable that the Government has recently begun to address some of these issues (GOSL, 2000).

It was also shown that the poor are very vulnerable to income fluctuations. This area received increased attention in the *World Development Report 2000–2001* (World Bank, 2001). One reason for this is that growth-promoting policies have been implemented unevenly, with insufficient emphasis on structural reforms in agriculture. All these problems have been viewed from a holistic perspective in the new poverty framework paper. The Government is geared to address these issues. In its *Vision for the 21st Century*, the Government has spelled out its aim of raising the income levels of the poorest 8 million by increasing their share of income from the current 4 percent to 15 percent by 2010.

References

ADB (Asian Development Bank). 1998. *Social Sector Development in Sri Lanka: Issues and Options.* A background study prepared for the 1998–2001 Country Operation Strategy. Manila.

———. 1997. *Emerging Asia: Changes and Challenges*, Asian Development Bank, Manila.

Athurupana, H. 1997. *Earning Functions and Rate of Return to Education.* University of Colombo, ISS Working Paper No. 9701. Colombo.

CBSL (Central Bank of Sri Lanka). 1999. *Central Bank of Sri Lanka—Annual Report, 1999.* Colombo.

Dissanayaka, S. B. 1995. Samurdhi Program: Concepts and Challenges. *Economic Review* 21(5).

Dunham, D., and C. Edwards. 1997. *Rural Poverty and an Agrarian Crisis in Sri Lanka, 1985–95: Making Sense of the Picture.* Poverty and Income Distribution Series, No. 2. Colombo: Institute of Policy Studies.

———, and S. Jayasuriya. 1998. Economic Crisis, Poverty and War in Contemporary Sri Lanka: On Ostriches and Tinderboxes. *Economic and Political Weekly* XXXIII (49, December).

Dutt, G., and D. Gunawardena. 1995. Some Aspects of Poverty in Sri Lanka: 1985–90. *Sri Lanka Economic Journal* 10(2). Written as a World Bank Policy Research Working Paper, No. 1738, and subsequently published in the cited journal.

GOSL (Government of Sri Lanka). 2000. *A Framework for Poverty Reduction in Sri Lanka.* Final Draft. Colombo. June.

Gunatilaka, R. 1997. *Credit-Based Participatory Poverty Alleviation Strategies in Sri Lanka: What Have We Learned?* Poverty and Income Distribution Series, No. 2. Colombo: Institute of Policy Studies.

———. 2000. Fiscal Decentralization, Rural Development, and Poverty Reduction. *Sri Lanka Economic Journal* 1(1).

————, and R. Salih. 1999. *How Successful is Samurdhi's Savings and Credit Program in Reaching the Poor in Sri Lanka?* Poverty and Income Distribution Series, No. 3. Colombo: Institute of Policy Studies.

————, and T. Williams. 1999. *The Integrated Rural Development Program in Sri Lanka: Lessons of Experience for Poverty Reduction.* Poverty and Income Distribution Series, No. 4. Colombo: Institute of Policy Studies.

Gunawardena, D. 2000. Consumption Poverty in Sri Lanka, 1985–1996. Colombo: External Resources Department, Ministry of Finance and Planning. Mimeo.

Herse, D., W. A. T. Abeysekera, and T. N. Wikramanayake. 1989. Food Consumption Behaviour of Urban Food Stamp Recipients in Sri Lanka. *Ceylon Journal of Medical Sciences* 32(2).

Kelegama, S. 1993. Distribution of Income and Ownership of Assets: Trends in Sri Lanka. *Pravada* (September/October).

————. 2000. Development in Independent Sri Lanka: What Went Wrong? *Economic and Political Weekly* XXXV (17, April 22–28).

Lakshman, W. D. 1997. Income Distribution and Poverty. In *Dilemmas of Development: Fifty Years of Economic Change in Sri Lanka,* edited by W. D. Lakshman. Colombo: Sri Lanka Association of Economists.

Rannan-Eliya, R., and N. de Mel. 1997. *Resource Mobilization for the Health Sector in Sri Lanka.* Cambridge, MA: Institute of Policy Studies/Harvard University Report.

Ravallion, M. 1997. Can High-Inequality Developing Countries Escape Absolute Poverty? Poverty and Human Resources Division, the World Bank. Mimeo.

Sanderatne, N. 2000. *Economic Growth and Social Transformations: Five Lectures on Sri Lanka.* Colombo: Tamarind Publications.

Sunday Leader. 2001. 20 January.

Tudawe, I. 2000. *Review of Poverty Related Data and Data Sources in Sri Lanka.* MIMAP-Sri Lanka Series, No. 4. Colombo: Institute of Policy Studies.

UNDP (United Nations Development Programme). 1997. *Human Development Report (Human Development to Eradicate Poverty).* New York: Oxford University Press.

UNICEF (United Nations Childrens' Fund). 1985. *Sri Lanka: The Social Impact of Economic Policies During the Last Decade.* Colombo.

World Bank. 1995. *Sri Lanka: Poverty Assessment.* Report No. 13431-CE, Country Department 1, South Asia Region. Washington, D.C.

————. 1999. *Sri Lanka: A Fresh Look at Unemployment.* South Asia Region, PREM Unit. Washington, D.C.

————. 2000. *Sri Lanka: Recapturing Missed Opportunities,* Washington, D.C.

————. 2001. *World Development Report.* Washington, D.C.

14. Pacific Islands: Is Poverty an Issue?

Christopher Lightfoot and
Anthony Joseph Ryan

1. Background

Most people do not associate poverty with the Pacific islands. It is usually
linked to images of suffering children in Africa or of the backbreaking peasant
labor of so many in Asia. Both are a far cry from the image of a Pacific populated
by healthy, smiling people living in a tropical paradise. But as the people of
the Pacific well know, the reality is not always as idyllic as the image.

The Pacific islands are vulnerable to natural disasters, most have few
resources, almost all are remote, and most have small populations. Over the
years, Pacific Islanders have learned to cope. They have developed cultures
based on both cooperation and sharing, with strong support systems that oblige
people to share what they have with their families and communities. In addition,
they have developed risk management strategies in traditional production
systems.

Pacific Islanders are proud of their cultures and, in particular, these
reciprocity obligations. So proud are they in fact that many have trouble
accepting that poverty is or can be an issue in their societies. But are they
correct?

2. Poverty of Opportunity

The overriding issue in the Pacific is poverty of opportunity. For
generations, many Pacific Islanders have struggled to achieve a reasonable
standard of living from the available resources, which are often extremely
limited. Traditionally, support from the extended family or community
went a long way toward alleviating poverty, but for this system to work, it
is necessary that the giver be able to improve the livelihood of the receiver.
If the whole family or community is poor, there may be little that can be
done to alleviate the poverty of any member. There are communities,
families, and individuals throughout the Pacific who, despite these social
support systems, live in hard-core poverty. One commonly held view is
that Pacific Islanders live in a state of "subsistence affluence." This is

certainly not true for all, and even when true, it is an economic dead end, with few opportunities for change and development.

There is little that is new in this. Unfortunately, the approach of the outside world has not widely introduced the means of improving livelihoods and standards of living. For some the gradual assimilation into the world economy has brought prosperity and opportunity, but most others remain trapped in a never-ending struggle just to survive. Today, despite a fairly widespread capacity to do something effective about it, poverty of opportunity persists, and in some cases is getting worse.

3. Evolution of Poverty of Opportunity in the Pacific

a. Resource base

Most Pacific island nations have very few natural resources. With the exception of Papua New Guinea, Vanuatu, and Fiji, agricultural land is very limited and can usually do little more than support the local population. The atoll islands have few resources aside from phosphates (and those are now close to exhaustion) and black pearls. Most are remote, which limits potential exports to nonperishable goods and services. A few countries have managed to develop tourist industries, but the remoteness of others limits this option. Tuna is an important resource to many countries and is contributing significantly to their economies. Timber resources have been plundered in recent times, an unfortunate reality of weak governance and uninformed communities.

Of critical importance to the persistence of poverty has been the virtual demise of the copra industry. Copra is one of the few exportable commodities that can be produced in the outer islands; the loss of this source of income has left many communities with little or no cash income.

b. Social system

In most countries, the traditional social system is based upon a hierarchy of power, with an elite group that controls the community's resources. Access to resources is determined by patronage; leaders allocate access rights according to a combination of need, tradition, and political expediency. The traditional system has checks and balances that act as constraints on the leaders, including a strong obligation to ensure that everyone has access to at least enough resources to provide a basic standard of living. This system works satisfactorily where the extent of the resources and the competing demands for those resources are clearly understood by all—that is, where there is transparency.

But as the Pacific island economies continue the transition toward monetized economies that are integrated into the world economy, the nature and extent of national resources, and the dynamics of political and social control, have changed. Today, it is those who control the monetary economy— who may or may not be the traditional elite—that have a marked advantage over those who are on the fringes. Three forces are leading to marginalization of some groups and individuals. First, in some countries, national politics operates as an extension of the traditional tribal system, with politicians supporting their own clan while ignoring others. Secondly, in other countries, as the leaders are becoming more removed from their communities, the obligations to support the community are being diluted. Finally, in general, the skills required to access the resources of the modern economy are different from those required to prosper under the traditional system, and the mix of "winners" and "losers" is changing.

Traditional systems are breaking down, but variations on this system survive in most countries, where the traditional or public service elite now dominates the public sector and continues to control access to and distribution of national resources. While this patronage system may have functioned fairly well in a small, tight-knit community, it is a far less effective method of managing complex, modern economies.

Other social issues that are marginalizing sections of the population include problems with civil and social order in several countries and, in many countries, the alienation of the youth, as a result of a failure to create meaningful employment, which in turn has led to a breakdown of law and order. The erosion of the rule of law marginalizes the weak and those without influence or power. It creates a society where those who can bully or bribe their way through the system prosper, while those without influence or power languish.

c. Capital

Typically, public sector investment dominates capital expenditure. Even in those countries with a significant private sector, there is little private sector investment.

The continued support provided by aid has been crucial to the maintenance of the economies of the region. Most countries rely on aid to fund public sector capital expenditure. For some, this is a carryover from the days when the colonial power funded infrastructure and other capital expenditure. For others, it is a matter of necessity, because domestic revenue is barely sufficient to meet the operating costs of government. In all cases, capital expenditure tends to be spasmodic and driven by donor priorities. It is also often concentrated on the "main" island or in the capital city. This leaves the remote communities underserviced and with even fewer opportunities for development.

Most of the economies have shown little if any real per capita growth for many years. Domestic activity is also constrained by low labor productivity and by the very limited opportunities that exist to add value to the primary products and minerals on which most economies are based, and hence for economic growth. Rapid population growth is also a factor, as is the capture of aid funds by the urban elite. In a few cases, the situation has been relieved by the outmigration of workers to Australia, New Zealand, and the United States. Several countries now rely on remittances from expatriate citizens to sustain the economy.

4. The Nature of Poverty in the Pacific

The Asian Development Bank's (ADB) report, *Fighting Poverty in Asia and the Pacific*, says:

> Poverty is a deprivation of essential assets and opportunities to which every human is entitled. Everyone should have access to basic education and primary health services. Poor households have the right to sustain themselves by their labor and be reasonably rewarded, as well as having some protection from external shocks. Beyond income and basic services, individuals and societies are also poor—and tend to remain so—if they are not empowered to participate in making decisions that shape their lives (ADB, 1999).

In the Pacific, these aspects of inequity and disadvantage are associated with limited opportunities to earn cash income; risks associated with change; shortage of financial, technical, and social services; the nature and quality of governance processes; and discrimination due to gender, ethnicity or status. These are discussed further below.

a. Limited opportunities to earn cash income

While the majority of Pacific Islanders rely on household production for their subsistence, they also need cash for education, health care, social obligations, etc. In addition, to rise above a basic standard of living, they must generate sufficient wealth to invest in training and assets. The combination of limited resources, a burgeoning population, and generally weak economic growth make it very difficult to meet these needs.

b. Risks associated with change

In the Pacific, being different is positively discouraged. Those who choose to follow another path risk losing the respect and support of the community.

They also risk failure. Where people are living close to the edge, the cost of failure can be catastrophic. Since the opportunities are limited, the benefits to be gained from taking a risk can be small, while the cost can be high. The real risk inherent in change is a powerful force against development.

c. Shortage of financial, technical, and social services

Throughout the Pacific, urban populations are better served than rural ones. This partly reflects the cost of servicing remote locations, but it also reflects the reluctance of professionals to locate outside the main centers. Priority is often given to the development and service needs of the main centers. Rural development often ends up taking a back seat to urban roads, higher education, and infrastructure. The result is a reduction in opportunities available to those who live in rural and remote areas.

There are also sometimes differences in the kind and quality of services available to ethnic communities and to men and women.

d. Nature of governance

Some Pacific island cultures have a strong tradition of participation in decision making. This tradition continues at the village and community levels, but weakens at higher levels of public administration because elected leaders often represent several communities. While some leaders are able to put aside their vested interests, many cannot or do not. The result is that a disproportionate percentage of national resources is channeled to the leader's clan.

Patronage is also a tradition. Many see it as right and proper for a leader to help friends, relatives, and colleagues. Most see nothing improper about petitioning politicians or public servants for goods and services. This system can work well in a small community, but it can have damaging consequences when applied in the complex environment of national or regional government. The use of patronage rather than more transparent systems favors those with influence and penalizes those without it. Small and remote communities are marginalized, thereby reducing their opportunities and increasing the incidence of poverty.

An associated issue is the rule of law. Several countries have experienced coups, military uprisings, attempted secessions, and serious civil disorder. These disruptions threaten lives and livelihoods. They discourage investment and reduce employment opportunities. The services and opportunities available to the majority decline, while a few who can either bully or bribe their way to success prosper. But even the prosperous usually invest much of their wealth offshore and hence reduce the funds available to develop the country.

e. Discrimination due to gender, ethnicity, or status

Most Pacific island populations are ethnically homogeneous, so there is no discrimination based on ethnicity. There is also little discrimination based on social status. The position of women is more complex. While some societies are matrilineal and women have considerable power and influence, in others women face systematic discrimination. Even in those societies where women have equal rights, they are often underrepresented in secondary and higher education, government, and management. They are confined to household activities, often combined with substantial subsistence workloads. They have few cash income opportunities and are frequently subjected to physical abuse.

5. Key Variables Influencing Poverty in the Pacific

The key variables for growth are vulnerability, political stability, good governance, capacity and skills, culture, population growth, and physical and financial infrastructure (ADB, 2000).

a. Vulnerability

Vulnerability is a characteristic of most small island economies. They suffer disproportionately from external shocks, such as climatic events or market failures. In a small country, a storm or earthquake can cause serious damage throughout the whole country. Equally, small countries often have a narrow economic base. They are susceptible to falls in the price of their few exports. The decline of the copra industry is a good example of the Pacific islands' vulnerability. Planning and investment can help mitigate adverse impacts, but their impact can never be fully offset.

b. Political instability

Political instability is common in the Pacific. Uninformed electorates, tribally based political systems, and corruption have all contributed to frequent changes of government. In fact, during the 12 months to mid-1999, there were changes of government in seven of ADB's 12 Pacific member countries. One present government contains eight former prime ministers! These changes of government and the associated changes of policy direction all too often result in development policies that marginalize the poor.

Nor is the region free from violence. Fiji experienced two coups in 1987 and an attempted putsch in 2000, followed by a military uprising. The Solomon Islands suffered a short civil war in 2000. Since 1989, Papua New Guinea suffered a military uprising, a long-running attempted secession of

Bougainville, and endemic civil and social disorder. In 1998, Vanuatu's police force rebelled and kidnapped the prime minister and other officials. This civil and social disorder reduces the effectiveness of government, absorbs scarce national resources, reduces employment opportunities, disrupts markets, damages property, frightens away tourists, and exposes people to the risk of injury. Usually, it is the weakest and most vulnerable who suffer the most in these situations.

c. Good governance

Good governance is characterized by predictability, participation, accountability, and transparency. Since 1995, ADB has led efforts to improve governance. These have been at least partially successful, leading to improvements in economic policy development and public sector management in all 12 countries. But predictability is still constrained by ad hoc, politically motivated expenditure decisions. In many Pacific island countries, the lines between the executive roles of public servants and the governance roles of politicians are blurred. Patronage remains common and the degree of accountability and transparency varies significantly between countries.

d. Capacity and skills

Capacity and skills at all levels are in short supply throughout the Pacific. This is a major constraint to equitable development. While top management is generally sound, the middle and lower echelons are often weak. Too often aid projects fail after foreign support is withdrawn because of poor management. This is partly because aid providers assign a low priority to technical and vocational training; they have tended to focus on postsecondary education through scholarships, most of which go to government employees wishing to study economics, political science, and other liberal arts. Technical and vocational training, on the other hand, is underfunded in local education systems and underrepresented in scholarships for overseas training.

There has been a serious decline in the quality of basic primary education in the rural regions of many Pacific island countries. If this continues, there is a risk that the resulting collapse of basic literacy and numeracy will cause rural communities to become even more mired in the poverty trap.

e. Culture

Culture has a major bearing, too, by affecting the opportunities available to people. Monetization is changing the nature and dynamics of local cultures. One important outcome is the gradual breakdown of social safety nets.

The customary ownership of land and common land use rights are deeply embedded traditions in most Pacific cultures. In most cases land ownership is legally restricted to the tribal owners. In practice, this means that investors and financiers have difficulty obtaining secure tenure and hence are unwilling to invest in development. A related issue is the uncertainty surrounding the actual ownership of land. Communities frequently recognize a variety of ownership rights and obligations over the same piece of land and it is not uncommon for these rights and obligations to vest in separate people. While these relatively complicated systems protect the land rights of tribal owners, they are a constraint to private investment, especially for land-intensive investments such as agricultural and tourism development.

Women are poorer than men in both rural and urban areas. In many countries, rural women work about 50 percent more hours than men, and get lower priority for access to food within the family. They do most of the agricultural work, including local marketing of surpluses, but are rarely the target of agricultural development initiatives. Women are far too often the victims of domestic violence.

The role of churches in Pacific societies is frequently overlooked. Many Pacific Islanders are Christian and are intensely religious. They contribute a large percentage of their income to maintaining the property and officers of their churches. For poor households, this commitment can absorb virtually their entire disposable income, yet there is strong pressure to contribute. Moreover, there is a tendency for these demands to expand or contract to absorb available cash in a given year, and they almost always take precedence over formal financial debt-servicing obligations. This places a considerable constraint on economic development. It also partly explains the generally low savings rates in Pacific island countries, and is a real factor in preventing poor families from improving their condition.

f. Population growth

Population growth rates are high in most Pacific countries and, in most cases, are outstripping economic growth. While the Polynesian countries and the Marshall Islands have offset the high population growth rates with equally high emigration rates, the other countries are failing to find productive employment for the growing work force. As populations continue to grow, the pressure on natural resources is increasing and the capacity of these resources to sustain those populations is under threat.

g. Physical and financial infrastructure

The physical and financial infrastructure is generally weak throughout the Pacific islands. The smaller and remote countries face problems in maintaining their international links. The larger countries are having trouble maintaining their road networks. And all must cope with providing interisland shipping services to small and remote communities. Inevitably, transport links are often unreliable, exacerbating the problems faced by remote communities. For example, only half of the 2000 coffee crop produced in Papua New Guinea reached markets.

The communications services also have a direct bearing on the quality of life. It is expensive to service small scattered communities, but if they are not given access to adequate communications, their opportunities to improve their situation will be reduced. There is a risk that many isolated communities will miss out on the information technology revolution, for example, even though they have the most to gain.

As for the financial sector, most rural communities are not well served. Few financial institutions are represented in country areas. In no small part, this is due to the land tenure systems that tightly restrict ownership of land. These restrictions prevent financial institutions from taking land as security for loans, constraining the opportunities for development.

In summary, while the incidence, depth, and severity of poverty vary greatly among countries, there can be no doubt that poverty is an issue across the Pacific islands.

References

ADB (Asian Development Bank). 1999. *Fighting Poverty in Asia and the Pacific.* Manila, Philippines.
————. 2000. *Pacific Strategy for the New Millennium.* Manila, Philippines.

15. Opening Doors to More Inclusive Societies: The Case of the Pacific Island Countries

Vijay Naidu

1. Poverty Denial Syndrome

There are still people in the Pacific island countries (PICs), usually the relatively advantaged, who deny the existence of poverty in the islands. They maintain that in the islands "subsistence affluence" and sharing and caring prevail so that everyone has the basic necessities of life. However, as the *Fiji Poverty Report* has shown, there is widespread rural poverty, even with the combination of subsistence produce, traditional exchanges, and cash income (UNDP and Fiji Government, 1997). Traditional social safety nets have been disintegrating with population mobility and new demands on individuals and households. Large income inequalities have emerged among rural households.

Relative poverty has emerged, with growing inequality between households. Living standard norms measured in terms of average household income are not enjoyed by more than 50 percent of the people of the Fiji Islands and the Solomon Islands. The *Pacific Human Development Report* (PHDR) of the United Nations Development Programme (UNDP, 1999: 20) points out that by 1986, the top 10 percent of wage earners in the Fiji Islands received 50 percent of all incomes, while in Honiara, the capital of the Solomon Islands, 70 percent of total income of households accrues to less than 2 percent of the population. In the Fiji Islands, the average weekly income in the highest 10 percent group of F$760 per week was 20 times that of the lowest 10 percent group earning an average of F$34 a week (UNDP and Fiji Government, 1997: 17).

The failure of redistributive mechanisms, including an absence of a modern social security system in all PICs, has resulted in larger numbers of individuals and families being unable to meet the basic necessities of life. Some 25 percent of the Fiji Islands' households are in absolute poverty and an almost equal number are vulnerable to poverty (UNDP and Fiji Government, 1997: 17).

Food poverty measured in terms of affording the least expensive but sufficiently nutritious basket of food for survival is becoming prevalent in the PICs, particularly in urban and peri-urban localities. Poverty of housing, as in the presence of overcrowded and substandard housing, has also become a feature. The expenses relating to education and health care, especially with the advent of the "user pay" principle, are beyond those in low-income categories. When other necessary expenses such as transportation costs and those relating to essential social obligations are taken into account, it is evident that many households in PICs do have considerable difficulties in surviving on a daily basis.

While poverty levels in the PICs have not reached the squalor and misery of other developing regions, impoverishment is becoming increasingly apparent with the appearance of beggars, street children, squatter settlements, and tenements and the increase in prostitution and destitution. Beyond these categories there are even larger numbers of islanders whose restricted access to opportunities denies them fulfillment as human beings.

2. Poverty of Opportunity

Poverty of opportunity has been defined as the "inability of people to lead the kinds of lives they aspire to" (UNDP, 1999: 34). Obviously, this has to be put within reasonable limits, as aspirations can be well beyond individual capabilities. The PHDR 1999 noted that the notion of poverty of opportunity was first used by the South Asia *Human Development Report* (HDR) 1997 and that it can be usefully applied in the Pacific islands. The PHDR 1999 further noted that while the South Asia HDR 1997 measured poverty of opportunity with respect to education, health, and employment, it could also include material well-being, access to markets, job security, political and social freedoms, and other indicators that are more difficult to quantify (UNDP, 1999).

It is evident that the concept seeks to capture the failure to fully develop human capital and the accompanying loss of social capital as the direct consequences of grossly unequal life chances of different social categories and classes of people in a society. In Oceania, as elsewhere in the developing world, poverty of opportunity has spatial, gender, age, ethnic, status, and disability dimensions. Island and archipelagic states have unique characteristics that make them vulnerable to both internal and external forces—anthropometric and environmental. High population growth rates have an immediate impact on the small land masses of atolls. They are extremely small players on the world stage and have no control over global markets for the commodities they produce. Environmental disasters such as cyclones, earthquakes, droughts, floods, tsunamis, tidal surges, and rising sea levels can wreak havoc on all forms of life in island territories.

3. Oceania is Diverse

Although regarded as a region, the Pacific islands are characterized by diversity—geomorphological, environmental, and cultural. Continental and volcanic high islands on the one hand, and atolls and raised limestone islands on the other, have different climatic conditions, degrees of ecological complexity, and widely variant resources. The former are relatively resource-rich compared to the latter. There is, for instance, a world of difference between the raised limestone island of Niue (258 square kilometers [sq km]) with its very limited natural endowments and the giant archipelagic state of Papua New Guinea (461,690 sq km). Niue has around 2,000 inhabitants, in contrast to Papua New Guinea's more than 5 million (SPC, 2000). Niueans are Polynesians, sharing a common language and culture. Papua New Guinea, on the other hand, has well over 700 languages and as many ethnic communities. Niue's physical resources are limited to a few inches of topsoil on the "rock," some scenic places, and a pristine marine environment. Papua New Guinea has a rich diversity of land forms and ecologies, from tropical mangrove systems to alpine forests, plentiful agricultural land, forests, and mineral resources, including oil and natural gas and extensive marine resources. Nuie's single major problem is to maintain a stable population so that it has a degree of sustainability. Its villages are deserted and many village greens are silent, thanks to the emigration of a great majority of Niueans to New Zealand. Reduced to a "MIRAB" economy and society,[1] Niue has an uncertain future with the tightening of aid from New Zealand. Papua New Guinea, by contrast, has to curb its population growth rate of 2.3 percent. However, it also faces numerous socioeconomic and political problems.

The above comparison between just two countries shows the danger of generalizing about Oceania. Yet generalize we must, if we are to identify regional patterns in socioeconomic conditions, structures, and processes, including globalization, that are impacting on and transforming PICs.

A word about the poverty/paucity of information and data, especially statistical data that would be timely at this stage in the chapter. Record keeping; research into and computation of systematic information on basic demographic trends; social indicators such as education, health, employment, and housing; economic statistics; and more technical information about public utilities and infrastructure are generally unsatisfactory and the available data grossly inadequate. Meaningful policy formulation, implementation, and monitoring under these circumstances is out of the question.

---

1. Some 8,000 Niue-born people have emigrated (ADB, 1995). The term MIRAB was coined by Bertram and Watters (1985) to denote dependant island economies characterized by migration (*mi*), remittances (*r*), aid (*a*), and a relatively large bureaucracy (*b*).

4. Patterns in Poverty of Opportunity in the Pacific

Spatially and culturally Pacific-wide, it is evident from the inadequate data that are available that poverty of opportunity is more prevalent and pronounced in the resource-rich Melanesian states than in the resource-poor states of Polynesia. Life expectancy in the former averages 61.5 years, compared to an average of 69.4 years in the latter; literacy rates, both in terms of adult literacy (number of years spent in school) and numbers of school-age children in schools, indicate considerable variation (see Table 15.1). Women's literacy rates are also lower in Melanesia. Similar differentials exist in rates of employment in the formal sector. While noncommunicable lifestyle diseases are rising throughout the PICs, causing premature disabilities and deaths among 40–50-year-olds, infectious, diarrheal, and respiratory diseases continue to afflict Kiribati, Papua New Guinea, and Solomon Islands. As well as being a cause of death, malaria causes long-term debility and lowers productivity in Papua New Guinea, Solomon Islands, and Vanuatu.

Between 90 percent and 100 percent of Polynesians have access to safe water, compared to only 24 percent of Papua New Guineans and 64 percent of Solomon Islanders. Access to sanitation is widespread in Polynesia and limited in Melanesia. Much of Micronesia, with the exception of Nauru and Palau, also has sanitation problems. Micronesian and Polynesian island states are integrated into the labor markets of Pacific rim countries and have high rates of migration. The limited opportunity within these island economies is enhanced by the access to wealthier rim country economies. Until recently, Melanesian people did not have the inclination or the capacity (skills) to emigrate. Throughout the PICs, the private sector is small and it is especially small in Melanesia and much of Micronesia.

Beyond these broad patterns, a closer examination of the different measures of poverty of opportunity is required. A person's life chances are determined primarily by his/her health, which in turn is influenced by the quality of nutrition, water, and physical and social environment.

5. Health Care

The 1995 Yanuca Island Declaration signed by the health ministers from PICs envisioned "the healthy islands" approach that perceived health in a holistic way: "Healthy islands should be places where children are nurtured in body and mind; environments invite leaving and leisure; people work and age with dignity; and ecological balance is a source of pride" (UNDP, 1999: 71). Unfortunately, over the last five or six years, the quality of the islands' physical and social environments has experienced deterioration. Rural areas continue

Table 15.1. Human Poverty Index for Pacific Island Countries

Country	Percentage of people not expected to survive to age 40	Percentage of adults who are illiterate	Percentage of people without access to safe water	Percentage of people without access to health services	Percentage of children >5yrs who are under-weight	Combined P3 value	Human Poverty Index
Niue	6.7	3.0	0	0	2	0.7	4.8
Tonga	8.4	1.0	5	0	2	2.3	5.9
Cook Is.	6.4	6.8	5	0	10	5.0	6.1
Tuvalu	9.8	5.0	15	0	0	5.0	7.3
Tokelau	8.3	9.0	6	0	0	2.0	7.6
Fiji Islands	7.4	7.1	23	0	8	10.3	8.5
Samoa	10.3	4.3	10	0	17	9.0	8.6
Palau	7.3	8.6	14	20	8	14.0	10.8
Nauru	17.4	5.0	0	0	0	0.0	12.1
Kiribati	16.3	7.8	20	0	13	11.0	12.6
Marshall Is.	13.2	25.6	24	5	17	15.2	19.5
Federated States of Micronesia	10.5	28.7	56	25	15	32.0	26.7
Vanuatu	12.2	66.5	13	20	23	18.7	46.6
Solomon Islands	13.7	69.7	36	20	21	25.7	49.1
Papua New Guinea	22.6	71.8	76	5[a]	29	36.7	52.2

Note: [a] This is the official figure; but many facilities lack essential drugs and personnel.

Source: UNDP (1999: 18).

to suffer from a lack of solid waste disposal services, inadequate provision of health services, and an absence of public and community health awareness. There is a scarcity of health care personnel, as they have increasingly moved to urban areas and to overseas destinations. There appears to be inertia in community and preventive health care.

A two-tier health service has emerged in a number of PICs: an insufficiently resourced public health sector for the poor and a private health sector with options for overseas treatment for the rich.

Over the last two decades, the rural-urban drift has intensified, as islanders in outer islands and interior areas of large islands recognize their geographical disadvantage with respect to opportunities for education, employment, and better social services. At present, more than 35 percent of the PICs' population is urban, with 8 of the 22 PICs predominantly urban. There are extremely high annual rates of urbanization in some PICs: 8 percent in Marshall Islands, 7 percent in Vanuatu, and 6 percent in Solomon Islands. Rapid urban population growth rates have resulted in congested towns and cities without adequate housing and basic utilities such as water supply and garbage and sewerage disposal. Informal housing or squatter settlements have mushroomed. In Solomon Islands, in the mid-1990s, 23 percent of the population of Honiara lived in squatter and informal housing. The figure for Betio in Kiribati is even higher at 25 percent (Walsh, 1996: 23). Overcrowding extends to schools, health facilities, and infrastructure. Generally, urban planning, limited in the best times, is in crisis. The question is whether these squatter settlements are slums of hope or slums of ongoing impoverishment.

The disintegration of rural communities and the transition to town dwelling has been accompanied by changing social behavior. There has been an increase in sexual promiscuity, as evidenced by premarital teenage pregnancies, an increase in sexually transmitted diseases, and—very worryingly—HIV/AIDS cases. Cancers of the cervix and breast are common among PIC women. Anemia and malnutrition are also prevalent among women and children.

Lifestyle diseases have soared in Oceania. Increased sedentary occupations, the consumption of nontraditional shop-bought foods, reduced physical activities, and the consumption of alcohol and cigarettes have led to a shift in the causes of morbidly and mortality. In the last decade and a half, noncommunicable diseases such as diabetes, heart disease, hypertension, stroke, and cancer have come to dominate the health picture for adults.

6. Education: Capacity-Building or Debilitating

In a recent paper, Hezel (2001) identified three apparently contradictory objectives of education: manpower training, cultural preservation, and academic skills inculcation. He maintained that all three objectives can be included in the curriculum, although culture is picked up at home and in the community and reinforced by school. He argued that there was a need for a new educational system that will meet new needs.

> We are educating young people who, although they may seem to lack some of the public service employment options that those before them had, are presented with other choices that their forbears may not have had. Young people today may move in any of three very different directions: they may return to the village and live a life on the land, or they may live in town and look for what employment they [are] able to find, or they can seek their livelihood abroad. Our clientele today may move in any of these directions. They are the heirs of the global economy (Hezel, 2001: 14).

As we have seen, access to education has been limited in Melanesian countries. Although the number of school-age children has increased significantly in these countries, a good 25–50 percent of children 10–14 years old continue to be denied access to education in Solomon Islands and Papua New Guinea. Moreover, with the possible exception of Cook Islands and Niue, statistics on adult literacy based on four years of schooling do not mean that people are indeed functionally literate or numerate. Likewise, the impressive data on school attendance in the PICs is misleading, as they do not indicate the quality of education and training. Rural schools generally have unsatisfactory facilities and untrained teachers, and are poorly resourced and managed. Certain elite schools in each of the PICs are relatively well endowed and service the educational needs of children from higher-income families. Such schools boast computer labs, while rural schools may not have even basic amenities such as reliable safe drinking water, sanitary toilets, or libraries.

Generally speaking, schooling has retained its colonial objective of training a small elite to fill administrative positions in the public service, even though Pacific island societies now require a much more complex range of human resources; educational systems are out of synch with the labor market. They remain exam-oriented and exclusive. Schooling costs are prohibitive. School fees, school levies, school uniforms, bus fares, and school lunches are beyond the means of most families. Without state subsidies, families with more children are compelled to keep some of them at home. Under such circumstances, it is likely that female children will be made to leave school. The "push out" rate remains high in most countries. In most PICs, 50–70 percent of children end their schooling between year 6 and year 8. There is a large attrition rate through secondary school and only between 2 percent and 20 percent go on to postsecondary studies.

In all PICs, there is an urgent need to reform education and training so that more quality and relevance can be introduced. There is an urgent need to provide second and third chances to push-outs and drop-outs. Vocational and technical subjects need to be taught. Nonformal and distant education, providing greater access and affordability, need to be introduced. Qualified and trained teachers are needed in all PICs.

7. Employment

A number of studies have shown that there is imbalance in the labor markets. The lack of fit between knowledge and skills dissemination and the labor market is reflected in the very large number of people who are unemployed or underemployed. This manifestation of the lack of realization of the full potential of young Pacific islanders is also partly an outcome of stagnant island economies. The "Pacific paradox," highlighted in the mid-1990s by the World Bank (1995), drew attention to the lack of economic growth in most PICs over the previous 10 years despite high per capita aid, access to preferential markets, and a relatively stable macroeconomic climate.

Most islanders emerge from schools without livelihood skills. Many aspire to white-collar public service jobs that have become scarce as a result of public sector reforms. It is estimated that anywhere between 5 to 12 persons will vie for a single job in Melanesia (Ahlburg, 1997: 19). In the Fiji Islands, it is estimated that 17,000 persons enter the labor market annually. As of May 2000, it was estimated that 8,800 of these job seekers were absorbed in the formal sector each year. A balance of 8,200 people is believed to have been absorbed into the informal sector as self-employed or irregularly/casually employed. The political turmoil since May 2000 has led to a significant decline in the absorption capacity of these sectors. Indeed, 8,000 formal sector employees have lost their jobs, while others have been required to work fewer hours or on reduced pay.

Semisubsistence agriculture remains the main source of livelihood for most Pacific islanders. This is particularly applicable to PICs that have predominantly rural populations, such as Papua New Guinea, Solomon Islands, and Vanuatu. Even for the Fiji Islands, Samoa, and Tonga, semisubsistence agriculture remains significant. However, socioeconomic policies generally and even agriculture policies are not designed to bolster subsistence livelihoods and productivity.

The low status given to smallholder farmers, uncertainty of land tenure arrangements, poor infrastructure, unreliable markets, fluctuating prices, limited access to credit, and the real threat of natural disasters all make agriculture an unattractive proposition. There is a shortage of rural-agricultural labor in the Fiji Islands, Samoa, and Tonga, as remittances and alternative sources of income compete with farm work. Agricultural productivity, which is low in the region, requires increased output per capita as well as acreage. The need to generate revenue for the State lends support to the commercialization of agriculture in PICs. Arable land, never extensive and always unequally distributed, is becoming even more unequally accessible and controlled, to the detriment of groups that are landless, migrants, and women whose labor power is central to agriculture but who do not own land.

In the Fiji Islands, among those in poverty are seasonal agricultural workers, particularly landless cane cutters. With the nonrenewal of agricultural leases, it is estimated that between 12,000 to 15,000 sugarcane farmers and their families will be deprived of their livelihoods. The impending collapse of the Fiji Islands' sugar industry will cause widespread unemployment and resultant social problems.

Customary or traditional forms of resource ownership have secured wider access and returns from land, mineral deposits, forest areas, and marine resources to Pacific islanders than would have been possible under a system of individual ownership. However, these forms of tenure have also impeded increased productivity gains and inhibited resource utilization by nonindigenous interests. Clashes between resource-owning groups have not been conducive to attracting investment.

In all PICs, women are underrepresented in formal employment and remain largely confined to the (unpaid) domestic and subsistence arenas (see Table 15.2). They are particularly underrepresented in decision-making positions and higher-paid jobs and are prevalent in a number of occupational ghettos, including secretarial, clerical and service work, nursing, teaching, and more recently, factory work. The full potential of PIC women is far from being realized despite well-intentioned policy statements on women's development and regional level commitment to a Pacific Platform of Action (Government of the Fiji Islands, 1998).

8. Social Exclusion

Social transformation in PICs has not empowered the broad masses of the people, instead it has concentrated power and wealth in fewer hands. Rural communities, squatters on marginal lands, rural and poor urban women, out-of-school youth, and the disabled have been marginalized and excluded. While in some situations of conflict, as in the Fiji Islands and Solomon Islands, some young men may acquire a sense of power and importance, the reality is that those in already vulnerable positions are even further disempowered and disadvantaged.

Holders of state power have tended to use their positions to benefit their own immediate family and networks of friends and kin. Where the private sector has taken root, it is not unusual for a nexus to emerge between business

Table 15.2. Employment Status of Pacific Island Women

Country	Women as percentage of overall population[a]	Women as percentage of economically active population[b]	Women as percentage of people in paid employment[b][c]	Women members of parliament	Women as percentage of people in administrative and managerial positions	Women as percentage of people in professional and technical jobs
Cook Is.	48.5	52	42	1	32	47
Fiji Islands	49.2	33	24	8	10	37
Federated States of Micronesia	49.0	35	32	0	15	32
Kiribati	50.5	43	46	0	9	42
Marshall Is.	48.8	27	22		7	32
Nauru	48.8	41	41	0	69	58
Niue	49.5	44	41	1	32	45
Palau	46.5	39	38	0	24	24
Papua New Guinea	47.2	42	18	2	12	30
Samoa	47.6	46	19	2	12	47
Solomon Islands	48.1	49	48	1	27	27
Tonga	50.2	51	21	0	19	44
Tuvalu	51.5	33	38	0	16	46
Vanuatu	48.5	49	46	0	13	35

Notes: [a]SPC (1994); [b]1986–1991 round of censuses; [c]Fiji Islands from 1996 national census.

Source: UNDP (1999: 25).

people, politicians, and senior bureaucrats. Lucrative contracts and subcon-tracts, membership in corporate and parastatal boards, and other benefits are shared in the close circle of the economically and politically powerful. Under these conditions, vested interests emerge to corrupt the political system and undermine democratic political processes.

With very rare exceptions, women, young persons, and those with dis-abilities (physical, vision, hearing impairment) are not found in positions of decision making. In the Fiji Islands, ethnic Fijian youth (between 17 and 25 years) constitute almost 80 percent of the prison population.

9. Ethnicity and Racism

Colonialism has left behind a number of vexatious ethnic problems. Melanesian PICs have sought to build nationhood in the midst of an emergent competitive market economy. Ethnic identification and the sense of belong-ing to an ethnic group is accompanied by in-group/out-group consciousness, stereotypes, and prejudices. Unequal integration into the mainstream politi-cal and economic structures and processes has privileged certain ethnic cat-egories over others. Interethnic competition for resources and opportunities (land, education, jobs, and political office) has, in some circumstances, spilled over into open conflict in the PICs.

Surprisingly, the problem of intergroup relations extends to monocul-tural contexts, as a consequence of internal migration and urbanization. Un-der conditions of overcrowding and land scarcity, migrants and traditional landowners often live in close proximity with some discomfort, the latter denying access of new migrants to their land and marine resources.

10. Substance Abuse

Betel nut, kava, alcohol, cigarettes, marijuana, spirits, and moonshine have been part of people's lives. Cocaine and other hard drugs also seem to be entering PICs, as the Fiji Islands' recent experience has shown. Consumed excessively, these substances result in additional grave social consequences. Loss of livelihood and productivity, family breakdown, domestic violence and criminal activities, mental illness, and suicides are associated with sub-stance abuse.

11. Governance

Although the PICs have adopted Westminster-type institutions, systems of government, institutional checks and balances, and other mechanisms for ensuring the accountability of politicians and public servants, these institutions are weak or do not function satisfactorily. Civil society organizations, the media, and the trade union movement, as well as political culture, have yet to evolve to a point where they can demand openness in government. In almost all PICs there have been well-publicized cases of corruption, abuse of office, and misuse of public funds, yet those responsible appear to be beyond the reach of the law. Moreover, a "culture of silence" permits traditional power holders and those aligned with them to use public office for individual gain.

While the "large governments" of the 1980s are being reformed, shedding excess employees, reducing public expenditure, and becoming more transparent, there is a need to increase the effectiveness of constitutional offices such as the auditor general, ombudsman, human rights commission, and attorney general's office. Sensitivity must be exercised in the reform process, as it can lead to conflicts of the kind experienced in the Solomon Islands.

12. Target Group

It is apparent that various degrees and forms of poverty are now found in the PICs. Absolute poverty is prevalent in the Fiji Islands: indicators such as grossly skewed income distribution, the prevalence of malnutrition and anemia; substandard housing; growing numbers of street children and out-of-school and unemployed youth; and abandoned elderly, deserted wives, and beggars in PICs' urban areas point to absolute poverty becoming widespread in the region. It is also evident that there is widespread denial of human opportunities to a broad mass of Pacific islanders. Those who are denied access to economic resources, education and health services, employment and credit, and infrastructure and markets include

- Rural communities, particularly rural children;
- Rural and working-class women;
- Out-of-school and unemployed youth—the push-outs and drop-outs;
- Landless people—outer-island and inland migrants to coastal towns and cities, Indo-Fijians in the Fiji Islands;
- Low-paid wage workers—the working poor who comprise 86 percent of the Fiji Islands' absolute poor, as they do not enjoy social security;

- Disabled persons, for whom facilities for education, training, and rehabilitation, including opportunities for employment, are limited;
- The destitute, including deserted wives, widows, single parents, the chronically ill, the severely disabled and the aged, for whom societies need to have social safety nets to meet short-term or long-term need; and
- Children of the poor, who require special attention with respect to health care and opportunities to education and training if the cycle of poverty is to be broken.

13. Strategies

Strategies that PIC governments could adopt to alleviate poverty in their countries include the following:

- Provide state support for capital expenditure on infrastructure, such as roads, ports, water supply, power, and communication.
- Upgrade education and training institutions by pursuing higher quality and greater relevance at all levels from preschool to postsecondary.
- Provide second and third chances to out-of-school youth in the form of vocational and technical training.
- Improve access to economic resources for disadvantaged groups, including the landless, women, and youth.
- Make finance available to those seeking to establish small and medium-sized businesses.
- Provide training support, advice, and marketing support for small businesses.
- Support informal sector entrepreneurship through outright grants, small amounts of financial credit, identification of opportunities, training, and marketing.
- Recognize that certain categories of extremely vulnerable persons require societal care.

14. Conclusion

The 1999 PHDR states that "the poverty of opportunity that exists in the Pacific is not an inevitable aspect of our lives. All forms of poverty can fade with the determined application of political will and community action" (UNDP, 1999: 93). While periodic natural disasters and pestilence have caused widespread suffering among Pacific islanders from time to time, the maintenance of structures and mechanisms, as well as cultures of exclusion that deny access to human opportunities to a vast majority of island people, particularly children, young people, and women, have caused and are causing long-term harm to individuals, families, communities, and society as a whole. Many have voted with their feet, shifting from rural communities to urban areas, while others have left island shores altogether for metropolitan rim countries in search of better opportunities for themselves and their children.

Pacific island societies pride themselves in being caring societies and indeed there is a strong traditional ethic of sharing and caring. However, contemporary realities have served to undermine or abuse the system of reciprocity and redistribution. A reversion to the ethics of a sharing and caring community, together with joint action and partnership by government, civil society, and business, can arrest and roll back the prevailing reality of poverty of opportunity in PICs.

References

ADB (Asian Development Bank). 1995. *Human Resource Development: South Pacific Island Countries.* Manila.

Ahlburg, D. 1995. *Income Distribution and Poverty in Fiji.* Suva: ESHDP, United Nations Development Programme.

Bertram, I.G. and Watters, R.F. 1985. The MIRAB Economy in South Pacific Microstates. *Pacific Viewpoint* 26(3): 497–519.

Government of the Fiji Islands. 1998. *The Women's Plan of Action 1999–2004.* Suva: Ministry of Women and Culture.

Hezel, F. X. 2001. *What Should Our Schools be Doing.* Vila: Economic and Social Council of Asia and the Pacific.

SPC (South Pacific Commission). 1994. *Rethinking Sustainable Development for Pacific Women Towards the Year 2000.* Noumea.

———. 2000. *Oceania Population 2000.* Noumea.

UNDP (United Nations Development Programme). 1999. *Pacific Human Development Report 1999: Creating Opportunities.* Suva.

———, and Government of Fiji. 1997. *Fiji Poverty Report.* Suva.

Walsh, A. C. 1996. *Informal Dwellings in Fiji, a Report for the UNDP Fiji Poverty Study.* Suva: United Nations Development Programme. Mimeo.

World Bank. 1995. *Pacific Island Economies: Building a Resilient Economic Base for the Twenty-First Century.* Washington, D.C.: World Bank.

Index

Abe, M. 160
agriculture
  growth, Asian developing countries
    238–9
  and information technology 132–5
  Pacific Islands 335–6
  Pakistan 273, 282, 285
  Sri Lanka 302, 307–8, 310
  see also Philippines, rural
    development
aid (development assistance) 40–41, 321
Andhra Pradesh, *see* information
    technology and poverty reduction,
    case study (Andhra Pradesh, India)
Arif, G.M. 264, 267–8
Arthashastra, The 7
Asian financial crisis, effect on
    Indonesian economy (computable
    general equilibrium/
    microsimulation models) 72–7
Azis, I. 72

balanced development, *see* development
    policy (balanced development)
Bangladesh
  poverty line 181, 188, 192
  social indicators 299
basic needs
  assessing 263–4
  cost of, poverty line estimation
    method 178–80, 212
  and gross domestic product (GDP),
    inclusion in 41–2
Basu, K. 17
Baulch, B. 268–9
Beng, C.S. 151
Berrian, D. 61
Bruno, M. 84
Bulír, A. 84

capabilities approach (Sen) 8, 22–4
capital
  evaluation of 35
  forms of, and 'AK model' 34–5, 36
  human, and export dynamism 118,
    120, 121

market distortions 144–5
and putty-clay vintage model 35
Cardoso, E. 84
child mortality 273, 294
China, People's Republic of, poverty line
    181–2, 188
churches, role in Pacific Islands 326
competitiveness, *see* manufactured
    exports, competitiveness/growth
Comprehensive Agrarian Reform
    Program (CARP) 248–9, 255
consumption, as measure of living
    standards 198–200
corruption 135–6, 336, 338, 339
cost–benefit analysis 16, 27–8, 35, 43
cost of basic needs method (CBN),
    poverty line estimation 178–80, 212

debt, external 26, 86
Decaluwe, B. 63–6
Deininger, K. 84
Demery, L. 88–9
Dertouzos, M. 126
devaluation, effects on poverty 46, 81–2,
    88–9
development
  assistance (aid) 40–41, 321
  as concept, evolution of 6–8
  goals of 6–12, 15–17, 18
development, measurement of 5–6, 7–8,
    9, 15, 29
  aggregate welfare measures 15–17, 24
  living standards, determinants
    of/levels of aggregation 22–7
  quintile income 9–11
  see also Human Development Index
    (HDI); living standards
development policy (balanced
    development) 20–22
  alternative approaches to 27–30
  government, role of 40–43
  living standards
    determinants of/levels of
      aggregation 22–7
    and human capital 30–34
  politics, role of 39–41

production technology 34–9
direct calorie intake (DCI) method,
    poverty line estimation 177
Dollar, D. 82, 87

economic growth
    and agricultural growth 238–9
    as goal 7–8, 20
    and household enterprises 143–4
    and inequality 67, 82–4, 91, 221, 303
    as measure of development 7–8, 20
    measurement of 23–4
    and poverty reduction 82–4, 91,
        99–100, 103, 109, 220–24, 261
    and social development 27, 28–9
    see also manufactured exports,
        competitiveness/growth; small
        and medium enterprises (SMEs),
        and equitable growth
economies of scale 146–7
education
    and information technology 127–9
    objectives of 333–4
    spending 100, 103, 222, 309–10
effective rate of protection (ERP),
    Philippines 251, 252
electricity regulation, and information
    technology development 140
employment
    and enterprise size 148–9, 151–5, 161,
        162
    and investment 38
    Pacific Islands 335–6, 337
    Pakistan 285–6, 287, 292, 294
    and policy reform/poverty reduction
        221, 227
    Sri Lanka 305–7, 314–15
    and wages 37
enterprises, small, see small and medium
    enterprises (SMEs), and equitable
    growth
environment
    deterioration of 4
    government, role of 42
exports, see manufactured exports,
    competitiveness/growth

factor proportions, small and medium
    enterprises (SMEs) 144–5, 157
Fields, G. 163, 176

Fiji Islands 328, 339
    employment 335, 336, 337
    Human Poverty Index (HPI) 332
    political unrest 324
finance
    capital projects vs. recurrent
        expenditure 43
    development assistance (aid) 40–41,
        321
    household credit 305, 311
    of investment 42
    lending, policy- and sector-based,
        impact of 220, 223–31
    small and medium enterprises (SMEs)
        165
    see also government expenditure
flood forecasting 135
food-energy intake (FEI) method,
    poverty line estimation 177–8, 180
foreign direct investment (FDI) 118, 119
forest management committees, use of
    information technology 132
Foster, J. 17, 59
functioning (Sen) 8

Garuda, G. 88
general equilibrium framework, see
        poverty analysis and measurement,
        computable general equilibrium
        (CGE) framework
globalization 3
    and marginalization 3–5, 17–18
    and technological capabilities 122
government
    and development policy 40–43
    and information technology 125,
        136–7, 139–42
    local 40, 313
    small and medium enterprises
        (SMEs), policies towards 148,
        155–66, 167–8
government expenditure
    education/healthcare 100, 103, 222,
        227, 308–10, 314
    and poverty alleviation 278
Greer, J. 59
gross domestic product (GDP), inclusion
    of basic needs 41–2
Gugerty, M.K. 82
Guhathakurta, S. 158–60

Gunatilaka, R. 311, 312, 313

healthcare
  and information technology 129–31
  spending 100, 103, 222, 309, 310
Heeks, R. 124
Hezel, F.X. 333–4
high-technology exports/production
    110–11, 112–13
  developing countries 113–15, 117
  newly industrialized economies
    (NIEs) 118
higher education, information
    technology 128–9
Hong Kong, employment/productivity,
    and enterprise size 149–51, 154
household enterprises 143–4
households, as consumers and producers
    31–4
human capital, and export dynamism
    118, 120, 121
human development 5–6, 9, 20, 27–9,
    43
  indicators of (national data) 245, 281,
    299, 304
Human Development Index (HDI) 89–90
  correlation with other poverty
    measures 90, 92–3
  and Gini coefficient 94
  national data 90–91, 95–7, 98–9,
    101–2, 245
Human Poverty Index (HPI) 90
  Pacific Islands 332
human resources development, and
    information technology 137–8
hydropower generation 133

inclusion, in development process 9; *see
    also* marginalization
income
  as measure of living standards 198–9
  per capita, national comparisons
    13–14
  see also living standards; quintile
    income/quintile income growth
income distribution
  determinants of 270
  and economic growth 82–4
  following external shock (computable
    general equilibrium (CGE)

    framework analysis) 67–71, 72,
    73–7
  functional 270
  and Human Development Index (HDI)
    90, 94
  and International Monetary Fund
    (IMF) programs 87–9
  Pakistan 269–73
  and small and medium enterprises
    (SMEs) 147–8, 163
  structural adjustment , effects of
    80–82
  see also inequality
India
  employment/productivity, and
    enterprise size 149–50, 153–4
  household enterprises 144
  poverty line 182, 187–8
  small and medium enterprises
    (SMEs), government policy
    towards 156–60, 167
  social indicators 299
  see also information technology and
    poverty reduction, case study
    (Andhra Pradesh, India)
Indonesia
  Asian financial crisis, effect of,
    computable general equilibrium/
    microsimulation models 72–7
  employment/productivity, and
    enterprise size 149–50, 153–4
  human development indicators 245
  poverty line 182–3, 186–7, 189–90,
    193–4
industrialization, and poverty alleviation
    60–61
inequality 6
  and economic growth 67, 82–4, 91,
    221, 303
  and inflation 84
  and International Monetary Fund
    (IMF) programs 87–9
  Korea, Republic of 161, 163
  and macroeconomic crises 86–7
  Pacific Islands 328
  Pakistan 269–73
  Philippines 205–7
  and quintile income growth 12
  richest people, limiting income of
    10–11

Sri Lanka 303, 304
see also income distribution; small
    and medium enterprises (SMEs),
    and equitable growth
inflation 84, 221–2
    Pakistan 284
information technology and poverty
    reduction, case study (Andhra
    Pradesh, India) 124–5
    agriculture 132–5
    capacity building/self-help groups
        131–2
    conclusion 142
    education 127–9
    electricity regulation 140
    emerging opportunities/IT-enabled
        services 126–7
    governance issues 136–7
    healthcare 129–31
    human resources development 137–8
    leadership 141
    lessons from experience 140–42
    network development 138–9
    potential benefits, IT 125
    public–private partnership 140, 141–2
    SMART government 139–40
    stakeholder involvement 141
    strategy adopted 137–40
    targeting the poor 135
infrastructure
    development program, Sri Lanka 305,
        306
    Pacific Islands 327
    nd rural poverty 256
International Monetary Fund (IMF) 87–9
    stabilization programs, impact
        assessment 223–4
investment
    and employment 38
    finance 42
    foreign direct (FDI) 118, 119
    marginal effect of 38–9
    and putty-clay vintage model 35, 37–8
irrigation
    Sri Lanka 307–8
    use of information technology 131,
        132–3
IT, *see* information technology and
    poverty reduction, case study
    (Andhra Pradesh, India)

Jafri, S. 265, 268
Japan, employment/productivity, and
    enterprise size 149–50, 151, 152–3,
    155–6
Jung, H.S. 53, 56, 60

Kakwani, N. 59
Kanbur, R. 175, 190–91
Kautilya 7
Kawakami, M. 160
Keynes, J.M. 38
Kim, L. 164–6
Korea, Republic of
    employment/productivity, and
        enterprise size 149–50, 152, 161,
        162
    manufacturing, factors affecting
        change in size distribution 163–4
    small and medium enterprises
        (SMEs), government policy
        towards 160–66, 167–8
    wage inequality 161, 163
Kraay, A. 82, 87
Kruger, D. 85

land
    ownership, Pacific Islands 326, 327,
        336
    reform, Philippines 247, 248–9,
        250–51, 258
    settlement, Sri Lanka 307–8
lending, impact of, *see* policy change
    (macro/sector level), and poverty
    reduction
Lipton, M. 83
literacy 16–17, 256
    and information technology 127–8
Little, I. 157
living standards
    determination of/levels of aggregation
        22–7
    households 31–4
    measurement of 29, 89–90, 198–200
    money metric approach 30–31, 33
    sustainable 42
    see also human development; Human
        Development Index (HDI);
        poverty lines
Living Standards Measurement Study
    (LSMS, World Bank) 30, 34

local government/ownership, and
    development policy 40, 313

macroeconomic policy and poverty
    reduction 25–6, 79–80
  debt, external 86
  economic growth 82–4, 91, 99–100,
    103, 109, 220–24, 261
  governments, actual behavior of 100,
    103
  inflation 84, 221–2
  and International Monetary Fund
    (IMF) programs 87–9
  macroeconomic crises 86–7
  research, suggestions for further
    103–4
  research review 80–89
  structural adjustment, effects of 80–82
  trade liberalization 85
  see also Pakistan, macroeconomic
    policies and poverty trends;
    policy change (macro/sector
    level), and poverty reduction
Malaysia
  employment/productivity, and
    enterprise size 149–50, 152, 155
  social indicators 299
malnutrition, Pakistan 273–4, 275, 294
manufactured exports, competitiveness/
    growth 109, 120, 122
  concentration levels 115, 116
  developing countries 113–17, 120
  foreign direct investment (FDI) 118,
    119
  high-technology production 110–11,
    112–15, 117–18
  newly industrialized economies
    (NIEs) 118–20, 121
  technical change 109–13, 120
marginalization 17–18
  globalization, as cause of 3–5
  see also quintile income/quintile
    income growth
market imperfections
  and factor markets 144–5
  and investment 39
market information, and information
    technology 134
'market route' poverty 4–5
Marx, K. 15

McCulloch, N. 268–9
microenterprises 143–4
  see also small and medium enterprises
    (SMEs), and equitable growth
mortality, child 273, 294
multinational enterprises (MNEs) 118
  and 'market route' poverty 5
  vertical disintegration 146–7

national accounts, and household survey
    data 34
natural disasters 134–5
Nepal, poverty line 183–4, 188, 189
newly industrialized economies (NIEs)
  agriculture 238
  competitive success, drivers of
    118–20, 121
NGOs (nongovernment organizations)
    40
Niue (Pacific island) 330, 332, 337
North American Free Trade Agreement
    (NAFTA) 115
Nugent, J.B. 163–6
nutrition, Pakistan 273–4, 275, 294

opportunity, poverty of 319–22, 329, 331

Pacific Islands, poverty issues 319,
    340–41
  agriculture 335–6
  capital expenditure 321
  cash income, opportunities to earn 322
  change, risks associated with 322–3
  culture 325–6
  data/information, inadequacy of 330
  discrimination 324
  diversity 330
  education/training 325, 333–5, 340
  employment 335–6, 337
  ethnicity/racism 324, 338
  governance 323, 325, 339
  growth 322
  health 331–3
  infrastructure 327
  key variables influencing poverty
    324–7
  nature of poverty 322–4, 328–9, 339
  opportunity, poverty of 319–22, 329,
    331
  political instability 324–5

population growth 326
resource base 320, 330
rural poverty 323, 328
social development/Human Poverty
    Index 331, 332
social exclusion 336, 338, 339–40
social system 320–21
strategies, poverty alleviation 340
substance abuse 338
urbanization 333
vulnerability 324, 329
women, position of 324, 326, 336, 337
Pakistan, macroeconomic policies and
    poverty trends 261–2
cross-section analysis 286, 288–9
data, availability and nature of 262–3
macroeconomic policies (structural
    adjustment/stabilization
    programs) 274, 276
  budget deficit 276, 277
  employment 285–6, 287, 292, 294
  fiscal system 276
  GDP growth 284–5
  monetary expansion 284
  public expenditure 277, 278, 281
  safety nets 282–3
  subsidies 282
  taxation 276–8, 279–81
poverty
  characteristics/identification of poor
    (cross-section analysis) 286,
    288–9
  child mortality 273, 294
  definition of 263–4
  depth and severity of 266–9
  determinants of (time series
    analysis) 289–92, 293
  functional income distribution 270,
    273
  incidence of 264–6, 292
  income distribution 269–73
  nutritional status 273–4, 275, 294
  social indicators 281, 299
  trends 263–4
time series analysis 289–92, 293
Papua New Guinea 324–5, 330, 332,
    337
Philippines
economic/human development 235,
    243, 245

employment/productivity, and
    enterprise size 149–50, 153–4
see also Philippines, rural
    development
Philippines, poverty measurement
    197–8, 208–10
inequality 205–7
poverty line
  and cost of living indexes 213–17
  and estimates of poverty change
    203–7
  and policy 190–91
  and provincial/regional poverty
    profiles 190, 194, 202–3,
    207–8, 209, 211–17
  setting 184, 187, 200–202, 203,
    211–13
poverty profiles 190, 194, 202–8, 209,
    211–17
welfare indicator, choice of 198–200,
    205–6
Philippines, rural development 235–7,
    256–8
agricultural growth 236–40, 249, 250,
    257
Comprehensive Agrarian Reform
    Program (CARP) 248–9, 255
deregulation 247–8
and economic development policy
    244, 246, 257
effective rate of protection (ERP) 251,
    252
government policies 244, 246–51,
    257–8
land reform 247, 248–9, 250–51,
    258
nonfarm sector 236–7
poverty reduction, determinants of
    251, 253–6
rural welfare outcomes 241–3
and sectoral policies 246–51, 257–8
tariff protection 249–50, 251, 252
policy change (macro/sector level), and
    poverty reduction 220–23
direct/indirect effects, distinguishing
    between 227–8
economic growth 220–24
employment 221, 227
government expenditure 222, 227
institutional change 223

lending, policy- and sector-based,
impact of 220, 223–31
macroeconomic stabilization 221–2
methodologies for assessing impact of
policy change 223–5
poverty impact matrix 225–31
relative price shifts 222, 227
see also macroeconomic policy and
poverty reduction
politics
and development policy 39–41
instability, Pacific Islands 324–5
local, and dynasties 256
participatory policymaking 79–80
poverty
causes of 24–7
definition of 30–31, 175, 263–4,
322
poverty, measurement of, *see* Human
Development Index (HDI); Human
Poverty Index (HPI); Philippines,
poverty measurement; poverty
analysis and measurement,
computable general equilibrium
(CGE) framework; poverty analysis
and measurement, social accounting
matrix (SAM) framework; poverty
lines
poverty analysis and measurement,
computable general equilibrium
(CGE) framework 45–7
budgetary rules, poverty minimization
61
example models
archetypal African developing
economy 63–72
Asian financial crisis, effect on
Indonesian economy 72–7
income distribution, following
external shock 67–71, 72, 73–7
policy change, impact of 224–5
social accounting matrix (SAM), as
basis of 62–3
poverty analysis and measurement,
social accounting matrix (SAM)
framework 45–7
accounting system/conceptual
framework 47–51
budgetary rules, poverty minimization
61

computable general equilibrium
(CGE) models, as basis for 62–3
distributional effects 57–8
example model (archetypal African
developing economy) 63, 64–5
interdependency effects 58
limiting assumptions 61–2
multiplier analysis 51–5
multiplier decomposition 55–61
policy change, impact of 224–5
poverty sensitivity effects 58–61
Poverty Assessments (World Bank)
30–31
poverty lines 30–31, 173–4, 191
Bangladesh 181, 188, 192
China, People's Republic of 181–2,
188
deriving, standard approaches 71,
177–80, 212
India 182, 187–8
Indonesia 182–3, 186–7, 189–90,
193–4
national methodologies 181–9, 191,
263–4
Nepal 183–4, 188, 189
Pakistan 263–4
and policy 189–91
specificity/relevance vs. consistency/
comparability 174–6, 186–9,
200–202
Sri Lanka 300, 301, 315
Thailand 184–5
Viet Nam 185–6, 188–9
see also Pakistan, macroeconomic
policies and poverty trends;
Philippines, poverty
measurement, poverty line
poverty reduction impact matrix 225–31
poverty transition matrix 268–9
Primary Agriculture Credit Societies
(PACS) 134
production
investment, marginal effect of 38–9
optimum plant size 146–7
putty-clay vintage model 35, 37–8
as a stock-flow relationship 34–5, 36
see also manufactured exports,
competitiveness/growth; small
and medium enterprises (SMEs),
and equitable growth

productivity
    and enterprise size 148, 150–51,
        152–5, 161, 162
    and wages 147–8
project evaluation 16, 35
    and marginal efficiency of investment
        schedule 38–9
    putty-clay vintage model 35, 37–8
Pyatt, G. 58

quintile income/quintile income growth
    definitions 10
    and development goals 9–12, 15–17,
        18
    national comparisons 13–14
    as welfare measure 12–13
Qureshi, S.K. 264

Ravallion, M. 82, 83, 84, 177
R&D, newly industrialized economies
    (NIEs) 120, 121
Report on the World Social Situation
    (1961) 27–30
'resource route' poverty 4
risk, and investment 39
Roemer, M. 82
Round, J.I. 58
rural development
    nonfarm sector 236–7, 312
    policies, effectiveness of 313
    and small and medium enterprises
        (SMEs) 143
    Sri Lanka 312–13
    see also agriculture; Philippines, rural
        development
rural poverty 83
    and agricultural growth 235–7
    China, People's Republic of 181–2
    and devaluation 88
    and information technology 132–5
    and infrastructure 256
    Pacific Islands 323, 328
    Philippines 204, 205–7, 210, 241–3,
        251, 253–8
    Sri Lanka 300, 301–2, 307–8, 310,
        312–14
    see also Pakistan, macroeconomic
        policies and poverty trends

savings 42

sector policy change, *see* policy change
    (macro/sector level), and poverty
    reduction
self-help groups, use of information
    technology 131–2
Sen, A. 8, 22–4
skill formation, and export dynamism
    118, 120, 121
small and medium enterprises (SMEs),
    and equitable growth 143–8, 166–8
    definition of SME 144
    and economic growth rates 145–7
    employment/labor productivity, and
        enterprise size 148–55, 161, 162
    factor proportions 144–5, 157
    and government policy 148, 155–66,
        167–8
    and income distribution 147–8, 163
    India, government policy towards
        SMEs 156–60, 167
    Korea, Republic of, government
        policy towards SMEs 160–66,
        167–8
    Taipei, China, government policy
        towards SMEs 160–61, 162
Smith, A. 15, 174
social accounting matrix (SAM), *see*
    poverty analysis and measurement,
    social accounting matrix (SAM)
    framework
social development, *see* human
    development; Human Development
    Index (HDI)
Solomon Islands 328
    employment, women 337
    Human Poverty Index (HPI) 332
    urbanization 333
Solow, R.M. 37–8
Squire, L. 84, 88–9, 175, 190–91
Sri Lanka, poverty issues/policy
    298–301
    education 309–10, 313–14
    employment/labor market 305–7,
        314–15
    government expenditure, social/public
        services 308–10, 314
    health 304, 309, 310, 313–14
    inequality 303, 304
    irrigation/land settlement 307–8
    politicization of poverty programs 311

poverty alleviation programs 303, 305, 306, 310–14, 315
poverty profile 299, 300, 301–3, 304
poverty strategy, problems 310–14
reform, need for 316–17
rural development programs 312–13
social indicators 299, 304
Stiglitz, J. 8
Streeten, P. 9
subsidies
   Pakistan 282
   and poverty alleviation 45–6
   Sri Lanka 303, 305, 306
substance abuse, Pacific Islands 338
Sutanto, A. 186

Taipei, China
   employment/productivity, and
      enterprise size 149–50, 151, 154,
      161, 162
   small and medium enterprises
      (SMEs), government policy
      towards 160–61, 162
taxation 41
   Pakistan 276–8, 279–81
teacher training, and information
      technology 128
technical change
   and competitiveness 109–13, 120
   and marginalization 4–5
technological capabilities, and
      globalization 122
technological learning 110
telemedicine 129–30
territorial control, as measure of national
      achievement 6
Thailand
   employment/productivity, and
      enterprise size 149–50, 154–5
   human development indicators 245
   poverty line 184–5
   social indicators 299
Thorbecke, E. 49, 50, 53, 56, 59, 60, 61,
      72
trade liberalization 85

transnational corporations (TNCs), *see*
      multinational enterprises (MNEs)

unemployment
   Pacific Islands 335
   Pakistan 285–6, 292, 294
   Sri Lanka 305–7, 314

VAT (value added tax) 41
videoconferencing 136–7
Viet Nam, poverty line 185–6, 188–9

wages
   and employment 37
   and size of enterprise 145, 147–8,
      151, 161, 163
   and structural adjustment 81
Warr, P.G. 190
'Washington consensus' 8
water resources, and information
      technology 131, 132–3
'weak transfer axiom' 12
weather information, and information
      technology 133, 135
welfare payments
   Pakistan 282–3
   Sri Lanka 303, 305, 306, 311
well-being, *see* human development;
      Human Development Index (HDI);
      living standards
Wiebe, F.S. 173
Winters, A.L. 85
Wodon, Q.T. 174
women
   Pacific Islands, position of, 324, 326,
      336, 337
   self-help groups, use of information
      technology 131
workhorse-dependent economy model
      81

Yoo, G. 163
Younis, M. 265

zakat (Pakistan) 283